BETWEEN WAR AND PEACE
The Potsdam Conference

OTHER BOOKS BY HERBERT FEIS

*The Road to Pearl Harbor: The Coming of the War
Between the United States and Japan*

*The China Tangle: The American Effort in China
from Pearl Harbor to the Marshall Mission*

*Churchill—Roosevelt—Stalin: The War They
Waged and the Peace They Sought*

The Atomic Bomb and the End of World War II
(originally published as *Japan Subdued*)

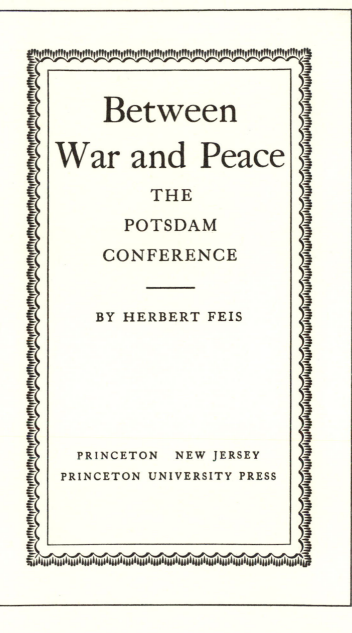

Between War and Peace

THE
POTSDAM
CONFERENCE

BY HERBERT FEIS

PRINCETON   NEW JERSEY
PRINCETON UNIVERSITY PRESS

PREFACE

THIS BOOK is a continuation of the narrative in *Churchill-Roosevelt-Stalin*. The first section tells how the surrender of Germany was effected, when the last attempt to divide her enemies failed. The next sections trace the flow of dissension within the coalition, the inner fractures that led to separation. The final section tells of the conference of the three Heads of Government at Potsdam—named Terminal. For it was conceived that at this meeting the situations left by the war would be resolved, and the nations would find, at the end of their sad journey, peace.

The time of war is one of effort, vigil, heroism, suffering. The brief season that follows is the time of determination: whether the struggle will have been just another match between nations—black against white, gray against gray—or whether it may be seen as the pangs of creation. I believe that these few months in the spring and summer of 1945 were crucial; and that knowledge of what happened then is essential to an understanding of the present.

I have been much aided in my task by others—to whom I wish to make acknowledgment here.

To the Department of State for enabling me to consult the collection of records on the Potsdam Conference which are being prepared for publication, and to members of its Historical Office, especially Dr. G. Bernard Noble, Dr. E. Taylor Parks and Dr. G. M. R. Dougall, for guidance in their use; to the Department of the Army for making available selected files; to the members of the Military Records Branch in the Federal Records Center for assistance in their use.

Again the records of the Honorable W. Averell Harriman, on his work and experience as Ambassador to the Soviet Union, were of much value; and their utilization was made pleasant by his generous encouragement. With patient kindness, former Secretary of State Byrnes put at my disposition many papers having to do with his participation in the Conference at Potsdam, and freely reviewed that experience with me. Similarly, the Under Secretary of State, Joseph C. Grew, was good enough to allow me to read and use his diary and memoranda. I am appreciative also of the enjoyed chance to talk over with the former Supreme Commander, President Dwight D. Eisenhower, some of the situations and events described in this book. Among the other members of the American Delegation at the Potsdam Conference, the Honorables James Dunn, Charles Bohlen, and George Allen have also dredged their memories, and so did George Kennan, then Counsellor of our Embassy in Moscow.

Miss Ruth Russell of the Brookings Institute was good enough to permit me to draw upon the manuscript of her comprehensive study of the history of the United Nations Charter, and to review critically the chapter on the San Francisco Conference. Assistant Secretary of State Francis Wilcox also did me the favor of reviewing that chapter. Professor Paul Y. Hammond of Yale similarly permitted me to learn from the manuscript of his excellent study of the origins of American policies in Germany.

For aid in research or in analysis of one sort or another, I am also obligated to Dr. Rudolph Winnacker, of the Office of the Secretary of Defense, M. Jacques Rueff, Professor Elting Morison, Dr. Robert Oppenheimer, Dr. Marshall Shulman, Dean McGeorge Bundy, Mr. Arthur Page, and Mr. Emilio Collado.

Mrs. Arline Van B. Pratt helped me much in research and in critical examination of the text; Miss Elizabeth Todd in the editing; Miss Rebecca Fuller in the tedious task of turning out the many versions of the manuscript.

Throughout, the effort was sustained by my wife, Ruth Stanley-Brown Feis, who as well went over the proofs with expert care and aided in the preparation of the index.

I am grateful to the Rockefeller Foundation for its supporting grant and to the Institute for Advanced Study for its appointment to membership and generous working facilities.

I wish again to repeat the statement in the prefaces to my other studies of this wartime era. "The aid given by persons in the government should not be construed as an indication of official sponsorship or approval, nor should that given by persons outside the government be taken to mean that they share responsibility for the contents of the pages that follow."

HERBERT FEIS

York, Maine

CONTENTS

CONTENTS

PART FOUR

Terminal: The Conference at Potsdam

SUPPLEMENTARY NOTES

PART ONE

The Time of Triumph

1. As the Germans Gave Up

MAY 1945: Hitler's Germany went down at last. Who does not remember the joy of the peoples who had won, and the prayers that mankind would never more have to go through the same anguish? Or the resolve that Germany should be so treated that it could not again bring war upon the world? Or the revived quest for a better ordered way of life among nations—secure and calm? This is the tale of these motions in the spirit of the winning nations when the war was over and they turned to the task of peacemaking.

The National Socialist structure of authority, in spasm, fell apart. The German people had been warned that they would have to admit complete defeat and offer total submission: the surrender would have to be unconditional. The victors had kept their right to deal with the German state and people as they should see fit. They would, it had been made clear, occupy and take control of the country in order to enforce their will. But this prospect had been made less fearful by the broadcast statements of the wartime leaders—Churchill, Roosevelt, and Stalin. All three had disavowed any intention of causing the German people brutally to suffer—or of enslaving them. "We come," Eisenhower had said on the day in 1944 that the Allied troops crossed the western frontier of Germany, "as conquerors, but not as oppressors." At their conference at Yalta, in the winter before the end, the three Heads of Government had declared: "It is our inflexible purpose to destroy German militarism and Nazism and to ensure that Germany will never again be able to disturb the peace of the world. . . . It is not our purpose to destroy the people of Germany, but only when Nazism and militarism have been extirpated will there be hope for a decent life for Germans, and a place for them in the community of nations."

The triumphing coalition had adopted rules to guide them in treating acts or offers of surrender by their common foe. The commanders of each segment of all combat fronts—west, east, south, north—were authorized to accept the surrender, unconditionally, of enemy units directly engaged against forces under their command. For such tactical surrenders in the field, as they were called, it was agreed that the military authorities in the west (Supreme Headquarters Allied Expeditionary Forces—SHAEF) and east (the Soviet High Command) need not first consult each other. But this military practice was under constraint. Each of these two top commands had promised to notify the other, and allow chance for consultation, if there was any prospect that a *main* German

[3]

force opposing it might stop fighting. And, in accord with pledges not to enter into any separate peace, it had also been agreed that the surrender of whole German armies on either of the two wide-ranging battlefronts—west or east—should not be accepted unless at the same time it was offered on the other. This was a mutual guarantee that the Germans should not be permitted to quit the fight in the west but keep on in the east, or quit it in the east but keep on in the west. The ultimate end would have to be one and indivisible.

The American and British governments had constantly to confirm to the Russians this accord against the Germans. The Nazi leaders and commanders did not bow to destiny in due season. Up to their last days they strove to escape the penalties of total defeat by securing an armistice in the west, which would enable them to maintain the fight against the Red Army. Some of them were genuinely surprised by their failure to corrupt the coalition, by the refusal of the western members to become quiet partners with them against Communist Russia. Even then these Germans were not aware of the aversion with which they were regarded. In their hearts they thought their own misdeeds justified. Why should not others? All through the war they had tried to imbue the western and eastern allies with greater fear of one another than of Germany. Why might they not yet manage to do so, when their western enemies realized they would have to face the Soviet Union alone unless they saved Germany from defeat?

Stalin, and those around and under him, scented the Nazi purpose. Their anxiety that it might succeed may be traced to their own conceptions—and preconceptions. In joining the infamous pact with Germany (the Molotov-Ribbentrop pact), which made certain the advent of the war, they had not been restrained by decency from doing what they deemed best for the Soviet Union and the cause of Communism. Why should not the West prove to be just as ruthless? In their book of beliefs about the nature of capitalist countries, the western allies were likely to act with guile, driven by relentless hatred of any Communist society.

Cooperation in the war had not really cleared the minds of those disciples of Communist dogma who ruled the Soviet Union of such ways of thinking and feeling. In the spring of 1945, when the drizzle of dissension began to fall upon their talks with their western allies about the arrangements for Europe after the war, this suspicion had revived. The objections made to Soviet designs for Poland and all other countries touching or near the Soviet Union had been construed as proofs of ill will. Whoever did not give in to the wishes of the Soviet Union must be its enemy.

The depth of Soviet distrust had been sharply revealed in the late March and early April that had just gone by. Then exploratory secret talks in Switzerland between American and British agents and mediaries for the German commanders in Italy, about the surrender of their forces, had brought forth from Stalin a blunt accusation of betrayal. Although Roosevelt was shocked, he had, in his last days alive, treated this as an aberration. At the time, the affair had come to nothing. But the experience had alerted the western military men to the frailty of Soviet faith in the pledged word that no peace would be made with Germany except a peace for all.

This shaped their course during the last weeks of battle, causing them to be most careful in their responses to German proposals, so as not to give ground for reproach. Even so, the friction over the measures that closed the war against Germany was a disturbing portent. It became clear that the ordeal had not joined the three great allies together in lasting trust and cooperation; that although their peoples were thankful of the end, the nations had separate strides and stances. The figures at the center of the concluding acts knew that the Soviet government was trying to make the Russian part in winning the war stand out supreme.

2. The Western Allies Prove Their Good Faith

THE next episode in the drama of surrender, after the trouble over the talks with German agents about surrender in Italy, was shaped by a wish to spare the Dutch people. By the middle of April, a Canadian Army corps had managed to expel the Germans from northeast Holland. But a large though isolated German force still retained its grasp on western sections of the country around Amsterdam. Its Commander had refused to give up, stating that he would fight on as long as the German armies elsewhere did. Reserve stocks, food, and other essentials for the Dutch civilians in the area subject to his will were almost gone, and two or three millions faced misery.

On April 10, in a message to Roosevelt, Churchill had described this prospect of near starvation. He had proposed that the two governments join in giving notice to the German government that they deemed that the German army had the duty to sustain the civilian population in those parts of Holland still under its control, but that it seemed to be failing to do so, and they were ready to provide what was needed. The German government was to be asked to facilitate this aid through the International Red Cross and other agencies. Should this offer be refused, Churchill thought the German Commander in Holland and all troops under him should be warned that by denying relief to the civilians in the area they would brand themselves before the world as murderers, and would be held grimly responsible for what befell the Dutch people. Truman had at once agreed to this program of protection.

The message calling on the German government either to see to it that the Dutch did not suffer or to allow the Allies to take care of them was sent through the Swiss government. It had led to talks between Seyss-Inquart, the German High Commissioner in Holland, and some of the leaders of the Dutch underground who were under arrest. Seyss-Inquart declared that he would not surrender the German forces in Holland as long as there was any effective military power in Germany. He urged instead that the Allied forces should suspend their attempts to advance past a designated line, and vowed that, if they did not, the soldiers under his command would obey their orders to fight to the end. He threatened to blast open the dams in the region and cause much of Holland to be flooded. The German forces in Holland, he boasted, would be able to resist long enough to ruin the country and starve those living in it. If the Allies would suspend their attack in Holland, however, he would refrain from these measures, and allow Red Cross ships or wagons to bring in supplies for the people. When and as the central German government might admit defeat, he would also.

The Dutch authorities (in exile in England)—including Gerbrandy, the Minister-President—saw salvation in this bargain. The problem was whether the Allies were to suspend their demand for unconditional surrender, and agree to this curious local truce, during which some of the opposing German forces might escape. Eden, in San Francisco, gave Stettinius a copy of a message from Churchill favoring acceptance. In the Prime Minister's view, the British and Americans ought not to be too stiff and proud when the life of a whole nation rested on a murderer's desperate push. He would "rather be blackmailed in a matter of ceremony than be haughty and see a free nation perish." The decision, he thought, lay solely between the American and British governments, but it would be well to let the Soviet government know what was in the wind. Let the three foreign secretaries discuss it while they were in San Francisco.

The State Department consulted the Joint Chiefs of Staff. General Marshall said that military prospects would not be hurt if operations against western Holland were suspended. But might there be, he wondered, other reasons for caution in thus trafficking with the enemy? The example might incite other Germany army commanders, those in Norway and Denmark perhaps, to make similar threats and propositions. The Joint Chiefs in their answer refrained from commenting on the political implications of this "apparent variation" from the rule that they would not deal with the Germans except on a basis of unconditional surrender. But they reminded the State Department that as our armies drew near to the Russians, need for closer touch was becoming imperative. They believed, therefore, that a Russian envoy should be present if the program was discussed with the Germans.

While President Truman, now Commander-in-Chief, was still gathering opinions, Churchill sent along a hint that the best way would be just to let Eisenhower act as he thought best. The idea had prevailed. The Combined Chiefs, on or about April 23, told Eisenhower they would leave the decision to him. He was not to depart from the unconditional-surrender policy; he was to see to it that his Soviet military associates knew what was going on; and he was to accord their liaison officers the chance to be in on any talks that might ensue with German agents. The Soviet government, he was also told, was being informed through the diplomatic route of the instructions being issued to him. Marshall penciled in a note at the end of this message: ". . . it being understood that General Eisenhower is to proceed without delay to carry out his instructions."

The American and British Ambassadors in Moscow advised the Soviet government accordingly. Neither the Soviet Foreign Office nor the Soviet High Command had any objection. By April 30, agreement was reached with Seyss-Inquart. The Allies promised to halt their military actions in Holland. Seyss-Inquart promised to flood no more areas of Holland, to end all his repressive measures against the Dutch, and to ease the entry of supplies. These supplies were quickly sent by land, sea, and air—to the grateful relief of the Dutch people.

While this special deal was being arranged, several major moves toward the surrender of the main German forces had taken a decisive turn.

The Americans and Russians had met on the Elbe. The British (Commonwealth) forces and Russians were about to meet near Lübeck on the Baltic. The German armies in Denmark and Norway, as well as those in Holland, were isolated; those in north Italy knew they were at the end; those in Austria and Czechoslovakia were near collapse and flight; the Russians were pounding against the last defenses of Berlin.

While that city writhed under its scourge of fire and smoke, Himmler took it upon himself to speak for Germany, on the score that Hitler was no longer able to do so, being cut off, gravely ill, or perhaps already dead. Himmler, that abhorred man, clung to the chance of saving himself by breaking the unity of the coalition. Having sought a meeting in Lübeck, he asked Count Bernadotte, head of the Swedish Red Cross, to arrange for him to see Eisenhower, so that he might offer surrender on the whole Western Front.

The Supreme Commander let it be known at once that he thought any reply to Himmler ought to insist that the Germans surrender to all three allies at the same time and everywhere, for he recognized Himmler's offer as a frantic attempt to create a schism. Churchill and Truman agreed with him. They then instructed the American and British Ministers in Sweden to have Himmler plainly so informed. In the course of telling Marshall that he was sure this was the only and right answer to make, the Supreme Commander reported that "In every move we make these days, we are trying to be meticulously careful in this regard"[1] —that is, to avoid any misunderstanding with the Russians.

[1] Truman, *Year of Decisions*, page 106.

To that end, Churchill and Truman hurried off messages to Stalin which, after telling him of Himmler's proposal, went on to say "There can be no question . . . of anything less than unconditional surrender simultaneously to the three powers." Within the day Stalin expressed his satisfaction. His answer to Churchill read, in part, "I consider your proposal to present to Himmler an unconditional surrender on all fronts, including the Soviet front, the only correct one. *Knowing you, I had no doubt you would act this way.*" When Churchill published the text of this message in his reminiscent account, he italicized the second sentence.[2] Could he have had in mind Stalin's accusation of deceitful purpose, made only a few weeks before, in connection with the talks about surrender of the German forces in Italy?

Bernadotte went back to Germany to pass on this answer. But by then Himmler, having thrown away his Nazi uniform and boots and decorations, was scurrying along dark back alleys.

Concurrently, and now with the confirmed support of General Vietinghoff, Commander of the German forces in Italy, a renewed effort was begun to find reprieve. General Wolff, the same SS officer who had taken the lead in the earlier talks, returned to Switzerland with full powers. The Combined Chiefs told Field Marshal Alexander that he might accept, as a tactical act in the field, the unconditional surrender of the German army opposing him in Italy. Churchill, on April 26, told Stalin of this authorization and asked that Russian envoys be sent at once to Alexander's headquarters to take part in any talks that might ensue.

The German envoys were brought to Caserta. There, on April 29, they signed the terms of unconditional surrender in the presence of British, American, and Russian officers. A few days later the fighting in Italy ended and nearly a million German troops gave themselves up as prisoners of war. Allied combat units were sped north in the direction of Austria.

On this same day, copies of Hitler's political will were being flung out of his last deep-down shelter in Berlin. In this Admiral Karl Doenitz was named Head of the German State and Supreme Commander of the German forces. In his first Order of the Day to the Armed Forces (issued on May 30) he said: "I assume command of all services of the Armed Forces with the firm intention of continuing the fight against the Bolsheviks until our troops and the hundreds of thousands of German families in

2 Churchill, *Triumph and Tragedy*, page 538.

our eastern provinces have been saved from slavery or destruction. Against the British and Americans I must continue to fight for as long as they persist in hindering the accomplishment of my primary object."

Doenitz concluded that the war had to be brought to an end as soon as possible. But he was determined to do his utmost to avoid a "corporate" unconditional capitulation on all fronts. Thus he resorted to a series of offers to surrender separate German armies to the western military commanders. In his *Memoirs* he avers that he neither sought nor expected to be able thereby to cause trouble between their governments and that of the Soviet Union.[3] His object was, he has explained, to postpone surrender in the east as long as possible, and gradually to retract the lines of resistance in the east to the demarcation line of the areas that were to be occupied by the British and Americans. But it is most unlikely that he failed to perceive that if the western allies allowed him to succeed in these tactics, the Soviet government would be resentful; and it is probable that he still hoped that the war alliance would at the last hour fall apart.

On the 2nd of May, Eisenhower got word that General Blumentritt, the Commander of the German Army Group between the Baltic Sea and the Weser River (in northwest Germany), wished to leave at once to see Field Marshal Montgomery in order to arrange the surrender of forces under him. Eisenhower decided that this tender also could properly be treated as a tactical military measure, and be dealt with as such. But in so advising Montgomery he cautioned that the only acceptable submission would be unconditional. The Soviet liaison officer at SHAEF, General Susloparoff, was told of this injunction.

Admiral Doenitz, however, changed his plans. On the next day (the 3rd) senior German officers, bearing written authority from Field Marshal Keitel, the Chief of the High Command of the Wehrmacht (OKW), with the consent of Admiral Doenitz, arrived at Montgomery's headquarters. They had come with an offer of surrender of the three German armies that were then *facing the Russians* between Berlin and Rostock on the Baltic, northwest of Berlin.[4] Montgomery told them that this offer should be made to the Russian commanders in the east— adding, however, that of course any individual soldiers or small groups from these three armies that came toward the Western Front would be accepted as prisoners. He also rebuffed pleas made by the scheming

---

[3] He has recounted his calculations and decisions in Chapter 22 of his *Memoirs*.
[4] Doenitz's subsequent account of his instructions to the senior member of the group, Admiral Friedeburg, is rather vague. "My instructions to Friedeburg," he writes in his

envoys for help in saving the many German civilians who were fleeing from the Russians. What the German envoys had in mind was a secret arrangement under which the German forces would take refuge in designated areas which still resistant German troops would give up to western armies as these went forward. Having made clear that he would have nothing to do with such a plan, Montgomery called upon the envoys of the High Command to surrender unconditionally to him all their forces on the western and northern lines of his area of command. The Germans said they would have to report back to Doenitz and Keitel. Montgomery wrote out his proposals and had the German envoys escorted through the lines to Flensburg.[5]

Forewarned, Eisenhower advised Montgomery that if the Germans should come back with an offer to give up their armies in Schleswig-Holstein, Denmark, Holland, and northwest Germany, without conditions, he could treat it as a tactical one and conclude the surrender on the spot. But should their proposal go beyond these limits they should be told they would have to present themselves to him, the Supreme Commander in the west. The Soviet High Command was informed at once of this guidance. Hardly had the message reached Montgomery when the German envoys were again brought into his presence.

He had been so sure of the answer that he had described to the press correspondents around him what was about to happen. This confidence was justified. Doenitz had been relieved at the acceptance of a separate surrender, which did not compel the instant abandonment of German soldiers and civilians to the Russians. Thus the German officers had returned that evening (the 4th) with authority from Doenitz and Keitel to surrender to Montgomery all their forces in these named battle lines and areas. It was arranged that fighting should cease on the following day, May 5.

Meanwhile, having learned that the German envoys were hurrying to his headquarters at Rheims, Eisenhower at once informed the Soviet High Command what he was going to say to them. With fateful finality, they would be told that the only way Germany could get peace was to surrender to him all forces on the Western Front, including Norway,

---

Memoirs (page 454), "were that he was to offer Montgomery the military surrender of the whole of north Germany and at the same time invite the Field-Marshal's special attention to the problem of the refugees and troops in retreat on the eastern boundaries of the area occupied by the British. He was in particular to do his utmost to ensure that the evacuations and withdrawals by land and sea were not adversely affected by the surrender, but would be allowed to continue."

[5] Montgomery prints the text of his terms in his *Memoirs*, page 302.

and to the Russian High Command all forces facing the Russians on the Eastern Front—at one and the same time.

This was the answer given to Admiral Friedeburg, speaking for Doenitz, when he offered to surrender only the forces on the Western Front. Nothing less than unconditional surrender *on all fronts,* he was grimly told, was acceptable. German troops were to stay where they were, hand over their arms intact, and surrender on the spot. A copy of an Act of Military Surrender, which had been written in Eisenhower's headquarters, was given to him. Commissioned to do so by the Soviet High Command, General Susloparoff listened and watched. In reporting to the Combined Chiefs, Eisenhower pointed out that this Soviet liaison officer had not objected to the stipulation that the German forces in Norway should surrender to him. He also saw to it that the Soviet High Command was at once informed, through the American and British Military Missions in Moscow, of what had taken place, and was given copies of the documents that had been handed to Admiral Friedeburg.

That depressed chief German envoy Friedeburg was convinced that the will expressed by Eisenhower could not be bent. He hurried off an aide to report to Doenitz asking permission to sign unconditionally a simultaneous surrender in all theaters.

While this talk with the messengers of the German High Command about the surrender of the German forces on the main western and eastern fronts was going on at Rheims, separate accords for ending the fighting in the north Alpine areas of Germany and Austria were being completed. But not without some confusion.

On May 4 Eisenhower heard from Alexander that General Kesselring, commanding all the remaining German forces in the west, was inquiring to what Allied headquarters he should address himself for the purpose of surrendering the German forces in the north Alpine region. Eisenhower told Alexander that Kesselring should address himself to General Devers, who was in charge of the U.S. 6th Army, then in the south of Germany. But Kesselring, without making clear what he had in mind, proceeded to ask consent to send an emissary to Eisenhower. The Supreme Commander sent word that unless Kesselring planned to yield all the German forces in Czechoslovakia, Austria, southern Germany, and the Balkans, and all those facing the Red Army —at the same time—it was useless to do so. If the purpose was merely to arrange a local surrender of forces in the Alpine area, that could be arranged with Devers. The Russian High Command was kept informed of each item in this correspondence. It ended when, on the 5th, the Commander of the German Army Group that was now scattered in or near the Alpine region of Bavaria, having been pushed back from the Palatinate, agreed with Devers to lay down arms at noon the next day.

Eisenhower, meanwhile, was tensely awaiting word about what the main German armies left in the west and east were going to do. On the 6th General Jodl came to join Admiral Friedeburg. The Russian liaison officer stayed close by.

Jodl had been instructed, if he found he had to offer a simultaneous surrender on all fronts, to suggest that it be carried out in two phases. During the first, to be as long as possible, all fighting was to end, but German troops were to be allowed freedom of movement. Once again the German envoys asked to be allowed to surrender only the forces on the Western Front; and they gave the impression that they were trying to gain time to move German soldiers away from the Russian front and German civilians from the areas that Russia was going to take over. Eisenhower, doing his utmost not to give the Russians any flicker of a reason for complaint, demanded almost instant capitulation. Speaking for the Supreme Commander, his Chief of Staff, General Walter Bedell Smith, repeated that only unconditional surrender at the same time on all fronts was acceptable. Unless they agreed to this, the Germans were told, all talks would be broken off and the Western Front would be sealed to prevent the frightened flow of German soldiers and civilians. In telling the Combined Chiefs of Staff what had been said, Eisenhower added that in practice, in order to save any needless loss of lives, all fighting would stop on the Western Front as soon as the act of surrender was signed. He was hopeful that the formal surrender could take place on the next day, the 7th; and that, if the program went through as planned, a proclamation could be made on the 8th, announcing Wednesday, May 9, as VE day.

"Eisenhower insists that we sign to-day," Jodl reported to Doenitz. "If not, the Allied fronts will be closed to persons seeking to surrender individually, and all negotiations will be broken off. I see no alternative —chaos or surrender."[6] Thus he asked to be enabled to sign on the understanding that actual fighting would stop forty-eight hours afterward (midnight May 8–9). In the early morning hours of May 7 Jodl was accorded the requested authority. Eisenhower agreed to this interval of forty-eight hours. At once the ultimate measure was completed.

[6] Doenitz, *Memoirs*, page 463.

A short Act of Military Surrender was signed.[7] Susloparoff put down his name for the Russians. The German envoys were also required to promise that appropriate German officers would execute a formal ratification of the act of surrender at another time and place, to be set by the Supreme Commander.

The first paragraph of the Act of Military Surrender read: "We the undersigned, acting by authority of the German High Command, hereby surrender unconditionally to the Supreme Commander, Allied Expeditionary Force and simultaneously to the Soviet High Command all forces on land, sea, and in the air who are at this date under German control." Thus ended in utter submission the effort of the Germans, under brutal Nazi direction and discipline, to make themselves masters of Europe and directors of an alliance that could sway the world. But nothing they might do then or later could heal the hurt they had done to the souls of individuals, the life of nations, or the stability of the western world.

A message, proud in its simple brevity, went from Eisenhower to the Combined Chiefs of Staff: "The mission of this Allied Force was fulfilled at 0241 local time, May 7, 1945." President Truman hastened to suggest to Churchill that they tell the world the news at the same time—at 9:00 a.m., Washington hour, Tuesday, May 8. They besought Stalin to time his announcement with theirs, since they did not think the news that the war was over could be held back longer; even then it was seeping out.

But the Soviet rulers would not be hustled. Their responses contained an echo of that note of annoyed accusation which was becoming familiar. The Allied Military Missions in Moscow had been asked by Eisenhower to let the Soviet High Command know as soon as the Act of Surrender was signed. But they were kept waiting two hours before given a chance to do so. In that interval General Antonov, First Deputy Chief of General Staff of the Soviet Army, replying to a previous message in which Eisenhower had outlined the final plans for handling the surrender, sent him a disturbed letter. Eisenhower learned what was in it early on May 7, a few hours after the surrender was sealed—as did also the Combined Chiefs of Staff. Antonov wrote that despite the fact that talks were going on (aimed to effect simultaneous surrender on all fronts), Admiral Doenitz, while ending

[7] See Supplementary Note 1, which traces the circumstances and ideas that led to the use of a short military Instrument of Surrender drawn up in SHAEF instead of the more comprehensive one on which the European Advisory Commission had been working for many months.

resistance to the Allied forces in the west, was ordering the German troops in the east to fight on. Such conduct was creating the impression among the Soviet people that he had already made a separate truce in the west. "You of course understand that such a truce would be a violation of Allied relationships."

Then, indicative of the Soviet wish to appear in first place in the drama, he went on to urge that the Act of Military Surrender be executed in Berlin, as it should be signed also by Marshal Zhukov. This point was verbally stressed by the member of the Soviet High Command when he gave the letter to the American Military Mission in Moscow, to be sent on to Eisenhower. The Soviet government preferred, he said, that there be only one ceremonial signing, and that this be in Berlin. And, contrary to their earlier assent, he also said that the Russian High Command did not approve of having Susloparoff sign a preliminary agreement. But that he had done hours before.

On reading this message Eisenhower flushed with anger. The drift of its language was unfair to him, and the Soviet wish overbearing. But his answer was calm and conciliatory. He did not deny that the German forces were acting in contrasting ways on the Eastern and Western Fronts in the brief passing interval (some forty-eight hours) between the signing of the Act of Surrender and the designated time when all fighting was to end. Remaining firm in his resolve that the great triumph of the coalition should not be spoiled by reproaches, he at once sped messages to the Russian High Command and to Washington. His reply to the Russian High Command was explanatory:

"I feel sure," he said, "you will understand that we have scrupulously adhered to the engagement of no separate truce on this front. When wholesale surrenders of enemy troops began taking place on our flanks, I ventured to keep on pushing in the right center until we should meet the Red Army. This movement was restrained because of the receipt of information from the Russian High Command that their commitment of large forces to the areas involved would certainly result in confusion and entanglement. We have consistently refused to discuss separate truce with anyone and have proceeded exactly in accordance with our understanding of Russian desires.

"While a brief instrument of unconditional surrender, of which you have a copy, was signed here at 0240 hours this morning, before receipt of your message above referred to, that instrument provides that the German High Command is required to report at a time and place fixed for a more formal signing. I should be very happy to come to

Berlin tomorrow at an hour specified by Marshal Zhukov who, I understand, would be the Russian representative. . . .

"My only desire is to get everything completed quickly in a clean-cut way in full cooperation with you."

His message to Washington informed the War Department of the letter from the Soviet High Command and of his reply. He added that he thought it becoming for him to go to Berlin for this formal signing if the Russian High Command wished it. Moreover, the course of events had altered his earlier ideas regarding the timing of the public announcement of the surrender; that, he now thought, had best wait until the Russians were thoroughly satisfied.

The Soviet top authorities were urging postponement. Stalin answered the messages from Truman and Churchill by saying he was not sure that the order of the German High Command to surrender unconditionally would be carried out at once by the German troops on the Eastern Front. He was afraid of a premature and misleading announcement. Thus he asked that any announcement be delayed until a formal surrender ceremony at Berlin had taken place and he was sure that the Germans meant to stop fighting. Antonov wrote still another letter to Eisenhower making a similar plea for postponement.

But Churchill and Truman both concluded that this could not and ought not be done. Rumors about the surrender were loose in Fleet Street and Whitehall. Lack of official confirmation might cause needless loss of life. So without waiting for Stalin, they went ahead and made their glad statements. Thus it came about that for a day, while western peoples were celebrating the event, the Soviet press ignored it. No flags were unfurled in the Russian cities.

On that same morning of the 8th, Eisenhower took still another step, however, to assure that the Russians would not suffer because the western allies were desisting from the fight. He told the Combined Chiefs of Staff he thought that since the Russian High Command was still worried lest the Germans fight on against the Russians after the fixed deadline, the American and British governments ought to set their minds at rest. This might be done, he suggested, by a statement that since the surrender of Germany had been made jointly to the Russian and to the Allied forces, any continuation of resistance after the agreed-on hour for its ending was an offense against all. Hence if any large numbers of Germans failed to surrender by that time, they would lose the status of soldiers. The Russian government might be assured as well, he thought, that the western armies would in any event continue to aid the Red Army in wiping out any lingering resistance. The Combined Chiefs of Staff approved this course.

The message telling the Soviet High Command of these intentions traveled ahead of the American group that was to take part in the formal ceremony of military surrender at Berlin. Eisenhower decided that the straits of precedence would be more easily avoided if he did not go. He assigned Air Marshal Tedder, his Deputy, to sign on his behalf. The personal message that the Supreme Commander hurried off to General Marshall, after watching the American mission take off for Berlin, is testimony to the strain he had been under in directing these momentous and touchy arrangements, and to the purpose that had guided him throughout:

"This meeting [at Berlin], completely concurred in by the Russians, finally relieves my mind of the anxiety that I have had due to the danger of misunderstandings and trouble at the very last minute. This anxiety has been intensified by the very skillful German propaganda that has been inspired by the German desire to surrender to us instead of the Russians. All the evidence shows that the Germans in the East are being paid back in the same coin that they used in their Russian campaign of 1941-42, and they are now completely terrified collectively and individually of Russian vengeance. . . .

"To be perfectly frank, the four days just past have taken more out of me and my staff than the past eleven months of this campaign. However, as I have noted above, I am at last reasonably certain that insofar as hostilities are concerned, the Russians and ourselves are in complete understanding and the meeting today should be marked by complete cordiality."

So it was. At 9:00 in the evening, General Keitel, as head of the German High Command, signed the second pledge of complete submission. Then, and then only, Stalin issued his victory proclamation telling the Russian people that the "great day of victory over Germany has come"; that the German troops were quitting and giving up their arms. "The Soviet Union," he added, "is celebrating victory though it does not intend either to destroy or dismember Germany."

But Eisenhower was called upon to take one more measure to end a last effort of the Germans to hold back the Russians a while longer. A few hours before the signature of the formal act of surrender at Berlin, Antonov again complained to Eisenhower that the Southern and Central groups of the German forces in the east had not yet given up; that some of them were still resisting while moving west. Thereupon the

Supreme Commander informed the German High Command that in view of these reports from the Red Army staff he had given orders to his troops to block all approaches to western lines and to impound all German forces moving from the east. They and their commanders, he added, would be turned over to the Soviet army as violators of the military act of capitulation. And, since he judged that actions of this kind were indicative of double-dealing by the German High Command, he ordered the instant arrest of the top officers of that command, including Keitel, Kesselring, Jodl, and Warlimont. These vigorous measures drew from Antonov, on the 10th, a letter of unusual warmth, expressing his "many thanks and sincere gratitude."

The attempted flight to the west of German combatants in organized units was thus checked. But soldiers, one by one or in small squads, still tried to get out of the reach of the on-coming Red Army. They plodded along the same roads as the pitiable columns of German civilians. Many of these had been thrust out of the towns, the land, and the villages into which the Poles, the Czechs, and the Russians were crowding; others were choosing to flee before the perils of oppression and revenge.

In following the discussions leading to the surrender of the main German armies in the west and east, we have passed by the concurrent and connected talks between the western allies and the Soviet government in regard to the bounds that should mark the areas of responsibility for dealing with the German forces in Austria and Czechoslovakia.

While dividing lines in Germany had been explicitly set in messages exchanged by Eisenhower and the Soviet High Command, none had been fixed in Austria. By the middle of April, the Soviet armies were in Vienna and the eastern part of Austria. There they had halted. A fortnight later American forces entered the country from the northwest, and French from the west. On May 4, the German garrison at Salzburg had surrendered to the American Field Commander. It was on the next day that the representative of the German Army Group in the Alpine region of western Austria and Bavaria had accepted Allied terms. Thereafter British forces, having marched up from Italy, entered Klagenfurt—on May 8—and joined with nearby Soviet troops in divided occupation of the province of Styria. Thus it came about that there were American troops in areas that were soon to be allocated to the Soviet Union as part of its zone of occupation in Austria, and Russian troops in areas soon to be allocated to Britain as part of its zone.

Czechoslovakia, it had been agreed, was to be treated as a liberated ally—to be freed of enemy forces and not kept under occupation. While the Russians were still fighting their way through the eastern sections of the country, American troops under General Patton had in late April crossed the western frontier and thrust southeastward along it. At the same time, due notice having been given the Russians, another column had begun to move east into Czechoslovakia as far as the Karlsbad-Pilsen-Budweis line. Churchill had advocated in messages to Truman that the U.S.-U.K. forces should seek to advance as far east as the Moldau (Vltava) River, which is a continuation of the Elbe and runs through Prague. Conformably, on April 28, the British Chiefs of Staff told General Marshall that the British government believed there would be much political advantage to be gained by doing so. They wished the Combined Chiefs to tell Eisenhower that while they were aware that the operation would be unwise if it meant he would have to lessen his efforts against the Germans in Austria and Denmark, he should use any improvement in his situation to keep going into Czechoslovakia.

Marshall was dubious, for, as he let his colleagues know, he was loath to risk American lives for purely political reasons. Thus he had revised the draft of an answer to the British Chiefs, to state flatly that the American Chiefs, for military reasons, did not take to the plan. The reason he gave was that Eisenhower's resources were fully engaged elsewhere, and probably would be to the end. But he had gone on to leave the way open by stating that Eisenhower might find he would have to move further into Czechoslovakia to complete the defeat of all German forces. The decision might best be left to him.

Marshall had asked Eisenhower what he thought about the move urged by the British Chiefs. In answer Eisenhower reported that he had been informed that the Soviet army was going to advance into the Moldau valley; that he was first moving into Pilsen and Karlsbad, and would not attempt any action he thought militarily unwise. He concluded, however—perhaps because the first German tenders of surrender in northwest Europe were about to free his forces for new ventures, or because the U.S. forces had moved on faster and further than he had expected, being only about sixty miles from Prague when the Russians were still over a hundred miles from the city—that he might safely attempt this advance. On May 4 he notified Antonov that he was willing, after occupying the Pilsen-Karlsbad area, to go forward to the region of Prague.

The State Department was hopeful that he would do so. On the 5th,

Acting Secretary Grew put before President Truman a memo giving the various reasons why the Department thought this extension of the American thrust into Czechoslovakia was wise and justified for political reasons. The flow of thought in its pages was more like Churchill's than any of the others that found their way to Truman's desk at the time. We had every reason and right to expect Soviet cooperation in regard to Austria and Czechoslovakia. But, on the contrary, the Soviet government was being ungiving and unhelpful. As examples, it had recognized a Provisional Government in Austria without consulting us or the British; it was refusing to allocate to the United States a zone in Austria that would contain an adequate airfield; it was pausing over a request that our diplomatic officials be allowed to go to the temporary seat of the Czechoslovakian government. Therefore the State Department believed that hard bargaining was needed, and that the present military chances should be used to serve our general policies. It recommended that the Joint Chiefs order the American armies to continue east to the Moldau River. In that connection it pointed out that the Soviet government was seeking our assent to a transfer to their zone of occupation of that section of Upper Austria north of the Danube into which the American Third Army had entered. The conclusion was that if our forces advanced to the Moldau, throughout its length, we would be able to deal with the Soviet Union on a basis of equality in regard to both Austria and Czechoslovakia, but otherwise it would probably continue to disregard our protests.

This operation was not attempted, however, for the answer Eisenhower received from Antonov repressed his impulse to go forward. The Soviet High Command asked that Allied forces in Czechoslovakia not be moved east of "the originally intended line." In the course of his comments Antonov pointedly recalled that the Red Army had stopped its advance to the Lower Elbe in Germany at Eisenhower's suggestion. Eisenhower complied with Antonov's request. The Red Army entered Prague. The German forces facing Americans surrendered in the field to American commanders, while those facing the Russians surrendered to Russian commanders. A period of separated military occupation of Czechoslovakia began.

The ordinary soldiers and civilians of the coalition did not know what care had been necessary to avoid a break among its members in the course of effectuating the group of surrenders. For them the days of victory were not darkened by somber forethought. In Britain the rejoicing was instant and deep. In the United States there was a surge of satisfaction and a soaring of spirits—restrained by thoughts of the war still to be fought against Japan. In Moscow the American Embassy was the scene of displays of friendly feelings by large and boisterous crowds. Members of the Embassy and the American Military Mission in Moscow were hoisted up and tossed about. Even the Dean of Canterbury, on the streets of Moscow, found himself on the shoulders of enthusiasts.

The three Heads of Government sent one another warm congratulatory messages and salutes. But even while soldiers embraced and crowds cheered and mothers wept in gratitude, the officials of the three great countries that up to then had stayed together were becoming estranged.

During the fortnight after the German surrender the American and British authorities were compelled to give intent thought to the wishes and pretensions of Moscow. They were worried over what Communist Russia had in mind for those parts of Europe and the Far East where it might extend its influence or control. Were these areas, emerging from the Axis reign of cruelty and arrogance, to pass under the Soviet reign of compulsion? Was the collaboration that had won the war so soon to dissolve? Or could it be preserved in support of a just and peaceful future? The differences between the Allies, after all the talks and vows of wartime, were enough, together, to affect relative power and realms of authority in the world thereafter. Past failures to reach agreement about them were beginning to turn mutual regard into offensive rudeness. And new issues were coming to the fore as soon as the demands of war ceased to be commanding.

These we must now review, and then follow the proposals and efforts by which the West sought to adjust them and reach a mutually fair and promising program for times to come.

PART TWO

The Time of Tension

3. Antiphony

THE antiphony in the performance of the coalition could be heard by trained listening ears in all three countries. Anxious doubts beat against the rhythm of the common cause. Now that the enemy of all was down would the coalition fall apart, each member beset by its own national history, aims, and fears? Or would enough sense of partnership be preserved to hold them together?

All would suffer if they did not remain as nearly at one as they had been during the war. Would the next—perhaps the last—mile along the banks of history be merely an elongation of the sad and violent annals of nation against nation? Or was there a turning and a change of vista ahead? Were the victors going to start rehearsing for another and more awful act in the human tragedy? Or could they this time make good by detachment and courage their avowals that the world must not again so suffer, and show at last that nations could long live at peace? It could not be hoped that mankind, congregated in their national shrines, would embrace the doctrines of St. Francis. But might they not become devoted to those that were being turned into a code of conduct at San Francisco?

History hints that what is done during the first few months after a great war ends is likely to determine the fate of the next generation, perhaps of many generations. Since prophets were not usable as diplomats, it was a time that called on diplomats to be prophets.

4. The Abrupt Slash in Lend-Lease Aid

No ACT of this time was more precipitate than the slash in Lend-Lease aid. The spell of comradeship in war was over. Hardly was ink dry on the Act of Surrender when the American government made known that it was not going to continue to provide its associates (the British Commonwealth, the Soviet Union, and the smaller allies) with weapons and supplies, except those needed to support the war effort in the Pacific. This measure would have been a shock no matter how managed. But because it was carried out abruptly, without prior notice or discussion, at a time of want and flux, the resultant tremor was regrettably great.

Generosity, even though serving a common purpose and joint interest, is hard to sustain. When tension comes between those who give and those who receive, the giver is apt to yield to the impulse to end the giving as soon as it is feasible to do so. Thus it happened in regard to the continuation of aid for the Soviet Union, under the Lend-Lease Act.

In the months after the Yalta Conference, when the conduct of the Soviet government began to provoke and worry, American officials had given thought to regulating the free and easy provision of products for that country and its people. The men who represented the United States in Moscow, Ambassador Harriman and General Deane, head of the Military Mission, had long since concluded that the time had come to do so. Both had become resentful of the Soviet indifference to what they regarded as fair American requests for cooperation.[1] They had urged that the American government should (1) require the Soviet government to give proof that each and every item on its list was needed for the effective conduct of the war; (2) be strict in its response to Soviet requests for products or machinery that might be put to use not in war but in Soviet reconstruction after the war; and (3) begin to ask definite return favors of some sort.

These proposals had been in the main resisted in Washington up to the end of the war against Germany. For this there were many reasons. American strategy and combat operations on the Western Front were conjoined with those of the Russians in the east; they must not be imperiled. Then Roosevelt and Hopkins had been determined to keep on proving our friendship in the hope of evoking a like disposition in

---

[1] Some of these requests—especially those made by our military departments—may not have been essential, or may not have taken into due account the hardships the Russian people were enduring or the difficulties under which the Soviet government was carrying on.

Moscow, for the sake of their great purpose—which was to lead the world into an era of prolonged peace. Another reason had been the coldness of the American military authorities in Washington toward any action that might cause the Soviet Union to delay its entry into the Pacific war. Still another had been the dislike of the State Department officials who were immersed in preparation for the coming conference at San Francisco of any step which might hurt that cause.

All but the first of these reasons remained valid even after Germany was defeated. But they were overborne by a wish or sense of duty to apply the law conscientiously.

Leo Crowley, the Foreign Economic Administrator in general charge of the Lend-Lease program, had been a public utility executive from Wisconsin. If the paths of politics had not led him into a detour, he probably would have been an isolationist, and against American support for Britain and the Soviet Union. Naturally, then, he believed that he was obligated, by the intent of Congress, to terminate that aid at the stroke of victory.

On the same day that the German surrender was announced, Crowley, along with Acting Secretary of State Grew, submitted to President Truman an order directing that Lend-Lease aid for our allies in Europe be ended at once. The President initialed it. By his own account he had not fully realized its import or effect. "What they told me," he wrote later, "made good sense to me; with Germany out of the war, Lend-Lease should be reduced. They asked me to sign it. I reached for my pen, and without reading the document I signed it."[2]

The subordinate officials to whom this order was sent carried it out with zeal.[3] They directed that goods waiting on the docks for shipment or in transport across the United States or still in factories were not to go forward. On vessels at Atlantic and Gulf ports and on the Pacific coast they interrupted the loading of all cargo except that consigned to the Soviet Union for use in the war against Japan. They even caused some of the ships at sea, en route to Russia with Lend-Lease cargo, to return to American ports. An instant protest was heard

[2] *Year of Decisions*, page 228.
[3] Harriman, who had advocated that we should not continue to provide the Soviet Union with Lend-Lease aid on the same lax basis as during the war, was taken aback at the abruptness and thoroughness of our action. To the officials of the War Department who directed the day-by-day execution of our policy, the wording of the original Presidential order seemed in very precise fashion to require them to do what they did. A good case can be made for their conclusion.

from Moscow, for the Soviet government had always regarded American aid as no more than its due, and construed the abrupt clipping of it as an attempt to force Russia to give in to us on other issues.

What had been done could be justified as an act of good faith toward Congress, and as an act of sense toward a country, the Soviet Union, that was devaluing our friendship as it pursued its own aims. But it was recognized at once that the way in which the measure had been put into effect gave just ground for grievance. So the American government hastened to make amends. On May 11, with Presidential approval, a corrected interpretation of the exigencies of the Lend-Lease law was adopted. The orders to return to the United States, given to ships at sea with Lend-Lease cargo for the Soviet Union, were cancelled; the ships were told to go on to their destination. All vessels on berth in American ports waiting for Lend-Lease cargoes were to be loaded and depart as scheduled. But, pending further review of both the law and the uses to which the products we sent would be put, it was directed that subsequent shipments were to be limited to weapons and goods for use of the Soviet Union in the war against Japan and in various previously approved programs therewith connected.

As a result of further examination of the question, in which the Joint Chiefs as well as the Secretaries of War and Navy participated, this policy was confirmed. Furthermore, the Soviet Union was to be asked to supply adequate relevant information to enable us to judge for ourselves in the future whether products requested were really needed for its war effort against Japan.[4] Against these legally correct and administratively sound measures the Soviet government did not protest. But, as will be seen, Stalin let us know later how displeased he had been by the first quick and ill-considered action.

Of all the recipients of Lend-Lease aid, Great Britain had the most reason to be offended by the abrupt termination. It had used up its resources without stint during the war, trusting in the American sense of partnership to enable it to make a fair start in restoring a tolerable peace-time life. Most of the British reserves of foreign investments and funds had been expended in the war effort. A substantial part of British shipping had been lost. Ordinary export trade had been forgone, and

---

[4] The actual rules adopted were more complex and flexible than this summary description. Since they were of consequence, a summary of their main features, as proposed by the Interdepartmental Committee concerned with the terms and ways of carrying out our Lend-Lease program (the Protocol Committee), and as approved by the President on May 15, are given separately, in Supplementary Note 2.

stocks of food and imported raw materials had been allowed to slump.[5] In contrast, needs during the period of transition to peace were going to be greater than ever before. Exceptional quantities of raw materials and equipment of all sorts would be required to enable Britain to get along, begin to restore industrial capacity, improve neglected railways and roads, and resume exports, so that it might again pay its way.

The British government had thought the country protected against a too severe and rapid reduction of American aid by the virtual promise that the President had given Churchill at their meeting in Quebec, on September 14, 1944.[6] Subsequently a committee of the Cabinet (Stettinius, Morgenthau, and Crowley) had recommended—subject to changing demands of strategy and conditions of supply—that the United States provide the British Commonwealth during the first year after the German defeat with about 2.7 billion dollars' worth of munitions and 2.8 billions of other products.[7] It had remarked that such a program would release British manpower and resources for reconversion, improve living standards, and aid in the revival of exports. Similar estimates had been given to the Senate Committee on Foreign Relations in the course of its hearings on extension of the Lend-Lease Act, which were held only a month before the end of the war against Germany.[8]

Little wonder then that the sudden and almost complete suspension of the flow of supplies had surprised and upset the British authorities. But they did not take quick offense or become sullen. The Chancellor of the Exchequer, Sir John Anderson, set to work to find out what, if anything, the American government was going to do to make good on

[5] For estimates of the deterioration in Britain's wealth, productive capacity, foreign investments, and gold, see Richard N. Gardner, *Sterling-Dollar Diplomacy*, page 178. He estimates that to compensate for losses in shipping and foreign-investment earnings, Britain's exports, which had dropped to one-third of their prewar volume, would have to be increased by about half over that volume to enable Britain to pay for same amount of imports as before the war.

[6] Roosevelt had initialed a memo calling for the provision to Great Britain, during the first year after Germany was defeated, of munitions in the approximate amount of 3.5 billion dollars, and other requirements—foods, raw materials, machinery, and shipping—of about 3 billions. This would permit Britain to transfer productive effort from the munitions industries to other branches of production. A thorough account of the commitments to the British is given in two Briefing Book memoranda, printed in Potsdam Papers, Documents 537 and 538.

[7] The joint public statement issued by the Committee on November 30, 1944, did not, however, specify any amount. It indicated an expectation that Lend-Lease deliveries to Great Britain would be reduced even before the defeat of Germany, and substantially thereafter. But it also stated it was likely "that both the United Kingdom and the United States will be able to reconvert part of their resources on an equitable basis to meet essential civilian needs in the period between the defeat of Germany and the defeat of Japan."

[8] See letter of Foreign Economic Administrator Crowley to Senator Arthur H. Vandenberg, April 4, 1945: U.S., 79th Congress, First Session, *Hearings . . .* , page 20.

the Quebec accord. While he sought to arrange a loan to enable Great Britain to procure vital necessities, Churchill and the British Chiefs of Staff exerted themselves to secure, as Lend-Lease, equipment and supplies for the extension of British war effort in the Pacific and the sustenance of British occupation forces in Germany and Austria.[9]

The expiration of the system of mutual support and aid bruised but did not rupture relations among the members of the coalition. Who knows how differently later events would have developed if the Lend-Lease program had been followed at once by another of equal dimensions in support of the peace-time efforts of the countries that had stood together against Germany? Conceivably this could have checked the warping of their attitudes which was by then well under way. But that is improbable, since the emerging subjects of dissension between the West and the Soviet Union were many and hard.

[9] A summary account of American policy in regard to the provision of Lend-Lease aid for Britain and our other Western European allies is given in Supplementary Note 2.

5. The Quarrel over Poland

OF ALL the quarrels within the coalition at the time of the German surrender, the one over Poland was the most taut and trying. The British and American governments were sure that the Soviet Union was bent on dominating the country. Despite all denials, its acts seemed to them clearly directed toward that end. Opposingly, the Soviet government chose to find malevolent intent in the stubborn resistance to its wishes. It professed to believe that the western democracies wanted the Soviet Union to remain exposed to assault from the west, and were bent on maintaining in Poland a government which, in the guise of independence, would be unfriendly. How closely aggression twines around fear; how frequently it feigns to be fear! It is in this dark tunnel in the nature of nations that peace is most often lost.

The three Heads of Government at Yalta, in February 1945, had agreed on the ways whereby the Polish Provisional Government, formed by disciples of Moscow, was to be reorganized so as to qualify for recognition by the United States and Great Britain, and on the general location of the new Polish frontiers. But the accord was ambiguous in the first respect, and incomplete in the second.

On what should be done about the government, the formula, to which Churchill and Roosevelt had given their resigned approval, read (in the Declaration on Poland): "The Provisional Government which is now functioning in Poland should . . . be reorganized on a broader democratic basis with the inclusion of democratic leaders from Poland itself and from Poles abroad." Whether Churchill realized that Stalin believed he and Roosevelt were assenting that groups loyal to Moscow would have dominant influence in the made-over government is hard to tell; in his memoirs the thought is not expressed. But Roosevelt knew it. His misgivings had been eased by the affirmation in the same declaration that the reorganized Provisional Government "shall be pledged to the holding of free and unfettered elections as soon as possible on the basis of universal suffrage and secret ballot." Any chance left that the Polish people might be free to choose their own government and fix their national policies depended on the honest fulfillment of this pledge. It had been arranged that Molotov and the American and British Ambassadors in Moscow (Harriman and Clark Kerr) should meet as a group to work out the steps by which this accord was to be carried out.

About frontiers the sustained argument at Yalta had been only partially resolved in that part of the Declaration which read: "The three Heads of Government consider that the Eastern frontier of Poland should follow the Curzon Line with digressions from it in some regions of five to eight kilometres in favour of Poland. They recognize that Poland must receive substantial accessions of territory in the North and West. They feel that the opinion of the new Polish Provisional Government of National Unity should be sought in due course on the extent of these accessions and that final delimitation of the Western Frontier of Poland should thereafter await the Peace Conference."

Stalin had been determined to extend Soviet territory westward to the so-called Curzon Line. He had insisted that the whole eastern segment of Poland, which he wanted, was not only Russian by habitation and historical heritage, but also vital for the protection of the Soviet Union. Churchill, whatever regrets he may have had that a former British Prime Minister had proposed this line as a just and suitable Soviet-Polish frontier, had not opposed it.[1] Roosevelt had agreed to it, in the belief that it was futile to try to deny to the Soviet Union what its armies could take and hold whether or not he and Churchill consented. But the Polish Government in Exile, resident in London and still regarded by the British and American governments as the only legitimate government of Poland, had been bitter about this turnover of territory to the Soviet Union. So had been the commanders of the valiant Polish armed forces who were fighting side by side with western soldiers and airmen.

Both Churchill and Roosevelt had been disposed to make up to Poland for this severance of its estate in the east. It would be amply compensated, they judged, if Poland received from Germany that part of East Prussia south of the Königsberg line, plus Upper Silesia and the area up to the line of the Oder River.[2] Thus bounded, the new Poland, it was reckoned, would be almost as large as the old and have a longer seacoast on the Baltic and greater sources of raw materials, especially coal. But at Yalta the President and Prime Minister had been faced by a claim for more by the Provisional Polish Government, backed strongly by Stalin and Molotov. Stalin urged that Poland's western frontier be

[1] The Curzon Line was named after Lord Curzon, the Secretary of State for Foreign Affairs, whose name was signed to the messages to the Polish and Soviet governments (July 1920) in which it was proposed. But actually it had been sponsored by Lloyd George, the Prime Minister. See the Supplementary Note on the origins of this line in Feis, *Churchill—Roosevelt—Stalin*, pages 657 ff.

[2] U.S. Proposal February 8, 1945: U.S. Dept. of State . . . , *The Conferences at Malta and Yalta, 1945*, page 972.

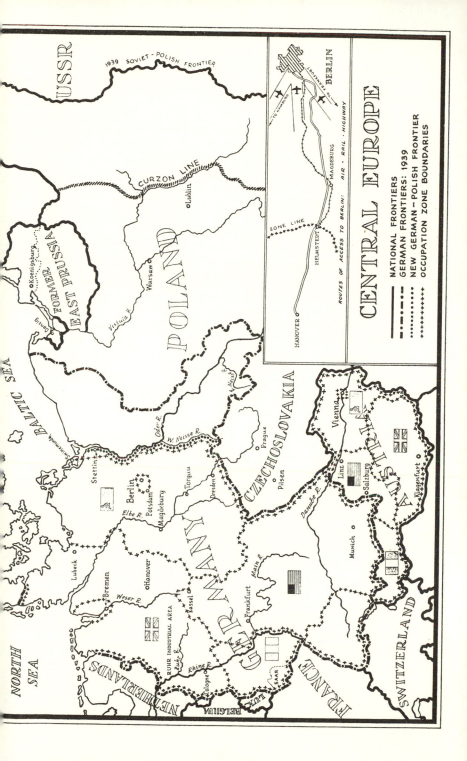

CENTRAL EUROPE

NATIONAL FRONTIERS
GERMAN FRONTIERS: 1939
NEW GERMAN – POLISH FRONTIER
OCCUPATION ZONE BOUNDARIES

USSR

1939 SOVIET - POLISH FRONTIER

CURZON LINE

Lublin

FORMER EAST PRUSSIA

Koenigsberg

Danzig

Vistula R.

POLAND

Warsaw

BALTIC SEA

Swinemünde

Stettin

Oder R.

W. Neisse R.

E. Neisse R.

Prague

CZECHOSLOVAKIA

Pilsen

Berlin

Potsdam

Torgau

Dresden

Magdeburg

Elbe R.

Lübeck

Bremen

Hanover

Kassel R.

Main R.

Frankfurt

GERMANY

Munich

Danube R.

Linz

Salzburg

Klagenfurt

Vienna

AUSTRIA

NORTH SEA

NETHERLANDS

Ruhr R.

RUHR INDUSTRIAL AREA

Weser R.

Rhine R.

Cologne

SAAR

BELGIUM

LUX.

FRANCE

SWITZERLAND

Inset map

BERLIN

TO HAMBURG

TO FRANKFURT

TO MAGDEBURG

Magdeburg

ROUTES OF ACCESS TO BERLIN: AIR · RAIL · HIGHWAY

ZONE LINE

HELMSTEDT

HANOVER

carried to that Neisse River (there was another of the same name further to the east) which flows south from the Oder River where that stream turns off to the southeast.[3]

Several million Germans lived in this large additional area, almost no Poles. These, presumably with the other six million or so Germans who lived east of the Oder, would be compelled to find new homes in the rest of Germany. That vulnerable country would be the more exposed to Soviet influence if Poland came under Communist control. Most significantly, it was foreseen that sooner or later this frontier might have to be defended by force. For these reasons Churchill and Roosevelt firmly refused to accede to this enlarged claim.

The issue had remained open. But the situation had not waited upon the consultations of the statesmen. During the spring many of the Germans had fled before the advancing Red Army and the Poles; and most of those who tried to stay were expelled.

In Moscow the Commission of Three had met many times. Their talks tore the Yalta accord apart, by distortion. The story of the tiring and repetitive arguments that wore out the patience of the American and British members has been told elsewhere. Harriman and Clark Kerr concluded that the Soviet government would not permit the emergence of any Polish government that might not be securely subject to its will; and that it was seeking to make Poland merely a protective and submissive projection of Soviet power.

After this failure Churchill and Roosevelt had sent distressed appeals to Stalin, and submitted several proposals that would allow the Commission to go on with its task. Stalin had answered them sternly. The Soviet position, he had alleged, conformed with the Yalta accord. It was they who were now trying to void it, by seeking to get rid of the Provisional Government in favor of a wholly new one. He had charged them with wanting to use persons who were known to be against all main points of the Yalta accord. Among those he had in mind was Mikolajczyk, the former Prime Minister of the Polish Government in Exile,

[3] The Matthews Minutes of the discussion in the Third Plenary Session on February 6, 1945 (*ibid.*, page 680), record Stalin as saying: "I prefer that the war continue a little longer and give Poland compensation in the west at the expense of Germany. I asked Mikolajczyk what frontier he wanted. Mikolajczyk was delighted to hear of a western frontier to the river Neisse. I must say that I will maintain this line and ask this conference to support it. There are two Neisse rivers. The east and the west. I favor the west." The other Neisse river, called the Eastern Neisse, branches off from the Oder south of Breslau and continues southward through the town of Neisse.

who despite his resignation was its leading political figure. Why should they not, Stalin and Molotov had urged, adopt for Poland the same terms on which a new government for Yugoslavia had been formed? Why not? Of the twenty-seven top places in that government, twenty were held by Tito's subordinates and only six by men of other groups and parties; and this minority were finding out that they had no influence and could not protect their supporters.

As a way of marking his displeasure at this resistance to his will, Stalin—on a pretext—had sent notice that Molotov would not be able to attend the San Francisco conference. The many Americans whose longings were centered on that venture in international creation were dismayed. But then, on an evening when he and Harriman spoke of Roosevelt's death, Stalin had relented. As a gesture he had said he would let Molotov go after all. The news that Molotov's flat but familiar visage would be among those around the head table at that assembly was strangely reassuring.

While Molotov was in Washington, not only the officials of the State Department but President Truman himself, in a blunt talk on April 23, had tried to get him to give ground on Poland. They had failed. All his responses had been akin to the one given to Stettinius when that affable but often inept Secretary of State solicited his approval of language to be used in a public announcement indicating to the world that "we are working in collaboration and unity particularly prior to the solemn task just facing us of setting up a world organization." The coral-like Soviet Foreign Minister had answered that we could "prove to the world our collaboration" when we had "achieved a settlement of the Polish question," but this could not be done "without first consulting the Warsaw Poles."

None of the later entreaties by Churchill and Truman had swayed Stalin. In the rejoinder he sent on April 24, on receiving Molotov's report of his talk with the President, Stalin asserted, after reviewing the record and the equities as they appeared to him, that the American and British governments were putting the Soviet Union in an unbearable position, trying to dictate to it. And he had been unmoved by the last lament (April 28) that Churchill addressed to him before the German surrender: "There is not much comfort in looking into a future where you and the countries you dominate, plus the Communist parties in many other states, are all drawn up on one side and those who rally to the English-speaking nations and their associates or Dominions are on the other. It is quite obvious that their quarrel would tear the world to pieces and that all of us leading men on either side who had anything to do with that would be shamed before history."[4]

The Soviet government was making surer each day that the Warsaw government could not be displaced and could not turn aside from Moscow. In the face of open American and British opposition it had signed a mutual-aid pact with that unrecognized regime. This action Molotov had defended, while in San Francisco, saying that since the Warsaw government was the only one functioning in Poland the Soviet government had to deal with it, to assure order as the Red Army fought its way into Germany.

And then, defiantly and without consulting the western allies, the Soviet High Command committed to the Warsaw government the control of the whole region to the Western Neisse—including areas within the designated Soviet zone. When first quizzed about this action, the Soviet government had argued that it did not conflict with agreements with the American and British governments about occupation and control of Germany, because "neither in the aforementioned agreements nor in the decisions of the Crimean Conference is the question of administration of occupied German territory touched upon." This contention, while literally true, was an abuse of good faith. While negotiating these accords, the Soviet government had never questioned the assumption that no one of the three occupying powers could transfer control of any part of its zone except by common consent.

The Soviet government avowed also that this step would not affect the determination of Poland's future frontiers. That opinion was shown to be false even as it was being uttered. The Prime Minister of the Provisional Government had said in a broadcast (on March 31) that "Besides Gdańsk [Danzig] we have received back the Masurian lands, Lower and Upper Silesia, and the hour is not distant when the Polish frontiers will be established on the Neisse, the Oder, and the Baltic shores." The Polish press construed the action similarly, telling of it in such headlines as "All Silesia unites with Poland!" In effect this area, as well as East Prussia (except that section kept for itself by the Soviet Union), was being taken over by the Poles.

But the American and British governments chose to treat the pretenses as sincere. Thus on or about May 8, the day after the German surrender, George Kennan, in charge of the American Embassy while Harriman was in the United States, left a memo at the Soviet Foreign

---

[4] This message is printed in full in Stalin Correspondence, vol. 1, pages 343-44.

Office, as instructed. This registered for the record the Soviet assurance that the transfer to Polish civil administration of territory that was German before 1939 had no relation to the question of the boundaries. It stated that the American government welcomed this assurance and assumed that the occupied German areas in question would remain effectively under Soviet occupation, with local administration entrusted as a matter of convenience to local Polish officials who were in no way responsible to the Warsaw government. On leaving this memo, Kennan reminded the Soviet recipients that the American government was against any change in the status of enemy territory without prior agreement of the several United Nations. Thus it was attempted to turn pretense into practice.

Meanwhile the Soviet secret police had arrested all the remaining leaders of the Underground Army who were attached to the Government in Exile and to the political parties still loyal to it. They were lured into coming out of their hiding places in Poland by hints that the Soviet government wanted to talk with them about the political future of their country, and by a guarantee of personal safety. For weeks the Soviet government had said it did not know where these sixteen men were. The British and American governments had continued to inquire, since rumors of what had happened were spreading. Then, after putting their prisoners through the usual secret inquisition, the captors accused them of being guilty of diversionary acts at the rear of the Red Army, and of terrorism and spying. They were to be brought to trial.[5]

Undeterred by the anger aroused in the American and British governments by the offensive Soviet treatment of their views, Molotov had persistently sought to get them to invite the Soviet ward, the Polish Provisional Government, to send representatives to the San Francisco Conference. Truman, aligning himself with Churchill, had bluntly refused the request, in his message to Stalin on May 4: "The meetings of the three foreign secretaries on the Polish matter have not yet produced a formula which is satisfactory. I consider it of the utmost importance that a satisfactory solution of the problem be worked out as soon as possible. I must tell you that any suggestion that the representatives of the Warsaw Provisional Government be invited to San Francisco, conditionally or otherwise, is wholly unacceptable to the United States Government. To do so would be the acceptance by the United States

[5] By this time a record of guilt had been made out of their confessions under detention.

[37]

government of the present Warsaw Provisional Government as representative of Poland which would be tantamount to the abandonment of
the Yalta Agreement."

Stalin had been just as plain-spoken in his rejoinder, saying that
"We insist and shall continue to insist, that only people who have
demonstrated by deeds their friendly attitude to the Soviet Union, who
are willing honestly and sincerely to co-operate with the Soviet state,
should be considered in the formation of a future Polish government."

Thus, as the war against Germany ended, the members of the coalition were sharply at odds over Poland. Both the American and the
British government had tried hard to reach a compromise accord clearing
the way to the formation of a Polish government that they as well as
the Soviet Union could recognize, thus mending this ugly rupture in
the coalition. They were to keep on trying. But a reflective reader, after
following the outcome of their effort, may wonder if they were well
advised to do so. Either of two other courses might have saved more
freedom for the Polish people: a fixed stance of opposition, backed by
American and British armies in Europe; or a complete dissociation, after
spoken protest, from the Soviet course in Poland.

6. The Tussle with Tito over Frontiers

NEXT in pitch to the row over Poland was the quarrel with Tito over his efforts to extend the realm of Yugoslavia.[1] He was bent on taking over the adjacent region that had been added to northeast Italy after the First World War. This was called by the Italians the province of Venezia Giulia; it bounded on Austria to the north, Yugoslavia to the east. In its southern section along the Adriatic were the port cities of Fiume and Trieste, on opposite sides of the base of the Istrian Peninsula. Railways and roads leading to Austria, Hungary, and the Balkans ran through the province in north and east directions. Thus the region was deemed to have both commercial and strategic value. In and about Trieste and the Istrian Peninsula there were many Croats, and in some more northern places many Slovenes mingled with greater numbers of Italians.

It had been foreseen that Yugoslav troops and partisans would have made their way into these areas before the war was over. Once there, it was feared they would not get out or give them up. This was a threat to the rule upheld by the American government that countries should abstain from grasping territory by force, and that all changes in frontiers should rest until they were passed upon at a peace conference. The historian who scans the whole horizon of the post-war world will observe how hard the State Department clung to this rule in regard to some of the disputed territorial questions in Europe. Even though Roosevelt at Cairo, Teheran, and Yalta had agreed that China was to have much of the Japanese Empire, and that the Soviet Union might reabsorb the Baltic states and have part of East Prussia and the eastern sections of Poland, the Department sustained the principle that fair foresight, not force or diplomatic bargaining, should determine the relocation of the national frontiers after the war was won.

There were also more definite reasons why the British and American governments were worried over this particular occurrence. A Yugoslav claim to the region would arouse resentment among the Italian people against their weak and faltering government, and cause a transfer of support to the Italian Communist Party. It might also hinder the main-

---

[1] Truman's *Year of Decisions* and Grew's *Turbulent Era*, vol. 2, are informative published sources of information about American policy, and C. R. S. Harris' book *Allied Military Administration of Italy*, especially Chapter 12, "Frontier Problems," is a lucid source about British policy. But none, in my opinion, adequately reveals the differences of judgment and wavering of decision both within each of the two governments and between them.

tenance of western military forces of occupation in Austria, because the port of Trieste and lines of communication from there to Austria were needed for the supply and movement of troops. Furthermore, if Tito was unchallenged, there were signs that he would also try to annex by similar methods adjacent parts of Austria.

Churchill and the new Supreme Commander in the Mediterranean, General Alexander, had, during the closing period of the war, sought to avert trouble by getting Tito to agree to the extension of Allied Military Government (AMG) over the whole of the province of Venezia Giulia as elsewhere in Italy. Tito had said he would not oppose the presence of Allied Military Government in the northern part of the area, or the line of communication to Austria, if the Yugoslav civil governments already installed in many localities were retained. He disputed, however, the need for Allied occupation of the Istrian Peninsula south of Trieste.

Seeking to obviate a clash, the British government had tried to get the American government to agree to the idea of dividing the disputed area into two zones, leaving the east and southeast section under Tito's control. But the State Department continued to oppose dissection as a solution. Thus as the fighting in Italy ended, there loomed the question of what to do if Tito would not give in. Should the Allies merely order their armies to take over, even if they had to drive out Tito's troops and partisans? And if they did so, how would the Soviet government react?

The differences of judgment between the British and Americans as to what had best be done had left Alexander without orders. Since he could not wait for them any longer, he informed the Combined Chiefs of Staff, on April 26, that unless otherwise instructed he would use an Anglo-American task force to take over those parts of Venezia Giulia essential to his military assignments. Thereafter he would proceed to set up Allied Military Government in this area. That organization would do its work through such suitable local personnel, whether Italian or Yugoslav, as were found on the spot. His thought was to explain his intentions to Tito before sending his troops into Venezia Giulia, and to say that any Yugoslav forces remaining there must necessarily come under his command. On the next day, April 27, Churchill urged Truman to approve this try of Alexander's. He said it seemed to him "vital to get Trieste if we can do so in the easy manner proposed, and to run the risks inherent in these political-military operations. . . . The great thing is to be there before Tito's guerillas are in occupation. Therefore it does not seem to me there is a minute to wait. The actual status of Trieste can be determined at leisure."[2] Acting Secretary of State Grew liked the tactic, and the Secretary of War went along with him. So, after consulting the Joint Chiefs, Truman answered Churchill: "The Combined Chiefs of Staff with my approval authorized Alexander to accomplish what I understand to be your idea regarding Trieste and other areas formerly under Italian rule as a matter of military necessity."[3]

Conformably, on the 28th, Alexander was instructed by the Combined Chiefs (in FAN 536) to occupy, and thereafter set up Allied Military Government in the whole of Venezia Giulia, including Fiume, the Istrian Peninsula, and the Quarnerolo Islands (except Zara). The combat forces and civil affairs officers were to be provided jointly by the British and the Americans. Tito was to be asked to withdraw his troops and partisans; and the Soviet government was to be asked to join in persuading him to do so. But Alexander was authorized to carry the plan into effect without waiting for Yugoslav or Soviet assent if he deemed such action necessary for military reasons. This release for action was braked by a caution that if any Yugoslav forces in the area began to resist, he was to ask the Combined Chiefs what to do next.

Alexander had informed Tito what he was going to do. Tito in turn informed him that as the situation had changed since the talks at Belgrade, the Yugoslav theater of military operations now went all the way west to the Isonzo River and north to the Austrian frontier— that is, over most of Venezia Giulia, including Trieste. In that area Yugoslav military and civil authorities would "naturally" continue to function. After this answer a direct clash between Allied forces and Tito's troops impended. The British Chiefs of Staff, through whom orders to Alexander were issued, decided to let him proceed, but with

[2] *Triumph and Tragedy*, page 552.
[3] *Year of Decisions*, page 244. But did Truman have a correct understanding of Churchill's idea at this time? That he may not is suggested by the fact that very soon thereafter Stimson and Marshall showed themselves confused about British wishes and intentions. They had thought briefly that the Prime Minister wanted to move U.S.-British forces into *the whole of the province*, as did the State Department at this time. But they found out otherwise. The entry that the Secretary of War made in his diary on May 2 (four days after FAN 536 was sent) indicates what happened: "I found out in the Staff conference that the British were strongly against our State Department's position in regard to the occupation of Venezia Giulia and were in favor of acting in concert with the Tito forces instead of acting against them; that the whole plan of the State Department was apparently based on a directive of Mr. Roosevelt before he died. This very strongly affected the position which I had misunderstandingly taken the other day in advising Marshall to back up the State Department. I thought the State Department was backed by the British instead of opposed by it." The records leave the reader puzzled as to who was confused and why; and whether or not Churchill was going through one of his rapid transitions of opinion.

care. He was told to go forward as far as he could, but if he met Yugoslav forces who refused to cooperate, he should halt, parley, and consult the Combined Chiefs. He should not use force except in defense.

Churchill, on this same day (April 30), sent Truman another running account of his impressions of the situation. He regarded as good what he called the military part of the instruction that had been sent to Alexander (FAN 536)—presumably having in mind the authorization to act without waiting for Soviet and Yugoslav assent if he felt there was military reason. In his opinion, Churchill said, it was a delusion to suppose that the Yugoslavs, with the Soviet government behind them, would agree to our entering or taking control of Venezia Giulia and Fiume. But the American and British governments, in their measures to clear Italy, including the Adriatic Provinces, of the Germans, had never undertaken to be limited by the approval of either the Yugoslavs or the Russians. Were not their forces as entitled to move freely into Trieste, if they could get there, as were the Russians to win their way into Vienna? "We ought if possible to get there first and then talk about the rest of the province." Let Alexander, therefore, carry out the plan that the Combined Chiefs had approved, do so as quickly and as secretly as possible, and above all else, take possession of Trieste from the sea before saying anything more to the Yugoslavs or Russians.

Even though the Americans had previously opposed the idea of an agreement with Tito providing for a dividing line of control, they now became upset by Churchill's bold attitude. Withered suspicions revived —that the British might be trying, for reasons of their own, to get us involved in fighting the Yugoslavs and maybe the Russians. Stimson, speaking both for himself and for General Marshall, warned Acting Secretary of State Grew of the danger just before Grew joined Leahy and others at a conference on the 30th with the President at the White House.[4] Either because he had formerly been merely sustaining the opinions of his staff, who were defenders of the Italian interest, or because he was unnerved by Stimson, Grew now wavered. At the conference at the White House, he, who up to then had favored a firm

---

[4] Grew prints the text of the memo of his talk with Stimson in *Turbulent Era*, vol. 2, page 1477. He recounts that Stimson read to him over the telephone an excerpt from a letter he was about to send over to Grew. This said that "Since present plans indicate the United States will have little or no military interest in the areas . . . once the Germans are eliminated therefrom, the continued presence of U.S. forces in these areas and their operations, become a political matter." It asked for clear-cut guidance at once from the State Department. Stimson then went on to tell Grew how worrried he and General Marshall were about possible developments, and remarked that in going along with Grew up to then he had gone against the wishes of his staff.

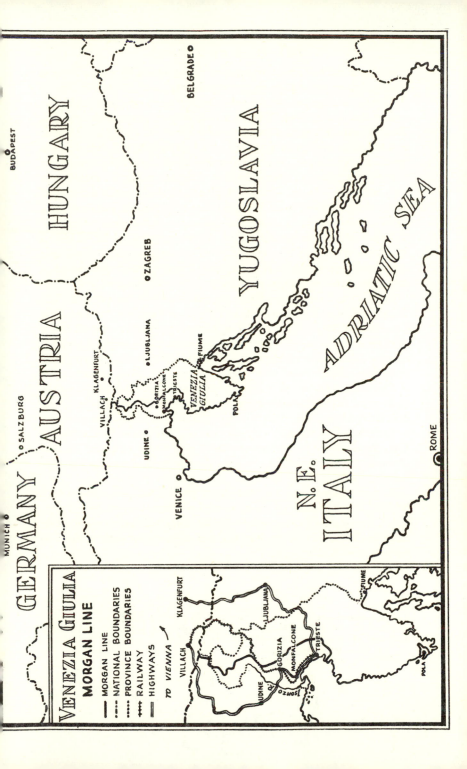

course, said that the State Department felt it would be most unwise to employ American forces to fight Yugoslavs.[5]

Truman was swayed by the anxieties and views of his advisers. His resultant answer to Churchill was a criss-cross of do's and don't's. The President was willing to have Alexander go ahead with his attempt to secure control of Trieste and the Istrian Peninsula and lines of communication to Austria. But the General should not fail to tell Tito what he was going to do, and before getting into a scrap he should communicate again with the Combined Chiefs. "I think this is important," he concluded, "for I wish to avoid having American forces used to fight Yugoslavs or being used in combat in the Balkan political arena."[6]

Alexander's troops were by then on the way to Trieste. Thus on May 1 he sent a warning to Churchill. He was now sure, he said, that Tito would not withdraw the Yugoslav troops from Trieste or Istria unless the Russians told him to do so.[7]

But during the night of May 1-2, Alexander continued to go forward. The division in the forefront of the advance, the Second New Zealand Division, met up with Yugoslav troops at Monfalcone, a few miles north of Trieste. The officer in command, General Freyberg, informed the commander of the Yugoslav forces on the spot that he was going to continue on to Trieste. So he had, receiving the surrender of the German soldiers that were in the town and taking control of the dock area. Yugoslavs were roaming over other sections of the town. Alexander's forces also went into Gorizia, although Yugoslav partisans were there before them. Thus, in much of Venezia Giulia, Allied and Yugoslav forces were in close contact as each strove to extend its area of occupation. As the last Germans fled, they seemed about to scrimmage.

At this juncture all the contestants paused and sent up rockets. Stimson and Marshall in effect warned the President to look out or Americans would be entrapped in the Balkans, and the Russians might come to the support of the Yugoslavs or even retract their promise to enter the war against Japan.

The Italian government bemoaned the situation, and implored the

[5] Grew, Admiral Leahy, William Phillips (a former Undersecretary of State who was temporarily serving in the State Department), and H. Freeman Matthews (Director of the Office of European Affairs) were present at this conference with Truman. Neither Stimson nor Marshall was asked to participate. The memo that Grew made of the talk is printed in *Turbulent Era*, vol. 2, page 1475.

[6] *Year of Decisions*, page 245.

[7] *Triumph and Tragedy*, page 553.

American and British governments to take control of all of Venezia Giulia. Cries of "Trieste is Italian" were heard in the streets of Rome. The American Ambassador, Kirk, reported that Allied prestige in Italy would be damaged if Allied Military Government was not maintained at least in Trieste and the surrounding areas. If it were not, he warned, the government of Italy might topple, and we might have to use American forces to keep order in that country. From his talks with his British colleague, Macmillan, he got the impression that our unwillingness to risk conflict with Yugoslav forces was disposing the British to give in.

Tito protested. He justified the earlier advance of Yugoslav forces on the ground that after Alexander made what he called a "truce" with the enemy forces in north Italy, the Germans could have transferred troops eastward toward Slovenia. Now that the Germans were gone, what military reason could there be for the Allied thrust into Trieste and nearby areas? He was willing, however, he told Alexander, to have SACMED use the ports of Trieste and Pola, and the lines of communication leading to Austria. Since the control of the government of the region had become a political rather than a military question, he, as Prime Minister, "must first of all take care of the interests of [his] country." Thus he kept his troops under orders to hold on to the territory up to the Isonzo River, and to try to establish civil control even in the eastern part of the adjoining Italian province of Udine. In sections of Trieste and elsewhere Tito's men were arresting the Italians of importance, conscripting others for forced labor, seizing banks, and requisitioning grain and other supplies. But they avoided clashes with Allied troops.

Alexander and his field commanders behaved with similar caution. While awaiting orders from the Combined Chiefs, they devoted their efforts to developing and operating the lines of communication from Trieste to Austria.

Now the British Chiefs again sought to get their American colleagues to agree to a dividing line, on one side of which there would be Allied Military Government and on the other side of which the Yugoslavs would be allowed to exercise control. The State Department then fell in with the idea of resolving the dangerous situation by making an accord of this kind with Tito. But, with the effect on Italy in mind, it maintained that Alexander's sphere of control must include a considerable area surrounding the city of Trieste. The Joint Chiefs thought it best to leave the determination of the line to Alexander, who could be counted on to do, and to do quickly, whatever could be done without getting into a battle with the Yugoslavs.

Having thus been granted latitude by the Combined Chiefs to compromise, Alexander sent his Chief of Staff, General Morgan, to confer with Tito in Belgrade on May 9. Morgan proposed an accord whereby SACMED would control the port of Trieste, the railways and roads from there to Austria via Gorizia and Tarvisio, and adjoining areas of Venezia Giulia. All regular Yugoslav military forces west of this line should be withdrawn, and all irregular forces either withdrawn or disbanded. But the Allied Military Government would use any local Yugoslav civil administration that was already in the area and working well. Morgan strove to make clear that this arrangement was to be regarded merely as one of military convenience, and that it should not prejudice the ultimate disposal of Venezia Giulia.[8] Thus deference was paid to the American attachment to a verbal formula, which in this as in other like situations turned out to be of little protective value.

Tito was not ready to forgo the chance to grasp the whole province. Civil government in all parts of it, he insisted, should be controlled by the Yugoslav National Liberation Committee. He suggested that military matters and operations, even in Trieste and along the lines of communication, should be jointly exercised. And instead of recalling the Yugoslav forces that were in the area Morgan reserved for SACMED, he sent in more.

Even more alarmed reports from our Ambassador in Rome were tumbling in. As summarized by Grew, for the President, these indicated that Tito was proceeding to dominate the entire region, which he admitted he intended to keep under the Peace Treaty; that Russia was undoubtedly behind Tito's move, with a view to utilizing Trieste as a Russian port in the future; that the Italian Socialists and Communists were arguing that the United States and Great Britain were no longer able to oppose the Soviet Union in Europe; and that the position of Ivanoe Bonomi (Italian Premier and Foreign Secretary) as President of the Council was endangered.[9] Truman now in turn was aroused by Tito's intransigence.

While Truman's previous messages to Churchill on the Venezia Giulia

[8] The text of Morgan's proposal is in Harris, page 337.
[9] Grew memo of conference at White House, May 10, 1945, in *Turbulent Era*, vol. 2, page 1479.

situation had been guarded, his next one (sent on May 11) was fired with indignation. He had come to the conclusion, he said, that they must now decide whether or not to hold Tito in check, for the Yugoslav leader not only was trying to grab control of Venezia Giulia, but had an identical claim for south Austria, in Carinthia and Styria; and he might even have similar designs on parts of Hungary and Greece if his methods in Venezia Giulia succeeded. The stability of Italy and the future orientation of that country with respect to Russia, he went on to remark, might well be at stake.

"I suggest," he concluded, "we instruct our ambassadors at Belgrade to inform Tito along these lines: that Venezia Giulia is only one of the many territorial problems in Europe to be solved in the general peace settlement. The doctrine of solution by conquest and by unilateral proclamation of sovereignty through occupation, the method used by the enemy with such tragic consequences, has been definitely and solemnly repudiated by the Allied Governments participating in this war . . . The plan of Allied military government for Venezia Giulia was adopted precisely to achieve a peaceful and lasting solution of a problem of admitted complexities. It is designed to safeguard the interests of the peoples involved . . . With these considerations in mind, and in view of the previous general agreement of the Yugoslav Government to the plans proposed for this region, my Government has instructed me to inform you that it expects that the Yugoslav Government will immediately agree to the control by the Supreme Allied Commander in the Mediterranean of the region which must include Trieste, Gorizia, Monfalcone and Pola, and issue appropriate instructions to the Yugoslav forces in the region in question to cooperate with the Allied commanders in the establishment of military government in that area under the authority of the Allied commander . . ."[10]

Churchill has told of his reception of this message: "I need not say how relieved I was to receive this invaluable support from my new companion." His answer began: "I agree with every word you say, and will work with all my strength on the line you propose. . . . If the situation is handled firmly before our strength is dispersed Europe may be saved from another bloodbath. . . . I trust that a standstill order can be given on the movement of the American armies and Air Force [toward home and to the Far East], at any rate for a few weeks."[11]

10 *Year of Decisions*, pages 247-48.
11 *Triumph and Tragedy*, page 555.

A copy of the text of the connected notes which the Ambassadors in Belgrade gave to Tito was sent, as Truman had suggested, to Stalin for his information.[12]

But what if Tito remained stubborn? Churchill was ready, perhaps even eager, to deploy all the divisions under Alexander's command (six British Commonwealth and Indian, seven American, two Polish, one Brazilian), if necessary to achieve the purpose.[13] But Truman was not. His impulse to act was dampened by the warnings of Stimson and Marshall, and by the wish for Soviet entry into the war against Japan. So he refused to promise to keep the same number of American divisions under Alexander's command as were there at the time. Nor would he join in an immediate order that would have enabled Alexander to use American divisions against Tito. Should they not, he asked Churchill, await Tito's response to the diplomatic presentations before deciding what forces if any to use? Unless Tito attacked it was impossible to involve the United States in another war.

Alexander was still under orders to ask for advice from the Combined Chiefs before taking any action against Yugoslav forces, although he was authorized, if attacked, to use in defense any or all troops in his command, including Americans. This left misty ground between active and passive policy—which puzzled Churchill. "I thought, from your number 34 [of May 11]," he observed to Truman, "that if [Tito] were recalcitrant, we should have to push his infiltrations east of the line you have prescribed. I presume his prolonged intrusion into these regions would, if persisted in, constitute 'an attack.' "[14] But Truman drew back from the attempt to try to commit him to this conclusion.

During this same period of suspense a race had been going on between the British Eighth Army and Yugoslav partisans for occupation of sections of Austria along the Yugoslav-Austrian frontier. The British had reached Klagenfurt, on the frontier, three hours before the Yugoslav partisans. But the partisans were hindering the Allied Military Government, entering hospitals, taking automobiles and food, and harassing the press. They were placarding the town with posters proclaiming that: "The Jugoslav Army has entered Carinthia in order to bring liberty and democracy to the Slovenes and Austrians and clean the land of Nazi criminals. Complete victory over Germany has now been gained by

---

[12] The message from Churchill to Stalin on May 15, conveying the text of the note to Tito, is printed in full on pages 352-56 of vol. 1 of Stalin Correspondence.

[13] See his message of May 12 to Alexander, in *Triumph and Tragedy*, page 556.

[14] *Year of Decisions*, page 248.

Jugoslav partisans also helped by the Soviet Union, England and America. We hereby make known that the military authority of the Jugoslav Army has now been established throughout all liberated Carinthia. The population and all branches of administration are to extend aid to our Army and to obey all published decrees unconditionally." In the town of Villach British troops were also in occupation, but the partisans were in control of many nearby villages inside Austria.

The two seemed on the verge of a clash when on May 10 the British Ambassador in Belgrade was instructed to urge Tito to withdraw all Yugoslav forces from Austria at once. This note emphasized that the American, British, and Soviet governments, all three, had stated in the Moscow Declaration of November 1, 1943, that they planned to restore a free and independent Austria within 1937 frontiers. Tito was asked to respect this line as a provisional boundary between Austria and Yugoslavia, pending final settlement at a peace conference. The Prime Minister had asked the President to stand by him in this demand, and the President had said he would. Tito's answer, given on the 15th, expressed the hope that the British government would consent to Yugoslav troops remaining in occupation of those parts of Austria they had seized, in view of great sacrifices Yugoslavia had made for the Allied cause. He was willing, however, that they be under SACMED's (Alexander's) command. This was equivalent to accepting the Allied ruling, and a few days later Tito agreed to evacuate all his troops from Carinthia.

But the situation in Venezia Giulia remained edgy, for Tito rejected the Allied proposals regarding that province. The essence of his answer was a restatement of his belief that the "honor of our army and our country demands the presence of the Yugoslav Army in Istria, Trieste and the Slovene coastline."[15]

Churchill again called for swift action. In his opinion, as conveyed to Truman, the situation could not be left to take care of itself. The Allied forces might be encircled or roughly handled. Pressure should be put on the Yugoslavs to force them to quit Trieste and Pola and return to the lines marked out.[16]

Now Truman was ready to take the risks of such a course. Perhaps he was just annoyed by Tito's defiance; perhaps he was touched by the

[15] *New York Times*, May 20, 1945.
[16] Churchill's message of May 19 to Truman is, with minor omissions, printed in *Triumph and Tragedy*, page 558.

continuation of anxious reports on the way in which the Italian political balance was being affected; or perhaps he was emboldened by word from Alexander's headquarters that Tito would be sensible when faced with enough determination and a large enough force. Whatever the reasons, at this juncture, in consultation with Grew and the Joint Chiefs, he determined (on the 19th and 20th) on several brisk measures. Grew was to give out at once a press release that would make it clear that the American government thought Tito's responses unsatisfactory. It was to repeat that in our view the dispute "involved the issue of due process as opposed to unilateral action that challenges agreements made among several powers."[17] Eisenhower was asked if he could send three American divisions under General Patton to the Brenner Pass north of Trieste; Admiral King was asked whether he could send some ships from the Mediterranean fleet into the Adriatic quickly; and General Arnold was asked to alert some squadrons for movement into the same area. All reported that they could.

The dispute had reached a climax. Stalin could avert it, if he would. Therefore, despite the fact that the Soviet government had not responded to an earlier statement of views and intentions, the President decided to bring Stalin up to date and solicit his support. He did so at once.[18] It may be surmised that there was little actual hope that Stalin would join in inducing Tito to give in; but in any case, communication with Stalin would ward off any later Soviet charge that we were acting without consultation, and avert possible harm to the prospects of the San Francisco conference.

Churchill, on learning from Truman what he had in mind, sped word that he was entirely in accord with the measures, with a view to making the preponderance of Allied force apparent.

But even while these steps were being taken, Tito began to show some inclination to end the quarrel and to restrain his supporters. The Yugoslav commanders moved their main headquarters out of Trieste, though not abandoning military control of the city. Tito let the American government know that he would agree to having AMG in the area west of the line that the Allies had proposed, provided that representatives of the Yugoslav army were included in the arrangements for military administration, and that AMG acted through the civil authorities

---

[17] The text of Grew's statement is in the *New York Times*, May 20, 1945.

[18] Texts of this message are printed in both *Year of Decisions*, page 250, and Stalin Correspondence, vol. 2, pages 235-36.

already set up in the area by the Yugoslavs. He proposed that talks should start at once to work out this arrangement.

Whether the change in Tito's address to the Allies was due, wholly or partly, to intimations that the Allies were preparing to make a show of force, or to Soviet advice, is not known. Stalin's answer to Truman's message, received on the 23rd, while moderate in tone, fitted in with the antecedent proposals of Tito and supported them.

Neither the British nor the American government was willing to accede to Tito's wish to have a share in the military or civilian administration of the area that was to be under the control of AMG. But while Alexander tried to convert Tito's latest offer into an acceptable arrangement, they anxiously waited to learn whether he would accept less than he wanted and thought he ought to have, or whether they might have to impose their terms against his will—and at the risk of another inflamed dispute with Moscow.

Such was the situation before Hopkins went to Moscow. The account of how it developed must wait upon the unfolding of other elements and strains in the association among the war Allies.

7 · Uncertainties about Germany

So often in history has the dilemma of how to treat an aggressive nation baffled its conquerors! With little transposition the words that passed long, long ago between the Persian, Cyrus the Great, and his prisoner Croesus, once King of the Lydians, might have been heard at this time in the talks of what to do about Germany:

"But no sooner had Cyrus marched away from Sardis than Pactyes made the Lydians to revolt. . . . When Cyrus had news of this on his journey, he said to Croesus, 'What end am I to make, Croesus, of this business? It seems that the Lydians will never cease making trouble for me and for themselves. It is in my mind that it may be best to make slaves of them; for now methinks I have done like one that should slay the father and spare the children. So likewise I have taken with me you who were more than a father to the Lydians, and handed the city over to the Lydians themselves; and then forsooth I marvel that they revolt.' So Cyrus uttered his thought; but Croesus feared that he would destroy Sardis, and thus answered him: 'O King, what you say is but reasonable. Yet do not ever yield to anger, nor destroy an ancient city that is guiltless both of the former and of the latter offense. For . . . it is Pactyes [Hitler] who does this present wrong; let him therefore be punished. But let the Lydians be pardoned; and lay on them this command, that they may not revolt or be dangerous to you; send, I say, and forbid them to possess weapons of war, and command them to wear tunics under their cloaks and buskins on their feet, and to teach their sons lyre-playing and song and dance and huckstering. Then, O King, you will soon see them turned to women instead of men; and thus you need not fear lest they revolt.' "[1]

The members of the coalition had made plans for divided but joint occupation and control of Germany. They had agreed that in matters of general scope the policies to be pursued in all zones were to be uniform. They had also confirmed certain prime and common purposes, such as the subduction of German capacity to make war, the extirpation of National Socialism, and the collection of reparations. But they had not worked out in the systematic detail needed for the conduct of joint control how otherwise they would treat the Germans—what, for example, they would do about ordinary tasks of government, or the problems of

[1] As told by Herodotus in the English translation by A. D. Godley, Book I, Paragraphs 154 and 155.

[52]

economic structure and production, transport, currency and banking, public health. Unless accord was reached on such vital matters, and unless persons and essential goods were permitted to move between zones, and there was a single monetary system for all, separation was almost certain. In short, there loomed the question whether, when avowals ended and actions started, the members of the coalition could reconcile their ideas and purposes sufficiently to control Germany as an integral country.

Conditions in Germany were in general miserable and in some ways chaotic. True, the Germans who were whole and well and had roofs over their heads were better off in some ways than the people of the countries they had invaded. Observers found many Germans, outside of the smashed and burned cities, looking healthier, fatter, less tired, and better clothed than the British—for they had taken away from their victims and unto themselves large quantities of food, all sorts of consumer goods, and stocks of machine tools. But great devastation filled the eye.

The most serious physical damage was in the destruction of housing, factories, office buildings, and warehouses, especially in the larger centers. The extent of this break-up is indicated by the fact that "On an average ten Germans . . . were living where only four had been living in 1939, even though some of the shelters and cellars in use hardly deserved the title of housing."[2] The railway system was wrecked. None of the main inland waterways, which carried so much of German traffic, was in use. Supplies of food were adequate for a short while, but the prospects of continuation of supply were precarious. The numbers of livestock had been much reduced (cattle, sheep, pigs, and goats). The potential production of cereal foods and potatoes was threatened by a lack of fertilizers and manpower; and delivery to market was restrained by doubt as to the future value of Germany currency. Coal and steel production was less than ten percent of pre-war capacity. But close inspection led to an estimate that for the whole of Germany only between fifteen and twenty percent of the industrial plant and mines had been ruined beyond repair.

Almost four million Germans had lost their lives in the course of the war, and two million more had been crippled. There was a great surplus of women. About seven million Germans under arms had surrendered to the Western armies, and either were in prison camps or

[2] Michael Balfour, in *Four-Power Control in Germany and Austria, 1945-46,* pages 7-14, portrays vividly and incisively the economic and social state of Germany at the time of surrender. I have drawn on his description, as well as on the reports of American civil affairs officers in Germany, for this summary sketch.

sealed-off areas or were on their way back to their homes. Other millions had surrendered to the Red Army, and were under detention or were being compelled to work for their captors.

There was a compulsive trudge of young and old on the roads. In the American and British zones were about three million who had fled west before the Russian advance. An uncounted number who had moved out of the cities into the country to escape bombing were now trying to return. Six million foreigners, almost all of whom had been kept at forced labor in Germany, were on the loose. Many were housed in barracks, where they were managing in summer weather to keep body and soul together. In some of these refugee camps or assembly points order was well maintained and the premises were clean; in others there was crime, disorder, fear, and filth. Many, dazed and distressed, were struggling toward their former homes in east or west, or some other place. Along with them, many soldiers of the United Nations who had been freed from German prisoner-of-war camps were wandering back toward their own lines.

The occupation authorities soon became aware that industrial revival depended on free movement between the several zones. Factories in each needed parts and raw materials to be had only from the others. For coal and raw materials the industries in the eastern zone had looked to the west to supplement what was had from their own regional resources. For foodstuffs the dependence was mutual. The country east of the Elbe in the Soviet zone (including that part that was being turned over to the Poles) had provided much of the bread grains, potatoes, and sugar wanted in industrial areas of the Ruhr and Rhineland. This source of supply was vital: it was reckoned that if the western zones were compelled to exist on their own production, individual food consumption during the rest of 1945 could amount to only about eleven hundred calories a day. But in turn the Soviet zone was deficient in beef, mutton, milk, butter, cheese, fruits, vegetables, fish, and eggs.[3]

[3] Of the 1937 German territory, 48 percent was now in the Russian zone (or under Polish control), 52 percent in the western zones; the corresponding figures for population were 42 and 58 percent. After the war, however, the relative population of the western zones was much greater than in 1937, because of flight and forced migration from the east. Between the two areas the percentage distribution of 1937 output was as follows:

	Russian Zone	Western Zones
Rye	60.5%	39.5%
Wheat	50	50
Barley	50	50
Oats	52	48
Potatoes	60	40
Sugar Beets	69	31

While dealing with this situation in Germany each of the occupying powers had to reckon with problems of adjustment at home—from the needs of war to activities of peace. Those of the United States were the easiest; it had, or could surely obtain, everything that was needed. The Soviet Union was in great immediate want, being short of many essential or useful components of production; but its people and government could count on acquiring these in time from their own resources. Great Britain could not; in order to feed its people and get most essential raw material and equipment, its export trade would have to be quickly restored. France, though little damaged, was in the throes of political and social turmoil. Belgium, Holland, Denmark, and Norway were all suffering the ravages of German occupation. Italy was finding it hard to meet minimal needs. Thus, as was well remarked in a later review of the experience, "Everywhere the processes of conversion from war to peace were fraught with problems, tensions and uncertainties. . . . Shortages of all kinds had to be reckoned with. Giving the German question the importance due to it was easily confused with favoring the cruel enemy at the expense of the unfortunate victim."[4]

American and British authorities were more aware of the hardships the Germans were suffering than they were of those borne by the Poles, the Russians, and the other peoples the Germans had assaulted. Several million American and British soldiers were living among the Germans—who had a way of earning pity for their troubles. In contrast, little was known at first hand of conditions in the countries to the east, for there, out of mistrust or pride, American and British observers were not given easy access and welcome. As for the Russians— the impulse to contribute to their welfare was repressed by their self-absorption. There was an impression that western aid and generosity during the war had not been fairly appreciated or acknowledged by the Russians, and there was resentment of the gruff, tough way in which the Russians took as their due whatever was given them. Moreover, the two western allies were influenced by contrasting anxieties: the harder

	Russian Zone	Western Zones
Cattle	39	61
Pigs	50	50
Coal	18.7	81.3
Brown Coal	69	31
Steel	14.5	85.5

Source: *Economist*, June 16, 1945.
[4] Balfour, page 14.

the life of the peoples of western Europe, the more possible that they might resort to revolution and perhaps even turn to Communism; and the faster conditions of life and work improved in the Soviet Union, the more effective its appeals and clamors might be.

Long before the surrender, several branches of the American government had been engaged in spirited disputes as to how to deal with the Germans. The tale of this wavering argument, which had many filaments, has been well told by others.[5]

To guide Eisenhower (and his deputy, General Lucius Clay) as Commander in the American zone and prospective member of the Control Council, the American authorities had been able to put together a succession of policy statements, mauled over and patched by many minds.[6] The various features had been reviewed with British civilian and military officials, who were not, however, in accord with some of them, especially the more harsh ones. These the British Chiefs of Staff

[5] Nowhere better, as far as I know, than by Professor Paul Y. Hammond in his careful, ample, and analytical accounts in *The Origins of American Occupation Policy for Germany*, which he has generously allowed me to read before publication, and by Hajo Holborn in *American Military Government, Its Organization and Policies*. Interesting information about preparatory work of the British government is given in E. F. Penrose, *Economic Planning for the Peace*.

[6] The first Interim Directive, J.C.S. 1067, had been sent to Eisenhower on September 27, 1944, for his use as Supreme Commander of the Allied Expeditionary Force. This was under almost continuous critical scrutiny and amendment in the following months.

A second Revised Directive, J.C.S. 1067/6, had been sent to Eisenhower on or about April 26, subject to final approval by the President. By this time it was foreseen that SHAEF would soon be dissolved; and that Eisenhower and General Clay, his Deputy, would put the new Directive into effect as Commanders of the U.S. army forces in the European Theater of Operations and as prospective American representatives on the four-power control council for Germany.

Only one other important change was made thereafter. On the morning of May 10 Grew informed President Truman that the final version was virtually complete and would be submitted to him later in the day. The President, who had not been in on the prolonged previous discussions of the subject, asked Grew to summarize its main elements. In doing so Grew said that one of the main purposes was to eliminate those industries in Germany that were able to make implements of war. The President asked whether this included light as well as heavy industry, and was told that except for a few specialized branches it did not. Then Grew related that Secretary Morgenthau had wanted to destroy the synthetic oil plants, but that the State and War Departments had not thought this advisable as long as the oil they could produce might be needed in the American zone. The President said he disagreed with Morgenthau. Actually the same question had been raised about the synthetic rubber and aluminum and magnesium plants. All these had been condemned to destruction in J.C.S. 1067/6. But this order was waived in the latest version, 1067/8.

That afternoon Assistant Secretary of State Clayton took to the White House Directive 1067/8, as approved by the Joint Chiefs and all members of the interdepartmental committee who had worked on it. Morgenthau, who was present, recorded his capitulation to superior authority. He said he concurred. The President then formally approved the Directive. It was sent to Eisenhower on May 14.

had refused to adopt and convert into a joint instruction. Hence the British government had issued its own Directive for General Montgomery (who was to be in command in the British zone and to be British member of the Control Council). This was similar in scope to the American, and like it in many but not all of its elements.

Even after the post-surrender Directive was sent to Eisenhower (on May 14), the furor in American official circles about some of the sterner aspects of our policy continued. Reports from the local commanders about conditions in Germany, and about the problems presenting themselves to the American army units there, impelled Stimson to urge further fast revision of the economic provisions. To President Truman he wrote on May 16:

"Early proposals for the treatment of Germany provided for keeping Germany near the margin of hunger as a means of punishment for past misdeeds. I have felt that this was a grave mistake. Punish her war criminals in full measure. Deprive her permanently of her weapons, her General Staff and perhaps her entire army. Guard her governmental action until the Nazi-educated generation has passed from the stage —admittedly a long job—but do not deprive her of the means of building up ultimately a contented Germany interested in following non-militaristic methods of civilization. This must necessarily involve some industrialization, for Germany today has approximately thirty million excess population beyond what can be supported by agriculture alone. . . . A solution must be found for their future peaceful existence and it is to the interest of the whole world that they should not be driven by stress of hardship into a non-democratic and necessarily predatory habit of life.

"All of this is a tough problem requiring co-ordination between the Anglo-American Allies and Russia. Russia will occupy most of the good food lands of Central Europe while we have the industrial portions. We must find some way of persuading Russia to play ball."

To Truman this slant of judgment seemed wise and prescient. As remarked by him later, in comment on his talk with Stimson about German prospects and policy, too many peace treaties had been based on the spirit of revenge.[7]

Churchill, after listening to Eisenhower describe Germany, said that his policy toward that country could be summed up in two words, "Disarm and Dig!" The Allies, he believed, should not assume full re-

[7] *Year of Decisions*, page 235.

sponsibility for Germany, but should only see to it that it could not start another war.

But how would the Russians regard this evolution of the Western attitude and this swerve of Western inclination? Were they really inclining to moderation toward those Germans not deeply dyed by Nazism, and to giving them another chance, once all elements of their military might were destroyed? Or would they regard this turn as a sign that the western governments wanted to use Germany as a make-weight, perhaps even as a threat, against the Soviet Union? And if so, would they perhaps be even more eager to secure undisputed control of all adjoining areas of Central and East Europe?

At Yalta, Stalin and Molotov had been stony in their gaze on Germany, and had not disguised their wish to break its strength once and for all. In their view there was right in revenge, sense in suppression, and fairness now in compelling the Germans to serve the victims of their aggression. In subsequent months, however, the Soviet attitude, or tactics, toward Germany, as reflected in the Soviet propaganda and press, had fitfully changed. The line had been softened and threats of punishment had been moderated. Only real Nazis were to be brought to book. The makers of Soviet policy seemed to have decided to leave the way open to a more positive and even half-friendly approach to the masses of the German people, though the Germans were to make some amends and be kept under various restraints. The Soviet government had not deviated in its support of the main standard features of the American program. But the Soviet spokesmen had carefully refrained from any indications of a desire to make the Germans suffer needlessly, or of intention to use the chance to turn Germany Communist. Who was to know whether this tolerance was genuine, or merely a way of fooling both the western allies and the Germans?

A clash over the amount of reparations to be obtained from Germany was in sight—or rather, a conflict of wishes and wills over whether the Soviet Union should be enabled to exact what it thought due and just, no matter how much the Germans might suffer, or how hard they might have to work, or how much expense might be caused the western allies.

The American government wanted no reparations payments except the retention of German assets in the United States. The British government hoped to get some German equipment and products that would enable Britain the more quickly to repair war damage. But it was disposed to adjust its demands to other aspects of policy toward Germany.

At Yalta a net of principles for a reparations program had been woven. This was incomplete, loose in meaning, and based on suppositions that turned out to be unreal, or at least unrealized. Roosevelt, Churchill, and Stalin had agreed that Germany ought to be compelled to pay reparations for the losses it had caused to the Allied nations in the course of the war. The preliminary plan they had approved there conceived that the reparations might be made in three ways. One was by the removal from Germany, and shipment to the beneficiaries, of factories, machinery, vessels, railway equipment, power plants, and the like, and shares in German industrial, transport, and other enterprises—all to be effected within two years after the end of the war. A second was by annual deliveries of goods to be produced in Germany during the following years. The third was by the services of German labor.

It had been agreed too that the flow of reparations should be measured basically *in kind* (as it was called)—that is, in terms of so many tons of steel-producing capacity, so many hundreds of optical lenses, so many man-days of work. But Stalin had sought to have stated also the total money value of what was to be obtained. Roosevelt and Churchill had given in to this wish. Then a stiff difference had arisen as to the sum to be named. Stalin had proposed twenty billion dollars, half for the Soviet Union. Roosevelt had agreed that such an amount might be used "as a basis for discussion" in working out the detailed reparations program. But Churchill had refused to go along. He had maintained that it was futile to try to fix a figure while the war against Germany was still being fought. Who could tell how completely German industry and transport might be smashed up or burnt out before the end? And what decisions would be made about detaching from Germany areas in the east and west, thereby affecting its capacity to pay reparations? In the Protocol of the Conference the two views had been recorded but not reconciled. This had not deterred the Soviet government from averring later on that in effect the twenty-billion-dollar total had been approved as an approximate objective.

This complex of contingent uncertainties was to provide a wide field for argument, mistrust, uncandid conduct. The task of dealing with them, of "working out on the above principles . . . a detailed plan for the exaction of reparations from Germany," had been consigned to an Allied Reparation Commission to be set up in Moscow.

But in the subsequent months, before the war ended, the Commission had not come together. The Soviet government was impatient at the delay. When Molotov was in San Francisco, not long before the German surrender, he quizzed Edwin Pauley, the appointed American member, about the reasons, and urged that the Commission get going quickly on its assignment. Pauley told him that the American government also wanted to get started but was puzzled over certain aspects of the question, such as the demands other European countries were making for equipment and products from Germany, the difficulties of evaluating industrial plants that might be removed and of forecasting the needs of the German civilian population. Molotov tried to pass over these problems lightly, saying that they would all be solvable with a little thought and cooperation.

In this same talk Molotov was asked about reports that the Russians were already moving material and equipment out of their zone and into Russia. He said they were only taking what they needed in the prosecution of the war—to which Pauley replied that he assumed there could be no objection if the commanders in the American and British zones did the same. This unregulated snatching of products from Germany (as war booty, as military equipment of possible use in the war against Japan, or as reparations) soon provoked a nasty squabble among the conquerors. The western allies protested at what the Russians were doing, because some of the equipment being taken away would be needed by the Germans living in the western zones, to get along, and therefore its removal would make more trying the task of the occupant powers in these zones. The Soviet authorities thought the protests indicated indifference to the great needs of the Russian people. They, in turn, were entering complaints against undisclosed shipments out of the western zones.

Then another worry flared up in American thought as the depressing state of all western Europe became better known. Would the United States again be under duress to provide relief and sustenance to all its portions, including Germany, as it had been after the First World War? This concern found outlet in the guiding instructions given to Pauley on May 18, which reaffirmed that "It is and has been fundamental United States policy that Germany's war potential be destroyed and its resurgence, as far as possible, prevented by removal or destruction of German plants, equipment and other property." But the instructions restrained the pursuit of this purpose by telling Pauley to oppose "any reparations plan based on the assumption that the United

States or any other country will finance directly or indirectly any reconstruction in Germany or reparation by Germany." Were we again going to have to pay in this way for our victory? The American officials were asking this question of one another in the discordant weeks after the German surrender.

The question was the more provoking because the Poles were being allowed to take control of a large section of the Soviet zone of occupation, without leave of the western allies. As will be seen, Stalin later passed by or over the protests of his western allies, on the ground of practical necessity. And the Americans and British resolved that if this area had to be forgone as a source of reparations and of supply for the rest of Germany, the Soviet Union as well as the western allies themselves would bear the loss.

8. Friction over the Former Axis Satellites

ANOTHER source of friction at this time was the former Axis satellite states of Bulgaria, Romania, and Hungary. The trouble went back to 1944, when the German armies were being expelled. The Soviet government had felt entitled to the decisive word in dealing with them, because they were in its neighborhood and because the Soviet Union had suffered most from their support of Germany. Thus it had taken over from its western allies the lead in the secret discussions about armistice terms—overruling them with sullen firmness.

Misgiving had been turned into mistrust by the course of political events in all three of these countries as they were liberated. Communist leaders and their local supporters or servants, with the help of Soviet officials, military and civil, won their way to the top, by any and all means. The Soviet government showed no patience with criticism of this political development. Was it not the small and selfish groups in control before the war that had brought these nations to disaster? Why should not more socially minded groups be elevated to office?

In consonance with their purposes and beliefs, the Soviet authorities insisted that their representatives, as chairmen of the joint Control Commissions formed under the provisions of the armistice accords with these countries, should have directive authority. When this attitude was challenged, the Soviet government flung back the charge that the American and British members of these Commissions had as much, or more, chance to share in the making of policies as was being accorded the Soviet representative on the control organization in Italy.

Roosevelt—taking over a favored proposal of former Secretary of State Hull—had managed at Yalta to get the Soviet government to approve a statement of principle called the "Declaration on Liberated Europe." This was an avowal of joint duty to aid the people in states regaining their freedom to restore conditions of internal peace, and through free elections to form governments responsive to the popular will. It stated that "when, in the opinion of the three governments [the American, British and Russian], conditions . . . make such action necessary," they would consult at once on the measures needed to discharge their responsibilities. The American government clutched at this wan promise as though it were a strong obligation.

The historian must ruefully remark that the history of these three countries leaves little evidence that they would have been likely to develop representative—democratic—free—peaceful—governments, the ideal in the political vision and doctrine of the West, even if aided to do so. At least two of them had never had governments of this sort, truly concerned with the welfare of the masses of the people. All had been ruled by small, hard-souled groups with royal and military affiliations. All had turbulent pasts, and while associated with Hitler had cruelly treated their political opponents and racial minorities. In sum, the remnants of the older order deserved little protection.

Even though these facts were taken into account, as they scantly were by the western diplomats, there were grounds for disliking and opposing what was being done. The effort of these nations to cast off bad and outworn ways and men was being diverted into a program for bringing them under Communist control. To this end the means used were detestable: suppression by the Communists not only of reactionary groups but of true democratic elements; brutality and excessive restraints on individual freedoms.

Even before the war was over the Soviet government had urged that peace treaties be concluded with the regimes it had fostered in these three Axis satellites. The American and British governments, however, regarded them as having been imposed on the people. They had refused to recognize them, and scorned the idea of entering into peace treaties with them.

The poor state of their affairs was kept in the fore by reports from the American representatives on the Allied Control Commission in Romania (General Schuyler) and Bulgaria (General Crane). Both confirmed, in a personal talk with the President on May 2, that the Communists, though in small minority, had managed to secure control of the local governments, because of Russian aid and support. They were convinced that the Soviet government was bent on getting and keeping control of these countries through subservient groups. They both recounted in detail the way in which they were ignored by the Soviet chairmen of the Control Commissions on which they served.

Truman's impulse, in accord with his wish to keep out of incessant political struggles in the Balkan area—as evidenced in the tussle with Tito—was to express our displeasure merely by recalling the American members of these Commissions. But he was persuaded by Grew that our interests called for a more active display of opposition; that instead of defaulting, the American government ought to exert itself to regain an effective part in the direction of the political life of these countries.

Churchill was more distressed at what was happening than the Americans. But he was cramped because in October 1944, in Moscow, he had agreed that while the war against Germany was going on the Soviet Union should have a dominant part in running the affairs of Romania and Bulgaria, in return for Soviet acquiescence in Britain's right to oversee events in Greece. They had agreed that in Hungary there was to be an equal division of influence.

In short, both the American and British governments were confounded by the Communist take-over of the Axis satellites. They saw no effective way of preventing it. But they were becoming more rather than less determined to resist and retaliate if Moscow ignored the vigorous protests forming in their minds.

9. Anxieties over Austria

THERE were anxieties over Austria too. Despite doubts as to how the Austrians could manage to get along within their small confines, the Allies had not wavered in their decision to detach the country from Germany and recreate it as a separate state. They had conceived their tasks there as quite different from those before them in Germany. Their aim focused on the revival of a nation rather than on the basic reeducation of a people, for they believed that a free Austria would turn to orthodox democracy, possibly of a socialist bent.

They had agreed that the occupation and control were to be jointly conducted, as in Germany. For this purpose similar accords were required, concerning zones of occupation and the system of control. But all three allies expected that the occupation would be relatively short, giving way to a freely elected Austrian government; and that their control would be correspondingly brief and relatively light.

Because of a wish to avoid any lasting immersion in the affairs of Central or Eastern Europe, the first inclination of the American government was to refuse the onus of a zone of occupation in Austria outside of Vienna. But in December 1944, Roosevelt had been persuaded to change his mind. By then it had been decided that the American zone in Germany would be in the southwest. Thus what was then planned as the American zone in Austria (the province of Salzburg and adjoining sections of Upper Austria on both sides of the Danube) was only an extension of the zone in Germany, as regards military and supply activities.

But even after American hesitation ended, the discussion in the EAC about zonal boundaries had lagged. In March the British member submitted a definite plan for partition. Soon afterward the Russians, not pleased with what the British offered, submitted another. The Soviet government asked to be assigned not only the northwest section of Austria but also areas toward the west, center, and south. The Joint Chiefs of Staff were willing to yield to the Russians two segments of the zone that had been marked out in earlier talks for the United States —the part of the province of Upper Austria that was north of the curving Danube River, and the fringe of the province of Burgenland (adjoining Hungary). But the Soviet wish to have also a section in the southeast corner of Austria, which in earlier talks had been marked for Great Britain, seemed to them to outrun reason. In opposing this the

American government stood by the British. Thus it came about that the compact between the allies on zones was still in analysis when the war ended.

So was the connected accord about the allocation of sectors in Vienna. Russian military authorities were in control of the whole region around that city. The Soviet idea was that the joint charge contemplated should extend only to the bounds of the city as they had been in 1938. The Americans and British wished it to include adjacent areas that had been incorporated into the city while it was under German rule. They found the smaller enclosure unsatisfactory for several reasons. There was only one airfield within its limits, and that would be in the Soviet sector. The western allies would not have enough space in their subdivisions for housing their garrisons, for training and recreation; nor would they have adequate facilities for communication or air traffic.

At the April 9 meeting of the EAC the American member had urged the retention of wider boundaries for the Vienna district, or, if that were not done, that one of the large airfields in the Soviet zone of Austria near Vienna be placed under American control. The British member had asked that one airfield in the greater Vienna area be assigned to each of the occupying powers. Both had proposed that the Inner City (Innere Stadt) of Vienna be not divided into sectors, but be regulated by the inter-Allied authority to insure equitable use of its facilities. The Soviet member had shaken his head twice or thrice.

During the following weeks the American and British Ambassadors in Moscow had tried to persuade Stalin and Molotov to permit small missions of inspection to visit Vienna. The American and British military authorities thought it essential, for the talks about allocation of sectors, to find out for themselves what condition the city was in, what facilities there were in its various parts. But in the letters that Harriman and Clark Kerr sent Molotov in support of this request, they hinted that the visiting missions, when in Vienna, might look into other matters of practice and policy—especially into the removal of industrial equipment from Austria to Russia that was known to be going on. Whether for that reason or not, the Soviet Foreign Office turned down the request, declaring that the allied missions would not be welcome until the accords on both Austria and the rest of Vienna were concluded. Thus the western allies were faced with the choice of coming to terms with the Soviet Union or reconciling themselves to an indefinite postponement of entry into Vienna and the inauguration of joint control of Austria.

That Stalin had reversed himself was made plain by the answers re-turned to personal requests sent him by Churchill and Truman early in May for permission to fly survey groups to Vienna at once. In a letter to Kennan on the 6th (the eve of the German surrender), Vishinsky explained that when Stalin had agreed to such a visit, the Soviet government had been confident that an agreement about both the zones of occupation in Austria and the districts in Vienna would have been concluded before the allied mission arrived in Vienna. Then, twisting the intent of the petitioners, he went on to say that the Soviet government could not consider having the zonal arrangement decided in Vienna, since it was within the competence of the EAC. And finally he averred that the Soviet government saw no need for these preliminary visits of inspection. After all, had not the EAC determined the zones for Germany and Berlin before western forces entered the city?

Churchill became more and more indignant over this willful exclusion from a country for which the western allies had so real an attachment. He informed Truman (on May 12) that although he was willing to have the ultimate determination of sectors in Vienna settled in the EAC, he felt that the British and American governments ought to keep on insisting that they be enabled first to survey the situation on the spot. He asked whether the President would be willing to join him in another and more blunt message to Stalin to that effect. Truman—while resisting other more positive measures urged on him by Churchill, as will be seen presently—agreed to this. So again they appealed to the man in the Kremlin, pointing out that since the Germans had been expelled from Austria, continued refusal of their request would not be understood.

Stalin thereupon made one of those occasional concessions to western wishes which nourished the belief that though tough, he was not immovable. First defending the Soviet wish to have the decision left to EAC, he went on to inform Truman that "I have no objection, however, to U.S. and Allied representatives going to Vienna to see for themselves the condition of the city and to draft proposals for its occupation zones. Marshal Tolbukhin will be instructed accordingly. The understanding is that the United States military representatives should come to Vienna at the end of May or the beginning of June, when Marshal Tolbukhin, now en route to Moscow, returns."[1]

This seemed to open the way to progress toward an accord. Churchill, however, continued to doubt whether the Russians would truly relax their grasp over Austria and Vienna unless compelled to do so.

[1] Stalin Correspondence, vol. 2, page 233.

And there was another current cause for recrimination. Dr. Karl Renner, the seventy-seven-year-old veteran Social Democratic leader who had been Chancellor of the Austrian Republic after the First World War, had been brought to Vienna by the Soviet Commander-in-Chief. He had been living in retirement in a small country town at the foot of the Semmering Pass. On Easter Sunday, April 1, he had left his house to try to find the local Soviet military headquarters in order to protest what the Russian patrols were doing in a house-to-house search for hidden weapons or German soldiers. He was asked by the Soviet Commander whether he was prepared to help the Red Army shorten the war. Renner had agreed to do so, saying, however, that he would not act as a Soviet agent. He wanted to speak to the Austrian people out of their common memory of his earlier leadership. In a letter to Stalin he said that he felt called upon "to assume the task of the liberation of Austria from Fascism."

Three weeks later Vishinsky had informed the American and British Ambassadors that Renner had presented to the Soviet government a plan for creating a provisional Austrian government; that he had the legal right to take this initiative; and that he was going to call together those former deputies of the Austrian parliament who could be reached and decide with them upon the composition of the new government. Vishinsky added that the Soviet government, since it believed that the creation of a provisional Austrian government could help in effecting the complete liberation of Austria, was inclined to help Renner in his effort. Thus assured, the Austrian party leaders, after only two days of conference, had agreed on the nature and membership of the new administration.

Both the American and British governments had advised Moscow that they did not want to be rushed into a decision. They asked the Soviet government to defer recognition of the Renner or any other group as the provisional government of Austria. Renner then proceeded to address himself directly to them. The new government, he averred, was a genuine national government with participants from all the Austrian political parties except those that supported the Nazis. It included Communists in the two ministerial posts that would deal day-to-day with the Austrian people—the Ministry of the Interior and the Ministry of Education and Culture. But it also included Leopold Figl (Catholic Party) and Adolf Schaerf (Socialist Party), who became Chancellor and Vice Chancellor of Austria after the elections. Renner asked the American and British governments not to keep their hands behind their backs.

But they would give no promises until they had adequate chance to find out for themselves whether the self-appointed group was representative of the Austrian people, and could and would act independently. The Soviet government did not wait for them to find out. In face of the dual requests for time to investigate, the Soviet government, through its commander-in-chief in Austria, had gone ahead and recognized Renner's group as a provisional government.

On April 30, Churchill and Truman, after consultation, sent separate notes, of similar tenor, to Stalin. They reproached him for not consulting them and for not deferring to their wish for time to consider and to concert policies. The hasty Soviet action, they concluded, made it the more imperative that their representatives proceed to Vienna at once, and that the agreements on zones of occupation and control machinery be swiftly completed in the EAC.

It was a fortnight later that Stalin agreed to admit the missions. In the interval the Soviet officials in Vienna continued to support and use the Renner administration. The Western Allies fretted over the possibility that the Soviet Union was bent on achieving in Austria, while it could, the same kind of dominance it was exerting over the Axis satellites. Where the Red Army was, would not the commissars be?

PART THREE

The Time of Testing

10. Differing Ideas about How to Deal with the Soviet Government

It was at Yalta, early in 1945, that the Allies adopted their plans about the future occupation of Germany. The nature of these plans was testimony to the wartime belief of the western allies, and especially of the Americans, that each member of the coalition would be responsive to the interests and wishes of the others. It was assumed that they would be able to agree on uniform policies to be pursued for all of Germany, with due leeway for local differences. Common combat experience and shared purposes would prevail, it was judged, over separate inclinations. Thus it was supposed that none of the several partners in occupation would strive for ascendance over the rest in the administration of Germany; and that there would be no contest in Germany between capitalist and Communist ways of living.

As Soviet egotism and transgression became increasingly apparent, British and American authorities began to diverge in their ideas of how best to deal with the emerging situation. While the assault on Germany was in its last phase, Churchill and his colleagues reverted to the ways in which Britain had constrained or confined Russia in the past. They urged that the armies on the western front be directed to secure positions as far into the center of Europe as possible, and along as many enclosing edges of Europe as possible, and then kept in place, in full strength. They thought that with Anglo-American diplomacy thus supported, the Soviet rulers should be confronted with a choice between moderation and coercion.

But Truman and his colleagues were not so excited about the rifts in the coalition, or so sure about their depth or import. They regarded disputes about the time-beaten boundaries and alliances between nations in the center of Europe more calmly. When had all the countries of the European complex ever been in stable accord on these questions? Should the United States, too, like so many other countries in the past, be led into elevating minor conflicts over complicated equities into causes of crises? Was it not saner to show patience and friendliness?

This trend of mind and diplomacy during so critical a period was in one aspect an avoidance of the realities of differences with Soviet Communism. In another, it was a search for a way to subvert these realities. When theory tyrannizes over facts, grief is apt to follow; but when facts of the moment tyrannize over theory, the chance of improvement is lost.

11. British-American Colloquy

THE assault of the allied forces had carried them beyond their allocated zones of occupation in Germany. When the war ended, western troops were lodged in an area within the Russian zone, extending about four hundred miles from north to south, and one hundred and twenty miles from east to west, at its greatest length. That they had not gone even deeper into it was due, as has been said, to American command rather than German resistance.

Churchill, aroused by Soviet actions and alarmed at indicated Soviet intentions, had begun to urge, early in April, that the American and British governments wait before redistributing their troops into the separate settled zones. Eisenhower proposed that after the armies from west and east had made contact, the commanders from each side should be free to suggest that the other withdraw within its assigned occupation zone; and that such requests should be heeded, subject to military necessity. Churchill, in his words, found "that this proposal was premature and that it exceeded the immediate military needs."[1] His reason for wanting to delay is clearly summed up in a memo sent to General Ismay for the Chiefs-of-Staff Committee, on April 14: "We consider that before the Anglo-American armies retire from any ground they have gained from the enemy, over and beyond the zones of occupation agreed upon, the political issues operative at that time should be discussed between the heads of Governments and in particular that the situation should be viewed as a whole and in regard to the relations between the Soviet, American and British Governments."[2] But in the affiliated message that Churchill sent to President Truman a few days later he did not reveal the scope of his thought so plainly. He suggested merely that western troops be not retired until the Allied Control Council for Germany had been set up and the Russians had agreed to share the anticipated food surpluses in their zone with the other zones.

Eisenhower and the Joint Chiefs of Staff were displeased at the Prime Minister's wish to "intrude" political purposes in what they regarded as a military matter. The difference had been abridged, however. Churchill accepted the principle that the American and British troops in Germany and Austria should retire to their respective zones as soon as the military situation permitted; the Americans agreed that

[1] *Triumph and Tragedy*, page 512.
[2] *Ibid.*, page 513.

this should not be done until the Control Councils for both countries were set up and the bounds of the zones of occupation in Austria were fixed.

Churchill had submitted to Stalin a plan combining these several actions, and Truman told Stalin he agreed with it. On re-reading this message, of April 27, it is hard to decide whether the two western allies were clear and at one about their purposes. The pertinent paragraph read: "When the fighting is finished the next task is for the Allied Control Commissions to be set up in Berlin and Vienna, and for the forces of the Allies to be redisposed and to take over their respective occupational zones. The demarcation of the zones in Germany has already been decided upon, and it is necessary that we shall without delay reach an agreement on the zones to be occupied in Austria at the forthcoming meeting proposed by you in Vienna."[3]

During the next week the Prime Minister's ideas roved over this area of decision. They were candidly expressed only, perhaps, in the message he sent to Eden (who was in the United States) on May 4— just three days before the German surrender: "First, the Allies ought not to retreat from their present positions to the occupational line until we are satisfied about Poland, and also about the temporary character of the Russian occupation of Germany, and the conditions to be established in the Russianised or Russian-controlled countries in the Danube Valley, particularly Austria and Czechoslovakia, and the Balkans."[4]

In a message to Truman two days later, he observed, after urging that as soon as possible there should be a meeting of the three Heads of Governments: "Meanwhile we should hold firmly to the existing position obtained or being obtained by our armies in Yugoslavia, in Austria, in Czechoslovakia, on the main central United States front, and on the British front, reaching up to Lubeck, including Denmark. . . . Thereafter I feel that we must most earnestly consider our attitude towards the Soviets and show them how much we have to offer or withhold."[5]

During the following days he propounded this advice over and over to Truman, as in his famous Iron Curtain message of May 12, in which

[3] The whole text of this important message, of which this quotation is only one paragraph, is in *Triumph and Tragedy*, pages 517-18.

[4] This section of the message to Eden is italicized in the account that Churchill published in *Triumph and Tragedy*, pages 502-03.

[5] For the first sentence Churchill again used italics in *Triumph and Tragedy*, page 501.

he concluded, "Surely it is vital now to come to an understanding with Russia, or see where we are with her, before we weaken our armies mortally or retire to the zones of occupation."[6]

But the American decision-makers, civilian and military, were not open to these pleas. None of them was ready to renounce past policies or methods, or to maintain large American armies in Europe and keep them where they were for a long time, until Russia met our terms and eased our anxieties. Churchill's bold program was judged by Truman and his counselors to be inadvisable, ineffective, and inexpedient: inadvisable because it was likely to provoke a harsh dispute with Moscow rather than to lead to a settlement; ineffective because the Soviet armies could shut us out of Berlin and Vienna and hinder the operation of the Control Councils for these two countries, and could force Soviet rule on Poland, Hungary, and Czechoslovakia; inexpedient because the American people expected a rapid return of veteran soldiers from Europe, and American military plans counted on them for the pursuit of the war against Japan.

So on May 14 Truman turned aside Churchill's appeals with the soothing answer that he would like to await events before adopting the course the Prime Minister was advocating. Whether the President and some of those near him were the more inclined to wait upon events because the world, including the Soviet Union, would soon learn that we had a vastly more powerful weapon than any known is still a subject that invites, but defies, speculation.

On May 16, Eisenhower, at this time still Supreme Allied Commander, met in London with Churchill and the British Chiefs of Staff, to review the situation. He asked the Prime Minister whether the Control Council for Germany might not be set up in the near future. He was finding it hard to carry out his duties, he explained, because he had to consult the Soviet commanders on many matters, and this meant long delay because they had to refer every question to Moscow. Once the Control Council was operative, he thought, this consultation could be carried on much more quickly and smoothly. His impression was that both the American and the British components of SHAEF were ready to organize and staff their sections of the Control Council, but that the Russians were not. Churchill agreed that the question was urgent. But he said he thought that SHAEF should continue for a while longer to be responsible for the control of those sections of Germany occupied by western troops. He was on guard against any change in the situa-

[6] *Ibid.*, pages 573-74.

tion that would give the Soviet government a chance to urge immediate troop withdrawal out of its zone.

Eisenhower waited a week. Then he tried again. He informed Washington that he could not carry out his mission much longer without making known the terms of the surrender imposed on Germany and issuing a Declaration stating that the Allies were assuming supreme authority over Germany in accordance with these terms. The British government acknowledged that necessity. On May 24 it proposed that the four Commanders-in-chief meet in Berlin not later than June 1, to take these measures. What it had in mind was that these military officials should act as the Control Council, and should thereafter meet as such, proceeding to develop their organization and to deal with questions as they arose. But at the same time the British government again urged that American and British troops should not be ordered back from their lines into the agreed zones of occupation until "outstanding questions" were cleared up with the Soviet government. Possibly the Foreign Office, if not the Prime Minister, thought that by agreeing to rapid constitution of the Control Council it might persuade the American government to defer to its inclination in this other matter. If so, it was disappointed.

The Secretaries of State, War, and Navy all favored the early issuance of the Declaration and prompt activation of the Control Council, for they were aware of the difficulties and dangers of coping with the situation in Germany without any operative organization that could bring all four sharers in the occupation in close contact. They were willing to defer briefly the retreat into zones while the effort continued to complete accords with the Soviet Union about the treatment of Germany as an economic unit and about occupation and control of Austria. But they thought that if the Soviet government became impatient, its wish, not Churchill's counsel, should prevail. So once again the British views were impounded. With the approval of the President and the Joint Chiefs, the War Department went ahead with plans to dissolve the combined American-British military headquarters in the west (SHAEF).

But during all these weeks, while resisting British pleas, the American officials, civil and military, were wondering whether they ought not show a changed mien toward the Soviet government, and perhaps seek release from the agreements with it into which they had entered. They were verging toward somber second thoughts—called in more solemn later days an "agonizing reappraisal."

12. The Urge to Re-examine the American Attitude toward the Soviet Union

Roosevelt, though troubled over signs of the Soviet will to dominate and expand, had clung to the conviction that the American government must continue to act with vigilant calm. He went on nursing the hope that Soviet mistrust, fear, and ill will could be tempered. Truman, on taking over the unresolved range of troubles with the Soviet Union, had adopted the same attitude. He regarded himself as pledged to go on with what Roosevelt had been trying to do, and in the same way Roosevelt had been trying—as long as there was a chance of success. And, as Roosevelt had been, he was fretted by thoughts of what would happen if the United States and the Soviet Union became alienated.

He refused to share Churchill's mood of grim pessimism regarding Soviet intentions. So did some of the advisers who had been closest to Roosevelt—Hopkins, Marshall, Stimson, and Byrnes. But others were yielding to exasperation over Soviet maneuvers and manners. Among them were the members of our diplomatic and military missions in Moscow—headed by Harriman and General Deane. They felt that in the elation of victory and pride of power the Soviet rulers had ceased to care about American friendship; that they were relapsing into scorn for our ways and ideals; and that they were bent on attaching western Europe and Asia to their cause. These officials, out of their daily efforts to win Soviet assent or cooperation, derived an impressive list of reasons why they believed it would always be hard to get along with the Soviet government.

In the State Department, judgment on the outlook was flickering and divided. The Secretary of State, Stettinius, who was intent above all else on bringing an international security organization into existence, avoided any conclusion that might severely strain relations with the Soviet government. The Under Secretary of State, Grew, was beset on one side by those members of his staff who leaned the same way as Stettinius, and on the other by those who believed that future war or peace would be decided in Moscow and Washington, not at San Francisco. Most aggrieved of all were the officials who were concerned with Soviet treatment of Poland and the smaller states of Central and Southeastern Europe.

Among the Joint Chiefs of Staff, judgment was still swayed by the wish to have Russian participation in the Pacific war early enough and on a scale great enough to save American lives. Stimson, as Secretary of War, eagerly shared this wish—one of the reasons why he kept under rein his dislike of the ways of the Russian Communist system. In contrast, Forrestal, the Secretary of the Navy, by this time was becoming set in his belief that the Soviet Union would turn into an enemy; the reports sent or brought from Moscow by Harriman, Deane, and others found in him vibrant response.[1]

These diverse attitudes coalesced into an impulse to re-examine the whole trend of our dealings with the Soviet Union. But this might not have led to action until later had not the need arisen to decide whether to go through with the secret accord about the Far East conceived at Yalta.

T. V. Soong, Prime Minister of China and head of the Chinese delegation in San Francisco, was seeking a chance to talk with the Secretary of State and the President about China's relations with the Soviet Union. Should they tell him of the existence and content of the Yalta accord? And if so, should Chiang Kai-shek be asked to concur in it? Or, alternatively, should Stalin be told that we now thought some of its provisions ought to be changed? If not that, should we at least ask additional political assurances from Stalin before using our influence to secure Chinese acceptance? The willful way in which the Soviet government was interpreting the agreement about Poland made it seem prudent to do so.

The State Department on May 12 summarized its ideas in letters to the War and Navy Departments. It urged that before taking any measures to carry out our part of the Yalta agreement we secure a group of fresh and more conclusive promises from the Soviet government. We might ask it to use its influence with the Chinese Communists to assist us in our effort to unify China under Chiang Kai-shek before we sought his concurrence in the Yalta accord. We might also ask it to express unqualified acceptance of the Cairo Declaration, promising the return of Manchuria to Chinese sovereignty. Similarly we might ask it to confirm the agreement to join in a four-power trusteeship for Korea—which would select

[1] In his *Diaries* (pages 47-48) Forrestal tells of listening on the night of April 19 to Harriman's apprehensions about our relations with Russia unless our attitude was marked by much greater firmness. The Ambassador predicted that the Russians, using the need of protection against Germany as the reason, would carry out their program of setting up all around their borders states that would adopt the Soviet ideology; and that this outward thrust of Communism might face us with a state of ideological warfare just as sharp and dangerous as that produced by Nazism. Two nights later Forrestal found Harriman's pessimism matched by that of Eden, who thought that the chief element of Russian policy was an effort to drive a wedge between England and the United States.

the temporary Korean government. Finally, it was suggested that before we gave final approval to Soviet annexation of the Kurile Islands, as specified in the Yalta accord, it might be desirable to get the Soviet government to promise to grant emergency landing rights for commercial planes on some of these islands.

Of all those who frowned over these questions, Stimson was the most perplexed. A person of noble conscience, he had a sense of deep responsibility. As chairman of the Interim Committee concerned with policies about the production and use of the atomic bomb, he had recently been told by his scientific advisers that the new weapon would almost surely be perfected soon. But before this was proved by actual test—which, in the phrase he used for his diary, would probably be "before the locking of arms came [with Japan] and much bloodshed"—he thought it premature to answer Grew's questions conclusively. If we had this stunning new weapon we would be in a much freer and stronger position in the event of a clash with Russia over Soviet pretensions in the Far East. We would have, again in his phrase, "a master card in our hand." The trend of his thinking is evident from the entry he made in his diary on May 14. In paraphrase, his thought was that we must regain the lead the Russians had taken away from us. S-1 was a royal straight flush, and we must not play it foolishly. The U.S.S.R. could not get along without our help and industry, and we would have a unique weapon. But we ought not get into unnecessary quarrels by talking too much, and not indicate weakness by doing so; let our actions speak for themselves.

So he thought it would be well if Harriman postponed his return to Moscow until the prospect was clearer; and he wanted President Truman to defer a personal meeting with Stalin and Churchill until then. Not that he was bent on having a showdown with the Soviet government. On the contrary, he doubted whether the Soviet Union was going to threaten our vital interests, and he was still disposed to continue the effort to adjust our relations with it in a friendly fashion, whether or not the new weapon became ours. Hence he was loath to consider yet any measures that would mean withdrawal from our engagements with the Russians, concerning either Germany or the Far East.

Marshall and McCloy concurred in Stimson's quest for balance.[2] This

[2] Eisenhower's views at about this time are recorded by his aide Captain Butcher: "Ike said he felt that the American and British relationship with Russia was about at the same stage of arms-length dealing that marked the early contacts between Americans and the British when we first got into the war. As we dealt with each other, we learned the British ways and they learned ours. A common understanding developed and eventually we became Allies in spirit as well as on paper. Now the Russians, who

prevailed over Forrestal's more pugnacious attitude, and shaped the answers that Stimson and Forrestal made on May 21 to Grew's letters. Shorn of verbal fleece, these consisted of three general observations. First, with or without our approval, the Soviet Union would have the military power to take all that had been promised it at Yalta, except perhaps the Kurile Islands, and any attempt by us to take these islands would be at the direct expense of other plans and involve an unassessable cost in American lives. But second, because of military reasons, there was no objection to reviewing this Yalta accord with Stalin, to the end of reaching a clearer and fuller understanding. And third, it would be desirable to obtain the Soviet promises that the State Department wished.

This bustle of consultation within the American government (going on at the same time as the exchange of views with Churchill and the British Chiefs of Staff about the maintenance of our advance lines in Germany) thus ended in mild conclusions. The American government would not proceed to disengage itself from any of the accords with the Soviet Union. But before going ahead with their effectuation we would make a new direct effort to ascertain the truth about Soviet intentions, to see whether Stalin did or did not confirm the principles thought necessary for sound settlements both in Europe and in the Far East. For this main purpose Harry Hopkins was asked by the President to go to Moscow on a grave special mission.

---

have had relatively little contact, even during the war, with the Americans and British, do not understand us, nor do we them. The more contact we have with the Russians, the more they will understand us and the greater will be the co-operation. The Russians are blunt and forthright in their dealings, and any evasiveness arouses their suspicions. It should be possible to work with Russia if we follow the same pattern of friendly co-operation that has resulted in the great record of Allied unity demonstrated first by AFHQ and subsequently by SHAEF." Harry C. Butcher, *My Three Years with Eisenhower*, entry for May 25, page 855.

13. Prologue to Hopkins' Trip to Moscow

THERE was another reason. Truman, while still learning how and why our quarrels with the Soviet Union had come about, and trying to make up his own mind about their gravity, was being drawn toward a personal meeting with Stalin and Churchill.

A few hours before the surrender at Rheims, Churchill, with Stalin's latest domineering message about Poland in mind, had radioed, "It seems to me that matters can hardly be carried further by correspondence, and that as soon as possible there should be a meeting of the three Heads of Government."[1] Truman answered on May 9 that while he agreed that such a meeting was desirable, he would like to have Stalin ask for it; perhaps the Prime Minister had some way of getting him to do so. Stalin, he added, could no longer have a valid excuse for refusing to come west "toward us."

The Prime Minister in several later messages pressed on with his project for meeting with Stalin at some "unshattered" town in Germany. In one of them he remarked "Time is on his [Stalin's] side if he digs in while we melt away."[2] In others he emphasized that if the United States and Great Britain, while postponing the conference, continued to move their troops out of their advanced lines and out of Europe, certainly the chance of persuading Stalin to heed their wishes would be poorer.

But Truman resisted all efforts to hurry him into such a meeting. Domestic tasks, such as the presentation of the budget message to Congress, were on his mind. He felt the need for more time to study and make up his mind about the disputed issues. He wanted to wait long enough to see how the San Francisco Conference was going. He intended to appoint a new Secretary of State, Byrnes, in place of Stettinius, as soon after that Conference was over as it could be done fittingly; and he wanted the successor to be present while decisions that would fall upon him were being discussed. And, though it is nowhere explicitly on record, it is probable that Truman wanted the meeting deferred because he, like Stimson, thought that decisions might be easier after it was known whether the United States had the new atomic weapon.

Besides, the President was being cautioned against Churchill's haste. He was being told by some about him, among them Leahy, Davies, and Marshall, that the great Prime Minister was often more concerned

[1] *Triumph and Tragedy*, page 572.
[2] *Ibid.*, page 572.

with the salvage of British interests than with world harmony. This caused him to wonder whether the chance of smoothing out our relations with the Soviet rulers might not be better if the Americans first saw and talked with them alone. Consonantly he was evading Churchill's cordial invitation to come first to England, an invitation extended with the idea that they might then move on to Germany together. In words so similar to those used by Roosevelt that they arouse the fancy that they were written by the same hand, he answered, "When and if such a meeting is arranged, it appears to me that in order to avoid any suspicion of our 'ganging up' it would be advantageous for us to proceed to the meeting place separately."[3]

Such was the complex of factors that caused Truman to want to wait a while before meeting with his two top associates—to wait until July, and even then, perhaps, to have some talk alone with Stalin before entering into the formal three-country conference.

But the two-month interval could not be a respite from change. Every situation with which the American government was faced, political and military, could turn quickly for better or for worse. Vital decisions could not be deferred. For these, Truman longed for more definite and up-to-date knowledge of Soviet intentions; and he thought the chance of convincing the Soviet government of the reasonableness of our own purposes worth the try.

No American except Roosevelt had done more to aid the Soviet Union during the war than Hopkins. Stalin and his colleagues were known to be appreciative of his contribution and convinced of his good will toward their country. So his selection for this special mission was natural, and he accepted, despite his miserably poor health. On May 19, after Harriman had returned from San Francisco and the State Department had heard from the Secretaries of War and Navy, Stalin was asked whether he would make Hopkins welcome.[4] The answer was quick and cordial.

The State Department, under Grew, was not over-pleased with the

---

[3] *Year of Decisions*, page 256. Churchill was hurt and disappointed at the rebuff; see *Triumph and Tragedy*, page 572. A month later, disturbed by press reports that the President intended to see de Gaulle in Paris before going on to Potsdam, he sent a message to Truman (June 16) saying that Roosevelt had several times promised he would not visit France before he visited England, and that he hoped Truman would bear this in mind before making any decision.

[4] Truman, in *Year of Decisions*, pages 257-59, retraces his idea of asking Hopkins to go to Moscow. According to this reminiscent account, it first entered his mind when talking with Hopkins about Russia on the journeys to and from Hyde Park for Roosevelt's burial ceremonies, and the plan was confirmed on May 4 or soon thereafter and virtually settled before Harriman arrived from San Francisco. Presumably Sherwood did not know

venture. Some of its permanent staff believed that Hopkins was too inclined to take the Russians at their word and to favor their views. The President prudently suggested to Hopkins that before he left he should study all the latest Russian developments with the State Department.

Truman did not seek Churchill's concurrence in the mission. Nor did he judge it useful to have some adviser to the Prime Minister join Hopkins in the talks with Stalin, as a way of assuring unity in policy.[5] But before Hopkins' actual flight, the President informed the Prime Minister of his errand. He also asked Harriman, to whom Churchill had a warm personal attachment, to stop off in London en route to Moscow

---

of these earlier talks when he wrote in *Roosevelt and Hopkins,* pages 885-86, his account of how it came about that Hopkins was sent to Moscow:

"However, less than a week after V-E Day, it seemed that the San Francisco Conference was going on the rocks. Molotov and Eden were both headed for home. Harriman and Bohlen were on an airplane flying eastward across the continent with a sense of despair in their hearts. They asked each other whether there was any conceivable way of saving the situation. With considerable hesitancy, Bohlen suggested the possibility that President Truman might send Hopkins to Moscow to talk things out directly with Stalin and Molotov. Bohlen's hesitancy was due to the thought that Harriman, as American Ambassador in Moscow, might resent the idea of Hopkins invading his own province and taking over his duties in direct negotiation with the Soviet Government; but Harriman was enthusiastic about the suggestion and, on his arrival in Washington, went immediately with Bohlen to see Hopkins in his Georgetown house to present this suggestion to him. Both Bohlen and Harriman have told me that Hopkins' response was wonderful to behold. Although he appeared too ill even to get out of bed and walk across 'N' Street, the mere intimation of a flight to Moscow converted him into the traditional old fire horse at the sound of the alarm. But he expressed the despondent conviction that Truman would never agree to send him on this mission.

"Harriman then went to the White House and presented the suggestion to the President, who said he was much interested in the idea but would need some time to think it over. Several anxious days followed with Hopkins fearing that it would all come to nothing, but then Truman sent for him and asked him if he felt capable of making the long journey; Hopkins' reply was an immediate, enthusiastic affirmative."

[5] This was probably in accord with Hopkins' own preference. On May 20 Forrestal wrote in his diary, concerning a talk at Hopkins' house at which Harriman and Bohlen were present, "Harry [Hopkins] said that he was skeptical about Churchill, at least in the particular of Anglo-American-Russian relationship; that he thought it was of vital importance that we not be maneuvered into a position where Great Britain had us lined up with them as a bloc against Russia to implement England's European policy."

But later on Hopkins appears to have regretted that there was no advance understanding with Churchill. As recorded in Sherwood, page 913, he wrote in a memo, after his visit to Moscow: "One of the difficulties in negotiating the Polish agreement in Moscow was that President Truman had sent me without discussing it in advance with Churchill. Altho, at the time of my departure, he acquainted him with my impending visit to Moscow, no British representative was present at any of my conferences with Stalin and I was in no position to deal directly with Churchill. Fortunately, Clark Kerr, the British Ambassador to Moscow, was an old friend of mine and quite in sympathy with my visit and I am sure he reported very fully to the British Foreign Office and Churchill. And, more than that, he was making recommendations to Churchill urging the British to back us up. I began to hear from Kerr that Churchill was obviously quite disturbed about the whole business but there was not very much he could say because it was probably to his political interest to get agreement on the Polish question before the British elections."

and explain to the Prime Minister the nature of Hopkins' trip. Harriman got to London on May 22. At dinner that night he did his best to persuade the Prime Minister that if Hopkins managed to accomplish what he was being sent to do, British wishes would be as well served as our own. The Prime Minister did not openly complain about the American initiative. But, as will be seen presently, he was aggrieved because more deference had not been shown to British views and interests, or possibly even to his own personal position. To this feeling he gave expression, in moderate measure, only after the mission was over. In the interval he had the disagreeable experience of being lectured to by Joseph E. Davies, a former American Ambassador to Russia, who had ever after bathed that country in fulsome praise. The Davies mission to London will be discussed later; Truman seems to have regarded it as a parallel step in his preparations for the meeting of the three Heads of Government.

Before following Hopkins to Moscow on his dramatic mission and Davies to London on his provocative one, it is imperative to bring into this May panorama the event that was in the center of American thought at the time: the conference at San Francisco. It had been convened to write a charter for a permanent organization to maintain peace by collective action. Most American officials were at one with the American people in believing this more meaningful than the troubles over European frontiers or the alignment of the smaller European states. History would have its willful way with these, as it always did, and its way would be war-bringing unless the nations could join in a new form of association, in which justice and humaneness would be parents of peace.

For the vitality of the conceived organization, even if not for its existence, Soviet cooperation was deemed essential. Therefore during the troubled weeks after the German surrender, the American government, as has been noted at several preceding points in this narrative, refrained from acts or statements that might lead the Soviet government to ignore the conference. With Molotov in charge, an able group of Russians had been taking an active part in the discussions and displaying devotion to the aim of the conference. But the Russians' defense of their own views and desires had aroused excited and anxious criticism in the American delegation. As they saw it, if the Russians had their way the new political prodigy would be deformed at birth. The thought that Hopkins, by personal explanation to Stalin, might be able to change the mind of the Soviet leader became another reason for sending him to Moscow.

14. Cooperation and Dissent at the San Francisco Conference

THE most absorbing purpose of those who directed American foreign policy was the creation of an organization in which the nations of the world would come together to maintain peace. We had failed in our foresight after the First World War; we had before us now another chance, perhaps the last good chance to repair the mistake. If an association of nations were formed, each would regard the mutual pledge of protection as the best sort of security; and all—even the tough Soviet Union—would be more amiable. Issues of frontiers, alliances, realms of control would be more easily settled, would not continue to be a plague upon peace. In other words, at least the more enthusiastic Americans "tended to think of the establishment of an international organization as a sort of talisman which would possess a powerful virtue to heal disputes among the nations."[1]

Most of the people in the British Isles and Commonwealth and many of the officials of the Foreign Office were touched by the same hopeful beliefs. Churchill, however, was doubtful whether the new organization would prove of much use either in bringing to an end the emergent causes of tension with the Soviet Union or in averting future ones. His liking for the project seems to have been in inverse proportion to what he thought the Soviet attitude toward it to be. In a note that he sent to the Dominions Secretary on April 3 he wrote: "If the replies [that is, Stalin's replies to Western proposals for the reorganization of the Polish Provisional Government] are wholly hostile, I think it most unlikely that Russia will come to San Francisco. She will prefer to fight it out on the side of the Lublin Poles. The question will then arise as to whether the San Francisco Conference should be held or not. We have not yet reached this point. But looking ahead at it, Anthony [Eden] and I both consider that it would be a great blow to our cause and prestige and also to the cause of a free Poland if the sulkiness of Russia prevented this World Conference from being held. The Russians would feel that their mere abstention paralyzed world action. Although I have never been at all keen on this Conference, I should in that event become very keen upon it."[2]

[1] W. H. McNeill, *America, Britain, and Russia*, page 501.
[2] *Triumph and Tragedy*, page 746.

Actually Stalin and his consultants were not unfriendly to the proposed creation. They were still resentful of what they regarded as the malign failure of the League of Nations to protect Russia from the assault of fascism. And Roosevelt's former idea of a close continuing alliance between the three great members of the coalition, who, acting by common accord, were to maintain peace throughout the world, appealed to them more than this large and poorly assorted association. Yet they were ready to play a part in it, if only to make sure that it did not turn into a grouping against the Soviet Union.

On the other hand, even if the new compact was brought into being, they meant to continue to rely primarily on Russian military might, the protrusion of Russian frontiers, and the exercise of control over adjacent countries. Moreover, the Soviet government was not willing, for the sake of bringing the collectivity into being, to take the risk of being compelled to accept verdicts it did not like. It was on guard against any and all attempts to get it to subscribe to a plan under which the Soviet Union might be outvoted or overborne.

At the Dumbarton Oaks Conference in 1944 the main lines of organization had been drawn. All governments, including the Soviet Union, had seemed fairly pleased with the main design. But many changes had been proposed. In regard to three vital features in particular, differences had still to be reconciled. How great was the basic authority of the organization to be? What was to be the balance of the large and small nations within it? Most troublesome of all, in what ways were its decisions to be subject to consent of each and every one of the large powers, the permanent members of the Security Council?

Others have examined more adequately than I can the structure of the preliminary proposals submitted to the nations, and their evolution after prolonged discussion at the San Francisco Conference into the United Nations Charter.[8] In this narrative I shall tell only of those few issues that became part of the pattern of strain within the coalition.

For a while, as has been mentioned, it was feared that the Soviet Union might dissociate itself from the endeavor. At the end of March, while quarrels over Poland and the satellites were fraying relations, the

---

[8] Of the many qualified studies, some reminiscent reflections of participants in the San Francisco Conference, some analytical, some factual, the recent book by Ruth B. Russell, *A History of the United Nations Charter*, is the most comprehensive and most thorough in its use of the records. I am indebted to its author for enabling me to read various chapters in manuscript, and for her critical examination of this chapter.

Soviet government had let it be known that its delegation to the San Francisco Conference would be headed not by the Foreign Minister, Molotov, but by its Ambassador in Washington, Gromyko. Did this mean that the Soviet government was going to disregard the results of the Conference? That it might do so had seemed the more possible since during these same days Stalin was accusing the American and British governments of deceiving him about the nature of secret talks in Switzerland having to do with the possible surrender of German forces in Italy.

It is hard to believe that anyone should wish for Molotov's rigid presence. But Roosevelt, determined not to allow any transient trouble with the Soviet Union to come into the way of his great purpose, had urged Stalin, on March 24, to let Molotov come to San Francisco if only for the vital opening sessions. If he were not there, said the President, the Conference would be deprived of a great asset. The whole world would construe his absence as protest or dissent. Stalin had answered coolly that Molotov was going to be needed in Moscow for a meeting of the Supreme Soviet of the Soviet Union. He could not let fear of inferences determine his decisions.

The first question that the American press had asked Truman, as President, was whether the Conference would meet later in the month as scheduled. He at once sent word out to them that it would. He deemed it, as he later wrote, ". . . of supreme importance that we build an organization to keep the future peace of the world." So his intent was not deflected on learning from Stimson, later that same first day of office, that the United States would soon have a weapon of "unbelievable destructive power." That night he determined to issue a statement assuring our allies of his support of the Conference.[4]

But on the next day (the 13th), Stalin had agreed to Harriman's request that, as a tribute to Roosevelt, Molotov be sent to San Francisco. Truman and the State Department enthusiasts were gladdened by this news. Stalin's gesture was read as a sign of a basic wish to remain in step with us. The appeal to have Molotov come to San Francisco was followed by a suggestion that he stop over in Washington for talks about Poland and other European issues. Earlier pages have told of the fractious course of these talks. The American officials found out that Molotov was the same man on this side of the Atlantic as on the other side—possibly even a little more resistant and glazed. His sojourn in Washington was an uneasy prelude to the sessions in San Francisco.

[4] *Year of Decisions*, pages 9-11.

The first rub had occurred in connection with an offending Soviet proposal that the Polish Provisional Government, unrecognized by the British and American governments, be admitted to the Conference and to membership in the prospective organization. This request the American and British governments bluntly rejected.

Then, at San Francisco, trouble broke out in the first days over the effort of the other American republics to have Argentina brought into the Conference. Under General Edelmiro Farrell that government had called itself neutral during the war, but in many ways it had been helpful to Nazi Germany. Just a few weeks before the end, it had recanted and stated that it would declare war on Germany. Thereafter it had been allowed to sign the Final Act of the Inter-American Conference on Problems of Peace and War, which had met in March at Chapultepec Castle (Mexico City). The other American republics were bent on restoring unity among all the countries of this hemisphere. They wanted to retain the existing security system of the Western Hemisphere and feared it might be submerged in the United Nations.[5] Thereupon Roosevelt, on April 9, had joined in recognizing this Argentine government and entering into diplomatic relations with it. But on doing so he had made it clear that the American government was not obligated to support Argentine admission into the United Nations until and unless that government took further action against the Axis and thereby qualified itself in the eyes of the other allies.

In short, there were valid grounds for making both the Provisional Polish Government and the Argentine government wait for inclusion in the United Nations. The Soviet government set about exacting recognition of the obedient regime in Warsaw in return for acceding to the wish of the American republics. Molotov, in the early committee work, angrily protested the admission of Argentina into the new organization, expatiating on the "fascist" nature of its government. In contrast he could and did stress that the Poles had fought the Germans hard. In rejoinder the western advocates could and did answer that they wanted Poland in their company; that their opposition was directed solely toward what would amount to acceptance of a temporary Polish administration slated for reorganization.

The American republics were determined to make good on the prom-

[5] For an analytical account of the discussions at the Chapultepec Conference on the question whether the American republics should retain authority to enforce peace and security in this hemisphere on their own initiative, see Russell, pages 554-72.

ise they had given the Argentine government at the Chapultepec Conference, that if their conditions were met it would be invited to San Francisco. They were the more set on doing so because they were being asked—not only by the Soviet government but also by that of the United States—to assent to an act that seemed to them unjust and contrary to the spirit of equality of members: they were being urged to agree to the admission of two of the constituent republics within the Soviet Union (Ukraine and Byelorussia, referred to usually as White Russia), even though these were not in any sense independent. The acknowledged reason was that the Soviet government thought itself entitled to at least three places and votes in the Assembly (having reduced its original request, made by Stalin to Roosevelt at Yalta, that all sixteen of the Soviet republics be accorded separate representation). In its view this demand was modest and fair, since it believed that all six members of the British Commonwealth that would be in the organization would follow British lead, and that most or all of the other American republics would follow that of the United States.

The United States delegation at San Francisco concluded that the other American members would assent to this assignment of two extra places to the Soviet Union if, and only if, their wish to have Argentina in was granted. It began to fear that in this case the Soviet government—aggrieved as it was at the refusal to invite the Provisional Government of Poland—might call its delegation back home and disrupt the Conference.

To avert that, the United States delegation joined in the decision to invite Argentina to San Francisco despite Soviet protests. But Molotov's criticisms put Stettinius enough on the defensive to lead him, when reporting to the nation over the radio on the progress of the Conference, to make it clear that "the vote of the United States in favor of seating Argentina did not constitute a blanket endorsement of the policies of the Argentine Government. On the contrary, with many of these policies both the Government and the people of the United States have no sympathy."[6]

Hopkins was to find when he got to Moscow that Stalin was still smarting over this defiance of his objections.

The fuss over the admission of Argentina had wider connotations. As suggested above, the other republics in this hemisphere wanted to be sure they would remain able to take any measures deemed necessary to protect their peace and security without having to reckon with the oppo-

[6] Radio broadcast, May 28, 1945, State Department *Bulletin*, June 3, 1945.

sition or veto of the Soviet Union within the Security Council. Inside the United States government there were two opinions as to whether an explicit sanction in the Charter for such regional enforcement action might be regretted. Some officials feared that if it were allowed, a variety of other regional arrangements would come into existence, and the world would presently be divided into competitive groups, each under the lead of some large power. Others were willing to take the risk in order to be sure that the American system would not be hindered in its operation; they argued also that whether or not this latitude was allowed, the Soviet Union would act on its own in any crisis in its relations with the smaller neighboring countries.

The President was asked to decide. As a result, the two groups within the American government were brought to accept a verbal formula that developed into Article 51 of the Charter of the United Nations: "Nothing in the present Charter shall impair the inherent right of individual or collective self-defense if an armed attack occurs against a Member of the United Nations, until the Security Council has taken the measures necessary to maintain international peace and security."

The United States delegation, especially its Republican members, Senator Vandenberg and senior Adviser Dulles, were under the impression that the Soviet government was seriously opposed to the adoption of any such provision.[7] But this may not have been so. The article is pliable. It is easy to believe that the authorities in Moscow foresaw that in the future it might be as useful to them as to the United States. If it provided a route along which the American republics could proceed without Soviet assent, it could also smooth the way for Soviet measures that others might not approve. The Soviet government was already forming its own system of regional accords with its weak neighbors.

The rambling discussion of the way in which regional accords and the new world arrangement should be geared into each other was connected with the issue that most incisively divided the main members of the coalition. This concerned voting procedure in the Security Council. It has become known as the veto question.

The three Heads of Government had left Yalta in February with the mistaken idea that the subject had been probed and settled. They had been in quick and firm accord that the unanimous approval of all its

---

[7] See, for example, the account given by John Foster Dulles in his book *War or Peace*, page 91, of the tactics by which in his judgment the Soviet government was brought to accept this text against its inclination.

permanent members (save any that chose to abstain) should be needed for any and all verdicts of the Security Council holding that a threat to the peace existed or that a breach of the peace had occurred, and that such unanimous approval should be needed before the Council could take any measures to enforce a decision.[8] But they had been puzzled as to whether it would be wise to have the Council similarly bound before engaging in preliminary activities; that is, before it could even take heed of a dispute, look into it, and try to settle it by peaceful means.

Roosevelt had proposed three rules to Churchill and Stalin: first, that decisions on "procedural matters" should be made by *any* seven of the eleven members of the Council; second, that the concurrence of *all* permanent members should be required on *all* other matters; but third, that while the Council was trying to bring about a voluntary peaceful settlement by advice, conciliation, or adjudication, any member of the Council, including the permanent members, who was a party to the dispute should abstain from voting.

In the correspondence before Yalta the Soviet government had at first shown dislike for the last segment of this proposal, whereby even the great powers would lose their chance to object to Council initiative in disputes in which they were themselves involved. The Soviet leaders had wished to maintain the rule that the dissent of any permanent member should debar the Council from taking any and all acts of a substantive sort. As expounded by Molotov, the Soviet position had been that the "principle of unity of action must be preserved from the inception of any dispute, it must never be diminished and there must be no exceptions to it; otherwise, the entire organization would be emasculated."[9]

And at Yalta, Stalin had tried hard to convince Roosevelt that this was the soundest provision, since the main task before them as Heads of Government, and before the organization, would be to avert or prevent future quarrels between the great powers. Roosevelt had once thought the same way, but he had been converted by Hull and others to another conception—that peace could best be assured by enabling all countries to act as guardians of it.

Abruptly, perhaps because of Churchill's persuasive explanations, the Soviet rulers had come about at Yalta. Both Stalin and Molotov had agreed that the American proposal would sufficiently safeguard the unity of the great powers. Their statements had bred the cheerful conclusion that the question was settled.

[8] Perhaps the American experts did not at this time conceive that the voting formula would allow abstention, as later interpreted in actual Security Council practice.
[9] Memo of Harriman-Molotov talk, December 27, 1944.

In the interval before the convening of the San Francisco Conference both Secretary of State Stettinius and Under Secretary of State Grew had construed the formulas conceived at Dumbarton Oaks and completed at Yalta. The Secretary of State had done so on March 5, at one of the sessions of the Chapultepec Conference. Grew's attempt, made on March 24 in an effort to clear away puzzled inquiries, was the same in substance.

The purpose of the Secretary of State had been to enlist the trust and support of the other American republics in the task of forming the world security organization by indicating that the few great powers did not intend to exercise undue restraint upon the judgment of the Security Council. After telling of the proposed provisions about the work of that body he had continued:

"This procedure means that whenever any member of the Council—including any permanent member—is a party to a dispute, that member can not vote in any decision of the Council involving peaceful settlement of that dispute. Consequently, the Council can examine the dispute thoroughly and the remaining members can make recommendations to all the parties to the dispute as to the methods and procedures for settling it. . . .

"This means that all members of the Security Council, when they are parties to a dispute will be on the same footing before this Council. It means that no nation in the world will be denied the right to have a fair hearing of its case in the Security Council, and that the equal, democratic rights of all nations will be respected.

"If a dispute is not settled by such means, the major question before the Council is whether force needs to be employed. In that event, it is necessary that the vote of the permanent members of the Council be unanimous. They are the nations which possess in sufficient degree the industrial and military strength to prevent aggression."[10]

This avowal was at the time misleading in its scope, though not intentionally so. In dispensing with the veto right of a permanent member engaged in a dispute, the formula of Dumbarton Oaks and Yalta intended this only as regards "recommendations . . . as to *methods and procedures* for settling a dispute, but not as regards the *terms of settlement.*" This was a point that was before long to mix up everybody.

---

[10] State Department *Bulletin*, March 11, 1945, page 395. The Secretary of State made this statement on the same day that the State Department publicly announced the invitations to the Conference at San Francisco. Later trouble might have been avoided if the American government had secured British and Soviet agreement on the text before issuing it. For Grew's statement see State Department *Bulletin*, March 25, 1945, page 479.

Even before the Conference met at San Francisco, comments had indicated that the governments of several smaller countries (Australia, New
Zealand, and various American republics) thought the three proposed
rules gave the great powers too preponderant a control over the actions
of the Security Council. Thus in the early sessions the smaller nations
presented a variety of amendments. These differed in range, but all
were aimed at enabling the Security Council to make decisions (some or
all) in regard to the pacific settlement of any dispute by a simple majority
of seven.[11]

The involved and fluctuating discussion of this question brought out
the fact that there was an important area of ambiguity in the formula
on the table, or at least an area in which the four sponsoring powers (the
United States, Great Britain, the Soviet Union, and China) were not
clearly on record as being of one mind. Was the admitted necessity for
concurrence of all permanent members (when not parties to the dispute)
to be applicable to any and all stages of an attempt to deal with a dispute
or situation by peaceful means? Even to the early stages, which would
ordinarily involve only a decision to take cognizance of the trouble? If
not, at what point in the sequence of possible action was it to become
effective? A Subcommittee was appointed to study this question "in order
to clarify the doubts that have arisen."

The Subcommittee decided that the practical way to make progress on
the subject was to submit a comprehensive questionnaire to the four
sponsoring powers and France; and to seek to have them agree on a
joint statement that the Subcommittee could use in composing a report
to the full Conference. This was done. But as soon as the specialists began
to consider the answers to the questions that had been posed, differences
appeared. All five powers were in accord that a mere decision to place
an item on the agenda of the Council for discussion should be regarded
as a procedural matter and therefore be determined by simple majority
vote. They also agreed that, at the other end of the range, unanimous
assent of the permanent members (except any that was a party to the
dispute) should be required for a decision of the Council to investigate

---

[11] The comment on this point that Senator Vandenberg entered in his diary for May 20,
1945 (page 196), is pertinent: "The Yalta 'veto' as *now* interpreted includes a 'veto' for
the Big Five even on preliminary discussion and investigation of disputes by the Security
Council. It does *not* apply, at this point, if one of the Big Powers is a defendant. But that
makes it all the more anomalous and fantastic that it should apply to the disputes of others"
(Vandenberg's italics).

His view of the veto power in the Security Council is in import, however, quite contrary
to his stand on questions of domestic jurisdiction and compulsory jurisdiction of the International Court of Justice—in both of which matters he was aroused at the danger that
the United Nations might consider a case despite United States protest.

and make recommendations on the pacific means of settlement. But what of the many possible intermediate actions? What, in particular, of the right to consider and discuss?

The British and United States representatives were of the opinion that the Council, in accord with other provisions of the Charter, would be under an unqualified obligation to go at least this far in carrying out its primary duty. Hence they were convinced that the decision whether to do so ought to be regarded as one of procedure, and as such decided by ordinary majority vote. But Gromyko—for by this time Molotov had returned home—said that before approving this statement he would have to consult Moscow. This came as a dismaying shock to the American government, for it had been taken for granted that the Soviet government had long since acceded to this judgment. Both Stettinius and Grew had so affirmed in the public statements to which reference has been made, and to which the Russians had not objected.

The Conference waited intently.[12] After hearing from Moscow, Gromyko said, on June 1, that the Soviet government believed the only correct answer was to require a "qualified" vote (that is, one in which all permanent members concurred) on this important question of whether the Council was to consider and discuss a dispute. The Soviet reasoning was fundamental and familiar. There was a vital need to assure the unity and unanimity of the great powers. But that might be impaired in any one of several ways if the Council were permitted to decide to consider a dispute despite the opposition of any one of them. If the discussion did not lead to any action the relations between the great powers might be strained. Or a discussion begun despite objection might launch a chain of events that would cause or require the Council to take action; and this might lead to dangerous dissension. Why the Soviet government retreated at this time from its earlier disposition to allow the Security Council to take heed of a dispute was then, and remains, a

---

[12] The anxiety of the American delegation is reflected in an entry that Senator Vandenberg made in his diary for May 26. An extract reads: "This time the problem [of the range of the veto power] is more perplexing than usual because the Big 5 is in disagreement itself over this particular interpretation. Speaking for Britain, Sir Alexander Cadogan says the Yalta 'veto' does not permit one of the Big 5 to 'veto' a discussion of *any* (that is, every) question brought to the Council. That, too, is our American position. China would accept this version. Once more the whole thing hangs on Gromyko who is 'awaiting instruction' from Moscow. He says he is 'inclined to go along'—but has to hear from home. It *might* be argued that when all the rest of us agree on an interpretation of Yalta, *our* view ought to govern rather than Russia's. That is *my* position. On the other hand, there is much to be said for *not* giving the Russians any excuse for running out on Yalta itself. (Of course [Russia] *has* run out; but the rest of us are demanding that it make good—and so we go to painful extremes to 'make good' ourselves.) At any rate, the answer is up to Moscow—and we are supposed to get the *answer* in the Pent-House tomorrow night."

matter for surmise. It may be that the stubborn resistance to the Soviet program for dominating Poland and nearby smaller states was regarded as a forecast that the Western powers, in combination in the Council, would be unfriendly to Soviet interests.

Not only the American but the British and Chinese delegations were unpersuaded by the Soviet argument. Stettinius let it be known on June 2 that the American government would never consent to such a curb on the right of the Council. Nor would the Conference itself, he predicted.

The Conference at San Francisco was at its most upsetting crisis. Unless the Soviet government could be brought to change its stand there would be no Charter, no world organization. Furthermore, failure at San Francisco would excite every other current cause of trouble with the Soviet Union. A sense of emergency ran through the corridors of government. Hence an urgent request was sent to Hopkins at Moscow, to do his utmost to make Stalin understand what was at issue and persuade him to go along with the American government in this matter.

15. Hopkins-Stalin Talks: The First Avowals

On the evening of the 25th of May, Hopkins, having stopped off to see Eisenhower, arrived in Moscow. The first talk with Stalin was set for the following night. In this and all that followed, Harriman and Molotov also took part.

Hopkins had been briefed by the State and War Departments on the main troubles they were having with the Soviet government. Whether or not he knew of the new impressive weapon we were soon to have is not of record.[1]

The first and second talks were given over to roving comment about the regrettable turn taken by American-Soviet relations, and the grievances that were leading from friendship toward separation.

Before starting on his statement of the purposes of his visit to Moscow, Hopkins tried the jocular tone he so often used in an effort to put either himself or the other fellow at ease before tackling a difficulty. He asked Molotov whether he had recovered from the battle of San Francisco. Molotov did not enter into the jest. He replied that he did not recall any battles, only arguments, at San Francisco. Then, turning to Stalin, Hopkins began to tell of Roosevelt's last moods and thoughts, and of his death; of how Roosevelt had often reviewed with him the results of the Yalta conference, and had come away from it with enlivened faith that the United States and the Soviet Union could work together in peace as they had in war. But recently that assurance had been ebbing. That was the real reason why President Truman had asked him to fly to Moscow: to talk over with Stalin the swiveling relationship between the United States and the Soviet Union. As later reported, he told Stalin:

"Two months ago there had been overwhelming sympathy among the American people for the Soviet Union and complete support for President Roosevelt's policies which the Marshal knew so well. This sympathy and support came primarily because of the brilliant achievements of the Soviet Union in the war and partly from President Roosevelt's leadership and the magnificent way in which our two countries had worked together to bring about the defeat of Germany. The American people at that time hoped and confidently believed that the two countries could work together in peace as well as they had in war. . . . He said he

[1] Harriman knew about it but thought of it only as a possiblity, pending actual test. It is likely that Hopkins had learned of it from him or someone else.

wished to assure the Marshal with all the earnestness at his command that this body of American public opinion who had been the constant support of the Roosevelt policies were seriously disturbed about their relations with Russia. In fact, in the last six weeks deterioration of public opinion had been so serious as to affect adversely the relations between our two countries. . . . The friends of Roosevelt's policy and of the Soviet Union were alarmed and worried at the present trend of events and did not quite understand why, but it was obvious to them that if present trends continued unchecked the entire structure of world co-operation and relations with the Soviet Union which President Roosevelt and the Marshal had labored so hard to build would be destroyed. Prior to his departure President Truman had expressed to him his great anxiety at the present situation and also his desire to continue President Roosevelt's policy of working with the Soviet Union and his intention to carry out in fact as well as in spirit all the arrangements, both formal and informal, which President Roosevelt and Marshal Stalin had worked out together. . . . He also said he would not have come had he not believed that the present trend could be halted and a common basis found to go forward in the future."[2]

Stalin did not interrupt him, so Hopkins talked on. It was not easy, he said, to identify the precise reasons for the current alienation of American opinion. But among the various incidents, the most troubling one seemed to be "our inability to carry into effect the Yalta Agreement on Poland." About the causes of this, he said, President Truman, as well as the American public, was bewildered.

At the mention of Poland—which was to engage more of their talk than any other issue—Stalin made his first pointed reply. The reason was clear: the Soviet Union wanted to have a free Poland but the British Conservatives were trying to prevent that, since they wished to revive the restraining alliance ("cordon sanitaire") around the borders of the Soviet Union. It may be surmised that Stalin, who never said anything aimlessly, thought that this version of the cause of the trouble would appeal to his American auditor. Hopkins said merely, and said it twice, that both the people and the government of the United States had no such intention as Stalin attributed to the British, and wished to see friendly countries all along the Soviet borders. If that were so, Stalin said, they could easily come to terms in regard to Poland. Hopkins remarked that he was glad to hear the Marshal say so.

Then, leaving that topic after a repetition of his belief that it was the

[2] Sherwood, pages 888-89.

greatest cause of disturbance in Soviet-American relations, Hopkins went on to inform Stalin of the other questions he would like to talk about. They were, first, Truman's wish to meet Stalin to discuss the problems arising out of the end of war in Europe, and the time and place of such a meeting; second, the setting up of the Control Council for Germany; third, the Pacific war and the future relations of the United States and the Soviet Union to China.

Having concluded his review of the matters he wanted to talk over, Hopkins said he would be glad to discuss any other issues the Marshal might have in mind. Stalin answered that, in fact, he had several. All but one, however, he left over until the next talk. That was whether there ought to be a peace conference to settle the European war. He said he thought that matter was, so to speak, knocking at the door. He felt the uncertainty was having a bad effect, and it would be wise to select a time and place well in advance. The Versailles Conference had been poorly prepared and as a result many mistakes had been made. It is to be wondered what mistakes Stalin had in mind. But Hopkins did not turn historian and ask him to explain that remark. He said that he thought the prospective meeting between the three Heads of Government would be a first step toward that peace conference, and that he had a general knowledge of Truman's views on the subject and would be glad to tell them to Stalin.

In their talk on the next night Stalin responded to Hopkins' invitation to tell him what matters concerning the United States were bothering him. Stalin's first remark had an edge to it. He would not try to use Soviet public opinion as a screen. He would talk of the feeling created in Soviet official circles by some recent actions of the American government.[3] They felt that these indicated a lessening of American regard for the Soviet Union, as though the Americans were saying that the Russians were no longer needed now that Germany was defeated. The bill of complaints that he went on to tote was long. I shall tell here only of the three that topped it.

One was the admission of Argentina to the San Francisco Conference. Stalin said he could not understand why this had been allowed, since it had been settled that only those states that had declared war on Germany before the first of March would be asked there. By this action the

---

[3] Stalin did not explain what "official circles" he had in mind. During all the years of the war he had not summoned one meeting of the whole Central Committee of the Communist Party or one party Congress.

value of agreements among the three major powers had been brought into question. What were they worth if they could be overturned by the votes of such countries as Honduras and Puerto Rico?

Another was the attitude of the United States toward Polish questions. He said it had been agreed at Yalta that the existing government was to be reconstructed. Anyone with common sense could see this meant that the existing government was to form the basis of the new. No other understanding of the Yalta accord was possible. Despite the fact that they were simple people, the Russians should not be regarded as fools —a mistake frequently made. Nor were they blind; they could see quite well what was going on before their eyes.

Then there was the manner in which Lend-Lease aid had been curtailed. This had been regrettable and even brutal; for example certain ships on their way to the Soviet Union had been turned about and unloaded. While that order had been cancelled, it had left offense. If, he continued, the refusal to continue Lend-Lease was meant as a form of pressure on the Russians "in order to soften them up," it was a great mistake; reprisals in any form would bring about exactly the opposite effect.

Hopkins, having listened patiently, tried to convince Stalin that there were no unfriendly or unfair intentions behind these and other American actions that Stalin deplored.

Since he had not been at San Francisco, Hopkins turned to Harriman to explain the reasons for the Argentine affair. In brief, Harriman said the United States representatives had found it necessary to go along with the other American republics in order to secure their assent to the extension of an invitation to the Ukrainian and White Russian governments to participate in the Conference. When Harriman then went on to suggest in his further remarks that perhaps Molotov had been in part responsible for the turn of events, he was answered with a grumbled denial. Stalin cut short the talk about this affair by saying that in any event what had been done could not be undone and that the question belonged to the past.

In regard to the slash in Lend-Lease aid, Hopkins exerted himself to counter Stalin's reproaches. He said he thought it had been made clear that the American government had to reshape its Lend-Lease program at the end of the war with Germany. The sudden turn-around and unloading of ships that were to have gone to the Soviet Union he attributed to a mistaken interpretation of the order by one government agency, and recalled that this had been corrected at once. He repudiated the notion that future Lend-Lease aid for the Soviet Union might be administered either arbitrarily or as a means of bringing pressure. He emphasized that promises to deliver military supplies that would be of use to the Soviet Union when it was in the war against Japan were being carried out.

Stalin struck a lofty note. He said he recognized the right of the United States to curtail Lend-Lease shipments. The Soviet government would not have complained if this had been done with suitable notice and gradually; but it certainly did not like the way in which it had been handled. After all, he said, an agreement between the two governments had been ended in a scornful and abrupt manner, and the absence of warning had upset Soviet plans. But he dropped this subject too, with the remark that he believed Hopkins and was satisfied with his explanations.

Thus neither Stalin nor Hopkins spoke all that was in their minds about this occurrence. In curtailing its aid the American government had wished to register its view that the Soviet authorities, by their actions, were losing their right to special treatment; but through mistaken zeal its intention had been exceeded. Stalin and his associates were displeased by our action not only because of the way that it was taken but because it reduced the generous, the carelessly generous, flow of supplies that would have been useful to them after the war.[4]

Lastly, Hopkins spoke at length about the Polish question, and Stalin answered him at length. But separate consideration is needed for this first outspoken exchange of views about that searing subject.

Since the mutual candor of these talks was accepted by each as a service to the search for friendship, it did not lead to rancor. Just before the visitors took their leave, Stalin said he was ready to meet the President at any time, and promised to announce Marshal Zhukov's appointment as Soviet representative on the Control Council for Germany at once, so that body might be able to start its work as soon as possible. The next talk was set for the following day.

---

[4] On May 28 (two days after this talk) Molotov and Mikoyan submitted to Harriman a large Soviet program for Lend-Lease material to be delivered in the period of July 1 through December 1945. See Supplementary Note 2.

16. Hopkins-Stalin Talks on Poland and the Satellites

HAVING said that of all the irritants between the two countries their quarrel over Poland was the worst, Hopkins, in his second talk with Stalin, stated the American view. With various turns of language he averred that the American government and people recognized the reasons why the Soviet Union wanted a friendly government in Poland. They were not seeking to prevent the realization of that wish. They deeply desired, however, that the Poles be allowed to choose their own government and their own social system, and that their country be genuinely independent. In American eyes the Soviet government, in concert with the Warsaw group, seemed to be bent on denying them these rights. Would not the Marshal help to find a solution for the Polish problem which would dissipate such suspicions?

Stalin began his justification of Soviet policy by a historical review. Needless to say, this did not contain any reference to the Molotov-Ribbentrop Pact, which in 1939 had cleared the way for the division of Poland between the Soviet Union and Germany. Twice in twenty-five years, he said, the Russians had had to endure horrible invasions through Poland, like the incursions of the Huns. The Germans had been able to use that country as a pathway because it had been "previous European policy" that "Polish governments must be hostile to Russia"; and because Poland either had been too weak to oppose the Germans or had let them come through. This experience, he concluded, had made it plain that Poland should be made both strong and friendly to the Soviet Union. He went on to say, however, "that there was no intention on the part of the Soviet Union to interfere in Poland's internal affairs, that Poland would live under the parliamentary system which is like Czechoslovakia, Belgium and Holland and that any talk of an intention to Sovietize Poland was stupid. He said even the Polish leaders, some of whom were communists, were against the Soviet system since the Polish people did not desire collective farms or other aspects of the Soviet system. In this the Polish leaders were right since the Soviet system was not exportable—it must develop from within on the basis of a set of conditions which were not present in Poland."[1]

He admitted the right of the United States and England to concern

---

[1] Sherwood, page 900.

themselves with what was done about Poland. But the Soviet government had been forced to act without their assent since they had refused to recognize the Warsaw government, and the Red Army had needed its aid. Had the Soviet government set up its own administration in these Polish territories, it would have looked like occupation and been resented by the local inhabitants. A further corner of his thought was revealed by one of his pendent remarks, that after all, the Soviet government had never been compelled to resort to the kind of repressive measures in Poland that the British government had taken in Greece.

These explanations appealed to Hopkins. They suited his devoted faith in popular democracy, his will to believe that the Soviet Union meant well, and his inclination to interpret British foreign policy as self-seeking. But the proposal which Stalin then made with an air of novelty let down his hopes, for it was the very one that he had been offering during all the previous weary weeks of argument. Why not, he asked, adopt the same type of arrangement that had been made for Yugoslavia? If that were done, out of the eighteen or twenty ministerial posts in the Polish government, four or five would be assigned to members of democratic groups not represented in the existing administration. If this was acceptable they could then go on to settle what persons should be selected for these positions. Perhaps it might be wise to ask some of the Warsaw leaders to come to Moscow while Hopkins was there, so that both of them might hear what *they* had to say. Again, as at Yalta, he bid for assent by implying that the arrangement in mind was only transitional. On this point too quotation is needed, as a reminder: "He [Stalin] added that if we are able to settle the composition of the new government he felt that no differences remained since we were all agreed on the free and unfettered elections and that no one intended to interfere with the Polish people."[2] Hopkins merely said that he would like to have time to think over Stalin's ideas.

That time was used in reporting to the President. The terse responses he got from Washington encouraged him to go forward along his opening line. This he did at the fourth meeting, on May 30. In that talk Hopkins started on an essay in persuasion. If a mutually acceptable accord on Poland were reached, it would serve Russia well. But if, on the contrary, Russia imposed a solution, it would remain a troubling or even threatening problem. Stalin did not dissent from the forecast, for he recognized, he said, that a settlement in which all three joined would

[2] *Ibid.*, page 901.

[103]

carry more weight.[3] Then, detouring around Stalin's proposal, Hopkins pointed to the cardinal elements that must be present (a combination of the principles of the American Constitution and Bill of Rights) if a real parliamentary system was to be established and maintained. He concluded that if both countries adopted these principles, which would be the basis for future free elections, "then he was sure we could find ways and means to agree on procedures to carry them into effect."[4]

Stalin's answer was substantiating enough to allow Hopkins to think —as he wished to think—that Stalin was in accord with his general view. Yet it was cleverly enough qualified to leave leeway for any deviations the Soviet supporters might make. To quote the record: "Marshal Stalin replied that these principles of democracy . . . would find no objection on the part of the Soviet Government. He was sure that the Polish Government, which in its declaration had outlined just such principles, would not only not oppose them but would welcome them. He said, however, that in regard to the specific freedoms mentioned by Mr. Hopkins, they could only be applied in full in peacetime, and even then with certain limitations."[5] Certainly, fascist parties, for example, whose aim it was to destroy democratic governments, could not be permitted full freedom. For further illustration of the possible need of restrictions, he recalled that during the revolution the Russian Patriarch and the entire then-existing church had declared the Soviet government an anathema, and had called on all church members to resist it in every way, thus leaving the Soviet government no choice but to declare war on the church.

At this juncture the long and earnest talk between the two left the upper regions of avowals and descended to details of what in another sphere is called "business." Stalin put Hopkins on the defensive by repeating his view that the British government secretly did not wish to see the Polish question settled. Why else should it and the American government suggest, as they had, that one of the leading agents of the reactionary Polish group in London (Jankowski), who directed the illegal internal work in Poland, be included in the new government? Hopkins denied any wish of the American government to have any present agents of the London Government in Exile, whether inside or outside of Poland, involved in the new Provisional Government. That, Stalin said, was "very good news." Hopkins pursued the point with vigor. He assured Stalin that Truman did not intend to name anyone,

[3] Bohlen memo of Stalin-Hopkins talk, May 30, 1945.
[4] Sherwood, page 906.
[5] *Ibid.*, page 906.

even for consultation, who was against the Yalta decision. Moreover, "he knew that President Roosevelt and now President Truman had always anticipated that the members of the present Warsaw regime would constitute a majority of the new Polish Provisional Government."[6] This was correct. But in admitting it so explicitly Hopkins must have hoped to induce Stalin to be yielding in return.

He followed up his remark by asking whether they might not agree on eight or ten men, outside of those connected with the Warsaw government, to be summoned to work with the Commission (Molotov, Harriman, and Clark Kerr) to form a new Provisional Government. Let the two of them—Stalin and himself—not try then and there to fix upon how many ministries might be assigned to Poles outside of the Warsaw government. Let this emerge from the consultations. This was Hopkins' way of refusing to accept the Yugoslav precedent, and of rescuing the Commission of Three from disuse. If it worked, the practice of coalition cooperation would be saved. Stalin seemed to fall in with the thought—saying that in their next talk they should try to agree on the persons to be invited.

Hopkins, pleased that Stalin was no longer insisting that the Warsaw government would have to approve all nominations for consultations, hurried to inform the President that "It looks as though Stalin is prepared to return to and implement the Crimea decision and permit a representative group of Poles to come to Moscow to consult with the Commission."[7]

Relying on Stalin's assurances that Poland, if friendly, could be free and independent, and leaving open the questions of distribution of offices and authority in the reorganized government, Hopkins pursued his suggestion in his next talks with Stalin and Molotov. They haggled about the number of independent Polish leaders—some in London and some still in Poland—to be invited to Moscow to talk with the Commission. They went over the roll of qualified individuals. For guidance in the effort to assure that the consultants could speak for all democratic elements in Poland, Hopkins turned to the American and British ambassadors and the State Department. The twists and thrusts in the bazaar-like barter for possible advantage in the consultations are no longer of interest. When the fifth talk ended, on May 31, agreement had been reached on the entries.

Hopkins at once cabled to the President: "This I believe is a satisfac-

---

[6] Bohlen memo of Stalin-Hopkins talk, May 30, 1945.

[7] Sherwood, pages 907-08. In the same message he reported that Stalin agreed to meet with Truman and Churchill in the Berlin area about July 15, six momentous weeks away.

tory list and I wish you will approve it. If you do, then I think it extremely important that you press Churchill immediately for his approval and have Schoenfeld [our diplomatic representative vis-à-vis the Governments-in-Exile in London] see Mikolajczyk at once in order to get his agreement." On the advice of the State Department, the President told Hopkins he endorsed the names. And he at once besought Churchill's concurrence. The arrangement Hopkins had made seemed to him an encouraging step forward, he told the Prime Minister, and thus he hoped for quick assent, that the next measures might be taken as soon as possible. And would Churchill also do his best to get Mikolajczyk, to whom the list was being submitted, to help carry Hopkins' program into effect?

Churchill has recalled his impression: "We of course concurred in these proposals for what they were worth."[8] His answer to Truman said he agreed that "Hopkins' devoted efforts have produced a breaking of the deadlock"; since this was the best deal Hopkins could get, he would join Truman in a message to Stalin telling him of their acceptance. Waiving any thought he may have had that Hopkins ought to have consulted him first, Churchill sent him too an agreeable personal message.

Mikolajczyk's response was compliant but admonitory. He said he would accept an invitation to take part in the Moscow talks, provided it was issued by the Commission of Three. Among his various comments on the list of individuals, the most important was his notation that it did not give any place to two of the most important former Polish political parties, the Christian Labor Party and the National Democratic Party; and he urged that a special effort be made to ask Stalin to include leaders from these groups. In conclusion, he said he was not hopeful of the outcome of the consultations, for he thought the Russians were merely giving way to pressure at the moment, in the knowledge that the subsequent steps in the formation of the new government were the ones of real consequence.[9]

In the messages that the British Embassy in Moscow was receiving from the British Foreign Office about the Stalin-Hopkins accord there was a similar note of pessimism. The belief was expressed that no real

---

[8] *Triumph and Tragedy*, page 582.

[9] Mikolajczyk, in the book he wrote later, *The Pattern of Soviet Domination*, page 128, reviews the submitted list and restates his doubts about it and the projected plan. This written account gives the impression that his response was more protesting and critical than it appears in the contemporary reports of it made by the American and British diplomatic representatives in London with whom he talked.

advance had been made, since the Soviet government would not allow the preliminary talks to result in the formation of a government that would give effective influence to independent elements, enough to enable them to see that the elections were conducted properly. On June 5, while Hopkins and Harriman at the American Embassy were reflecting on this sober estimate, Truman asked them to try to get Stalin to agree to certain small changes on the list which would be very helpful and create a favorable reaction among Polish circles abroad. But they were authorized to go ahead on the best basis they could reach, for the President thought that Hopkins was doing "a grand job," and told him so.

In his last talk with Stalin, Hopkins won him over to some of the desired changes. They agreed that the Commission should promptly issue invitations to those on the revised list. As a last act of precaution, Hopkins confirmed his understanding that in the prospective consultations no decision would be reached by the Commission of Three, of which Molotov was Chairman, except unanimously.

The President and the State Department were much relieved that a way out of the Polish morass had been sighted. They were pleased by reports of Stalin's amiability.

What Hopkins had obtained from Stalin was an affirmation (1) that the Soviet government did not intend to interfere with Polish affairs; (2) that it would not oppose the inclusion of independent political elements in the Polish government; and (3) that it would join with the American and British governments in seeing to it that the reorganized Polish government held free elections and respected individual rights and liberties.

In return, Hopkins had agreed (1) that only Poles who had accepted the Yalta accord were to be invited to consult with the Commission of Three; (2) that the Soviet government retained the right to dominate the outcome, since all members of the Commission of Three would have to approve any agreement reached by the Polish Commission (and if no accord was reached, the Red Army and the subservient Warsaw regime could continue to extend their control); and (3) that the Warsaw government was to have a dominant place in the reformed government. Also, Hopkins had refrained from challenging two decisive acts that the Soviet government had taken on its own. These were the turning over of part of its zone in Germany to the Poles, and the signature of a treaty with the Warsaw regime.

The chance that this accord might eventuate in an unhampered Polish government depended on the good faith of the Soviet authorities in seeing to it that free and honest elections were carried out. That was the only route by which the Polish people might be able to determine the form and policies of their government.

Hopkins did his animated best to induce Stalin to release arrested leaders of the Polish underground who were being examined as a preliminary to trial. Forgiveness toward them, he tried to impress upon Stalin, would gratify American public opinion and make it easier for the American government to gain the support of the Poles in the United States for an ultimate settlement of the Polish question. It would also, he emphasized, lessen the bitterness in the circles of the Government-in-Exile in London and among the Polish forces that had fought with the allies, for these felt deeply that the captives had been engaged in a patriotic and courageous struggle. And, he said, though without any ring of accusation, it was the general belief that it would be just to release these men, who had acted, he thought, without bad intent.

On the evening of May 31, after the formal dinner that Stalin gave him, Hopkins made the point that he thought it would be much easier for him to secure approval of the list of persons who were to be invited to come to Moscow for consultation if the Soviet government released at least those prisoners who were charged only with minor misdeeds. Stalin was unrelenting, saying he knew that all the prisoners had engaged in what he called "diversionist" activities. Then, no doubt aware of Hopkins' disposition to be critical of the British, he said he thought that Churchill had misled the American government in regard to the facts, causing it to believe the statements of the Polish government in London though just the opposite was true. With vehemence he declared he did not intend to have the British manage the affairs of Poland, which was exactly what they wanted to do. When all the evidence was published, it would look very bad for the British. Still, to please American and British public opinion, he would do what he could to ease Churchill out of a bad spot. At the end he told Hopkins that although the men must be tried, they would be treated leniently.

Both Churchill and Mikolajczyk, when approving the arrangement for consultations, had deplored the need to do so while these men were kept under detention and in jeopardy. Thus on June 5, Hopkins tersely told Churchill: "I am doing everything under heaven to get these people out of the 'jug.' But the more important thing, it seems to me, is to get these Poles together in Moscow right away."[10]

He had been authorized to separate the two questions. But in his last talk with Stalin, marked by a mutual sense of accomplishment and accord, Hopkins once again pleaded for the arrested Poles and once more urged Stalin to try to please American feeling. Stalin stood fast, promising only that he would give thought to the views and statements Hopkins had expressed. There can be little doubt, in retrospect, that Stalin was dead set against doing anything that might spare anyone associated with the Polish government in London. He hated and feared it, and was determined to crush it out of existence.

While Hopkins was striving to work out a solution for Poland, the situation in the former satellite countries was being discussed between the Heads of Government. On the 27th of May Stalin sent similar messages to Churchill and Truman. Eight months had passed, he recalled, since Romania and Bulgaria had broken with Hitler's Germany and gone into the war on the side of the allies. They had thereafter contributed to the defeat of Hitlerism. Thus, he believed, it was about time that diplomatic relations be restored with their governments. As for Finland, it would be well to do the same with that country, since it was now "taking the democratic way" and perhaps also with Hungary, a little later.[11]

The President, on June 2, sent Hopkins and Harriman his reply, for transmission to Stalin. Truman also wanted the armistice periods to be short. He too thought that they ought quickly to reward the efforts of these countries to line up with the principles of the allied nations. Thus he was ready to exchange diplomats with Finland at once, since its people had proved their true devotion to democratic ways and precepts. He did not find the same remedial tendencies in Romania and Bulgaria or in Hungary. There democracy was being repressed, and there the groups in power were neither representative of the popular will nor responsive to it. But the American government was prepared to engage at once in consultation with the Soviet and British governments, with a view to concerting policies and actions vis-à-vis these three satellites. That could lead to a restoration of normal relations with them as independent states.

[10] *Triumph and Tragedy,* page 583.
[11] Stalin Correspondence, vol. 2, page 361.

Hopkins and Harriman, afraid that the difference delineated in Truman's answer might set them back, asked permission to defer delivery of this response until after the talks about Poland were concluded. They were told that they might choose their time. Harriman did not delay long. On June 7, just after Hopkins got on his plane to leave Moscow, he passed the President's message along to Stalin. The Marshal, as will be told later, argued back.

17. Hopkins-Stalin Talks on Far Eastern Situations

NEXT to the search for an acceptable accord about Poland, the foremost purpose in sending Hopkins to Moscow had been to ascertain what Stalin was going to do about Far Eastern matters.[1] Hopkins was asked to extract from talk with Stalin knowledge that would be of use in deciding whether it was to American advantage to continue to place our trust in the secret agreement reached at Yalta, and whether we should try to secure Chinese concurrence in it. Doubts had sprouted into two confluent sets of questions.

One concerned Soviet intentions in Chinese affairs. Would the Russians really respect Chinese sovereignty? Would they be friendly to the National government and abstain from aiding or encouraging the Chinese Communists? Would they cooperate with the American government to bring about political and military unity in China, the purpose upon which our policy focused?

The other set concerned the military plans of the Soviet government. Would it enter the war against Japan, and in time to save American lives? The laggard and evasive responses to American requests for joint advance military measures had aroused our impatience and, curious as it now seems, caused worry over Soviet designs. Despite the swift advance of our forces toward Japan and our self-sufficient plans to defeat Japan, which had been conceived by the middle of May, Soviet entry into the war was still wanted by the American military authorities.

Hopkins along with Harriman, who knew most about the talks both before and at Yalta that had led to that accord, and who had urged Roosevelt at the time to seek a clearer version of its ambiguous clauses before signing, had been asked to find out the answers. In his third talk with Stalin on May 28, Hopkins tried to do so (while still thinking over Stalin's proposals about Poland). He said that the American government was most interested in unity in China. But he did not know of any definite American plan for bringing this about, and he would like to hear what Stalin thought of the prospect of Chinese unity

---

[1] The telling of the events, decisions, and policies in the Far East during this crucial period from May to the Japanese surrender in September 1945 is being left for another volume. Thus they will figure in this narrative only when and as they directly entered into or influenced the members of the coalition in their talks and treatment of affairs in the western world.

and how it could be achieved.[2] Stalin said that he too thought it desirable that China should be unified and become an integrated state, and that "we should all occupy ourselves with helping China to achieve unity." And at a later point in the talk he remarked that "The United States must play the largest part in helping China to get on their feet; the Soviet Union would be busy with its own internal reconstruction and Great Britain would be occupied elsewhere."[3]

By such open and amiable assent to American aims and American stardom in China, he had, months before, convinced our Ambassador in China, Patrick J. Hurley, that we could count on his aid.[4]

Harriman then went on to ask a series of pointed questions. What would the Soviet attitude be if China was not unified when Soviet troops entered Manchuria? Would the Marshal consider it possible in that case to make the necessary arrangements with Chiang Kai-shek? Stalin answered without pause. The Soviet government did not propose to alter the sovereignty of China over Manchuria or any other part of China; and the Soviet Union had no territorial claims on China, either in Sinkiang or elsewhere. "In regard to the Generalissimo, . . . he knew little of any Chinese leader, but he felt that Chiang Kai-shek was the best of the lot and would be the one to undertake the unification of China. He said he saw no other possible leader and that for example he did not believe that the Chinese Communist leaders were as good or would be able to bring about the unification of China."[5]

Was Stalin going to ask Chiang Kai-shek to organize the civil administration when Soviet troops entered Manchuria? He would, Stalin replied; in Manchuria, as in any part of China where Soviet troops went, the Chinese civil administration could be set up by Chiang Kai-shek. "Chiang could send his representatives to set up the Kwantung regime in any areas where the Red Army were . . . . the Soviet government was prepared to talk with the Chinese and if they wanted representatives in the areas where the Red Army would be they would be quite prepared to accept them."[6]

Who except the most unbelieving would have doubted promises so frontal and explicit? They were deemed to be of enough value to China and the Kuomintang government to warrant them in concurring in

---

[2] Hopkins had not been told in Washington of any detailed plan for bringing about Chinese unity, in cooperation with the Soviet Union. One was worked up by the State Department, however, while Hopkins and Harriman were on their way to Moscow.

[3] Potsdam Papers, Document 26, Bohlen memo of Stalin-Hopkins talk, May 28.

[4] Feis, *The China Tangle*, pages 284-89.

[5] Potsdam Papers, Document 26, Bohlen memo of Stalin-Hopkins talk, May 28.

[6] *Ibid.*

the Yalta accord, thus rewarding the Soviet Union for entering the Pacific war. Would these promises not enable China to regain possession of Manchuria and Formosa? Would they not mean that China would be protected against superior Soviet force? Would they not influence the Chinese Communists to come to terms with the National government, accepting a conjunctive political and military place?

If such boons would flow from Chiang Kai-shek's assent to the Yalta accord, why continue to hesitate to carry it through? What reason was left for not seeking thereby to make sure that the huge Red Army would crush the Japanese in Manchuria, and leave the American combat forces free for other tasks, and bring the war to an end sooner?

About his intentions in that regard Stalin was also asked directly. He forecast that the Red Army would be properly deployed in its Manchurian positions and ready to attack by August 8. But he added that the actual date depended on China's approval of the Yalta accord. He was willing to clarify and complete its terms and application by a firm agreement with the Chinese National government. For that purpose he would like T. V. Soong (the Chinese Premier and Foreign Minister) to come to Moscow, not later than the first of July.

In his report to Washington about this long talk on May 28, Hopkins said that in the light of what Stalin had said about Far Eastern matters, he believed it desirable that the American government adopt the procedure suggested by the Marshal. Truman, all the more relieved by this report because of the predictions of the military of the losses we might suffer in the final battles against the Japanese, gladly agreed.[7] In doing so he discarded the idea of waiting to seek Chiang Kai-shek's concurrence in the Yalta accord until the outcome of the test of the atomic bomb was known, or until he met with Stalin.

---

[7] Thus in *Year of Decisions*, page 265, Truman recalls: "I was reassured to learn from Hopkins that Stalin had confirmed the understanding reached at Yalta about Russia's entry into the war against Japan. Our military experts had estimated that an invasion of Japan would cost at least five hundred thousand American casualties even if the Japanese forces then in Asia were held on the Chinese mainland. Russian entry into the war against Japan was highly important to us."

His satisfaction with what he thought Hopkins had achieved is reflected in his talk with Stimson a week later. Then he told the Secretary of War, according to an entry in Stimson's diary for June 6, that there was a promise *in writing* (my italics) that Manchuria would remain fully Chinese except for a ninety-nine year lease on Port Arthur and the settlement at Dairen. When Stimson warned him that Russian power, with control of the railways running across Manchuria, would probably outweigh Chinese, the President said the promise was perfectly clear and distinct. Did he have in mind only the Yalta written accord? Did he think Hopkins and Stalin had put their interpretive application of the Yalta accord in writing? Or had Stimson either misunderstood Truman or been hastily careless in his diary entry?

He authorized Hopkins to inform Stalin that Soong would be told Stalin would like to see him in Moscow before July 1, and that we would provide a plane to get him there. On Soong's arrival in Moscow, the President added, he would have the American Ambassador in China take up with Chiang Kai-shek the promises held out to the Soviet Union at Yalta. If the Sino-Soviet talks went well, they would, it was anticipated, be over before the scheduled meeting of Heads of Government at Potsdam.

On the night of June 6, as Hopkins was starting off on his last talk with the Marshal, Stalin again told him that the Soviet Union would enter the war against Japan only if and after Chiang Kai-shek concurred in the Yalta accord. He had not yet heard, he remarked, when Soong would get to Moscow. Harriman let him know that he and Hopkins believed Soong should plan to arrive before the end of June—and implied that they were so advising the President.[8]

On the same day (June 6) Stettinius in San Francisco relayed Stalin's message to Soong: come to Moscow before July to talk with me. Before saying yes or no Soong wanted to learn what was going to be asked of him. So it was arranged that he be flown to Washington straight away.

Truman within the next week told him what was in the secret Yalta accord. But both he and Grew resisted Soong's efforts to get them to interpret the meaning of some of its capacious clauses. Disquieted, Soong set off on his quest to Moscow via Chungking. The American government went ahead with plans for conquest of Japan by its own and British forces alone, if need be. But it continued to value highly the reaffirmed assurance of Soviet cooperation in ultimately converging assaults. Plans for adjusting Russian operations to our own were made ready for discussion with Stalin and the Soviet Chiefs of Staff at Potsdam.

Our wish to have the Soviet Union join in the Pacific war was not affected by the fact that in the consequential talk on May 28 Stalin made it clear that he would like to have a say in what was done about Japan. After he and Hopkins had agreed on the program for Sino-Soviet talks to effectuate the Yalta accord, Stalin said he thought that Japan was doomed and the Japanese knew it. Since peace feelers were being put out by certain elements in Japan, he continued, he believed the time had come to "consider together our joint attitude and act in concert about the

---

[8] The Chinese Ambassador in Moscow had informed Harriman that Soong wanted to wait in the United States until Hopkins got back to Washington, in order to consult with him. But Hopkins was not anxious to see Soong. So he suggested to Washington that if Soong was going to return to Chungking before going on to Moscow, it would be best that he leave the United States at once.

surrender of Japan."[9] He feared that Japan would try to divide the allies. Hopkins did not comment on this remark, but probably Washington meditated over it. Was it a hint that the Soviet government might make a deal with Japan if its desires were not satisfied? Was it an attempt to detect whether the American government might soften its attitude toward Japan and offer peace on easier terms unless the Soviet Union entered the war?[10]

The second possibility is suggested by Stalin's following remarks. He expressed a strong preference for stiffly maintaining the demand for unconditional surrender and all it implied. He was also in favor of extinguishing imperial institutions, for he thought that unless the military might of the Japanese was once and for all thoroughly destroyed, they would start at once to plan a war of revenge. But he foresaw that if we did retain the unconditional-surrender formula the Japanese would not give up, and the allies would have to overcome them completely, as they had the Germans. Should the Japanese offer to surrender on easier terms, and should the allies be prepared to accept a modified surrender, then (as phrased by Hopkins in his report to the President) "Stalin visualizes imposing our will through our occupying forces and thereby gaining substantially the same result as under [unconditional surrender]. In other words, it seemed to us that he proposes under this heading to agree to milder peace terms but once we get into Japan to give them the works."[11]

Stalin also indicated that he expected Russia to share in the actual occupation of Japan. The American and Soviet governments would have to have "serious talks about Far Eastern problems, particularly in regard to Japan, including such questions as the zones of operations for the armies and zones of occupation in Japan."[12] Washington was eager to discuss zones of military operations, but was by then loath to contemplate any zonal plan for occupation.

The mention of Korea was brief. Hopkins said the American government thought it would be desirable that the four most interested powers share in the trusteeship over Korea—the Soviet Union, the United States, China, and Great Britain. Its duration might be left open. It would certainly run for five or ten years, perhaps as long as twenty-five. Stalin said he fully agreed.

[9] Sherwood, page 903.
[10] On this very day, May 28, Acting Secretary of State Grew was urging President Truman to try to stimulate Japan to surrender by letting it know that we would not oppress it and would allow it to retain imperial institutions, if the Japanese people so decided.
[11] Sherwood, pages 903-04.
[12] Potsdam Papers, Document 26, Bohlen memo of Stalin-Hopkins talk, May 28.

After these talks—of which I have given only a skimming version—the American and British governments ought to have been able to discern how the Soviet government conceived its position in the Far East in relation to their own, after the defeat of Japan. The Soviet Union would acquire the southern half of Sakhalin, the Kurile Islands, extensive rights in Manchuria, and a naval base at the end of the Kwantung peninsula at Port Arthur. Japan would be so diminished it need not be feared. As one of the controlling and occupying powers in Japan the Soviet Union would have an active chance to convert the Japanese to its side, or to keep them down, as it should later decide. China might or might not be unified under Chiang Kai-shek's real or nominal control. Even if it were, China and the Chinese government would be weak for a long time; and even if the Chinese Communists accepted for the time being a secondary place in the Chinese government, they could continue their struggle for control. In Korea there was to be for an indefinite period a trusteeship, in the administration of which the Soviet government would have much influence.

Even assuming that the prospect was viewed this way in Washington and London, the authorities there had to reckon with the probability (noted in the answers that Stimson and Forrestal had made to Grew not long before) that the Soviet Union could obtain all these advantages without going to war, except perhaps the Kurile Islands and a part in the occupation of Japan.

18. Relief for the San Francisco Conference

ONE reason why Hopkins' reports were read in a receptive mood was that he got Stalin to whisk away a barrier stalling the Conference at San Francisco.

It will be recalled that the Conference had been cast into a crisis over the issue whether any one of the permanent members should be able to prevent the Security Council from discussing a dispute or situation (when it was not directly involved). The Soviet delegation had clung to the view that this right ought to be reserved, as essential for unity among the great powers. It had forewarned that if the Council was authorized to engage itself in a dispute against the wish of any one of the permanent members, their relations would be exposed to strain. The American government and those of kindred outlook were willing to take that risk. The legally minded thought it to be small, since the requirement of unanimity was so well protected in other sections of the Charter. The morally minded thought that proposed restraint offended against the sense of equal chance and standing before the tribunal that should prevail in the organization. The politically minded tended to want many nations, not only the few strongest ones, to be able to exert effective influence in the treatment of disputes. All agreed that this check on Council action would be so resented that many countries—including the United States—might refuse to join the new organization.

Was Stalin about to spoil the vision of enduring peace for which we had fought two wars? Truman decided to put the question hard and directly to Stalin. In the instruction that was hurried off to Hopkins and Harriman an overtone of indignation can be heard. After reviewing the issue it observed: "The Soviet proposal carries the principle of the veto . . . even to the right of a single nation to prevent any consideration and discussion of a dispute. We feel that this would make a farce of the whole proposed world organization."

The American envoys were asked to find out whether Stalin fully realized what the advices sent to Gromyko meant, and how they would affect the character of the organization that was being formed: "Please tell him in no uncertain words," the message said, "that this country could not possibly join an organization based on so unreasonable an interpretation of the provision of the great powers in the Security Council. Please tell him that we are just as anxious as he to build the organization on a foundation of complete unity but it must be unity of action in the light of a maximum of discussion. At no stage in our discussions relative to creation of the world organization at Dumbarton Oaks or at Yalta or at any other time was a provision ever contemplated which would make impossible freedom of discussion in the Council or Assembly. This is a wholly new and impossible interpretation."

Gromyko, it may be noted, had on the contrary been maintaining at San Francisco that the American position was "new."

The memo of the talk that Hopkins and Harriman had with Stalin and Molotov on June 6, at their sixth and last meeting, may or may not be as straight as the trail of discussion itself.[1] But it is not so lucid as the student of this question (which under its technical dress is of real political importance) might wish. And it may be that some of the things said are not recorded in its loose chain of sentences.

Molotov spoke up before Stalin. What he said sustained the instruction by which Gromyko had been guided, and the reasoning behind it. The memo goes on to relate briefly that a conversation took place in Russian between Molotov and Stalin, from which the American interpreter and recorder, Charles Bohlen, gathered that Stalin had not grasped the question before; and that he told Molotov he did not think the issue to be significant and the American view should be accepted.

Stalin prefaced his own response to Hopkins by observing that there was a tendency among the small nations to exploit and even to create quarrels between the great powers for their own ends. The great powers, he warned, must be on guard lest this again cause trouble. "After all," he observed, "two world wars have been begun over small nations."[2] There were statesmen who sought to get hold of the votes of small nations, and this was a dangerous and slippery path. But still, in the words of the memo, "Marshal Stalin then stated that he was prepared to accept the American position on the point at issue at San Francisco in regard to voting procedure."[3]

There was rejoicing in Washington and San Francisco when the news that Stalin had deferred to the American view was received. It was hailed, as Sherwood wrote, as "the real news that the San Francisco Conference had been saved." The President was delighted. Stettinius was excited. Grew recorded in his diary that he was "immensely happy" about it. All sent to Hopkins and Harriman buoyant messages of praise. Stalin's terse comment was regarded by others as it was by Senator Vandenberg:

[1] The text is printed in Sherwood, pages 910-12.
[2] Hopkins and Harriman did not suggest to Stalin that it might have been more just and correct to say that the two wars turned into world wars because great powers were in rivalry for control over small nations.
[3] Sherwood, page 912.

". . . a complete and total surrender. No attempt at any weasel-worded compromise. Just a straight-out acceptance of unhindered hearing and discussion regarding any dispute brought before the Security Council. That *ought* to clear the track for a quick and successful conclusion of the Conference."[4]

However, to foretell, when the representatives of the sponsoring powers met anew at San Francisco to express the presumed accord into an exact statement of their ideas for the information of the Conference, areas of unsettled intention re-emerged. An adequate analysis of these would carry us into long scrutiny of the texts over which committees once again pored.[5] Here it is perhaps enough merely to record that in final form the joint statement identified the types of decisions on which a "qualified" vote would be necessary and those for which only a procedural vote would suffice (that is, a vote of any seven members).

In one sentence of this text there was what appeared to be a clear confirmation that the Council was to be unrestricted by the veto in deciding whether or not to take cognizance of a dispute. It read: "Further, no individual member of the Council can alone prevent consideration and discussion by the Council of a dispute or situation brought to its attention . . . Nor can parties to such a dispute be prevented by these means from being heard by the Council." But tucked away in a later part of the text there was a statement that in "the unlikely case" of a difference of opinion as to whether one or the other type of vote should be required, this "preliminary question" must be settled "by a vote of seven members of the Security Council, including the concurring votes of the Permanent Members."[6]

In reality, this four-power statement was a hazy blend of the Anglo-American view of freedom of discussion and the Soviet view on the "preliminary question." Moreover, it was not enlarged into a formal international agreement. The Conference refused to vote on it, and its contents were only in part made explicit in the Charter.

An issue of similar import, which caused almost as crucial a crisis in the Conference, concerned the scope of the authority of the General

[4] Vandenberg, entry for June 7, 1945, page 208.
[5] They are considered with fullness and competence in Russell, Part Five.
[6] The title of this statement was: "Four-Power Statement at San Francisco Conference on Voting Procedure in the Security Council, June 7, 1945." The text may be found in United Nations, *Documents on . . . Conference on International Organization*, vol. 2, pages 710-14. Because it is oblique in its method of exposition, no summary interpretations can be conclusive. The one on which I have drawn is that made by Francis O. Wilcox in the *American Political Science Review* (October 1945).

Assembly. Several smaller nations, led by Australia, were determined upon a paragraph that in original form read: "The General Assembly shall have the right to discuss any matter within the sphere of international relations, and (subject to specified exceptions) . . . to make recommendations to the members of the organization or to the Security Council, or both, on any such matters."

Gromyko stood out against any such broad license. He voiced the fear that the Assembly might interfere in matters of purely domestic concern. The suggested language, he warned, would encourage the impulse of any nation, with any kind of complaint, to arouse trouble.

The American and British groups at first sought to avoid another affray by refraining from support of this paragraph, since they thought that authority of the Assembly was well enough set forth elsewhere. They tried to persuade the Australian delegation and its supporters that this was so; but to no avail.

Thus during the first two weeks of June a stubborn and intense exchange of arguments ensued over a variety of proposed textual changes far too numerous and detailed to be recounted here. Then, on the 16th, the Soviet delegation, for the first time, agreed that the right of the Assembly to *discuss* any dispute or situation would be unrestricted. But it continued to insist that the right to *make recommendations* should be circumscribed. Though not pleased by the Soviet proposal, some of the American group at San Francisco might have assented to it in order that the issue should no longer keep the Conference unsettled and postpone the finish of its work. But the advocates of the original statement would not yield. No less grimly, Gromyko turned aside the pleas of both major and minor delegates by just saying over and over that "The Soviet government does not agree" and that he was under firm instructions not to sign the Charter unless the language met Soviet wishes. It was at lunch after a morning marked by such reiteration that the Earl of Halifax said to Gromyko that he now understood how his countrymen had managed to hold Stalingrad against apparently hopeless odds.[7]

There ensued a last spasm of fatigued effort to hit on phrases that all might adopt. Again the task of excavating out of the voluminous minutes the details of this drama of constitution-making must be left to others. On the 19th, all other ways having failed, Stettinius, anguished, asked Harriman to try to win round the Soviet government. He was told to see whether it could be induced to accept any of three alternative texts, which were sent on from San Francisco. He was authorized to let the

[7] Halifax, *Fulness of Days*, page 292.

Soviet government know that if it would not do so, the American government saw no choice except to allow the Conference to adopt whatever rule it preferred—even if as a consequence the Soviet government should refuse to join the organization.

For the American officials the following night was another worried one. They were convinced that they could not give in on what they conceived to be a vital issue, one that could determine whether or not the Assembly might become the "town-meeting of the world."[8] But what if the Soviet government maintained its refusal and let the Conference end under this threatening cloud of dissent? So there was great relief when Gromyko made it known, on the 20th, that he had been given permission to accept one of the three formulas.[9]

With the removal of the last serious obstacle to the adoption of the complete text of the Charter, the way was open to move on to its signature. The conflict of views with the Soviet government was indicative of Soviet unwillingness to repose trust in the impartiality of the majority of the countries in the United Nations. The American and British governments felt that by and large they could count on a concordance of judgment and interest between themselves and most of the members of the new organization. The Soviet government felt that it must be on guard against the enmity of many or most of the other members—or if not their enmity, their will to resist Soviet aspirations.

The prolonged contention at San Francisco expressed itself in debate between strong sovereign nations over involved written texts. But words

[8] This tenacity, however, was true only to a degree. The American government warded off all proposals that it thought might enable others to try to get the United Nations to intrude into fields regarded as wholly in the domain of domestic decision (such as trade and immigration). It was determined to reserve the right to draw the line for itself. Had the American government been consistent, it would have become engaged in a similar argument with the Soviet government over some of the provisions in the Charter which defined the realm of jurisdiction of the International Court of Justice. Many countries wished to accord to the Court compulsory jurisdiction over certain kinds of legal disputes among the members. But in opposing any such provision, even though carefully circumscribed, the American delegation found itself aligned with the Soviet delegation. The main reason for this departure from the general attitude was the fear aroused by memories of the defeat by the Senate of the United States of the determined attempt made in 1935 by President Roosevelt to secure approval for American membership in the World Court.

[9] This enveloping compromise formula, as written into Article 10 of the Charter, read, "The General Assembly may discuss any *questions or any matters within the scope of the present Charter* . . . and, except as provided in Article 12, may make recommendations to the members of the United Nations or to the Security Council or to both on any such questions or matters" (compromise formula italicized by me). It had already been agreed, and was so provided in Article 12, that the Assembly should abstain from making any recommendations with regard to a dispute or situation that was under active consideration in the Security Council, unless the Council requested it to do so.

in a document do not always control conduct, even when their meaning is clear. This will remain so until or unless the more exalted elements in the complex of purposes that inspired the creation of the United Nations come to prevail among the people and the decision-makers of the major powers.

The Charter was unanimously adopted on June 25. The spirit of the occasion was exhibited in President Truman's address to the final session, in which he said: "The Charter of the United Nations which you have just signed is a solid structure upon which we can build a better world. . . . Between the victory in Europe and the final victory in Japan, in this most destructive of all wars, you have won a victory against war itself." Few of those who took part in the Conference and few commentators openly stressed that the future of the new organization would vitally depend on the way and the extent to which the West and the Soviet Union would give in to each other on the matters over which even then they were at odds. Nor did many find it appropriate to emphasize the need for self-restraint and self-inspection on the part of all nations, great and small. But it may be assumed that beneath the resounding cheers with which the veterans of this conference hailed the completion of their work, all but the inexperienced were aware of such elementary truths.

The vibrating question for the future was whether the essential rules of good conduct would be sufficiently heeded to dominate national egotisms, ambitions, fears, and compulsions. Before another month had passed, that question was to become more vital than ever in the history of mankind, as nuclear explosive weapons were perfected and the human power to destroy made absolute.

The conclusion, in cheerful concord, of the Conference at San Francisco cleared the way for the meeting of the Heads of State at Potsdam. It confirmed the decision of the American people to play the part proffered them in the affairs—twisted and touchy—of the whole world.

The effect on American official outlook of the presumed success of the Hopkins mission and the easing of various other situations, traced in other chapters, is visible in the summing up that Acting Secretary of State Grew made for the British Chargé d'Affaires on June 8, the day after Hopkins left Moscow. He said he did not want to crow before the sun had risen, but surely the international scene was brighter than it had been before. Russia had yielded in the question of veto in the Security Council, and thus it was all but sure that a satisfactory charter for the permanent organization of the United Nations would be completed;

Hopkins' visit to the Soviet Union had gone off well, bringing other solutions into sight and improving the state of feeling; the allies were about to sign an accord with Tito that would end the danger of an armed clash over control of northeast Italy; de Gaulle had receded from his attempt to take over a small fringe of northwest Italy, and the trouble with him about the Levant states was quieting down.

These happenings seemed to Truman to indicate that his general course was sound. They revived his drooping belief that through personal talk with Stalin the two countries could get back on good terms and deal with their differences in honest and friendly fashion. The mood in the White House became briefly blithe.

The date for the meeting with Stalin and Churchill had been set. Studies of its subjects were coming off a hundred typewriters. But before telling of the way in which that conference was arranged we ought to turn aside to London. There another special envoy of the President, Joseph E. Davies, was talking to Churchill—trying to convince that man of spirit that he ought to soothe the Soviet rulers rather than challenge them.

19. Davies' Visit to London

CHURCHILL did not share the turn of feeling and expectation. He still feared Soviet purposes and acts, and at moments verged on depression over the European prospect. The great warrior who had stood alone before 1940 felt that he had again to battle for his views against obtuse or inert associates. Besides, he was facing an election at home. Though acclaimed by the British people he had led to victory, he was not sure of the way they might lean now that the exhausting ordeal was over.

Davies had been sent to London to bring the ardent Prime Minister to realize that the American government was not going to adopt the measures he was urging; that it was not going to give way to mistrust of Russia. He was to be talked into being more patient and conciliatory. As Davies expressed it in the memo he gave the President after his return, he told the Prime Minister that Truman "conceives it to be the duty of the three nations which won the war to leave nothing undone in an effort to solve their differences, and through continued unity make possible a just and durable peace structure."

Churchill was given to understand that Truman wanted to meet with Stalin alone somewhere in Europe before the three of them got together for their conference. As Davies awkwardly exposed this wish to the Prime Minister, the President thought the situation was the more serious because the Soviet rulers believed Britain and the United States were "ganging up on them," a suspicion that ought to be dispelled. This could be done only if the parties had a chance to talk frankly, and to know and estimate each other. On that score the President was at a disadvantage, since both Churchill and Eden had had the benefit of frequent past contacts and friendly association with Stalin and Molotov. The President wanted, in view of the responsibility he must assume, to have a similar chance. He therefore "desired an opportunity to meet the Marshal immediately before the scheduled forthcoming meeting."

Just what program Davies had in mind for these introductory talks between Truman and Stalin is not clear, even after scanning his testimony and the record as remembered by the Prime Minister. Churchill gathered, rightly or wrongly, that Truman had in mind more prolonged private talks than the informal chats à deux that the Heads of Government had had with each other before the regular sessions of the conferences at Teheran and Yalta got under way.[1]

---

[1] Churchill, in *Triumph and Tragedy* (page 577), expressed his understanding as follows: "The crux of what [Davies] had to propose was that the President should meet

It must have been hard for Churchill, who was spurting cautions that Russia might become the new oppressor of Europe, to listen to Davies' comments on the source of current tensions, for they were akin to personal reprimands. In effect he placed the blame for Soviet suspicions and misconduct on the American and British governments, and pointed to the Prime Minister as the chief malefactor, or at least the most active cause of the worsening trouble and the recent swerves in Soviet policy. Davies' attitude is evident from his written report: ". . . frankly as I had listened to [Churchill], inveighing so violently against the threat of Soviet domination and the threat of Communism in Europe, and disclosing such a lack of confidence in the professions of good faith of Soviet leadership, I had wondered whether he, the Prime Minister, was now willing to declare to the world that he and Britain had made a mistake in not supporting Hitler, for if I understood him, he was now expressing the doctrine which Hitler and Goebbels had been proclaiming and reiterating for the past four years in an effort to break up allied unity and 'Divide and Conquer.' "

Davies had ready explanations for the Prime Minister's vehement response to his accusations. "Obviously, [Churchill] was upset and concerned over two situations which he saw developing which I could understand. First, the possible effect of the proposal [Truman-Stalin meeting] upon his election, and second, the confirmation of his fear of the withdrawal of the U.S. from Europe and particularly that Britain might be deprived of our military strength in trading with the Soviets."

Churchill was shocked to learn that while he had had the impression that the United States and Great Britain were united on the main measures to govern the peace, important American officials did not think so and were causing the new President to keep his distance. It may be assumed that the Prime Minister sensed what Davies thought and was going to tell the President, Leahy, and others: "The Prime Minister is a very great man, but there is no doubt that he is 'first, last and all the time a

---

Stalin first somewhere in Europe before he saw me." Truman, in *Year of Decisions* (page 260), has explained that his intention was merely to suggest to Churchill "that when we arrived at our meeting place, I would have an opportunity to see each separately."

Doubt about how Davies explained Truman's intention to Churchill is enhanced by a passage in a letter sent by Molotov to Harriman on May 26, in which Molotov referred to a message that Davies had recently sent him, raising the question of "the meeting of the *two* heads of Government and also of a place of this meeting" (my italics), and to Molotov's answer to Davies. No mention of such an exchange of messages between Davies and Molotov on this subject is to be found either in the various printed accounts of Davies' oral report to Truman on his mission (Truman and Leahy books) or in Davies' supplemental written report to the President.

great Englishman.' I could not escape the impression that he was basically more concerned over preserving Britain's position in Europe than in preserving peace. In any event he had convinced himself that in serving England, he was best serving peace." About this, the comment that Admiral Leahy later wrote in his book is telling: "This was consistent with our staff estimate of Churchill's attitude throughout the war."[2] Among the other impressions that Davies conveyed to the President were these:

"The Prime Minister was tired, nervous and obviously working under great stress. The vehemence and bitterness of his expressions would undoubtedly be much modified with considered judgment.

"He [the Prime Minister] was bitterly disappointed by the President's decision and the fact that American troops were already being diverted from Europe to the Eastern Theater, and would be withdrawn (retreat, as he called it) to the occupational zones agreed upon. . . . It has been his purpose, and so avowedly stated, to employ the presence of American forces and their position in advance of their lines, as trading material to induce concessions from the Soviets. His policy is based on the 'tough approach.' He was willing to run the great risk which such a gamble entails.

"He [the Prime Minister] was bitterly hostile to the Soviet. . . . His attitude must be known to or at least suspected by the Soviet government. It is undoubtedly responsible for the suspicion voiced in the interchange of cables in connection with the surrender of Germany's troops in Italy; the situation in Austria, the suspicion that secret arrangements have been made on the Western front at the expense of the Russians on the Eastern front, and other troublesome situations. It could and does undoubtedly account for much of the aggressiveness and so-called unilateral action on the part of the Soviets since Yalta. . . . They are protecting their position."

But Davies predicted that from then on the Prime Minister would be docile. He reported him as saying at the end of their talks that "(1) He will not oppose the American policy toward Russia and (2) he is entirely in accord with the policy of trying to exhaust all means consistent with self-respect to resolve the differences between the Big Three."[3]

The sense of affront given by Davies' suggestions and lectures was repressed in the brief message that Churchill sent Truman, on May 31,

[2] Leahy, *I Was There*, page 380.

[3] In this account of Davies' talks with Churchill I have not followed the unsystematic way in which Davies strung out his conclusions in his report to the President, but have combined what seemed to be connected parts.

DAVIES' VISIT TO LONDON

after his talks with Davies. "I had agreeable talks with Mr. Davies which he will report to you when he returns. I must say, however, at once, that I should not be prepared to attend a meeting which was a continuation of a conference between you and Marshal Stalin. I consider that at this victory meeting, at which subjects of the greatest consequence are to be discussed, we three should meet simultaneously and on equal terms."[4]

Before answering, Truman waited for Davies to get back and report to him personally. Then on June 7, when sending thanks for Churchill's acquiescence in the later date—July 15—for the conference, he said he concurred that all three should meet at the same time.

Davies' visit may have served to make Churchill aware of the way in which his proposals were disturbing the civilian members of the American government who thought continued cooperation with Russia essential for peace; and how keenly they were worrying the military members who wanted such cooperation in order to bring the war against Japan to the quickest possible end. It may have shaken his stand on some of the momentous matters that were to be discussed at the coming conference. But on the other hand, among the small American upper circles of decision, Davies' version of Churchill's aims, and tales of his violence of feeling, nourished suspicion of the Prime Minister's balance and motives.

[4] A paraphrase of this message is in *Year of Decisions*, page 260. Churchill does not include it in *Triumph and Tragedy*. The Prime Minister had given free expression to his indignation in a long note intended for Truman, which he had dictated on May 27 after his first talk with Davies, and which, according to his later recollection, he gave to Davies. This note is printed in *Triumph and Tragedy*, pages 578-80, with the strongest passage italicized. Churchill, in his account of the episode, states that the President received this note in a kindly and understanding spirit. But Davies, in his report to the President, explicitly stated that at their last talk he and Churchill agreed that it would be wiser (mainly in the interests of secrecy) *not* to exchange *aide-mémoires* as they had previously agreed to do, and it is probable that Churchill did not actually give Davies the note he prints. No reference to any such document is to be found in *Year of Decisions* or in the available American archives.

20 · Discord with de Gaulle

WHILE Hopkins at Moscow was sealing the edges of the protocol for the encounter of Heads of Government, and Davies in London was reproving Churchill, General de Gaulle was wanting to visit Truman. His purposes were diverse. First of all, it was surmised, was the wish to gain entry to the coming conference, at which the future form of Europe might be set. His bid for inclusion in the Yalta gathering had been ignored, and he believed that thereby French interests had been hurt and French honor slighted. Was he again to be left out, even though this time matters of vital concern to France would be settled, as for example, what was to be done about Germany?

De Gaulle must have known that the welcome he wanted could be had only if Churchill and Truman were able to revoke Stalin's scornful sentence that France was not entitled or qualified to share in the momentous decisions ahead. Both the Prime Minister and the President regarded de Gaulle as a man misled by visionary pride into asking too much for France. Still, their vexation over the person and his pretensions were offset by traditional friendship for France and a wish to have it reemerge as a virile power.

The quest for an invitation to the conference had been pursued through every diplomatic route in Washington, London, and Moscow. On May 18 the President had told the French Ambassador that he would bear in mind de Gaulle's wish to be present when and if he met with Churchill and Stalin. On the 29th, in a cordial letter, de Gaulle wrote in effect that he would be glad to come to Washington whenever the President wished, to talk over the many matters of common concern to their two countries. Truman at first frowned at this extra call on his time and energy. But Grew persuaded him not to put off this determined applicant just because of his avidity to be present at the conference with Stalin and Churchill. Could not the President honestly say that this could not be decided without the consent of the other two? It was agreed that de Gaulle should be informed that the President was willing to see him in mid-June. A message so saying was typed in the State Department. But it was not sent. Concurrent affronts led Truman to conclude that he would rather defer the visit and evade the request for admission to the conference.

The American government was being provoked most of all by de Gaulle's willfulness in keeping French troops in an adjoining sector of northwest Italy. In order that the German divisions on the Franco-Italian frontier might be held there as long as could be, French forces under Eisenhower's command had been authorized at the beginning of April to patrol to a distance of twenty kilometers inside Italy. They had penetrated much further,[1] and had engaged in unusual and purposeful activities. They were trying to attract the civilians living in the Val d'Aosta away from Italy and to get them to clamor to be taken into France.[2] Preparations had been made for plebiscites. Extra rations were issued to those who used a French identity card. To the French this course seemed just and justified. During the first phase of the war, Italy had compelled France to keep many divisions along that frontier. Then in June 1940, when France was going down into the depths, the craven Mussolini had joined the attack and invaded France.

But de Gaulle's venture was regarded by the American and British governments as another sign of his willful ambition. Moreover, it was a serious threat to the principle they were trying to uphold against Yugoslavia and the Soviet Union.

General Alexander was under orders from the Combined Chiefs to extend Allied Military Government (U.S. and British) in Italy up to the frontier with France. So he had asked Eisenhower to order all French troops out of Italy. The Supreme Commander passed on the request to General Doyen, who was in command of the French contingents in Italy. Doyen answered that he could not withdraw unless so ordered by the French government. The State Department then asked our Ambassador in France, Jefferson Caffery, to get de Gaulle to tell Doyen to comply.

[1] French troops had advanced east into Italy to Ivrea, in the Val d'Aosta, and Rivoli, only twenty kilometers west of Turin; they had gone into Liguria, where they occupied quite a part of the province of Imperia—fourteen communes, including Ventimiglia—and even into Savona on the Ligurian coast.

[2] De Gaulle in his *Mémoires*, vol. III, pages 183–184, professes that his main intention was to acquire some enclaves on the French slopes of the Alps, to incorporate in France two cantons that had once been part of Savoy-Tende and La Brigue—and perhaps the same with Ventimille, if the inhabitants favored. But although France had the best of ethnic and linguistic reasons for absorbing the Val d'Aosta they would be satisfied if Italy recognized its autonomy. Moreover, he adds, the Italian government had allowed the French representatives to believe it was resigned to accepting its conditions.

The Val d'Aosta, though it had for centuries been part of the dominions of the House of Savoy, had not been incorporated into France in 1860, when the rest of Savoy and Nice were taken as the price exacted by the French from Victor Emmanuel II for an alliance that enabled him to defeat the Austrians in the Italian War of Liberation in 1859. Many of the inhabitants of the Val d'Aosta spoke French and had been much opposed to Mussolini's attempt to enforce Italian customs on the region and to stop the teaching of the French language in the schools. There was some sentiment in favor of separation from Italy, especially on the part of a few partisan groups. But what the local population would have really liked was to become part of Switzerland.

On May 6, just before the German surrender, de Gaulle assured Caffery that France wanted only minor adjustments on the frontier. To these he was hoping the Italians would agree without much furor.

But the news from the region had grown more disturbing. French forces were being increased; French propaganda was becoming more flagrant; Italian flags were being taken down; the natives were being urged in conspicuous posters to declare their wish to be annexed to France, and they were being compelled to accept French currency. The Italian government, fearful of losing Venezia Giulia in the northeast to Tito, was talking in an excited way of this French invasion.

Truman had concluded that plain speaking was in order. So when Georges Bidault, the French Foreign Minister, came to see him on May 18 to ask consideration for several French wishes, among them that de Gaulle be asked to take part in the coming conference, Truman had let him know that American patience was being abused. He reminded his visitor that the American people were providing food for the liberated countries of Western Europe, including France, and that the American government was going to give up a part of its zone in Germany to France. Then in several ways he conveyed his displeasure with the French course of conduct in northwest Italy. To give point to his remarks he told Bidault that we would accede to the eager French wish to participate in the war against Japan only if sure that the French troops would obey the orders of our commanding general; he did not want to have the experience we were going through in Europe repeated.

Grew had gone into the situation again with Bidault, the next day. The Foreign Minister tried to explain it away as a matter of *amour-propre*, since Italy had in 1940 occupied part of France. Like de Gaulle, he disavowed any intent at annexation—only minor frontier adjustments. But soon afterward General Juin, Chief of Staff for National Defense in the French government, informed Eisenhower that "the question of the withdrawal of the Army detachment of the Alps to the Franco-Italian frontier of 1939 can no longer be handled directly between the Supreme Command and the French Command, and should be dealt with on the diplomatic plane." The French troops had been left where they were, and their presence hindered Alexander's efforts to extend Allied Military Government in the western part of the province of Imperia and elsewhere.

General Doyen's next defiant utterances—made while Hopkins was in Moscow—had aroused Washington. On May 30 he wrote to General Crittenberger, who was in command of the U.S. IV Corps in northwest Italy: "I have been ordered by the Provisional Government of the

French Republic to occupy and administer this territory. This mission being incompatible with the installation of any Allied administrative agency in the same region, I find myself obliged to oppose it. Any insistence in this direction would assume a clearly unfriendly character, even a hostile character, and could have grave consequences."[3] Then on June 2 he added: "General de Gaulle has instructed me to make as clear as possible to the Allied Command that I have received the order to prevent the setting-up of Allied Military Government in territories occupied by our troops and administered by us, by all necessary means without exception."

The unsigned invitation to de Gaulle to come to the United States was sent to the files. A note of quite different tenor was sent out in its place. Addressed to the French government, this plainly implied that what it was doing in northwest Italy was regarded by the American government as exactly what Tito was doing in Venezia Giulia and Trieste, and would be opposed in the same way. In Washington, thought was given to a straight and hard stroke against de Gaulle himself, in case this warning was not heeded. The Joint Chiefs were proposing that Truman and Churchill publicly condemn his course in north Italy. But Stimson objected on the score that this might either bring about de Gaulle's downfall and political disorder in France, or have the opposite effect of causing the French people to rally to his support. With Grew he persuaded the President to forbear a while longer. And then Marshall began to have second thoughts, since a clash with the French might interfere with the transfer of our troops from Europe to the Pacific. Stimson, McCloy, and Grew composed instead a letter for the President to send to de Gaulle privately. Truman subscribed to its severe strictures. A stern review of the record was followed by the statement that Doyen had made an "almost unbelievable" threat, one that would profoundly shock the American people if they heard of it. The President begged de Gaulle to reconsider before his threat became public knowledge. The concluding sentence defined the penalty: "While this threat by the French Government is outstanding against American soldiers, I regret I have no alternative but to issue instructions that no further issues of military equipment or munitions can be made to French troops." Pursuantly, orders were issued at once suspending all transfer of military supplies for French forces, except such as were to be used in the war against Japan. The provision of food and gasoline was continued, however, while Washington waited to see what was going to happen.

[3] Churchill, in quoting the same excerpt from Doyen's reply, italicized the last sentence. *Triumph and Tragedy*, page 567.

How much the French leader was trying the temper of the Prime Minister, as well as the President's, is indicated by Churchill's message on learning that Truman was going to defer the public statement: "the publication of your message would have led to the overthrow of de Gaulle, who after five long years of experience I am convinced is the worst enemy of France in her troubles . . . [and] one of the greatest dangers to European peace."[4] Churchill, it may be hazarded, was thinking more about the row he was having with de Gaulle over French actions in the Levant states than about northwest Italy.

It may be interjected that on the day this letter was sent off to de Gaulle (June 6), Bidault was letting Grew know that he considered French intrusion into Italy not only against the rules, but foolish: "I was born very near that region. It is not worth the skin of a cat."

In Truman's terse phrase, the warning "brought results." The French Ambassador brought in de Gaulle's answer on the 8th. This belittled the trouble. Were not American troops actually side by side and in good comradeship with the French troops? Why should France's allies want to exclude her from this area? How could he but regret being asked to evacuate it? But unfair and unperceptive as the request was, he would comply with it. "In any case I intend to give you satisfaction insofar as that is possible for us. Tomorrow morning, General Juin will proceed to Field Marshal Alexander's headquarters to deal with this matter in the broadest aspect of conciliation in order that a solution may be found."

This response ended the clash. It was welcomed by Truman. But it was regretted by some of his advisers, for example Admiral Leahy, who thought that if de Gaulle had refused to give in, he would have been finished. Grew had a different notion: that de Gaulle was on the downgrade, and that if we had caused him public humiliation, he would have regained support.

A few days later an agreement was concluded for the retreat of all French troops out of Italy by the 10th of July. The American government waited until this was done before resuming the provision of military supplies for the French troops. But meanwhile a concurrent quarrel over French effort to regain control of Syria and Lebanon simmered on, giving off unpleasant fumes.

---

[4] De Gaulle avers, however, that the ultimate arrangement left France in possession of what he wanted her to have. For, according to him he did not approve the agreement entered into by General Juin's representative, agreeing merely that small allied detachments should have access to the disputed communes; that the cantons of Tende and La Brigue elected governments which proclaimed their return to France, and in the Italian enclaves we attached fields and woods to the nearest French villages. Only at Ventimille was the situation let slide. *Mémoires*, vol. III, pages 183–184.

These two small Arab countries had been French mandates under the League of Nations, but during the war the French forces had lost control over them. Native governments had emerged, which the United States, Great Britain, and Russia had recognized. As new and independent states, they were included in the number of those named to take part in the Conference at San Francisco.

But de Gaulle was trying to impose his will on them. Talks about a new treaty to regulate French-Levantine relations had begun in March. The French negotiator, General Beynet, had sought of both Syria and Lebanon extensive and special concessions, political, cultural, and military. During an interruption in the discussions the French had sent in more troops. The Syrians and Lebanese took their arrival as a threat.

Both the British and the American government had been startled. They had informed the French government they were afraid that fighting in these countries might spread throughout the Middle East and interfere with allied war efforts in the Far East. They had deplored the possible effect on the work of the Conference at San Francisco—by arousing Arab opposition and mistrust of the greater powers' intentions to act in accord with the principles there being advocated.

These reproofs had been without effect. Strikes and demonstrations had spread. Lives were lost in Aleppo. The Syrian government ordered conscription. French troops and native forces fell to fighting, and the French shelled Damascus and bombed other towns.

The Syrian government had appealed to the British Ninth Army in the Middle East to arrange a truce. Churchill later remarked about his decision: "It was now impossible for us to stand aside."[5] Before acting he told Stalin and Truman what he was about to do. He said he was convinced the fighting in Syria would cause trouble in the Middle East and harm communications to the Far East. Thus he was going to tell the British Commander-in-Chief to interpose. He was seeking their approval and support. When a favoring answer was received from Truman, or maybe even before, General Paget was ordered to act to stop the fighting. At the same time, to ward off de Gaulle's wrath, Churchill informed him (on May 31) that:

"In view of the grave situation which has arisen between your troops and the Levant States, and the severe fighting which has broken out, we have with profound regret ordered the Commander-in-Chief of the Middle East to intervene to prevent the further effusion of blood in the interests of the security of the whole Middle East, which involves com-

[5] For de Gaulle's version of his intentions, see *ibid.*, pages 184–185.

munications for the war against Japan. In order to avoid collision between British and French forces, we request you immediately to order the French troops to cease fire and to withdraw to their barracks.

"Once firing has ceased and order has been restored we shall be prepared to begin tripartite discussions in London."[6]

The next day or two were anxious ones. British troops might fall to fighting either the French or the Levantines. With the thought of impressing the contestants, the British government asked that American naval vessels be sent to join those that Britain had in the area. Admiral Leahy has recounted that: "This request had come from Sir Andrew Cunningham. I had such confidence in this brilliant British commander that I had no hesitancy in advising that it be granted. The President directed me to inform the Navy that there was no opposition to giving Cunningham such assistance by American war ships as he might request and we might spare."[7]

But hardly had the order gone out—an order that directed an American warship to proceed to Beirut, not to do any shooting but simply to show the American flag—when Grew advised the President against this open signal of our judgment. He thought it wiser not to impair the chance that we could, if need be, act as mediator between Britain and France. The President revoked the order.

Churchill was doing his best to spare French pride and calm Syrian excitement. He instructed Paget to seek a peace "without rancour," and asked the President of Syria not to make his task harder by anger and exaggeration. Whether or not as a direct response to these British initiatives, de Gaulle gave way.[8] He ordered his troops to cease fire, and later on when a British detachment entered the city, instructed them to leave Damascus. The President of Syria, in thanking Churchill, explained that his message had been written under stress of bombardment and deep emotion; that he wanted to cooperate with the British to restore order and security in Syria.

[6] *Ibid.*, page 564.

[7] Leahy, page 373.

[8] The French Ambassador in Washington later told Grew that de Gaulle's order that the French troops should cease fire and stay in their positions had been sent from Paris at 11:30 p.m. on May 30, and that de Gaulle had not read Churchill's message until the afternoon of the 31st. Churchill (*Triumph and Tragedy*, page 564) corroborates the time when his message got to de Gaulle, explaining that because of an error of transmission it was read in the House of Commons on the afternoon of the 31st, about three quarters of an hour before it reached de Gaulle.

De Gaulle accuses Eden and Churchill of deception, of knowing that he, de Gaulle, had not received Churchill's message before it was read in the House of Commons, and, so as not to get official notice of the order to cease-fire, of having ignored requests of the French Ambassador for an interview. *Mémoires*, vol, III, pages 191–192.

Even as the American and British officials were relaxing in the belief that the way forward was clear, the French shook them up again. Before hearing of the truce, the Soviet government had tried to get into the act. On the 1st of June the Soviet Embassy left a note at the State Department which observed that events in Syria and Lebanon did not match the spirit of the United Nations. Thus the Soviet government urged that steps be taken to end the fighting. In talking with Grew the Soviet Chargé d'Affaires pointed out that this note implied that the Soviet government wished to start consultations regarding possible joint policy.

In any case, the French government, endorsing the idea that the Soviet government had advanced, proposed a meeting of the five main powers (the fifth was China), to deal not only with the situation in Syria and Lebanon but with the whole Middle East. The presence of all was needed, averred the French Foreign Minister, because it was unlikely that a settlement could be reached by direct talks between the French and British alone. The French troubles in Syria and Lebanon were attributed to influences active everywhere in the Middle East, including Egypt, and therefore they could be ended only in connection with a general arrangement for the whole region.

Was this proposal, the specialists in the Foreign Office and the State Department asked each other, merely a tactic in negotiation? Or was it an attempt at reprisal? Or was it an effort to extort admission to the coming conference? It could be any or all of these.[8a]

Truman did not want to get drawn so deeply into this sea of trouble. So when asked at his press conference on June 7 whether he favored the French proposal he answered "No."

The French government was trying hard to get the coalition to grant its right, on the score of proximity and vital interest, to an equal share in the occupation and control of Germany and Austria and in the determination of policies toward them. To those who had fought in the French resistance it seemed utterly wrong that their leader should not be there when these matters were discussed at the coming conference at Potsdam.

France had already been promised a zone of occupation in Germany, to be formed out of parts of the American and British zones. But de Gaulle was aggrieved that the original agreement about zones had been made without consulting him or his colleagues. This had moved him to refuse,

[8a] De Gaulle candidly states that in his opinion "the way in which the Anglo-Saxons were behaving toward us justified us in throwing a stone in their diplomatic sea," and virtually admits that he was aiming to make use of the fact that Egypt, Palestine and Iraq wished to free themselves from British control. Mémoires, vol. III, page 198.

for a while in April, to evacuate French forces that had taken Stuttgart, so that an American army unit, as agreed, might take over the city. When he was called to account, through Caffery, the American Ambassador in Paris, de Gaulle had answered: "Such incidents could be avoided if the allies of France would only recognize that questions so closely touching France as the occupation of German territory should be discussed and decided with her."[9]

During the weeks before and after the German surrender, discussions went on with the French government in regard to the section of Germany to be allotted to France as a zone of occupation. France had sought large areas on both banks of the Rhine.[10] Once installed therein, it would get a better hearing for its wish that Germany be permanently shrunk back in the west. But de Gaulle was opposed to combining the areas that France wanted to occupy into a single state, since this might become the center of a movement to unify Germany; moreover, he did not want the Soviet Union to share in the control of any domain touching France. He conceived of three separate arrangements. The area on the west bank of the Rhine from the Swiss frontier as far north as Cologne, and one or two bridgeheads to the opposite bank, might be put under French control without any restrictive international supervision; this was proposed because this region had so often been the path of invasion. Second, the Saar might be linked to France in a way that would enable it to control the mines, but without annexation. And third, the Ruhr might be placed under an international regime.[11]

Grew had said he could not comment on these proposals since American ideas about the treatment of Germany in the west were still in flux. That was so. But he knew that the intent of both the American and the British governments was veering toward leaving Germany in the

[9] *Year of Decisions*, pages 238-39.

[10] The two general areas in mind, as far as can be learned from Bidault's description to Grew on May 19, were in the Ruhr and in Rhineland-Württemberg.

The Ruhr area, as customarily bounded, embraced parts of the Rhenish and Westphalian provinces of Prussia, centering in the Ruhr river basin and extending west of the Rhine. Before the war this territory had about 5.3 million population, and produced about 70 percent of total German coal and iron and crude steel. It contained other major industries as well—steel manufactures, machinery, electro-chemical products, synthetic oil and rubber plants, chemicals and textiles—and normally accounted for about one-third of Germany's industrial exports. Ruhr production was highly important for all of western and central Europe.

The Rhineland-Württemberg area apparently included, on the west bank of the Rhine, most of the Rhineland province, the Palatinate, and the Saar, and on the eastern bank part of Württemberg. These had in 1939 a population of about 6.5 million. Possession of the west bank of the Rhine and bridgeheads across it would enable France to dominate the Ruhr strategically, and to command the gateways into central Germany.

[11] Grew memo of talk with Bidault, May 19, *Turbulent Era*, vol. 2, pages 1509-11.

west intact. Moreover, the war record did not warrant belief that France would long be able, by itself, to keep control of any part of Germany. While the western allies were willing to turn over part of their zones to the French as temporary occupants, they did not want to have the prospective discussion about the longer future of Germany subjected to French desires.

Also still unsettled at this time were the location and dimensions of the sector in Berlin to be turned over to France. The Soviet government had assented to such an assignment only on the understanding that it would be taken out of the American and British sectors. The Soviet members of the EAC had averred that this was fair since the Soviet sector had suffered the greatest destruction. Actually, the western allies were not sorry to partition their area of responsibility and have the French as company in Berlin. But the lines of subdivision had not yet been finally drawn and approved.

Then there was the question whether France was to have a place on the Reparation Commission. To this Stalin had been strongly opposed, even though he had agreed that France was to have a zone in Germany and a seat on the Control Council for Germany. Thus when Stettinius solicited Molotov's views on this subject at San Francisco, he was surprised to be told that the Soviet government would not object if Poland and Yugoslavia were granted the same privilege. Had they not fought Germany harder, suffered more, and won a better right to reparations? The American and British governments could not gainsay this pertinent observation. But they upheld their request for the admission of France, as a practical necessity; as master of a zone and member of the Control Council, France would in any case have to be consulted before a program of reparations could be carried out. When Hopkins tried to win over Stalin, in his second talk, on May 27, Stalin complained of the American pressure. In view of the fact, he said, that France had concluded a separate peace with Germany and opened its frontiers to the German armies, the American wish to give France a place on the Reparation Commission equal to that of the Soviet Union looked like an attempt to humiliate the Russians. Hopkins soothingly said he did not think we would insist on it.

During these same days the Foreign Office was urging the State Department to agree to hold up the departure for Moscow of the British and American representatives on the Reparation Commission, as a way of bringing Stalin around. Grew and Clayton told Roger Makins, Counselor of the British Embassy, that although the American government also wished for French participation in the Commission, it did not believe, in view of the Yalta accord,[12] that the talks could be delayed indefinitely in an effort to induce Soviet assent.

This repertory of troubles during the period of arrangement for the conference had confirmed the view in Washington and London that de Gaulle's presence would hinder rather than help, even if Stalin could be persuaded to include him. It would make the task harder and confuse, if not destroy, the progress of discussion. So neither Truman nor Churchill propelled de Gaulle's request. Truman, moreover, may have been restrained by fear that if they did so Stalin might think that the three western democracies were forming a coalition against him at the conference.

When it was settled that de Gaulle was not to be asked, the President thought it well to abate his disappointment.[12a] He invited de Gaulle to come to Washington after the conference. De Gaulle professed to be pleased with this plume of recognition. But on the day that the President and the Secretary of State sailed for Potsdam the French Ambassador called at the White House once again to protest against the disbarment of the head of his government. With earnestness amounting to admonition he said he hoped that no final step would be taken on matters affecting France until the French government was consulted, especially about reparations and German territory. Truman could not promise that this wish would be heeded, but he said he thought it would be.

The time and place for the conference had been set. But the advance arrangements for the coming together of the three Heads of State lagged. They were entwined with the spray of loose ends of the accords about the entry of national forces into the allotted zones in Germany and Berlin. Before the arbiters of Europe could proceed to their rendezvous these had to be tied together.

[12] The Yalta Protocol on Reparation had provided that the Commission to be set up in Moscow "will consist of three representatives—one from the Union of Soviet Socialist Republics, one from the United Kingdom and one from the United States of America."

[12a] But in his *Mémoires* (vol. III, pages 201–202) de Gaulle writes that although irritated by the exclusion, really he ["we"] thought it best not to be drawn into discussions that could, at this stage, only be superfluous.

21. Clearing the Way to the Potsdam Conference

CHURCHILL had continued to urge that the meeting take place as soon as possible, for he thought western wishes would be respected only as long as western forces confronted the Russians in full strength. He was afraid, as explained to Truman on May 21, that Stalin might "play for time in order to remain all powerful in Europe when our forces have melted." But even though Stalin told Hopkins that he too thought that the three should meet soon in view of the many urgent matters awaiting discussion, Truman clung to his wish to put it off until mid-July. And in the next flight of messages back and forth it was so set .

The mind retreats before the complexities of the question whether if the Conference had met, say, a month earlier, the resultant accords would have served Western interests better and been more lasting. But a few of the many considerations that could haunt anyone bold and curious enough to engage in pursuit of an opinion may be noted.

The American and British troops would have been still in their advanced lines, not yet back within the limits of their zones. This would almost surely have meant that the start of the conference would have been quarrelsome. Stalin would probably have refused to discuss other issues about Germany or Poland until the realignment was effected. Churchill would have striven to get him to do so before agreeing on a program of withdrawal. Would Truman have continued to think that the accord on zones had to be carried out in line with Soviet demands, or would he have changed his mind? Would the conference have reached a compromise or broken up?

Certainly it would have been over before the American government became so nearly sure, after the test in New Mexico, that it was the possessor of a weapon no enemy could withstand. Knowledge of this possibility ought to have strengthened Truman's will in negotiation and served to bend the outcome of the conference toward our wishes. (Whether it actually brought any marked changes in either our proposals or denials at the conference will emerge in later pages.)

In what ways, had the conference met sooner, might our strategy in the Pacific, our plans for Soviet entry into the war, our policies about surrender terms for Japan, have been different?

The middle of July, then, it was to be. But where were the eminent ones to meet? Stalin had told Truman—through Hopkins—that he thought the most convenient spot would be Berlin; there would be adequate quarters in the suburbs of that ruined city. Truman had remarked in talk with his intimates that since Stalin had caused Roosevelt and Churchill to come east to see him, it was Stalin's turn to come west to see them; but he had agreed to travel to Berlin. That meant that he would be dwelling within the confines of the Soviet zone in Germany.

It had been assumed by the Americans that by the time the conference met the respective national forces would have been directed into their assigned zones in Germany and their sectors in Berlin. It had also been anticipated that the former German capital would be under joint military control; that each of the three (or four) allies would have garrisons there; and that routes of access to it by road, rail, and air from the Western zones through the Soviet zone would be freely open and in use. But the talks about how and when each of these occurrences was to be effected turned out to be so long and delaying that they became entangled with arrangements for the conference.

On May 28, the same day on which Truman had asked Hopkins to tell Stalin he would come to the Berlin area about July 15, the President had brushed past Churchill's objections to having Western forces retreat into their zones before the conference. But Eisenhower and his staff were reporting that while the Germans, having been living off the fat of Europe, seemed in good physical condition, a program was needed at once for the whole of Germany to prevent hunger, disease, and disorder when winter came.[1] So Winant had been instructed to propose to his colleagues on the EAC that the Commanders-in-Chief of the four zones meet in Berlin not later than June 1, to sign and issue the declaration on the defeat of Germany and the assumption of supreme authority over the country.[2] The further thought of the American government was that after doing this, the Commanders-in-Chief should at once constitute the Control Council and begin to deal with matters affecting Germany as a whole. The Soviet government fell in with this proposal. Eisenhower hastened to tell the British and French of Molotov's assent. But he recommended that the meeting be postponed a few days, the better to get ready.

[1] A State Department survey team, after a field trip into Germany at Murphy's and Clay's request, submitted similar reports, which were well summarized in a memo from Donald C. Stone to the Secretary of State on June 7, 1945.
[2] Instruction, Acting Secretary of State Grew to U.S. Embassy, London, for Winant, May 26, 1945.

He hurried off (on June 2) a request for instructions, for he anticipated, whether the President did or not, that "one of the questions which will be raised at the Berlin meeting [of Commanders-in-Chief] to sign and issue the declaration will be the date on which our forces will begin their withdrawal from the Russian zone. It is possible that Russians may establish such withdrawal as a corollary to the establishment of the Control Council on a functioning basis in Berlin and to turning over the several zones in Berlin to the forces to occupy these zones. Any cause for delay in the establishment of the Control Council due to delay in withdrawal would be attributed to us and might well develop strong public reaction. We have as yet no instructions covering such withdrawal. It is believed desirable that separate instructions be given to me, as American Commander, and to the British Commander prior to the Berlin meeting as to how we should reply to this question if it is raised."

The Joint Chiefs of Staff, with Truman's approval, told Eisenhower that re-deployment into zones should not be required before the Control Council was functioning and sectors in Berlin taken over. If the Russians raised the point, he was to maintain it was one of the matters to be arranged by the Control Council. If asked about the timing of the actual movement of United States forces, he might state as his opinion that it was a matter of military convenience.

The four Commanders-in-Chief met in Berlin on June 5. There they signed a Four-Power Declaration regarding the defeat of Germany and the assumption of supreme authority.[3]

Then General Zhukov, the Soviet Commander-in-Chief, as chairman of the session asked whether there were any proposals for the order of business. Eisenhower spoke up: "The installment of the Control Council in Berlin." "No," said Zhukov, "not until your troops will have been evacuated from the areas in the Soviet zone they now illegally occupy." "Why not, then," suggested Eisenhower, "talk about both questions?" "No," said Zhukov, "I cannot discuss the first until the second is settled." He said he could not do so until all forces in Germany had been homed within their zones, or at least until a date was fixed for that event. And also, he added, until the division of Berlin—including the unsettled boundaries of the French zone—was determined.

This meant that the Control Council could not get started on its

---

[3] On the same day the four allied governments made known in two published joint statements the main points of the accords they had reached about zones of occupation and the system for the control of Germany.

work at once. There was to be no operative joint organization for the control of Germany during the following crucial weeks, in which the policies of each of the three occupants, in its own zone, were being set and connections with the defeated Germans were being formed.

Eisenhower advised the Chiefs of Staff that he thought the American government would have to satisfy Soviet authorities in both these matters before they would join in the activation of the Control Council.[4] He threw out the thought that it might be well to consider variations in the planning for Germany. Perhaps the system of control might evolve into a joint arrangement between the three Western powers for their zones, plus a separate zone run by the Russians, or even into four separate zones.

Both the Supreme Commander and his political adviser, Robert D. Murphy, thought there was little to be gained and something to be lost by trying to keep our forces in the Russian zone of Germany any longer.[5] Hopkins, having stopped off to see them near Frankfurt, informed the President and Marshall on June 8 that Eisenhower was convinced that uncertainty about the date for withdrawal of allied troops from the area assigned to the Russians was sure to be misunderstood by them, as well as at home. This would continue to stand in the way of the wish to get the Control Council to work and develop a unified program for the direction of German affairs.

Hopkins suggested, however,—and in doing so he was probably leaning on Eisenhower's (or Murphy's or General Smith's) opinions—that in connection with arrangements for withdrawal, we should insist on getting firm engagements from the Soviet government on several related actions. These were that Western troops be allowed to enter Berlin at the same time; and that unrestricted access to Berlin from Frankfurt and Bremen, by air, rail, and highway on agreed routes, be guaranteed. If, Hopkins

---

[4] Montgomery reached the same conclusion as Eisenhower; see his *Memoirs*, pages 338 and 340.

[5] Murphy's report to the State Department after this meeting in Berlin concluded: "For the Department's secret information, I believe that General Eisenhower does not consider that the retention of our forces in the Russian zone is wise or that it will be productive of advantages. I believe that it is pretty obvious to all concerned that we really are desirous of removing our forces and that it is only a question of time when we will inevitably do so. The Russians on the other hand may well be content temporarily to consolidate their present position in the territory they hold. In the interim, no progress would under such a circumstance be made in the organization of the quadripartite control of Germany, to which we are committed. I do not believe there is ground here for new discouragement but on the contrary I find that definite progress has been made. I am convinced that the Russians believe the Control Council necessary and that it is in their own interest to have it operate."

added, the President believed a settlement of remaining differences over zones in Austria and Vienna should also be prerequisite to realignment of forces in Germany, he should advise Stalin of our conditions on these matters as well.

The American government adopted this Eisenhower-Hopkins program. The British went along with it, Churchill muted but still murmuring wait and see.[6] Truman on June 12 bluntly told the Prime Minister that he did not feel it possible to delay the drawback of American troops as a weapon of diplomacy; if we waited until the meeting in July our relations with the Soviet Union would be greatly hurt. He submitted a text of a message—written by Marshall—that he was going to send to Stalin. This stated that he was ready to order all American troops in Germany to start their return to the American zone by June 21—in accordance with arrangements to be made between the commanders. These were to provide for the simultaneous movement of the national garrisons into Greater Berlin, and for free access to Berlin by air, road, and rail from Frankfurt and Bremen; there were also to be provisions for turning over to the respective local commanders the task of defining zones for Austria and Vienna.

"This," Churchill later recalled, "struck a knell in my breast, but I had no choice but to submit."[7] He was concerned most of all over the inadequacy of the provisions about Austria and Vienna. He did not think, he advised Truman, that Stalin would agree to authorize the Soviet Commander in Austria to settle the Austrian problem, which he thought of equal urgency to the German one. Why not, he proposed, make the same conditional stipulations for Austria and Vienna as for Germany? He wanted to be sure above all that the Russians who were occupying part of the British zone in Austria would get out at the same time as the American and British forces evacuated the Russian zone in Germany.

Leahy's reminiscent comment on his reaction to this obliging answer reflects remembrance of past differences over military strategy: "Churchill's action in agreeing to our withdrawal was entirely unexpected. His acceptance of the President's decision after repeated British insistence that we remain in the Soviet zone, indicated to me a possibility that the great Englishman was not in vigorous health. It was not in his nature,

---

[6] In his minutes to the Foreign Office on June 11, he wrote (*Triumph and Tragedy*, page 604): "I am still hoping that the retreat of the American centre to the occupation line can be staved off till 'the Three' meet. . . . We ought not to let ourselves be hurried into a decision which touches issues so vast and fateful."

[7] *Triumph and Tragedy*, page 605.

or in accord with his past performance to give up so easily, even when he was plainly wrong—as he was in this matter."[8]

Truman accepted Churchill's suggestion. The message to Stalin was sped on its way. Churchill let the Marshal know he was ready to give corresponding orders to Montgomery.

Stalin took both Truman and Churchill aback by asking that the start of these several movements be postponed until the 1st of July. The reason he gave was that Zhukov was wanted in Moscow for a parade and would not get back to Berlin until the end of the month. He also remarked, incidentally, that more time was needed to clear Berlin of land mines. Were these the real reasons, rather than a wish for a protracted chance to remove "war booty" from East Germany and Berlin, unobserved? He also thought the final sectioning of Austria could not be begun before Zhukov's return to Berlin. And if the American and British governments wanted the relocation to take place in the two countries at the same time, they both had better hasten to complete the accords with the Soviet government about zones in Austria (including the zone in which French troops were to be) and sectors in Vienna. Stalin, it was plain, was going to strike a hard bargain for admission into Vienna.

Grouped orders were issued by the Combined Chiefs to Eisenhower and Montgomery to get ready to move troops under their command out of the Soviet zone in Germany, and to Alexander to move the troops under his command into the British zone in Austria. The shifts were to start on July 1.

The program for Germany was carried through roughly in accord with this timetable. All the American and British troops were back in their zones, and their garrisons were in their sectors of Berlin, by the 4th of July. But their entry into their zones in Austria was delayed.

The day after Truman sent Stalin his proposals for concurrent movements of national forces in Germany and Austria, Eisenhower asked General Deane to secure permission to send a large advance party to Berlin to consult with Zhukov's deputies. It would have two assignments: to talk over plans for living and working arrangements for the American delegation during the conference; and to prepare for the entry of American troops into Berlin, and for their accommodations, security, signals, and supplies. The British Mission presented a similar request. Consistently the Soviet High Command answered that it was

[8] Leahy, page 382.

no use having these groups come to Berlin until the end of June, since no one but Zhukov could do what they wanted.

But Eisenhower correctly contended that if so little time was allowed to get ready for these events, he would not be able to make sure that the auspices of either the conference or the entry of Western forces into Berlin were going to be satisfactory. So the Ambassadors in Moscow, Harriman and Clark Kerr, were asked to turn to the Soviet Foreign Office. Vishinsky told them not to worry, since preparations for the conference would be rushed after Zhukov got back to Berlin. Harriman said that would not do. Unless the advance parties were allowed to start for Berlin at once, he warned that the President would find it necessary to postpone the conference with Stalin and Churchill and make the reasons known. On the 21st notice was received that the wish was granted, and that those subordinate Soviet military commanders who were in Berlin would aid the advance groups. But Vishinsky's letter to Harriman contained the retort that "the threat contained in your letter . . . is ill-advised. The Soviet Government has no intentions to limit the freedom of the American press but it considers it necessary to draw the attention of the American government to the fact that there is a press in the Soviet Union which will be able to give a proper reply to such a type of statement in the American press."[9]

The American and British groups were well received in Berlin by the Russians. They had little trouble in working out the arrangements necessary for the work, security, and comfort of the expected delegations to the conference. They also made helpful progress in planning for the entry and presence of the garrisons that were to start on their way to Berlin early in July. But they found no one authorized to discuss an agreement for permanent routes of access to the city from the west. That was left in suspense until the last possible thrust in negotiation, when it would be too late for the western allies to reverse their promise to pull back westward into their zones, leaving Berlin enclosed within many miles of the Soviet zone.

The desirability of obtaining formal and precise assurance from the Soviet government about access to Berlin had not been out of mind when the other accords on Germany were being written. But the Joint Chiefs had thought this a simple military task, merely a matter of securing adequate routes of transit, supply, and communications for the garrisons

[9] Potsdam Papers, Document 84.

in Berlin. They had not then foreseen that the western allies would also have to send in food, coal, and raw materials to sustain the German civilians in the city. So they had passed up Winant's offer to insert provisions about access into the accord negotiated in the EAC about zones.[10] They judged that it would be wiser to wait until they knew just what roads and railways would be usable at the end of the war, and just how large the movement back and forth would be. With this surer knowledge, the military commander could arrange, after Berlin was captured, for use of the routes required for the exercise of occupation.

Truman, as has been told, included in the program of concurrent transfer of forces in Germany and Austria, which he proposed to Stalin on June 14, a request for "provision of free access for United States forces by air, road and rail to Berlin from Frankfurt and Bremen."[11] Churchill made a similar reference to free ways from the British zone. Stalin, on proposing postponement until July, had not made reference to these stipulations—allowing the belief to thrive that the right of access was taken for granted.

In the major directive that Marshall sent Eisenhower on June 25, regarding the movement of American and British troops into their zones in Germany and Austria and their segments of Berlin, he thought it best not to give definite orders about transit rights to these two cities: "It will be noted that the proposed . . . directive . . . contains no action to obtain transit rights to Berlin and Vienna on a combined basis. In accordance with the President's message to Stalin [of June 14th] . . . these should be arranged with Russian commanders concerned simultaneously with arrangements for other adjustments, by Eisenhower for Berlin and Clark for Vienna. It is assumed that appropriate Russian commanders have been instructed accordingly . . . and it is desired that [General] Deane confirm this with the Soviet staff."[12]

The Soviet High Command had passed Deane's inquiry on to their political mentors. On this same day, June 25, Vishinsky told Harriman, and two days later Antonov told Deane, that Zhukov had been authorized to discuss the subject of access with General Clay (Eisenhower's Deputy in Berlin) and General Weeks (for Britain). Deane thought there would

[10] General Clay, in his book *Decision in Germany*, page 15, attributed the default to Winant. But Philip Mosely, Winant's deputy on the EAC, in an article in *Foreign Affairs* for July 1950, gives a systematic account of discussions on the question within the American government; this indicates that the decision not to try to settle the matter in the EAC was made by the American military authorities in the face of the Winant-Mosely offer to take it in hand.
[11] Stalin Correspondence, vol. 2, page 245.
[12] *Year of Decisions*, page 306.

be little trouble in working out adequate arrangements. The conference with Marshal Zhukov was set for the 29th.

On the day before, Eisenhower, through Air Marshal Tedder, sent on to American military headquarters in Berlin a summary of American-British wishes, with the request that it be delivered to Zhukov at once. Among its main features were: first, the immediate and unrestricted right to use several designated automobile roads from the west to the American and British sectors of Berlin, including the right to repair and construct the surfaces and bridges; second, a similar right to use several designated rail lines, including the maintenance of rights of way, the control of the rolling stock operated by the Americans and British, and authority to introduce into the Russian zone American- and British-trained rail crews and American- and British-supervised German railroad civilians; third, a similar right to unrestricted air travel, including fighter escort, between the British and American zones of occupation and Staaken, Tempelhof, and Gatow airfields in the Berlin area, with exclusive use and occupancy of the first two; fourth, an agreement that all road, rail, and air traffic on authorized rights of way be free from border search or control by customs or military guards. In short, American and British authorities wanted the right to have their contingents in Germany, and whatever equipment and supplies they might need to carry out the tasks of occupation, traverse the eastern zone to and from Berlin in whatever form of transport was most convenient, by many converging routes, and almost at will.

The Russians, they learned the next day, would grant much less than was wanted, and even less than was needed. Furthermore they regarded this allowance as a privilege rather than a right. Zhukov faced down Clay and Weeks with a summary of the requests that had been made of him: for unrestricted use of two highways, three railway lines, and two broad airlanes. He said all these would traverse Russian lines of communication and it would be hard to protect them.

In his opinion one highway and one railway would be adequate for the movement and supply of the small garrisons that the United States and Great Britain planned to have in Berlin—about 50,000 men. This was their own estimate; the coming of families to keep them company was not then contemplated. He thought the one road and the one railway that went from Berlin through Magdeburg would be most convenient for both the American and the British forces, since they were centrally located; and would also be the most economical, since the two converged at Magdeburg. But, he continued, if the Americans and British did not like this route, "it can be changed." Clay explained the need for several roads, since the American occupation zone was toward the southwest of Germany but its port would be Bremen in the northwest and its administrative center would be in Berlin. Zhukov, however, was under orders that he could not expand.

So Clay and Weeks accepted the use of the single railway via Magdeburg (to Helmstedt, on the border between East and West Germany), on the understanding that the gauge would not be changed without advance notice and that the bridge at Magdeburg would be rebuilt with American materials and Russian engines. They also decided to accept for joint U.S.-British use the one autobahn running from Hanover through Magdeburg to Berlin. Clay in so doing went against the advice of General Parks, the head of the American advance party, to stand fast for the right to use also the more direct southern route from Berlin to Frankfurt via Halle. But he reserved the chance to reopen the question in the Control Council if in use this one road turned out to be inadequate. Zhukov said of course—all the arrangements made by them might be changed.

Clay and Weeks also thought that for the time being it was best not to reject the scanty offer of one main airlane from Berlin to Magdeburg, with one branch southwest from Magdeburg to Frankfurt, and another westward to Hanover, though this confined flight route did not satisfy the Americans or the British. In the following November, it is in point to record, they managed to get the approval of their Soviet colleague on the Control Council for a paper authorizing the use of three twenty-mile air corridors between West Germany and Berlin, along which flights could proceed without advance notice.[13]

As for airfields in the Berlin area, allied wishes were well met. The Americans were to have the use and control of Tempelhof field. During the conference the Americans and British together were to have full use of the Gatow airdrome (which Zhukov called the best), and thereafter it was to be assigned to the British, being in their sector according to the Soviet map. When Weeks said that the British map did not so locate it, and that he had counted on having the use of the Staaken airfield,

[13] This was one of several papers approved by the Control Council defining the general arrangements that had been discussed in the meeting of the commanders on June 29. The three airlanes were Hamburg-Bremen-Berlin, Hanover-Berlin, and Frankfurt-Berlin. An account of the way in which this agreement was reached and carried into practice is given in the informative study by W. Phillips Davison, *The Berlin Blockade*, pages 33-37. See also "Department Press Release on Legal Aspects of the Berlin Situation, December 20, 1958," in Appendix to U.S. Dept. of State, *The Soviet Note on Berlin: An Analysis*.

Zhukov agreed that this might be considered later, either by their governments or in the Control Council.

It was clearly understood that the American and British right to use these airlanes and airfields was to be unrestricted; they were to make their own regulations, and except for an obligation to give advance notice of their flights, were not to be subject to any formalities. A rather jumbled American memo of the conference, from which some of these details are derived, leaves a slight whiff of uncertainty as to whether the accord on the conditions that would govern use of the roads and railways was wholly clear. The Americans certainly understood that all allied military traffic on roads and railways would be free from border search or control by customs or military authorities, but was to conform to Russian police control in the normal way.[14]

These provisional delineations of the routes and conditions of access to Berlin were not inscribed in any official agreement. One probable reason is that Clay and Weeks thought if they were, it might be harder to obtain amplifications of them later. Another is that an attempt to write them out with completeness might have taken many sessions, many days; and the movement into zones and into Berlin was to start in two days. Having waited that long, over-long, to secure a reliable definition of the rights of access, the western allies now had no choice but to trust in the accommodating spirit of the commanders who together were to control Germany and Berlin.

Meanwhile negotiations in the EAC about the final demarcation of the four zones of occupation in Austria had been dragging along. In the outcome the Soviet realm was stretched to include the part of upper Austria north of the Danube, but reduced a little elsewhere; it enveloped Vienna and bordered on Czechoslovakia and Hungary. The American

---

[14] This memo, which records in a hasty and rather disconnected way the course of discussion at the meeting on June 29, was unsigned but was manifestly written by one of the American participants or listeners. For whatever reason, it was not forwarded to the State Department until three years later, with a brief note of transmission by Murphy.

However, Murphy himself had sent in to the State Department a report summarizing the agreements reached at the conference the very next day, June 30, 1945. In this he stated that the Russians agreed that "with respect to roads, Autobahn Hanau-Magdeburg-Berlin will be used by U.S. and British troops without restrictions"; and with respect to rail transport they agreed "to exclusive use by U.S. of standard gauge line Greine-Gottingen-Belra and unrestricted use by the allies of line Goslar-Magdeburg-Berlin." He further said: "It was agreed that all road, rail and air traffic on authorized routes would be free from border search or control by customs or military authorities; but traffic to conform to Russian police control in the normal way." Potsdam Papers, Document 112.

realm was in the province of Salzburg and the section of upper Austria south of the Danube; this area adjoined the American zone in Germany. The British realm covered most of Carinthia and the province of Styria in the south, running along the frontiers of Italy and Yugoslavia. The French area was in the Tyrol and Vorarlberg, running along the northern edges of Italy and Switzerland, and connecting with their zone in Germany. All in all, it was a sensible division.[15] But before taking its roving armies out of sections of the British and American zones, the Soviet government insisted not only on formal completion and ratification of the accords about zones and control in Austria, but also on final full agreement on sectors in Vienna.

It was understood that the city, though divided into national parts, should be treated as a unit under a four-power Council, as was Berlin. But a difference of desire persisted about where the limits of the city were to be. This was reduced when all agreed that the center of the city (Innere Stadt) should be common ground. Stubbornly the Western governments maintained that each of the four occupants of Vienna ought to have unrestricted use and control of its own airdrome, and equally stubbornly the Soviet government maintained that one airdrome ought to be enough to serve them all.

The first scheduled date (July 1) for simultaneous movements went by. The Russian High Command maintained its refusal to allow Western troops to take over the whole of their zones or enter Vienna. The British member on the EAC threatened to end all talks about Austria unless the Soviet authorities were more considerate. Thereupon the Russians offered a compromise: one airfield (Tulln) for the American forces, one (Schwechat) for the joint use of the British and French forces. This was accepted. The accords were signed *ad referendum* in London on July 9, while the President and the Secretary of State were on the way to Potsdam. Possibly this was the reason for the delay in recording official American approval. So it came about that Churchill and Truman were greeted on their arrival in Germany by news that their troops were still being debarred from Vienna. It was a sharp lesson in Soviet intransigence.

It had been left to the Soviet authorities to select the exact locale for the conference. Since the city of Berlin was in ruins they chose the district of Babelsburg, close to Potsdam and some sixty kilometers southwest of Berlin. Here each delegation would have its own living area and offices.

[15] The text of the final agreement on zones in Austria may be found in U.S., *Treaties and other International Acts*, Series No. 1600, 61 Statutes (3) 2679.

The meetings would be held in the former palace of the Crown Prince in Potsdam. The walls of the conference room were decorated with a paper pattern of flowers and pheasants. This the Soviet hosts liked. But in the dining room there hung a painting in which a dark cloud loomed over a ship. That they deemed ominous. So where the cloud had been, their official decorators painted in a shining star. The Chief of the Soviet press section in Potsdam explained to the reporters that this was symbolic of Russian-American unity, since the star appeared in the heraldry of both nations.[16]

The letters and memoirs of some of the main Western figures at the conference leave the impression that the selection of this location within the Soviet zone may have colored their future attitude toward the Soviet Union. They were oppressed by the rigid and heavy-handed police methods by which the Russians ruled the area. They were not happy in the air they breathed. They were annoyed at having to satisfy Soviet guards and patrols whenever they left their assigned residential areas. This was their first personal brush with the manners and practices of the Soviet regime. How different these were from their own they appreciated more keenly when they left Potsdam than they had when they arrived.

[16] *New York Times*, July 16, 1945.

PART FOUR

Terminal: The Conference at Potsdam

22. Preparatory Work and Attitudes

EVEN before the date of the conference was fixed, the American and British officials had been studying the topics that ought to be, or would be, discussed.

On May 29 the British government had turned over to the State Department the syllabus it had in mind. In a measure this bore out what Churchill had said to Truman in explanation of his wish for an early meeting: that in reality nothing had yet been settled. But some of the subjects of controversy on the British list were being determined either by agreement or by some irreversible development.

On June 14, when Grew sent to the President the views of the State Department on the British proposals, he commented: "While in general the subject matter covered by Mr. Churchill is satisfactory and deals with a number of problems requiring urgent clarification, the form of presentation, I feel, is unfortunate. Mr. Churchill's list is so drawn as to give the appearance largely of a bill of complaints against the Soviet government, which hardly seems the proper approach to the forthcoming meeting. Presumably he would wish to reword his list of subjects prior to any communication of it to Marshal Stalin."[1]

Parallel work in the American government had been retarded because Secretary of State Stettinius was off in San Francisco. Also, the comment of the Joint Chiefs had to be solicited on many subjects. But on June 30 Acting Secretary of State Grew sent to the President a draft of a usable American statement on the agenda for the conference, with copies for Leahy and Byrnes. In his letter of transmittal he wrote: "Since there is at the present moment no Secretary of State it has been impossible to obtain for the attached memo and documents the clearance I should have desired, but in view of your request and the shortness of time remaining before the meeting I thought it best to submit the material without delay."

Three significant differences can be discerned between the nature and scope of American official ideas about the main objects of interest and those of the British. The Americans assigned prime importance to settling on the ways and means for carrying forward preliminary talks about the peace settlements. The British seemed to be willing to let arrangements to this end emerge as they would from discussions about current situations. The Americans wished to avoid decisions on territorial questions at the conference; they thought it would be better,

[1] Potsdam Papers, Document 152.

[155]

whenever it was possible, to remand issues of this sort to the Council of Foreign Ministers that was to be formed, or to leave them for the peace conference. The British were sure that they could not and would not wait. The Americans anticipated that attention would be given to a program for defeated Japan. The British prospectus did not include any Far Eastern topics—except those having to do with the distribution of military tasks and commands—leaving them for the Americans to bring forward. Neither mentioned the atomic bomb, which was to explode as the conference was assembling.

After active comment on each other's proposals, and revisions by each, the American and British governments, by July 11, separately let the Soviet government know what topics they wished to discuss. The President and the Prime Minister made it clear that their lists were not comprehensive or exclusive. Each said he would be ready to talk about any other questions that the Soviet conferees might wish to raise.

The Soviet government did not object to any item on the American or British programs for business, and it did not submit a corresponding program. Stalin waited until he arrived in Potsdam to reveal what other matters he wanted to present.

Such were the advance signs of the differing trends of interest and purpose that led the three Heads of Government to Potsdam. The British government sought first of all to make sure that the disquieting situations in and around Europe would be discussed. The American government realized that this was the realm of difficulty that made the convocation of the conference necessary at the time, but it was intent on using this good chance to further joint policies for the conduct of the war in the Far East and to foster the preparation of peace settlements. The Soviet government centered on a variety of definite and immediate desires.

Informed observers of the situation—two months after the coalition triumph—did not have to be in on these preliminary exchanges of agenda to know that there would be a complex contest at the conference. The *Economist* of July 14 described the actuality well: "The agenda that awaits [the three Heads of State] is a stiffer proposition than that for either of their previous meetings. Then, their united purpose in the military field served to gloss over the deviations of view. Now every item conceals a sore point for someone."

Perhaps this was why none of the three Heads of Government looked forward to the meeting with a buoyant sense of likely achievement.

Each seemed more drilled in knowledge of the ways in which the others would be troublesome than of the ways in which they might be helpful.

Lord Halifax, the British Ambassador in Washington, showed shrewd perception in his forecast of the American line at the conference, sent to Churchill on July 7: "I am sure you will find Truman most anxious to work with us, and justly alive to the long-range implications as well as the short-term difficulties of the decisions we have to make. I judge that American tactics with the Russians will be to display at the outset confidence in Russian willingness to co-operate. I should also expect the Americans in dealing with us to be more responsive to arguments based upon the danger of economic chaos in European countries than to *the balder pleas about the risks of extreme Left Governments or of the spread of Communism.* They showed some signs of nervousness in my portrayal of Europe (whatever the facts) as the scene of a clash of ideas in which the Soviet and Western influences are likely to be hostile and conflicting. At the back of their minds there are still lingering suspicions that we want to back Right Wing Governments or monarchies for their own sake. This does not in the least mean that they will be unwilling to stand up with us against the Russians when necessary. But they are likely to pick their occasion with care, and are half expecting to play, or at any rate to represent themselves as playing, a moderating role between ourselves and the Russians."[2]

These impressions would have been confirmed if Halifax could have read the recommendations in the Briefing Book paper submitted by the State Department in July for the use of the President as an analysis of British policies. This began with an excerpt from a letter the Joint Chiefs of Staff had sent as long ago as May 16, 1944, to the Secretary of State: "The greatest likelihood of eventual conflict between Britain and Russia would seem to grow out of either nation initiating attempts to build up its strength, by seeking to attach to herself parts of Europe to the disadvantage and possible danger of her potential adversary. Having regard to the inherent suspicions of the Russians, to present Russia with any agreement on such matters as between the British and ourselves, prior to consultation with Russia, might well result in starting a train of events that would lead eventually in [to] the situation we most wish to avoid."[3]

This Briefing Book paper then continued: "However, it must be

[2] *Triumph and Tragedy*, pages 611-12; Churchill's italics.
[3] The full text of this letter is in U.S., Dept. of State, *The Conferences at Malta and Yalta*, pages 106-08.

[157]

recognized that the Russians have already gone far to establish an effective sphere of influence in Eastern Europe. Our definitive position with respect to a British sphere in Western Europe must await further clarification of the Soviet Union's intentions. In the meanwhile our policies should be to discourage the development of rival spheres of influence, both Russian and British. . . . We should direct our best efforts towards smoothing out points of friction between Great Britain and Russia and fostering the tripartite collaboration upon which lasting peace depends."[4]

It was not that the American officials were ignorant of or indifferent to Soviet attempts to extend their control and influence. As summarized in another segment of this same Briefing Book paper: "The Russians have taken steps to solidify their control over Eastern Europe. They have concluded bilateral treaties of alliance with the Lublin Poles (in spite of our objections) and with the governments of Yugoslavia and Czechoslovakia. They have taken unilateral action with respect to the formation of the Austrian Government and have acted independently in Rumania, Bulgaria and Hungary without consultation with the American and British representatives in those countries. An exclusive economic agreement has been concluded with Rumania which makes possible extensive Soviet Control over Rumanian industry and which may virtually cut off Rumanian trade with the rest of the world. The Russians have rejected British-American proposals that discussions should take place in regard to the political situation in Rumania and elections in Bulgaria. These actions are not in accordance with the Crimea Declaration on Liberated Europe whereby the Big Three agreed to concert their policies in assisting the liberated peoples to solve their pressing political and economic problems by democratic means. Eastern Europe is, in fact, a Soviet sphere of influence."

Other Briefing Book papers contain affirmations of the opinion that the dissolution of the Communist International (Comintern) was not genuine; that in reality none of its former sections had ceased to exist or to be active; that foreign members of Communist parties who had been connected with the Comintern were emerging as leading political figures in their own countries; that they were all obedient and loyal to the Soviet government; that they were set in their militant line; and that they were doing their utmost to take advantage of the state of Europe at the end of the devastating war to exploit the suffering for their own purposes. Yet the desire for accord persisted.

The British officials regretted the refusal of the Americans to enter

4 Potsdam Papers, Document 224.

into an advance concert on joint policies. Most of them shared Churchill's belief that the ultimate Soviet intentions were ominous, and that any conciliatory words or acts of the Kremlin were ruses. The Soviet rulers were convinced that the leading purpose of the British government was to surround the Soviet Union with unfriendly states in order to confine it, and cheat it of its fair reward for victory. While they did not attribute the same fixed purpose to the American government, they thought there was little chance that in direct contest over any issue in this sphere the American government would range itself against Britain. They were counting on Russian power to grasp and hold what it most wanted, rather than on the chance of winning willing assent.

President Truman set off for Potsdam with sober will rather than with the elated sense of a great occasion with which Roosevelt had gone to Teheran and Yalta. His mood on leaving the White House was reflected in two of his letters to his mother, on July 3: "I am getting ready to go and see Stalin and Churchill, and it is a chore. I have to take my tuxedo, tails . . . preacher coat, high hat, low hat, and hard hat, as well as sundry other things. . . . Wish I didn't have to go, but I do and it can't be stopped now." And on July 12, from shipboard on his way to Potsdam: "I wish this trip was over. I hate it. But it has to be done."[5]

Churchill was glum as he left Downing Street, worried about the frustrations and refusals he might face, as well as a little unsure of the outcome of the voting in Britain. In his gloomier moods and stances, he predicted that Stalin would table "several important things . . . during [the] course of the Conference and it should not be excluded that even a *fait accompli* or two might be presented."[6] But not even this dark vista entirely subdued his enjoyment in the activities of governing and disposing of great matters.

Stalin, though not feeling well, looked forward to the meeting with calm assurance. The struggle in Europe was won; the acquisitions he wanted most for the Soviet Union were within his grasp; and he could feel fairly sure of getting almost all he wanted in the Far East, in one way or another.

Churchill and Stalin were familiar with the past developments of the situations that were going to be considered at the conference. But Truman had had to acquaint himself with them in quick flashes. Sep-

[5] *Year of Decisions*, pages 331 and 338.
[6] Potsdam Papers, Document 225.

arate and compact studies on all of them had been prepared for his use. Each summarized the history of the problem, analyzed it as it appeared in American official vision, and outlined recommendations. Much of the time while these studies were being worked on, he was away from Washington. They were waiting for him when he entered his cabin on shipboard, "a briefcase all filled up with information on past conferences and suggestions on what I'm to do and say."[7] The voyage was his first sustained chance to study them. This he used in his own fashion. It was not the way of a patient student of pondering mind, but rather the way of a person who habitually sought simple versions from which he could arrive at quick decisions. The great and grave chore did not prevent him from spending much time in informal talk with his friends and with the newspapermen who were on board, or interfere with his enjoyment of dinner concerts and movies and card games. All in all, as he wrote to his family (on the 12th): "the trip has been most pleasant and restful."[8] But the next day, as the ship neared Europe, he devoted to shaping up with Byrnes and Leahy a final American version of an agenda for the conference, and to poring over a written summary brief on various questions that would arise.

The Secretary of State, Byrnes, had taken office only a few days before sailing. Of some of the subjects that were to require the utmost exertion of thought and persuasion at the conference he already knew much. Of others he knew little. But in prolonged sessions with his staff each day on the way over he did his conscientious utmost to prepare himself.

The American delegation to the conference was conventionally composed. Harry Hopkins, the man who had worked most intimately with Roosevelt at Cairo, Teheran, and Yalta, stayed home. No longer could his will conquer his sick body. "I had to stop this running around the earth at some time," he explained to Winant, "and this seemed as good a time as I could possibly find. While I am feeling better, I have a long way to go to be in the kind of shape I want to be in and I don't want to have to get started all over again." Thus he was spared the experience of witnessing for himself with what few scruples Stalin infringed the avowals made to him only a few weeks before.

The President had wanted to take along Stettinius, the departing Secretary of State. But he was kept in Washington because Congress

[7] Letter to his mother and sister Mary, written July 3, *Year of Decisions*, page 331.
[8] Letter to his mother and sister Mary, written on shipboard July 12, *Year of Decisions*, page 338.

would be holding hearings to decide whether or not the American government should sign the charter for the United Nations.

In contrast to the American groups that went to Teheran and Yalta, most of the civilian members of the delegation to Potsdam were career officers of the State Department and the Foreign Service. In addition, Byrnes took along two persons in whom he reposed great trust, Benjamin Cohen and Donald Russell, the first of whom became his most usual official scribe. Davies, the most soothing interpreter of Soviet actions, was next to the President at the round table, but was only a whispering commentator. That Harriman had to propose himself was indicative of the desire of both the President and the Secretary of State to leave themselves free to make up their own minds about the spirit in which to deal with the Russians. The Ambassador in Moscow was given little to do after arrival. Stimson, the Secretary of War, arranged to be close by on momentous special business.

Except that no Davies was on its roster, the British delegation came from similar circles of officialdom. But Churchill had invited Attlee, the head of the Labour Party and deputy head of the War Cabinet, to come with him as friend and counselor, and to help "on all the subjects on which we have so long agreed."[9] After consulting his principal colleagues in the House of Commons, Attlee had accepted. Like Churchill, he saw advantage in preserving and showing to the world the unity on foreign affairs that had been maintained during the war, and in giving assurance that if the British elections should put him in office, the continuity of British policy would not be broken.

Of the Soviet group all that need be said is that Stalin was there, and Molotov, always present, "like the north star."

Churchill had looked in the lexicon for a code name to identify the conference. He chose Terminal. This he conceived to be appropriate for several reasons. Would not the conference mark the end of the perilous journey on which Britain had started in 1939? Would its decisions not complete the transition from war to peace in Europe? Both Truman and Stalin thought the name well suited to the historical circumstance. In retrospect, however, it has taken on a connotation other than the one the Prime Minister had in mind. The conference did not lead to a restful destination. It turned out, rather, to mark the end of the line of close collaboration by which the coalition had achieved victory.

[9] Potsdam Papers, Document 73.

The British Chiefs of Staff had for some time past been seeking a full and formal meeting with the United States Joint Chiefs of Staff. The Americans had not been eager to be drawn into arguments about military dispositions in Europe, and had not been ready to discuss military plans and operations in the Pacific. But as soon as the conference of Heads of Government was set for mid-July, it was hailed as a convenient and timely occasion for the convocation of the two top groups of military officials. By then the Joint Chiefs expected to have their strategy in the Pacific fixed, and their ideas about theaters of command and coordinated operations in order.

The British Chiefs had proposed, as had Churchill to Truman, that their American colleagues stop off in London for three or four days before going on to Potsdam. But the American Chiefs had avoided this close preliminary engagement with the British alone. They had answered that if the British Chiefs had matters in mind that ought to be settled before the conference, these could be discussed in Washington; and that if all common business could not be finished at Potsdam, they would stop off in London *after* the conference.

On June 20, Truman, at the request of Marshall and Hopkins, and having in mind the possible Japanese reaction, had asked Harriman to ascertain whether Stalin would object if he brought along his Chiefs of Staff to Berlin. Stalin said there was no objection; in fact, their presence would be of use in discussions of military operations in the Far East.

In the advance list of subjects for discussion submitted by the British Chiefs, one was regarded by the Americans with reserve: "Russian participation in the war against Japan." The Joint Chiefs doubted whether it would be necessary to discuss this with the British Chiefs. In any case they did not want to do so until after anticipated talks with the Russians. At Potsdam, with the Soviet Chiefs of Staff, they hoped to review American operations in the Pacific, past and prospective, and to learn about Soviet plans. In mind was an accord for concerted actions in all the areas around Japan. The British, it was expected, would be campaigning in the South Pacific and South Asia; the Russians and the Chinese would be advancing on Japan from the north and center, in assaults more closely conjoining with our own. In military matters, as in political ones, with the ending of the war in Europe, it was what the Russians did that counted most in American official reckoning.

23. The Secret That Traveled to Potsdam

THE Americans left for Potsdam with a momentous secret—which they kept out of their memos as well as off their tongues. They knew that some day soon the first test was to be made of the atomic weapon that had been long in the making.[1]

Secretary of War Stimson, who bore the focal responsibility for the decisions that would have to be made at once if the test went well, was planning to go to Potsdam. The President agreed that he should be close at hand when the results were known. Moreover, as Stimson told Byrnes, he wanted to learn for himself more about the task assigned to the Army in the American zone in Germany and in the four-power administration.

Stimson's thoughts about S-1 (as the atomic weapon was identified), like those of the President, circled around its possible use in the war against Japan, rather than its bearing on the matters that were to be discussed in the conference at Potsdam. Its first great impact was the issuance of a last warning to Japan—the Potsdam Declaration. The extended account of the many talks, before and after Potsdam, about its use against Japan and about plans for its control will be left for future narration. But before entering into the lanes along which the work of the conference flowed, we ought to summon the stirring reports that reached Potsdam about the test in New Mexico just as the conference was starting.

The formal opening of the conference was put off from July 16 to 17 because Stalin had suffered a slight heart attack.[1a] Truman used the liberated day to drive into Berlin from his quarters at Babelsberg. "In that two hour drive," he later wrote, "I saw evidence of a great world tragedy."

Upon his return Stimson hurried over to tell him and Byrnes of a message just in from George Harrison, who was acting as Chairman of the Interim Committee on S-1 while Stimson was away.[1b] This was

---

[1] Smyth, the historian of the project, was writing in his notes, "the end of June finds us expecting from day to day to hear of the explosion of the first atomic bomb devised by man." Henry De Wolfe Smyth, *Atomic Energy for Military Purposes*, page 223.

[1a] When Stalin called on Truman he apologized for causing this delay, explaining that the doctors would not let him fly because of "weakness in the lungs." But it is virtually certain that he was suffering from heart trouble.

[1b] In writing later about the first report given him by Stimson of the results of the test, Truman seems to have been confused in his memory of detail. As recounted in *Year of Decisions*, page 415, "The historic message of the first explosion of an atomic bomb was

the first flash about the detonation of the bomb in Alamogordo. In code expression it read: "Operated on this morning. Diagnosis not yet complete but results seem satisfactory and already exceed expectations. Local press release necessary as interest extends great distance.[2] Doctor [General] Groves pleased. He returns [to Washington] tomorrow. I will keep you posted."[3]

Harrison did so in another short message that reached Stimson the next day or evening (the 17th). This read: "Doctor Groves has just returned most enthusiastic and confident that the little boy is as husky as his big brother. The light in his eyes discernible from here [Washington] to Highhold [Stimson's house on Long Island, 250 miles away] and I could have heard his screams from here to my farm [at Upperville, Virginia, 40 miles away]."[4]

Stimson at once discussed the latest news with Byrnes, and passed it on to Churchill. The Secretary of War noted in his diary that the Prime Minister had not heard of the great event from British officials in Washington, that he was much cheered up, and that he was strongly against disclosing information about the weapon to the Russians.

On the next day, the 18th, Stimson talked over with the President the import of Harrison's second message. In his diary entry for that day he noted that the President seemed to him "highly delighted . . . [and] very greatly reinforced over the message from Harrison, and said he was very glad I had come to the meeting."[5]

---

flashed to me in a message from Secretary of War Stimson on the morning of the 16th. . . . Stimson flew to Potsdam the next day to see me and brought with him the full details of the test." But Stimson was in Babelsberg on the 16th, and took the first brief message in person to Truman that same evening.

[2] The flash and noise of the explosion, seen and heard far away, aroused excited curiosity. The Commanding Officer of the Alamogordo Army Air Base, General Ericson, gave the press a statement, which said that the explosion had occurred in a remotely located ammunition magazine. For its text see *Albuquerque Tribune* of July 16, 1945. The explanation seems to have been accepted calmly and without question. No mention of either the explosion or its cause is to be found in the issues of the *New York Times* or *Herald Tribune* of July 17, probably because of voluntary censorship.

[3] Potsdam Papers, Document 1303.

[4] Potsdam Papers, Document 1304.

[5] Here this historian runs into another instance of conflicting records of chronology, which is left for other researchers to clear up. Stimson's diary does not mention any general convocation of military and civilian heads to confer about the news on either the 17th or the 18th. But Truman, *Year of Decisions*, page 415, wrote that on the 17th, after having heard Stimson's report of the test, he at once called in Byrnes, Leahy, Marshall, Arnold, and King, to review our military strategy in the light of this revolutionary development. The Joint Chiefs did meet on the morning of the 17th, but not with the President.

Churchill, *Triumph and Tragedy*, pages 638-39, wrote that on the morning of the 18th "a plane arrived with a full description of this tremendous event in the human story,"

On the 21st, just before noon, a courier put in Stimson's hands the special report that General Groves had prepared. Stimson found it "an immensely powerful document, clearly and well written, and with supporting documents of the highest importance," and believed that "it gave a pretty full and eloquent report of the tremendous success of the test and revealed far greater destructive power than we expected in S-1."

This report from the scene of the explosion is longish, but in order to appreciate its impress, it should be read in full, as it was by the recipients at Potsdam:

MEMORANDUM FOR THE SECRETARY OF WAR

(July 18, 1945)

Subject: The Test

1. This is not a concise, formal military report but an attempt to recite what I would have told you if you had been here on my return from New Mexico.

2. At 0530, 16 July 1945, in a remote section of the Alamogordo Air Base, New Mexico, the first full scale test was made of the implosion type atomic fission bomb. For the first time in history there was a nuclear explosion. And what an explosion! . . . The bomb was not dropped from an airplane but was exploded on a platform on top of a 100-foot high steel tower.

3. The test was successful beyond the most optimistic expectations of anyone. Based on the data which it has been possible to work up to date, I estimate the energy generated to be in excess of the equivalent of 15,000 to 20,000 tons of TNT; and this is a conservative estimate. Data based on measurements which we have not yet been able to reconcile would make the energy release several times the conservative figure. There were tremendous blast effects. For a brief period there was a lighting effect within a radius of 20 miles equal to several suns in midday; a huge ball of fire was formed which lasted for several seconds. This ball mushroomed and rose to a height of over 10,000 feet before it dimmed. The light from the explosion was seen clearly at Albuquerque, Santa Fe, Silver City, El Paso and other points generally to about 180 miles away. The sound was heard to the same distance in a few instances but generally to about 100 miles. Only a few windows were broken although one was some 125 miles away. A massive cloud was formed which surged and billowed upward with tremendous power, reaching

---

and that the President invited him to confer "forthwith," Marshall and Leahy to be present. That Churchill did have some sort of talk with Truman on the 18th is verified by the note bearing that date written by Churchill for the War Cabinet (*ibid.*, pages 640–41). But the report containing the "full description" was not put in Stimson's hands by courier until the 21st.

the substratosphere at an elevation of 41,000 feet, 36,000 feet above the ground, in about 5 minutes, breaking without interruption through a temperature inversion at 17,000 feet which most of the scientists thought would stop it. Two supplementary explosions occurred in the cloud shortly after the main explosion. The cloud contained several thousand tons of dust picked up from the ground and a considerable amount of iron in the gaseous form. Our present thought is that this iron ignited when it mixed with the oxygen in the air to cause these supplementary explosions. Huge concentrations of highly radioactive materials resulted from the fission and were contained in this cloud.

4. A crater from which all vegetation had vanished, with a diameter of 1200 feet and a slight slope toward the center, was formed. In the center was a shallow bowl 130 feet in diameter and 6 feet in depth. The material within the crater was deeply pulverized dirt. The material within the outer circle is greenish and can be distinctly seen from as much as 5 miles away. The steel from the tower was evaporated. 1500 feet away there was a 4-inch iron pipe 16 feet high set in concrete and strongly guyed. It disappeared completely.

5. One-half mile from the explosion there was a massive steel test cylinder weighing 220 tons. The base of the cylinder was solidly encased in concrete. Surrounding the cylinder was a strong steel tower 70 feet high, firmly anchored to concrete foundations. This tower is comparable to a steel building bay that would be found in a typical 15 or 20 story skyscraper or in warehouse construction. Forty tons of steel were used to fabricate the tower which was 70 feet high, the height of a six story building. The cross bracing was much stronger than that normally used in ordinary steel construction. The absence of the solid walls of a building gave the blast a much less effective surface to push against. The blast tore the tower from its foundations, twisted it, ripped it apart and left it flat on the ground. The effects on the tower indicate that, at that distance, unshielded permanent steel and masonry buildings would have been destroyed . . . I no longer consider the Pentagon a safe shelter from such a bomb. Enclosed are a sketch showing the tower before the explosion and a telephotograph showing what it looked like afterwards. [Neither picture reproduced.] None of us had expected it to be damaged.

6. The cloud traveled to a great height first in the form of a ball, then mushroomed, then changed into a long trailing chimney-shaped column and finally was sent in several directions by the variable winds at the different elevations. It deposited its dust and radioactive materials over a wide area. It was followed and monitored by medical doctors and scientists with instruments to check its radioactive effects. While here and there the activity on the ground was fairly high, at no place did it reach a concentration which required evacuation of the population. Radioactive material in small quantities was located as much as 120 miles away. The measurements are being continued in order to have adequate data with which to protect the Government's interests in case of future claims. For a few hours I was none too comfortable about the situation.

7. For instances as much as 200 miles away, observers were stationed to check on blast effects, property damage, radioactivity and reactions of the

population. While complete reports have not yet been received, I know that no persons were injured nor was there any real property damage outside our Government area. As soon as all the voluminous data can be checked and correlated, full technical studies will be possible.

8. Our long range weather predictions had indicated that we could expect weather favorable for our tests beginning on the morning of the 17th and continuing for 4 days. This was almost a certainty if we were to believe our long range forecasters. The prediction for the morning of the 16th was not so certain but there was about an eighty percent chance of the conditions being suitable. During the night there were thunder storms with lightning flashes all over the area. The test had been originally set for 0400 hours and all the night through, because of the bad weather, there were urgings from many of the scientists to postpone the test. Such a delay might well have had crippling results due to mechanical difficulties in our complicated test set-up. Fortunately, we disregarded the urgings. We held firm and waited the night through hoping for suitable weather. We had to delay an hour and a half, to 0530, before we could fire. This was 30 minutes before sunrise.

9. Because of bad weather, our two B-29 observation airplanes were unable to take off as scheduled from Kirkland Field at Albuquerque and when they finally did get off, they found it impossible to get over the target because of the heavy clouds and the thunder storms. Certain desired observations could not be made and while the people in the airplanes saw the explosion from a distance, they were not as close as they will be in action. We still have no reason to anticipate the loss of our plane in an actual operation although we cannot guarantee safety.

10. Just before 1100 the news stories from all over the state started to flow into the Albuquerque Associated Press. I then directed the issuance by the Commanding Officer, Alamogordo Air Base of a news release as shown on the inclosure. With the assistance of the Office of Censorship we were able to limit the news stories to the approved release supplemented in the local papers by brief stories from the many eyewitnesses not connected with our project. One of these was a blind woman who saw the light.

11. Brigadier General Thomas F. Farrell was at the control shelter located 10,000 yards south of the point of explosion. His impressions are given below:

Impressions of Brigadier General Thomas F. Farrell at control shelter 10,000 yards south of point of explosion:
"The scene inside the shelter was dramatic beyond words. In and around the shelter were some 20-odd people concerned with last minute arrangements prior to firing the shot. Included were: Dr. Oppenheimer, the Director who had borne the great scientific burden of developing the weapon from the raw materials made in Tennessee and Washington and a dozen of his key assistants—Dr. Kistiakowsky, who had developed the highly special explosives; Dr. Bainbridge, who supervised all the detailed arrangements for the test; . Dr. Hubbard, the weather expert, and several others. Besides these, there

were a handful of soldiers, two or three Army officers and one Naval officer. The shelter was cluttered with a great variety of instruments and radios.

"For some hectic two hours preceding the blast, General Groves stayed with the Director, walking with him and steadying his tense excitement. Every time the Director would be about to explode because of some untoward happening, General Groves would take him off and walk with him in the rain, counselling with him and reassuring him that everything would be all right. At twenty minutes before zero hour, General Groves left for his station at the Base Camp [almost ten miles from the point of explosion], first because it provided a better observation point and second, because of our rule that he and I must not be together in situations where there is an element of danger, which existed at both points.

"Just after General Groves left, announcements began to be broadcast of the interval remaining before the blast. They were sent by radio to the other groups participating in and observing the test. As the time interval grew smaller and changed from minutes to seconds, the tension increased by leaps and bounds. Everyone in that room knew the awful potentialities of the thing that they thought was about to happen. The scientists felt that their figuring must be right and that the bomb had to go off but there was in everyone's mind a strong measure of doubt.[6] The feeling of many could be expressed by 'Lord, I believe; help Thou mine unbelief.' We were reaching into the unknown and we did not know what might come of it. It can be safely said that most of those present—Christian, Jew, and Atheist—were praying and praying harder than they had ever prayed before. If the shot were successful, it was a justification of the several years of intensive effort of tens of thousands of people—statesmen, scientists, engineers, manufacturers, soldiers, and many others in every walk of life.

"In that brief instant in the remote New Mexico desert the tremendous effort of the brains and brawn of all these people came suddenly and startlingly to the fullest fruition. Dr. Oppenheimer, on whom had rested a very heavy burden, grew tenser as the last seconds ticked off. He scarcely breathed. He held on to a post to steady himself. For the last few seconds, he stared directly ahead and then when the announcer shouted 'Now!' and there came this tremendous burst of light followed shortly thereafter by the deep growling roar of the explosion, his face relaxed into an expression of tremendous relief. Several of the observers standing back of the shelter to watch the lighting effects were knocked flat by the blast.

"The tension in the room let up and all started congratulating each other. Everyone sensed 'This is it!' No matter what might happen now all knew that the impossible scientific job had been done. Atomic fission would no longer be hidden in the cloisters of the theoretical physicists' dreams. It was almost full grown at birth. It was a great new force to be used for good or for evil. There was a feeling in that shelter that those concerned with its

[6] All parts of the structure and detonating mechanism had been well proved; but the physics of the process of atomic fission, as embodied in the bomb, had not been experimentally tested, and the scientists were anxious lest some element might have been overlooked, or incorrectly calculated.

nativity should dedicate their lives to the mission that it would always be used for good and never for evil.

"Dr. Kistiakowsky, the impulsive Russian (Interpolation by Groves at this point, 'an American and Harvard professor for many years'), threw his arms around Dr. Oppenheimer and embraced him with shouts of glee. Others were equally enthusiastic. All the pent-up emotions were released in those few minutes and all seemed to sense immediately that the explosion had far exceeded the most optimistic expectations and wildest hopes of the scientists. All seemed to feel that they had been present at the birth of a new age— The Age of Atomic Energy—and felt their profound responsibility to help in guiding into right channels the tremendous forces which had been unlocked for the first time in history.

"As to the present war, there was a feeling that no matter what else might happen, we now had the means to insure its speedy conclusion and save thousands of American lives. As to the future, there had been brought into being something big and something new that would prove to be immeasurably more important than the discovery of electricity or any of the other great discoveries which have so affected our existence.

"The effects could well be called unprecedented, magnificent, beautiful, stupendous and terrifying. No man-made phenomenon of such tremendous power had ever occurred before. The lighting effects beggared description. The whole country was lighted by a searing light with the intensity many times that of the midday sun. It was golden, purple, violet, gray and blue. It lighted every peak, crevasse and ridge of the nearby mountain range with a clarity and beauty that cannot be described but must be seen to be imagined. It was that beauty the great poets dream about but describe most poorly and inadequately. Thirty seconds after the explosion came first, the air blast pressing hard against the people and things, to be followed almost immediately by the strong, sustained, awesome roar which warned of doomsday and made us feel that we puny things were blasphemous to dare tamper with the forces heretofore reserved to The Almighty. Words are inadequate tools for the job of acquainting those not present with the physical, mental and psychological effects. It had to be witnessed to be realized." (End of General Farrell's account)

12. My (General Groves') impressions of the night's high points follow: After about an hour's sleep I got up at 0100 and from that time on until about five I was with Dr. Oppenheimer constantly. Naturally he was very nervous, although his mind was working at its usual extraordinary efficiency. I devoted my entire attention to shielding him from the excited and generally faulty advice of his assistants who were more than disturbed by their excitement and the uncertain weather conditions. By 0330 we decided that we could probably fire at 0530. By 0400 the rain had stopped but the sky was heavily overcast. Our decision became firmer as time went on. During most of these hours the two of us journeyed from the control house out into the darkness to look at the stars and to assure each other that the one or two visible stars were becoming brighter. At 0510 I left Dr. Oppenheimer and

returned to the main observation point which was 17,000 yards from the point of explosion. In accordance with our orders I found all personnel not otherwise occupied massed on a bit of high ground.

At about two minutes of the scheduled firing time all persons lay face down with their feet pointing towards the explosion. As the remaining time was called from the loud speaker from the 10,000 yard control station there was complete silence. Dr. Conant said he had never imagined seconds could be so long. Most of the individuals in accordance with orders shielded their eyes in one way or another. There was then this burst of light of a brilliance beyond any comparison. We all rolled over and looked through dark glasses at the ball of fire. About forty seconds later came the shock wave followed by the sound, neither of which seemed startling after our complete astonishment at the extraordinary lighting intensity. Dr. Conant reached over and and we shook hands in mutual congratulations. Dr. Bush, who was on the other side of me, did likewise. The feeling of the entire assembly was similar to that described by General Farrell, with even the uninitiated feeling profound awe. Drs. Conant and Bush and myself were struck by an even stronger feeling that the faith of those who had been responsible for the initiation and the carrying on of this Herculean project had been justified. I personally thought of Blondin crossing Niagara Falls on his tight rope, only to me this tight rope had lasted for almost three years and of my repeated confident-appearing assurances that such a thing was possible and that we would do it.

13. A large group of observers were stationed at a point about 27 miles north of the point of explosion. Attached is a memorandum written shortly after the explosion by Dr. E. O. Lawrence which may be of interest.

14. While General Farrell was waiting about midnight for a commercial airplane to Washington at Albuquerque—120 miles away from the site—he overheard several airport employees discussing their reaction to the blast. One said that he was out on the parking apron; it was quite dark; then the whole southern sky was lighted as though by a bright sun; the light lasted several seconds. Another remarked that if a few exploding bombs could have such an effect, it must be terrible to have them drop on a city.

15. My liaison officer at the Alamogordo Air Base, sixty miles away, made the following report:

"There was a blinding flash of light that lighted the entire northwestern sky. In the center of the flash, there appeared to be a huge billow of smoke. The original flash died down, there arose in the approximate center of where the original flash had occurred an enormous ball of what appeared to be fire and closely resembled a rising sun that was ¾ above a mountain. The ball of fire lasted approximately fifteen seconds, then died down and the sky resumed an almost normal appearance.

"Almost immediately, a third, but much smaller, flash and billow of smoke of a whitish-orange color appeared in the sky, again lighting the sky for approximately 4 seconds. At the time of the original flash, the field was lighted well enough so that a newspaper could easily have been read. The second and third flashes were of much lesser intensity.

"We were in a glass-enclosed control tower some 70 feet above the ground and felt no concussion or air compression. There was no noticeable earth tremor although reports overheard at the Field during the following 24 hours indicated that some believed that they had both heard the explosion and felt some earth tremor."

16. I have not written a separate report for General Marshall as I feel you will want to show this to him. I have informed the necessary people here of our results. Lord Halifax after discussion with Mr. Harrison and myself stated that he was not sending a full report to his government at this time. I informed him that I was sending this to you and that you might wish to show it to the proper British representatives.

17. We are all fully conscious that our real goal is still before us. The battle test is what counts in the war with Japan.

18. May I express my deep personal appreciation for your congratulatory cable to us and for the support and confidence which I have received from you ever since I have had this work under my charge.

19. I know that Colonel Kyle will guard these papers with his customary extraordinary care.

L. R. Groves[7]

Stimson at once sought an engagement with the President. It was fixed for half-past three that afternoon. In the interval he told Marshall of the main features of Groves' report. When Stimson got to the "Little White House," he asked the President to call Byrnes in, and read the message in full to them. The President was, in the words of Stimson's diary, "tremendously pepped up by it . . . and said that it gave him an entirely new feeling of confidence." Why the report was such an elixir will be clearer after reading the later pages telling of the tussles that were going on around the conference table.

Stimson then hurried over to Churchill's quarters and gave him the typed memo from Groves. The Prime Minister could not read it through before he had to leave for the Fifth Plenary Session with Truman and Stalin. He asked Stimson to come again the next morning.

Before going over to see the Prime Minister that next forenoon (the 22nd) Stimson stopped by the "Little White House" to pick up a paper he had left with the President the day before, summarizing his ideas about sharing knowledge of the new weapon with the Russians, and the possibility of bringing the new force—atomic energy—under effective international control. As he was leaving he told Truman that Harrison had just assured him that a bomb would be ready for use against Japan early in August.

Then on he went to the residence of the Prime Minister, and stood by while the message from Groves was being read in full. On putting it

[7] Potsdam Papers, Document 1305.

down, Churchill, all animation, leaned forward in his chair, waved his cigar, and said: "Stimson, what was gunpowder? Trivial. What was electricity? Meaningless. This atomic bomb is the second coming in wrath."[8]

The Chairman of the British Chiefs of Staff did not share the Prime Minister's exuberance. "At 1:30 p.m.," he noted in his diary, "we went round to lunch with the P.M. He had seen the American reports of results of the new 'Tube Alloys' secret explosive which had been carried out in the States. He had absorbed all the minor American exaggerations and, as a result, was completely carried away. It was now no longer necessary for the Russians to come into the Japanese war; the new explosive alone was sufficient to settle the matter. Furthermore, we now had something in our hands which would redress the balance with the Russians. The secret of this explosive and the power to use it would completely alter the diplomatic equilibrium which was adrift since the defeat of Germany. Now we had a new value which redressed our position (pushing out his chin and scowling); now we could say, 'If you insist on doing this or that, well . . .' And then where are the Russians!"[9]

The consequent questions of whether, when, how, and how much to tell the Russians about the new weapon had perplexed the informed American officials ever since the scientists and engineers had forecast its being.

In 1943 at Hyde Park, Roosevelt and Churchill had entered into an agreement stating: "(1) The suggestion that the world should be informed about Tube Alloys, with a view to international agreement regarding its control and use is not accepted. The matter should continue to be regarded as of the utmost secrecy; but when a 'bomb' is finally available, it might perhaps, after mature consideration, be used against the Japanese who should be warned that the bombardment will be repeated until they surrender."[10]

The Interim Committee, without knowing of the accord, had agreed early in June that the American government ought not reveal the existence of the weapon to Russia or anyone else until after it was proved in use against Japan. When reporting to the President on June 6th about

---

[8] Harvey H. Bundy, who was present at this talk with Churchill, in the *Atlantic Monthly* (March 1957).

[9] Extract from diary of Field-Marshal Lord Alanbrooke, July 23, 1945, in *Triumph in the West*, by Sir Arthur Bryant.

[10] Potsdam Papers, Document 1306.

the points of agreement reached in the Interim Committee, Stimson had stressed this conclusion. He had then said he was perplexed as to what might happen when the President met with Stalin and Churchill. Truman had remarked that the postponement of the conference until the middle of July would give the wanted time. The Secretary of War had not been wholly reassured. What if the tests were delayed?

Stimson had then summed up for the President the discussions that had been going on in and out of the Interim Committee on future control of this new force. The only suggestion the Committee had advanced, he said, was that countries should promise to make public all the work they were doing in this field, and to form an international control group with full powers of inspection in all countries. Presciently, he remarked that he realized that this plan was imperfect and the Russians might not agree with it. If they did not, all we could do, he thought, was to accumulate enough fissionable material as insurance. In any case, he reiterated his conviction that no disclosure ought to be made to anyone until an agreement on control was working effectively. Marshall had been of the same determined opinion.

Could the United States, the President wondered, get something of value in return for sharing information about atomic fission with the Soviet Union? Might we be able to get greater cooperation in arriving at accords in regard to Poland, Romania, Yugoslavia, Manchuria, for example?

On July 4, two days before the American group left for Potsdam, the Combined (U.S.-British) Policy Committee had pondered over the same problem of what, if anything, to tell the Russians. The British and Canadian members (Field Marshal Sir Henry Maitland Wilson, liaison for the British Chiefs of Staff, and the Honorable C. D. Howe, Canadian Minister of Munitions) had gone along with Stimson's ideas of what had best be done. As recorded in the Minutes of this discussion:

"The Chairman [Stimson] said he was thinking of . . . the forthcoming meeting with Stalin. His own opinion had been very much influenced by the probable use within a few weeks after the meeting. If nothing was said at this meeting about the T.A. weapon, its subsequent early use might have a serious effect on the relations of frankness between the three great Allies. He had therefore advised the President to watch the atmosphere at the meeting. If mutual frankness on other questions was found to be real and satisfactory, then the President might say that work was being done on the development of atomic fission for war purposes; that good progress had been made; and that an attempt to use a weapon would be made shortly, though it was not certain that it would succeed. If it did succeed, it would be necessary for a discussion to be held on the best method of handling the development in the interests of world peace and not for destruction. If Stalin pressed for immediate disclosure the President might say that he was not prepared to take the matter further at the present time."[11]

All these questions had been left hanging in the air. There they had stayed until the President reached Potsdam and the news of the results of the test in New Mexico overtook him and Stimson and Byrnes. When they learned that it would soon be available for use against Japan, they had to make up their minds. The quest for the correct course led them into even more intense talk about how much to tell the Russians.

All recognized that it would be sensible as well as proper to let Stalin know of the achievement, for of course he would learn of it as soon as the bomb was used against the Japanese—which would be in about a fortnight. But how much should he be told of its nature? Above all else, should we share the knowledge as to how the new weapon was made? On that question, as has been told, the ruling official opinion had been steady from the start: we must not do so until or unless an agreement was reached for international inspection and control. The only notable challenge to this conclusion was that offered by some of the scientists who were convinced that the Soviet Union could easily and quickly learn how to make the new weapon, whether or not we told them what we knew. If that were true, they had argued, by sharing our knowledge we would be showing trust, and so win trust; while if we concealed what we knew, we would, by showing mistrust, stimulate their hostility, suspicion, and rivalry.

Stimson meditated over this dilemma, fretted over it during sleepless hours of the night. He had taught himself to live by the maxim that the way to win trust is to give it; and this clashed with the dark lessons of history about the ways of absolute dictatorship. The President took the view that it was common sense to wait until we were sure. Byrnes thought unguarded openness would bring advantage only to the Russians.

But at Potsdam these longer and more lasting aspects of the question were thrust into the background by thoughts of more immediate

[11] Potsdam Papers, Document 619. The members of the Committee were Stimson, Wilson, Howe, and Dr. Vannevar Bush. On this occasion there were also present the British Ambassador (the Earl of Halifax), Sir James Chadwick, General L. R. Groves, and George Harrison, as well as the Joint Secretaries, Harvey H. Bundy and Roger Makins.

consequences. How would opening the doors to knowledge about the weapon, or keeping them closed, affect the Soviet attitude in the disputatious talks on European questions that were going on? How might the Soviet decision about entering the Pacific war be affected? Or the timing of Russia's entry? Or its attitude toward the situation in China?

On July 18, when Truman talked with Churchill about the new weapon, they reviewed these quandaries. Truman's attitude and Churchill's response are recorded in a note the Prime Minister made for the War Cabinet:

"The President showed me telegrams about the recent experiment, and asked what I thought should be done about telling the Russians. He seemed determined to do this, but asked about the timing, and said he thought that the end of the Conference would be best. I replied that if he were resolved to tell it might well be better to hang it on the experiment, which was a new fact on which he and we had only just had knowledge. Therefore he would have a good answer to any question, 'Why did you not tell us this before?' He seemed impressed with this idea, and will consider it.

"On behalf of His Majesty's Government, I did not resist his proposed disclosure of the simple fact that we have this weapon. He reiterated his resolve at all costs to refuse to divulge any particulars . . ."[12]

On further thinking the matter over, Churchill developed a positive disposition to let the Russians know we had the new weapon. After Stimson talked with him again on the 22nd, he wrote in his diary that Churchill "now not only was not worried about giving the Russians information on the matter, but was rather inclined to use it as an argument in our favor in the negotiations. The sentiment of the four of us [Stimson, Bundy, Churchill, Cherwell] was unanimous in thinking that it was advisable to tell the Russians at least that we were working on the subject and intended to use it if and when it was successfully finished."[13]

But Stimson's impulse to be trustful and revealing was still checked by his view of the system of dictatorship under which the Russians lived. His worry and his sense of being on the sidelines had found outlet in a memo that he had given to the President the day before. In this he had expressed the opinion that the basic difficulty in our relations with Russia was that there was no personal or political freedom in that country, that it was ruled by an arbitrary autocracy, and there could not be

[12] *Triumph and Tragedy*, pages 640-41.
[13] Potsdam Papers, Minutes, July 22, 1945.

close and reliable relations between such a system and ours. Thus he had urged that we try to get Stalin to take the lead in introducing freedoms into the Soviet Union. Otherwise he feared that a new war was inevitable, one that would bring about the destruction of our civilization. The memo concluded:

"The foregoing has a vital bearing upon the control of the vast and revolutionary discovery of 'X' [atomic energy] which is now confronting us. Upon the successful control of that energy depends the future successful development or destruction of the modern civilized world. The Committee appointed by the War Department [the Interim Committee] which has been considering that control has pointed this out in no uncertain terms and has called for an international organization for that purpose. After careful reflection I am of the belief that *no* world organization containing as one of its dominant members a nation whose people are not possessed of free speech but whose governmental action is controlled by the autocratic machinery of a secret political police, [can] give effective control of this new agency with its devastating possibilities.

"I therefore believe that before we share our new discovery with Russia we should consider carefully whether we can do so safely under any system of control until Russia puts into effective action the proposed constitution which I have mentioned. If this is a necessary condition, we must go slowly in any disclosures or agreeing to any Russian participation whatsoever and constantly explore the question how our headstart in 'X' and the Russian desire to participate can be used to bring us nearer to the removal of the basic difficulties which I have emphasized."[14]

In other words, even if our head start were only temporary, could it not be used to influence the Soviet Union to make life safer for the world by converting itself into a constitutional democracy, in which citizens were free and rulers under restraint? How grand the purpose, how far away the chance! But to Stimson, as Elting Morison observes, "That these difficulties could, with care and time, be removed was not 'an idle dream.' "[15]

On the morning of the 24th Stimson showed Truman the most recent message from Harrison, giving the probable date when all would be in order to use the bomb against Japan, then being assembled in Tinian. The President was delighted and said that it gave him his cue

[14] Potsdam Papers, Document 1157.
[15] Morison manuscript.

for issuing the final warning to Japan to accept the terms we and the British were offering, as the only way to escape utter destruction. He wanted to issue this summons to surrender as soon as he heard from Chiang Kai-shek, who had been asked to approve the text. At lunch Truman talked over with Byrnes how Stalin might be told enough to invalidate any future reproach that information of military importance had been kept from him, but no more. They agreed that it should be done in a rather off-hand way.

That afternoon the Combined Chiefs of Staff had what was deemed a rewarding session with their Soviet associates. The Plenary Session of the Heads of State was rather unproductive, and at moments discordant, but Stalin showed some disposition to heed Western wishes. The conferees rose from their places with amiable nods, after approving the worksheet for their next meeting. As they were standing around in small groups waiting for their cars, the President sauntered over to Stalin. His own later account of their very brief chat is as off-hand, as humdrum even, as his act was made to appear: "On July 24 I casually mentioned to Stalin that we had a new weapon of unusual destructive force." The better to give the impression of speaking in a "by the way" manner, he did not ask Bohlen to come with him. So what the President said was translated by Pavlov, the Russian interpreter. We are left to wonder what Pavlov, whose grasp of English was not perfect, understood Truman to say, and what translated version he passed on to Stalin.

Whatever it was, the Generalissimo seemed pleased rather than surprised. Truman thought that he showed no special interest. All he said was that he was glad to hear it and hoped we would make 'good use of it against the Japanese.' "[16]

Churchill was standing perhaps five yards away, and watched with the closest attention to measure the effect of what the President was going to tell Stalin. His impression was more enlivened by his dramatic imagination: "I can see it all as if it were yesterday. He seemed to be delighted. A new bomb! Of extraordinary power! Probably decisive on the whole Japanese war! What a bit of luck! This was my impression at the moment, and I was sure that he had no idea of the significance of what he was being told."[17]

When Churchill asked Truman how the talk had gone, the President told him that Stalin had been pleased but not inquisitive. And when

[16] *Year of Decisions*, page 416. As Truman later wrote to Professor James L. Cate: "Premier Stalin smiled and thanked me for reporting the explosion to him, but I'm sure he did not understand its significance" (Craven and Cate, page 712).
[17] *Triumph and Tragedy*, page 670.

Byrnes asked the same question the President answered in effect that all Stalin had said was "That's fine, I hope you make good use of it against the Japanese."[18]

What had been feared had not come to pass. Stalin had not tried to find out what the nature of the new weapon was, or how it was made. He had not suggested that Soviet officers or technicians be allowed to examine or witness its use. But was this only because he did not realize the significance of what Truman was telling him? He was not dull in grasping the meaning of even the most passing remark, or incurious about any improvement in weapons. It did not occur to any of the American and British officials who were at Potsdam that Stalin might already have knowledge of the production and testing of the new weapon. Possibly he did not.

But it would be curious if he had not, in view of the secret and illicit reports that had been sent by Soviet agents to Moscow about the problems solved in making the bomb, the engineering difficulties mastered, and the method of detonation. It is conceivable, though unlikely, that the Soviet intelligence organization had not sent this information to the top, or that Stalin's military-science experts had not credited it. A better surmise—still only an unsupported surmise—is that he knew, before he was told, that this weapon was being made, knew even that it was all but perfected, but had not learned of the satisfactory test in New Mexico.[19]

In any case, Truman's statement did not seem to either the American or the British observers to influence the Russian attitude toward the situations that were being talked about at the conference. Nor can the historian going over the record of the conference discern signs that it did so. But this steadiness may have been dissimulation. Stalin was quite able to conceal any glimmer of an idea that the diplomatic or military balance between the West and the Soviet Union might be affected by the new weapon. Or he may have been certain that the American government would not use the weapon against the Soviet Union because of any current difference. It may be that his technical advisers were already telling him they could in due course repeat the production. These are some of the reasons that can be conjectured for Stalin's response, for the way in which he matched Truman's casualness.

---

[18] Byrnes, *All in One Lifetime*, page 300.
[19] This surmise is derived from examination of the published record of Soviet atomic espionage; see *U.S. Congress, Report of Joint Committee on Atomic Energy.*

After his first quick and interrupted scanning of Groves' long and vivid report on the New Mexico bomb test, Churchill had told Stimson he had noticed during the session of the conference the afternoon before (the 21st) that the President was evidently much fortified by some news or event. To that alert observer Truman had seemed to be a changed person, maintaining his stand against the Russians in a most emphatic and decisive manner. And so, Churchill added, he too was a different man.

Some of the President's attendant staff had the same impression of new gusto and greater firmness. But alas, this is not detectable in the dull monochrome tone of the American minutes of the conference. Nor can I discern that any change in mood or attitude or judgment lasted through the following days of the conference. Certainty that we would be able to defeat the Soviet Union in war did not cause Truman or his advisers, military or civilian, to be more demanding. It apparently did not lead them to anticipate that the Russians would be more yielding after the great destructive power of the weapon was proved in use against Japan.

As will be seen in the following chapters, the secret knowledge appears to have caused the Americans and the British to be firm in their resistance to Soviet wishes that they thought excessive or perilous. It was a buttress for the policy of fairness and friendliness to which they were clinging. But the Americans at Potsdam either did not know how to use their command of the new weapon effectively as a threat, or chose not to use it in that way.

Was not the American government resting the whole structure of its policy on a conviction that situations and disputes were to be settled only by peaceful means and orderly procedures? The intention was to find ways to use the technical triumph in New Mexico for the service of the ideal principles that had been endorsed at San Francisco. Even if Russia could be frightened or coerced by the bomb to give in against its will on matters before the conference, would the West be well served if in consequence it turned against the United Nations? Such, in so far as I can gather, was the trend of the sober reflections of those who guided American diplomatic and military decisions in Potsdam.

Nor was our wish to have Russian cooperation in the war against Japan dispelled. After the receipt of the Groves report Stimson told Marshall that the President would like to know wether Marshall still thought we needed the Russians in the Pacific war or whether we could get on without them. The answer was neither direct nor conclusive. Marshall said that the fact that the Russians were amassing large forces on the Manchurian frontier was already serving one of the purposes for which we wished them to come into the war: to cause the Japanese to keep their army in Manchuria. He also pointed out that even if we defeated the Japanese without the Russians, or before they entered the war, they could, if they wished, march into Manchuria and take what they wanted. In sum, Marshall gave Stimson the impression that since we had the atomic bomb, Russian aid was no longer really needed to conquer Japan, or much wanted; but it would bring the end more quickly and with smaller loss of life; and since in any event the Soviet forces could obtain control of Manchuria (and possibly Korea and the Kuriles) it was still expedient to solicit Soviet entry.

In sum, the light of the explosion "brighter than a thousand suns" filtered into the conference rooms at Potsdam only as a distant gleam. It was the fire, however, concealed in the final call for Japanese surrender that was issued from Potsdam. And its full glare was to flash over Hiroshima not many days later.

24. Toward a Peace Conference

TERMINAL: where war ended and peace was to start. As soon as all were in their seats at the round table for the first time, Truman led off in that direction. He asked attention for a proposal aimed to accelerate the preparation of peace treaties with some or all of the defeated Axis countries.

Memories of the dissension among the allies who had come together at Versailles after World War I had hung heavy over all discussions in Washington about the task ahead. By what means and methods different from those used in 1919 could the toil be shortened, the inevitable conflicts of desire softened, and the ultimate arrangements improved? Only, it was concluded, if there were adequate advance consultation—first between the larger powers, and then between them and the smaller ones.

In a memo that Stettinius had sent to the President on June 19 these thoughts were developed into a plan of procedure. It first cautioned against the convocation of a formal peace conference to deal with the enormous range of questions that were left in Europe at the end of the war: if all of the interested countries were invited to take part the proceedings would be slow and unwieldy; while if only a few were invited the others would object and challenge the decisions. A better way to start on the task, it was suggested, would be to have a small Council—composed of the five Foreign Ministers of the United States, United Kingdom, the Soviet Union, China, and France—first go over the most important problems. Stettinius urged that the Heads of Government at Potsdam create such a Council, fix the time and place of its first meeting, and indicate the items they thought ought to be discussed first. After the Council had gone over a situation or treaty, as for example the peace treaty with Italy, it might be advisable in some cases for the governments who were members of the Council to call a conference of all states chiefly concerned; but in others ordinary diplomatic methods might suffice.

The State Department had named the first tasks on which the Council had best engage: to draw up the terms of peace with Italy, Romania, Bulgaria, and Hungary; and to propose settlements of open territorial questions.

Early in July the American government had notified the British and Soviet governments that Truman at Potsdam would present a proposal along these lines. The British government had found no fault in it. The Soviet government had found one. On July 11 Molotov told Harriman that he saw no reason why China should be in the Council when it discussed peace treaties with European countries, for China's interest in European affairs was remote and its knowledge of them small. Harriman had countered that the war was worldwide in its effect; and that since China was one of the permanent members of the Security Council of the United Nations it was advisable that any deficiency in its knowledge of European affairs be quickly made up by informed experience.

No doubt the Soviet government thought that the Chinese member of any such Council of Foreign Ministers would usually agree with the United States in case of differences of opinion with the Soviet Union. It may be surmised that the American government figured the probabilities in the same way. History was going to surprise them both—to shock the United States and delight the Soviet Union.

The proposal that Truman submitted at the First Plenary Session of the conference conformed to the earlier notice. It read in part: "The experience at Versailles following the last war does not encourage the belief that a full formal peace conference without preliminary preparations on the part of the leading powers is the best procedure. Such a conference without such preparation would be slow and unwieldy, its sessions would be conducted in a heated atmosphere of rival claims and counter claims and ratification of the resulting documents might be long delayed. I therefore propose as the best formula to meet the situation the establishment of a Council composed of the Foreign Ministers of Great Britain, the Union of Soviet Socialist Republics, China, France, and the United States."[1]

The first task to be assigned to this Council of Foreign Ministers, it was suggested, should be to draw up peace treaties with Italy, Romania, and Bulgaria. The next would be to propose settlements of outstanding territorial questions in Europe. Later on the Council should be used to prepare a peace treaty with Germany. The Council should be allowed to adopt its procedure of consultation to each situation. It was contemplated that any and all states should be given a fair chance to discuss with the Council any questions of direct interest to them.

Stalin said he had no objection to the principles in Truman's proposal. But, as had Molotov before, he questioned whether China should be drawn into the treatment of European affairs. It may be inferred that Churchill was no more pleased at that prospect than Stalin. But instead of directly opposing Truman he sought a way around the disagreeable

[1] Potsdam Papers, Document 711.

point. He approved the idea of bringing into being a Council of the Foreign Ministers of the five powers. But this new group should not supersede or lead to the disuse of two existing agencies of consultation, the regular quarterly meetings of the three Foreign Ministers, and the European Advisory Commission; China was not on either. Let the three groups coexist and cooperate.[2]

In a series of meetings that went into the next week, the three Foreign Ministers present at Potsdam—Byrnes, Eden, Molotov—and their staffs struggled to smooth over these divergent ripples of interest and intent. Stalin and Churchill were induced to pay a formal tribute to the American wish to elevate the status of China. Truman was induced to accede to their opinion that China should not be given the chance to meddle in the preparation of peace treaties with European countries or the settlement of territorial questions in Europe. This was done obliquely, by providing that "For the discharge of each of these tasks the Council will be composed of the Members representing those States which were signatory to the terms of surrender imposed upon the enemy state concerned."[3] China was not a signatory to any of the acts of surrender in Europe.

But what about France? Was it to be enabled, even though it had dropped out of the war, to share in the preparation of peace treaties with all the European members of the Axis? The Americans and British wanted to grant it that chance. Stalin and Molotov were willing to concede it the right to participate in the work on peace treaties with Italy and Germany, but not on those with Hungary, Romania, and Bulgaria. Their opposition was effective.

Was it to be stipulated that the terms of these peace treaties, after the Council had agreed on them, be submitted to the United Nations? The President proposed that it should be so provided. And Byrnes argued that they were all obligated to this course by the original United Nations Declaration of January 1, 1942. But Churchill said he had misgivings about making any such procedure compulsory, since it might cause the business of peacemaking to be too protracted and laborious. Stalin's ambiguous comment (this was at the Second Plenary Session) enabled the negotiators to express themselves as being of one mind. He said that the provision under consideration would not make any differ-

[2] Subsequently, however, the conference agreed to recommend to the member governments that the EAC be dissolved and that its work be taken over by the Control Councils in Germany and Austria.

[3] Potsdam Papers, Document 714. For final text see the Protocol, reprinted below as Supplementary Note 7.

ence since the three powers would represent the interest of all (presumably of all the United Nations).

Churchill seems to have taken this remark to mean that the text of the treaties would be referred to the United Nations only if and after all members of the Council of Foreign Ministers had given their stamp of approval. That being understood, he said the stipulation was acceptable. And, Truman, possibly not grasping the import of Stalin's remark, closed the discussion by saying that then the procedure for peace settlements was agreed to by all.[4] The pertinent provision in the text of the agreement as finally adopted read: "As its immediate important task the Council shall be authorized to draw up, with a view to their submission to the United Nations, treaties of peace with Italy, Rumania, Bulgaria, Hungary and Finland . . . The Council shall be utilized for the preparation of a peace settlement for Germany to be accepted by the Government of Germany when a Government adequate for the purpose is established."

". . . with a view to their submission"! The bridge builder, in his specification of materials and structures, makes allowance for sway. So does the diplomat, by fluidity of language.

This was the first accord reached at Potsdam. It was regarded as a cheering sign that the wish to cooperate would rule. But actually, while this agreement about future procedure in peacemaking—which committed no one to any fact or act of substance—was being conceived, a cold and separating argument was going on about the attitude to be assumed toward Italy and the smaller Axis satellites. It started when the Americans urged that Italy be treated no longer as a former enemy, but as a reformed and friendly associate in the United Nations.

[4] The American minutes of this talk at the Second Plenary Session on July 18 leave the whole subject in obscurity, and so do the later references to it by Churchill and Truman in their memoirs. Churchill records his interpretation (*Triumph and Tragedy*, page 650) as follows: "Mr. Byrnes said we were so bound by the United Nations Declaration, but both he and Stalin admitted that reference to the United Nations could only be made after the five Powers had agreed among themselves. I left it at that." Truman's sole comment is even more glancing. Referring to Stalin's statement that the three powers would represent the interests of all, he wrote (*Year of Decisions*, page 352): "That was Stalin's viewpoint all the way. His viewpoint was that Russia, Britain and the United States would settle world affairs and that it was nobody else's business. I felt very strongly that the participation of all nations, small and large, was just as important to world peace as that of the big Three."

25. The Former Satellites of Germany

THE armistice with Italy was twenty months old. The country was being treated by the allies in some respects as a former enemy, in others as an associate in the struggle against Germany, and in still others as a ward. Its people were abashed rather than ashamed over their jackal behavior while under the spell of Mussolini. They were suffering from humiliation, though in the adaptable, self-accepting way of Italian nature. Many were without work and hungry, or sick, on the edge of despair. They lacked the means of paying for the coal, oil, raw materials, machinery, trucks, and railway equipment needed to revive industrial production. Fascist suppression was past. Social inequality and neglect were as present as ever.

The first coalition government that had been formed after liberation was conscientious, but directed by individuals who did not have the needed vitality or boldness. The Communists, by their bravery in their partisan activities against the Germans, had earned esteem and popularity. They were well organized, and were bent on securing control of the country either by taking advantage of the parliamentary system of government or by subversion. At the other edge of Italian political life a Fascist spirit and loyal supporters survived.

Allied forces were still in occupation of part of the country, and still entitled under the armistice terms to direct its political and military affairs. But they were also acting as supporters and guardians: providing essentials to avert disease and unrest and to alleviate misery; keeping the Yugoslavs from taking over the northeastern provinces; teaching compromise in Italian politics.

In the earlier stages of the war Great Britain had held the initiative in shaping policy toward Italy and the Italians. British Commonwealth forces (and their Polish comrades under British command) had endured most of the weight of the prolonged, punishing campaign from Sicily and the boot of Italy up to the Apennines. A British officer, Field Marshal Alexander, was Supreme Commander of Allied Forces in the Mediterranean Theatre. But by the time of the German surrender the lead had passed to the United States. It alone had the means to aid the country to revive, an intent wish to have it do so, and enough influence among the Italian people. Impatiently pushing the American government on were the large numbers of Americans of Italian origin, and the influential Catholic church officials and members, to whom Rome was the center of the spiritual world. American opinion was open to the belief that the Italian people wished to return to the ways of freedom and fairness.

Proof was seen in the formation of an abler and more representative coalition in June. This had been hailed by Grew on June 21 in a public statement of encouraging warmth, which said: "This government is happy to learn that Italy has succeeded in forming a new government in which the newly liberated north joins hands with the south and all the parties of the Committee of National Liberation participate. This union of forces, under the presidency of Signor Ferruccio Parri, a leader of the resistance movement—an outstanding soldier in the long fight for Italian freedom from the early days of Fascism to the last days of German invasion—is a good augury for the new government as it faces the many problems ahead. Not least among these is the historic task of preparing the machinery whereby the people of Italy can at long last freely and fully express their political will. . . . The people of the United States will therefore follow its progress with interest and sympathy."

Not only with interest and sympathy, but with active support. The American government had determined to prop up the authority of the new Italian administration, repair the Italian economy, and regenerate the self-respect of the Italian people.

On the whole, Churchill welcomed this surge of American purpose because of his lively fear that the Italian people, having tolerated Fascist domination for twenty years, might easily slide into Communist control. But Eden found it harder to forget how Italy, by assaulting Ethiopia, had smitten the League of Nations; how it had then, in 1940, repudiated its bonds with the West and struck England a blow that might have been mortal; and how the British army and navy had been forced, at utmost risk to the nation, to devote their combat reserves to preventing Italian conquest of Suez and loss of vital connections with the East.

Some of the measures conceived in Washington the Americans and British could take quickly and without consulting the Soviet government. Others required time and Soviet (and perhaps French) assent.

The first step in mind was the reform of the Allied Commission (nominally an agency of the United Nations but really run by its British and American members). This was to be converted into a civilian organization, with many of its duties and powers given over to the Italian government. The next step was to replace the instrument of surrender, signed in 1943, by an interim agreement that would relax many of the allied controls and restraints. While these measures to turn control of Italy back to the Italian people were being taken, the American government would be striving to secure admission for Italy into the United Nations, and doing what it could to hurry on the negotiation of a peace treaty that would discharge Italy from allied custody.

This program, it was realized, would work out well only if there were steady and strong political leadership in Italy and a rapid improvement of the conditions of daily life. For these purposes it was essential to enlist popular support. This in turn could be achieved only by the introduction of a new government by fair and free elections; and by giving the Italian people an unhindered chance to decide for themselves by popular vote whether they wanted Italy to remain a kingdom, under the former king in exile, or any king. The American and British governments might see to it that these elections were properly conducted. And this political effort was to be sustained and supplemented by measures to relieve economic and social distress, and enable Italy to become self-supporting.

The American government visualized the rapid departure of allied troops from Italy. Even as it was vowing that all forms of military organization must be banned forever in Germany, it seems to have been willing to consider the formation of an Italian military force as well as a civilian police force. As approved in June by the Joint Chiefs, the American plan of redeployment contemplated that by the end of the year only 2,500 American troops would remain in Italy, other than the division that was to continue to share in the occupation of Venezia Giulia. But Alexander regarded this rush to get out as dangerous; and Churchill, it was known, intended to urge Truman when they met to retain larger numbers in the country. The State Department recommended to the President shortly before he left for Potsdam that: "the principle should be established that the Allied troops will not be wholly withdrawn from Italy until after the Italian people would have had an opportunity . . . to choose their form of democratic government. It is thus recommended that at least a token force of United States troops be left in Italy."[1]

Similarly the British Chiefs of Staff wanted to maintain a Combined (U.S.-British) Command in Italy, at least until the Allied Commission had been dissolved and the allied military assignments in Venezia

[1] Potsdam Papers, Document 473.

Giulia and Bolzano had ceased. The American Chiefs were eager to dissolve the existing Combined Headquarters, but agreed to postpone decision.

Truman made the scope of his purpose plain at the First Plenary Session. There he introduced a proposal that stated the essentials of an interim arrangement to regulate relations with Italy while the peace treaty was being prepared and negotiated.[2]

The surrender terms were to be replaced by a voluntary accord with the Italian government. The allies would agree to end all their controls over Italy except those justified by two special purposes. One of these was the elementary one of servicing and protecting such allied military forces as might stay in Italy. The other was to make sure that the dispute with Tito about control of Venezia Giulia was settled fairly and peaceably. The Italian government would pledge itself not to take any hostile actions against any of the United Nations, and not to maintain any military forces except such as might be approved by the allies.

Churchill listened with a scowl—especially to Truman's prefatory remarks devoted to the admission of Italy into the United Nations. He recalled the Italian "stab in the back" and warned against deciding such important matters in haste.

Stalin on this occasion said nothing. But three days later (July 20), when Truman asked for action, it became clear what other skeins the Marshal wanted to wind about the same bobbin. Stalin said that in principle he was not against what the President was proposing. Why not have the three Foreign Ministers examine the main points carefully, *and at the same time consider whether they should not also transform in a similar way the relations with other satellite states*—Finland, Hungary, Romania, and Bulgaria? He saw no reason to single out Italy. Truman brought up two: Italy had surrendered first; and the armistice terms imposed on it had been harsher than those imposed on other satellites. But he curtly agreed that the situation of the other satellites might also be reviewed.

Churchill's usual magnanimity—or fear of Communism—came slowly to the fore again. He said he was willing to have the Council of Foreign Ministers begin to prepare a peace treaty with Italy. But he could not wholly agree to the proposed interim arrangement, for it would not cover the existing rights of allies to control the future of the Italian

[2] *Ibid.*, Document 1089.

fleet, the disposition of Italian colonies, reparations, and other matters; and if these were lost the allies would not be able to get the peace
terms to which they were entitled. He added, however, that he was more
inclined to conclude peace with Italy than with Bulgaria, which "lay
crouching in the Balkans fawning on German aid. She had also committed many cruelties in Greece and Yugoslavia. She had prevented
Turkey's entering the war when this would have been most helpful."

This rainbow discourse did not appeal to either Truman or Stalin.
The President has recalled his impressions as he listened: "Churchill
always found it necessary in cases of this kind, particularly where the
Mediterranean was involved, to make long statements like this and
then agree to what had already been done. . . . He was apparently
making a record for use later by the British when the peace treaties
were really and actually negotiated. He did the same thing when we
were talking about France and Spain. On several occasions when
Churchill was discussing something at length, Stalin would lean on his
elbow, pull on his mustache, and say, 'Why don't you agree? The
Americans agree and we agree. You will agree eventually, so why
don't you do it now?' Then the argument would stop. Churchill in the
end would agree, but he had to make a speech about it first."[3]

It is true that Churchill was not forgetting the British imperial highways to the East: there was no Truman Doctrine then for Greece and
Turkey. Nor was Stalin forgetting the countries on Russia's borders
that were being absorbed into the Soviet sphere of control. What the
three of them did at Potsdam, he moralized, should not be warped
by complaints or desires for revenge. It should be shaped by the purpose of separating all these countries from Germany for all time. So the
Russians were willing to subdue their memories of injuries, inflicted not
only by Italy but also by the other satellites. The time had come, he
thought, to ease the positions of these countries too, though not in the
same measure as in Italy. "With regard to the satellites, he did not
propose that peace treaties be signed with them nor even that some
intermediate position be accorded them as the President had proposed
for Italy." But why should they not start by resuming diplomatic relations with them? As for the objection that they did not have freely
elected governments, neither had Italy, France, nor Belgium, with which
the United States and Great Britain were consorting. Truman answered
vaguely that he thought an agreement could be reached regarding not

[3] *Year of Decisions*, page 363.

only Italy but all the satellites. He wished to bring about a feeling of peace in the world as soon as might be, and to make it possible for all these countries to be self-sustaining.

Let the Foreign Ministers, it was agreed after some vagrant argument, discuss not only the American proposal about Italy but also the situation of the other satellites. Discuss they could and did. Agree they could not. Trouble erupted when they tried. The reasons may be clearer if we briefly review the immediately preceding turn of events in the satellite countries.

Hungary had taken a brutal part in the Nazi program and the assault on the Soviet Union. Yet it was still thought to be by history, nature, and wish attached to the West; and the American government was eager to rescue it for the West. The existing Provisional National Government was a coalition of various anti-Nazi groups, controlled by party leaders and organizers, the strongest of whom were Communists. The more moderate elements were living in fear of the political police and ultimate suppression. Moreover, the people were being kept in a state of distress because of Soviet requisitions for the Red Army and reparations.[4]

These trends, the American government decided, could not be combated or reversed unless there was a thorough transformation of the Control Commission. Two main changes were deemed crucial: to limit the action of the Commission to the execution of the armistice terms; and to procure for the American and British members of the Commission as much chance to determine policy as the Soviet Chairman (or President, as he was called in some documents).[5] Harriman, in the weeks before Potsdam, had not been deterred from urging these reforms by Molotov's coldness or by his studied carelessness in answering letters on the subject.

Then on July 12, just a few days before the conference was to start,

---

[4] Although the American government did not learn of it until a month later, the weak Hungarian government had on June 15 been induced by the Soviet government to sign an agreement (under Article 12 of the armistice) whereby Hungary promised payment of 200 million dollars of reparations in goods and services over the next six years. This was a moderate fine. But it was topped by the Red Army's direct seizures of capital equipment and stocks, as "war booty," and its requisitions of food and other supplies. Furthermore the Yugoslav and Czechoslovak peoples whom the Hungarians had also maltreated were demanding reparations—another 100 million.

[5] These were only two of the leading features of comprehensive plans of reorganization —drawn up by General Key, American representative on the Commission, and Arthur Schoenfeld, the American political representative in Hungary—which guided American representations in Moscow and at the Potsdam conference.

General Voroshilov, the Soviet Chairman of the Control Commission, informed his two colleagues of substantial changes in procedure, which his government was going to introduce.[6] These—and the similar changes defined in notices sent by the Soviet members of the Control Commissions in Romania and Bulgaria[7]—could be of real value and enable the Western governments to have effective influence. But they were ambiguous in some main details. Our representatives in Hungary had been of the opinion that unless they were clarified and enlarged, the will of the Soviet member would continue to dominate. The proposed changes would not in themselves clear the way for free political institutions in Hungary, or assure their survival.

In Romania a coalition government headed by a well-worn politician, Petro Groza, had been imposed by Moscow. It included only left political parties, and excluded several conservative ones that had substantial popular support. Bribes were being offered for the conservatives' cooperation. The king was being cosseted by the Soviet government, awarded high decorations and promised equipment for a large army— though secretly he was pleading with the American and British governments to help him get rid of the Groza administration. When the Americans and British criticized this contrived regime the Soviet government defended it as democratic and representative.

What could be done against the will of Moscow? There were a million Soviet troops in the country, with the avowed purpose of supervising the armistice agreement. The Romanians were being compelled to provide them with food, shelter, and other supplies. Trains were carrying off industrial equipment, as war booty or reparations. The Russians were acquiring control of many Romanian enterprises transformed into state monopolies. They were demanding the shares that the Germans had owned in Romanian banks and oil companies.

[6] Among them were these provisions: 1) that the Soviet President (or Vice-President) would convoke meetings at least once every ten days; 2) that "Directives of the Allied Control Commission on questions of principle were to be issued to the Hungarian authorities by the President or Vice-President . . . after agreement on these directives with the English and American representatives"; 3) that the latter two representatives and their aides were to be allowed to participate in all staff conferences and commissions; and 4) that they were to be permitted, after advance notice, to travel freely in the country. Potsdam Papers, Document 796.

[7] One main difference between the procedure proposed for the Control Commissions in Bulgaria and Romania and that intended for Hungary is of interest. In the letter sent to the American and British members of the Commission in Hungary the language used could be taken to mean that their assent would be needed for decisions on policy; but the notice sent to the Western members of the Commissions in the other two countries said that the Soviet President was to issue directives after preliminary *discussion* with them.

The Soviet government had an actual need for these requisitions of Romanian supplies and resources. But its combined impositions would lead to the destruction of private industry throughout the country and the impoverishment of the wealthier groups—many of whom had been Nazi supporters and sympathizers. Thereupon the elements that were attached to Moscow would the more easily gain control. And since Romania would not be able to enter into trade or financial relations with Western business interests or governments, it would be dependent on the Soviet Union.

While these conditions were being brought about, the American and British members of the Control Commission were not being consulted about interpretations placed on the armistice agreement or the measures taken to compel compliance with Soviet demands. Most aggravating was the refusal of the Soviet member of the Control Commission, General Susaikov, to give them any information on the arrival, location, or length of stay of the Russian troops in Romania, even though they were being housed and fed by the Romanian government.[8] But, as in regard to Hungary, the American and British members of the Control Commission had been informed, a few days before the Potsdam conference began, that the future procedure would be more to their satisfaction. The American member advised the State Department that perhaps, but only perhaps, he would henceforth have a chance to compel discussion of offending policies.

In Bulgaria, Communist control was being imposed by similar methods. The American and British members of the Control Commission in that country had not even been able to find out what was being done in their name. The American and British political representatives in the country had also been ignored. Loud and angry, almost to the verge of hysteria, were their daily reports to Washington concerning repression and brutality by Communist elements while the Soviet

---

[8] The Romanian government that had negotiated the armistice agreement had tried at the time (September 1944) to secure a definite stipulation that Russian troops would leave Romania after the end of the war with Germany. But it was told that this was unnecessary since, as Molotov expressed it, "What the Romanians wanted was implicit in the whole Convention." The Romanians did manage, however, to have it recorded in the minutes of negotiations that it was "unnecessary to add to the proposed articles," because it was "a matter of course" that the Soviet armies would "leave Romanian soil at the end of hostilities."

At the time Harriman had predicted to Washington that the armistice arrangements would mean that the Soviet High Command would obtain unlimited control of the economic life of the country and police power throughout the land—at least during the armistice period.

mentors watched passively. Thus they had scrutinized with scathing mistrust the Soviet notice of changes to be effected in the procedures of the Commission. They were sure that the changes had been conceived only to blunt Western complaints at Potsdam and to fool the American and British governments into acceptance of the existing regime.

In short, the American effort before Potsdam to bring about drastic reforms in the operative methods of the Control Commissions, and to head these three satellites toward representative democracy, had failed. But the Americans could at least refuse to condone what was being done by denying recognition to the regimes that had imposed themselves under the shield of the Red Army.

The British government, while viewing the scene in these countries of eastern Europe in much the same way as the American, did not have faith in the effectiveness of our policies. Would the mere refusal of recognition prevent the extension of Communist control? It did not think so. Why not then grant the desired recognition and go ahead as fast as possible to conclude peace treaties with these former satellites? By so doing, the rule of the Control Commissions would be ended and the withdrawal of Soviet forces hastened.

But American officials, both in the local capitals and in Washington, had not been persuaded. It was their belief that if the regimes in power were recognized, all resistance to Communist control would soon fade away. They had girded themselves to argue in the conference at Potsdam for basic reforms in the constitution of all three Control Commissions, and basic reorganizations of all three governments. They had in mind a program similar to that for Poland.

The British Foreign Office had let the State Department know it would "come along behind us" in our efforts to win Soviet acceptance of this program—but with a candid statement of disbelief in its success. There was little reason to think that Stalin would agree to it; and no reason to think that he would subject Soviet policies and actions toward these satellite countries to the approval of the United States and Great Britain. Any attainable measure of reorganization of the Control Commissions, the British forecast, would be ineffective. And anyway, when had these peoples ever of themselves gone in for representative democracy? So, with a shrug, the Foreign Office had given the State Department to understand that when it went aground, the British group at Potsdam might again advocate the other course.

[193]

Passing notice ought to be taken of another cause of American displeasure over Soviet policies in these countries. American financial interests in them were being dispossessed, and the chance of Americans to carry on trade with them was being foreclosed.

In Romania and Hungary the Soviet masters had trundled away capital equipment (especially oil refinery and transport equipment) owned in whole or in part by Americans (or British or French or Belgians). They had maintained that they could properly do so because the equipment had been used to serve Nazi Germany, and because much of the existing plant to which the Western investors claimed ownership had been built by the Germans. They had similarly defended their demands upon American (or British or French or Belgian) owned companies to provide reparations for Russia out of current production. The American government had protested these practices as rough depredations of American property. It urged that removals of capital equipment belonging to Americans cease, that the equipment already taken away be returned, and that the enterprises be relieved of the obligation to make current deliveries.

In the trade field American objections were directed against the secret agreements that the Soviet government had signed with the obedient governments of Romania and Bulgaria. These governments had ceded to the Soviet Union command over the economies of their nations. Russia would get most of their exports and would control their production of raw materials. Through joint government monopolies, in which the Soviet government was to have a half or greater share, the Russians would run the most important branches of industry: oil, lumber, metals, water and rail transportation. These newly formed monopolies were absorbing properties that had been wholly or partly owned, before the war, by Americans, British, French, and Belgians.

Such was the riddled ground onto which the conference entered when our efforts in behalf of Italy became linked with Soviet efforts in behalf of the governments of these three smaller satellites.

The contest centered on two texts, the one submitted by the Americans regarding Italy, the other by the Russians regarding the satellite states. In order to secure Soviet assent to the adoption of a benign policy toward Italy, Truman and Byrnes were willing to agree that a start be made on the preparation of peace treaties for the satellites. They were also ready to assent to easing the controlling armistice terms. But Stalin and Molotov wanted more. The premium they asked was diplomatic recognition of the existing governments. That the Americans were not then willing to pay. At the end of the Fifth Plenary Session of the Heads of Government on July 21, after a traveling circular argument, it was agreed to pass by the question. In effect this meant that the determination of future events in Italy fell to the West, and in the other satellites to the Soviet Union. Both were to be a continuing subject of mutual accusations.

Similarly, the American effort at Potsdam to win consent for the admission of Italy into the United Nations was matched by a Soviet effort to secure advantage for the satellites.

The American government had wished to announce—without waiting for the conference at Potsdam—that it would favor the admission of Italy into the United Nations. On July 15, the better to qualify, the Italian government had declared war on Japan, former companion in the Tri-Partite Pact. The State Department had hastened to tell the British Foreign Office that it would "accordingly announce on July 17th (Tuesday) the intention of the United States Government to support officially Italy's admission into the World Security Organization," and that it hoped the British government would "feel able to support this decision." On that day, the opening day of the conference, the British Embassy in Washington left at the State Department (and a Foreign Office official gave to a State Department member of the American delegation at Potsdam) an aggrieved acknowledgement. Such short notice of American intention, and on a more or less take-it-or-leave-it basis, was deemed inconsiderate. The proposed action was thought to overlook the close connection between Italy's admission into the World Security Organization and the question of making a peace treaty with Italy. Could the action not be suspended, the Foreign Office asked, until the question could be discussed at Potsdam?[9] The Secretary of State heeded the protest. He decided to submit the statement in mind to his allied associates at Potsdam, and to invite the Soviet government to join in it.

Byrnes did so in a proposal that began, "The Three Heads of Government will support the entry of Italy into the United Nations."[10] Eden asked whether they ought not add the phrase "on the conclusion of peace." Molotov asked whether the admission of Italy should not be conditioned also on its payment of reparations. And in subsequent

[9] Potsdam Papers, Documents 243 and 722.
[10] *Ibid.*, Document 727.

sessions of the Foreign Ministers he urged that the other satellite states, which had since become co-belligerents, be included. Had they not done more to win the war than neutrals like Switzerland or Portugal, which were to be admitted, or than Italy, which was to be admitted after the conclusion of peace? By this test, perhaps, they qualified equally. But by another they did not. Byrnes and Eden firmly maintained that there was a genuine difference that debarred the other satellites. To grant them admission would be to recognize their existing governments, which were not, as the Italian government was, representative of political opinion in their countries. They bluntly asserted that for this reason the American and British governments would not recognize them, make peace with them, or support their admission into the United Nations. This hot argument between the Foreign Ministers, ignited at their session of July 24, died down when Molotov asked that the question be referred to the Big Three, for they were "more reasonable people than we" and would "find a way out."

Thereupon the Big Three took over the question, discussing it later that same day. Stalin spoke like a patient man provoked. By treating the other satellites like "leprous states" the Western nations were discrediting the Soviet Union. He contradicted Truman's and Churchill's criticisms of their governments, asserting that they were as democratic as the Italian and closer to the people, and as willing to grant access to American and British agents as Italy was to admit Russian agents.

Churchill rather than Truman bore the brunt of Stalin's pressure. When the Prime Minister averred that freedom had re-emerged in Italy while in the satellites the British representatives were "penned" within an iron fence, Stalin said without raising his voice: "all fairy tales." Truman was inclined to end the altercation by acceding to a proposal made by Molotov: that each of the three governments be obligated to consider soon, for itself, the resumption of diplomatic relations. But Churchill would have none of it. He thought that if this and nothing more were said, the very real differences between the West and the Soviet Union would be concealed, and the world would receive a false impression of the British and American attitudes. Stalin argued that it was inconsistent to agree, as the three of them had by then, to start work on peace treaties with these countries, but to refuse them recognition. Not so, said Churchill; the treaties might be put in shape, but the British government would not conclude them except with governments resting on popular consent, meriting recognition.

So the talk spun on, more and more confusingly. No one would want now to follow its wearisome turns.[11]

The conference was lurching toward its close, with the Western allies and the Russians still frontally separated on two issues of deeper import for Europe than that of the satellites: what Poland's western frontiers were to be; and what reparations were to be exacted from Germany, and under what system. In a private talk with Molotov on the afternoon of July 30, Byrnes came forward with what was called a "package proposal," about which more will soon be told. In it there was included, as one of its three elements, a new text concerning the course to be pursued toward Italy and the smaller satellites. There evolved, after much more wasted debate over clauses and phrases, an approved version that was included in the Protocol.

What this seemed to say in its involved parts was (1) that the three conferring allies favored the preparation of a peace treaty for Italy, and its admission into the United Nations after the treaty was concluded; (2) that the Council of Foreign Ministers should also prepare peace treaties for the other satellites, but they would not conclude them with Bulgaria, Hungary, and Romania until these countries had "recognized democratic governments." Support for their applications for membership in the United Nations would follow. But others may find fault with this extraction of the text's meaning.[12]

As an item of historical bookkeeping, if for no other good reason, it should be noted that the Americans countered the Russian efforts to win recognition for the existing governments in the smaller satellites by requests that the Soviet Union honor an earlier promise to join in transforming those governments.

This promise, the American authorities thought, had been made at

[11] Byrnes retraced them for the Heads of State at one of their later plenary sessions, on July 28. First, the American government had asked support for the admission of Italy into the United Nations. Second, the British had asked the resolution to be extended to include all neutrals in the war except Spain; we had agreed. Third, the Soviet government had insisted on a provision about the admission of the other satellites—different, however, from the one on Italy; we had agreed but the British had not. Fourth, we had been asked to change the language about Italy to conform to that about the other satellites; again we had agreed but the British had not. "Unfortunately, we find that when we agree with the Soviets, the British disagree, and when we agree with the British, the Soviets disagree." Potsdam Papers, Cohen Notes.

[12] Let the reader try for himself. The text is Section IX, entitled "Conclusion of Peace Treaties and Admission to the United Nations Organization," in the Protocol, printed in Supplementary Note 7.

Yalta, on acceptance of the Declaration on Liberated Europe. In the proclaimed creed, Stalin had joined Roosevelt and Churchill in an avowal that the policies of the three allied governments would be concerted in an effort to help both liberated countries and satellites to solve their problems by democratic means, and to aid them in steps toward the formation, after free elections, of governments responsive to popular will; and the three had agreed to consult when necessary in discharging these joint obligations.[13]

The Soviet government had brushed by this hedge of phrases as it went on its way to lordship over the smaller satellites. Those in the State Department who had believed in the covenant watched with deep indignation. They had tutored Truman in the growing record of disrespect for both the terms and the concepts of this memorial of Roosevelt's hopeful purpose.

Before the proposal that the Americans submitted at Potsdam was formally discussed, Stalin reproached Churchill for supporting what was in substance a demand for a change in government in Romania and Bulgaria.[14] After all, he said, he was allowing the British government to manage the affairs of Greece without meddling. This was a not-so-oblique way of reminding the Prime Minister that in October 1944, in the course of a long night of talk in Moscow, the two of them had marked out spheres of responsibility in southeastern Europe during the war, whereby Romania and Bulgaria had been assigned to the Soviet Union, Greece to Britain. Churchill sought to re-locate the issue in broader and later geographic and historical perspective. He called the roll of the capitals east of a line from the North Cape to Albania which were in Russian hands. Did that not look as though Russia were rolling on westward? Stalin denied any such intention, saying that on the contrary he was bringing back his troops from the west as fast as railway cars could be found to carry them.

In subsequent discussions between the Foreign Ministers, Molotov led a counter-offensive directed against Greece. In that country, he averred, terrorism ruled, not law, democratic elements were being oppressed, and Albania and Bulgaria threatened. Why not a recommendation to act at once to establish a genuinely democratic government in Greece? When Eden denied the statements as "a complete travesty of the facts," pointing out that all the world could go to Greece and see

---

[13] The text of the Declaration is in U.S. Dept. of State, *The Conferences at Malta and Yalta*, pages 977-78.
[14] *Triumph and Tragedy*, pages 636-37.

what was going on, and that the Greek government had invited others to observe the coming elections, the Soviet Foreign Minister merely expanded his accusations to include Italy.

Byrnes tried to reconcile their differences. With Eden's warm approval he proposed that the three agree to join in supervising elections in all five of the countries they had been discussing—in Italy and Greece, as well as in Romania, Bulgaria, and Hungary. At Truman's wish, the provision for "supervising" the elections was softened to "observation," but even then Stalin would not agree to it. He stood firm on the ground that such interference in the affairs of the satellites was not called for, and would be offensive.

So all that came out of the Potsdam discussions about the former satellite states was an expression of mutual acceptance of the revised ways of conducting the business of the Control Commissions in the three smaller satellites in southeastern Europe.[15] These made no difference in the long run. The Western governments failed to arrest the gradual extension of rigorous control over these states by Communist supporters, working in concert with the Soviet government. Old injustices and oppressions were being replaced by new ones. The peasants and workers would survive, and in some ways have a better life than during former days of party strife and minority domination. But individual freedom and national independence were lost.

[15] See text of Protocol, Supplementary Note 7.

26. Spain

CONCURRENTLY with this American effort to release Italy from restraints and the Soviet effort to obtain recognition for the new order in the eastern satellites, the proponents were also at odds over what to do about Spain. That they should have come to differ over this question was perhaps a clearer signal than any other that their mutual animosity was defacing their common experience.

Hitler's Germany was suffering in ruins. Mussolini's Italy was repudiating its past. But Franco, who had been helped by them to control Spain, and had sided with them as long as he had found it prudent to do so, remained in power. His was an avowed dictatorship, relying on the army, the police, and one political party to enforce his will. How could tolerance for the Franco government be justified while the western allies were assailing other governments for suppressing the popular will? But how could the regime in Spain be displaced without grave risk of another agonizing civil war and of opening the way for Communists—with cruel and perilous consequences? This was the dilemma that the British and American governments faced at Potsdam when they were called on by Stalin to condemn and repudiate the Franco government.

Stalin directed attention to the situation at the first session of the conference. He explained his interest on the score that the Franco regime had not originated in Spain but had been imported and forced on the Spanish people by Germany and Italy. He spoke of it as a danger to the United Nations. For these reasons would they not be doing well to create conditions that would enable the Spanish people to have the government they wanted? If so, why should Churchill and Truman not join him in a recommendation to the members of the United Nations to break off all relations with the government of Franco, and to enable the democratic forces in Spain to establish a satisfactory regime?[1]

But both drew back. Churchill expressed distaste for the Franco government. As reported in the minutes, "He had been misrepresented as having been friendly to this gentleman. All he had said was that there was more to Spanish policy than drawing rude cartoons of Franco." He recalled that when Franco had proposed to him that he organize the western states against "that terrible country, Russia," he had "sent him

[1] The proposal submitted by the Soviet Delegation on July 19 is in Potsdam Papers, Document 1177.

a chilly reply." But Churchill thought that if they took the step proposed by Stalin it would so arouse the proud and touchy Spanish people, who were now deserting Franco, that they would come to his support. The breaking of relations was not a satisfactory process. He was ready to take every measure by all proper diplomatic means to speed the departing guest. But he was not ready to use force, as might be necessary if this reproof was disregarded; and he would deplore anything that would lead Spain into another civil war. In short, the British would be unwilling to intervene actively, as a government, in the Spanish affair at this juncture. Forces there were working for a change for the better.

Truman spoke in a similar vein. He had no love for Franco but he had no wish to have any part in starting another civil war in Spain. The Spanish people must be left to find another government for themselves.

Stalin questioned all the cautionary reasoning. He thought Franco was gaining, not losing, strength. He believed that the existence of his regime, nurtured by the Axis, was a matter of international, not merely Spanish, interest. He denied that his proposal would mean either civil war or military intervention. But if the Prime Minister and the President did not want to be severe, if they were not willing to break relations, were they content that everything just be allowed to go on in Spain unchanged? Or was there some more flexible means of letting the Spanish people know that the three governments were in sympathy with them and not with Franco? Silence would be considered approval of the dictator.

Churchill gave other reasons for going slow and being tolerant. Britain had an old and substantial trade with Spain: unless he was sure that a move would bring about the desired result he did not want to risk the loss. Furthermore, while Spain had molested Russia during the war, having had the audacity to send a Spanish division to the eastern front, it had refrained from taking action against Britain when this could have been disastrous.

Stalin continued to urge that they must say something to indicate that the aspirations of the Spanish people were just, and he proposed that the Foreign Ministers try to devise a milder measure than his first suggestion. Truman said he was willing to have them do so. But Churchill was not. He asserted that as a matter of principle he was against interfering in the internal affairs of other countries, and as a matter of policy he thought it dangerous—and in this instance likely to rivet Franco in his place. Neither Stalin's refutations nor Truman's inclination budged him—either at this session or at the later ones when talk returned to the subject. In his subsequent account of the Potsdam conference Churchill accorded the discussion of Spain only a few lines and referred to his part most tersely: "I resisted [Stalin's] suggestion and eventually the subject was dismissed."[2]

But Byrnes, in connection with his attempt to win Soviet approval for the admission of Italy into the United Nations, proposed to the other Foreign Ministers that the conference go on record that its participants "will not support the entry of Spain into the UNO, so long as Spain is under the control of the present regime in that country."[3] Eden thought the idea good. He suggested that if they recommended the admission of all other neutral governments the reference to Spain would be more pointed. It was so agreed, and written into the Protocol as follows:

"The three Governments, so far as they are concerned, will support applications for membership from those States which have remained neutral during the war . . .

"The three Governments feel bound, however to make it clear that they for their part would not favor any application for membership put forward by the present Spanish Government, which, having been founded with the support of the Axis powers, does not, in view of its origins, its nature, its record and its close association with the aggressor states, possess the qualifications necessary to justify such membership."

This borrowed some of Stalin's words without giving them the decisive effect on action he had sought. By then all proposals for joint action to down dictators or up democracies encountered the question: whose cause or position would be served, that of the West or the Soviet Union?

2 *Triumph and Tragedy,* page 654.
3 Potsdam Papers, Document 730.

27. Poland: The Consultations before Potsdam

IF THE affairs of any one European country ruled the conference at Potsdam, it was those of Poland. The problem of its frontiers was in itself enough to dismay any group of diplomats who knew history. On the east they would limit the Soviet Union, on the west, Germany. The Soviet Union had been promised the area that had been the eastern part of Poland before the war; how much of Germany was to be ceded to Poland as compensation? The settlement might end the centuries-old struggle between Russians, Poles, and Germans over their place in this heartland of Europe, or might lead to its continuation. But was there any that all three would in time accept as permanent—since they never had before?

Whether Poland emerged as a genuinely free and independent state would affect the balance of control in central Europe, maybe in all Europe, maybe in all the world. The development of its economic and social life would infringe on that of all nearby countries. The treatment of the Germans who had lived in areas that might become part of the new Poland would determine how many became refugees to the west. Not least significant, the Poles have a long memory and the Western peoples an abiding emotional interest in their fate. The United States had been midwife at the rebirth of Poland in 1919, and Britain, linked to it by a treaty of alliance, had gone to war in its defense.

The accord reached between Stalin and Hopkins at Moscow, opening the way for carrying into effect the Polish provisions of the Yalta Agreement, had been acted on quickly.

In contrast to its previous caution, the American government had played an alert and vigorous part in the subsequent consultations. The British government had been more on guard, lest it become responsible, or at least be deemed responsible, for an outcome that would be disliked not only by most of the Poles but by most of the British people. Churchill, in his comment to Truman about the Stalin-Hopkins accord, had said only that he agreed that Hopkins had obtained the best solution to be hoped for in the circumstances. This reserve had tinged the instruction sent by the Foreign Office to Clark Kerr, the British member of the Commission of Three. He was told not to obligate the British government, before the talks among the Poles themselves began, to any formula regarding the proportion of key positions to be given to groups *not* in the Warsaw government. He was reminded that it was essential that any accord be acceptable to British public opinion and Parliament; and that the British government should not expose itself to the charge of having followed the Munich pattern by imposing on an unwilling people a settlement agreed upon in advance among the great powers.

"We must," this instruction had affirmed, "above all else, maintain the position that the role of the Commission is to act as mediators only, assisting the Poles to reach among themselves a settlement which can then be endorsed and approved by the Poles. No doubt the settlement will inevitably be 'based upon' the present Warsaw government. But so far as public appearances are concerned, it is one thing for the Poles themselves to reach the conclusion that this is the logical outcome, and quite another for them to be told before they begin their discussions that this is what they must accept."

Behind this wariness was perhaps the same judgment of the Stalin-Hopkins accord as that recorded in the reminiscent comment of General Anders, Commander of the Polish Forces: "What did all this mean? . . . It was the total surrender of even the semblance of political independence."[1]

Within a week the Commission of Three had issued invitations to the list of Poles chosen to come to Moscow to consult.[2] They were expected in three separate groups, one consisting of members of the existing Provisional Government in Warsaw, the other two of Polish political leaders who were not affiliated with the government, some of whom were living in Poland and others abroad. Harriman and Clark Kerr had agreed with Molotov that the Commission might meet first with the representatives of the government. It was left to the three Polish groups to make arrangements for meeting with each other.

The Soviet government had seen to it that the members of the Provisional Government in Warsaw got to Moscow. It had gone to pains to make plain its favor and friendship. When President Bierut and his colleagues arrived at the Moscow airport on June 13, they were met not only by Molotov and Vishinski but also by Bulganin (the Secretary of the Presidium of the Supreme Soviet), the Commandant of

[1] Anders, *An Army in Exile,* page 274.
[2] They were representatives of the Polish Provisional Government in Warsaw (B. Bierut, E. Osubka-Morawski, W. Kowalski, and W. Gomulka); democratic leaders who were in Poland (W. Witos, Z. Zulawski, S. Kutrezeba, A. Krzyanowski, and H. Kolodziejski); and democratic leaders from abroad (S. Mikolajczyk, J. Stanczyk and J. Zakowski).

Moscow, and other Soviet officials. The next day the Moscow papers reported their arrival on the first page, and published pictures of the delegates reviewing the guard of honor at the airport. No public notice whatever had been taken of the arrival or presence of the two other groups.

Among those not in the Warsaw government who had been invited to come from Poland to Moscow, the most esteemed political figure, Wincenty Witos, head of the Peasant Party, had declined. He was not well enough to come, he had explained, and this may well have been true.[3] His refusal was one more reason why the leader of the group that was to come from London, the former Prime Minister of the Government-in-Exile, Mikolajczyk, had wavered about going. He was outraged at the detainment of the leaders of the Polish underground who had served under his orders, and he foresaw that he would be urged to consent to a disliked deal. Then Witos' refusal to take part in the consultations and share responsibility for the outcome seemed to him to make his position impossible—in the involved and sensitive web of Polish politics.[4]

His reluctance to leave for Moscow unless assured in various ways had worried Harriman, the American member of the Commission, who feared that without Mikolajczyk's personal effort and thawing influence the Polish groups would not agree. Stalin's remark that Mikolajczyk "has missed the bus every time and will continue to do so" rang in his memory. He got the State Department to instruct the American Embassy in London to do whatever it could to get Mikolajczyk to change

[3] Witos had been Prime Minister of Poland three times. In 1939 he had been wounded by a German projectile, and then taken by the Germans into a Gestapo prison near Potsdam. Becoming dangerously ill there, he had been allowed to return home under guard, had managed to escape and join the underground. The Russians had treated him rudely, and he was living in poverty when routed out by the Warsaw authorities, who thought he might bring them helpful support. They had compelled him to make a five-or-six-day automobile trip through various provinces and to Warsaw. Members of the Warsaw branch of the Peasant Party, which was under the control of the Provisional Government, had urged him to make appearances and statements; but he had refused to do so and had been sent back to his home.

[4] Mikolajczyk had received a secret report from Witos some weeks previously (probably before the Hopkins-Stalin accord) telling him that Witos had been consulted by the Russians and had been offered the Prime Ministership of a reorganized Polish government and six portfolios for his followers; Witos had answered that the proposal must be made through the Moscow Commission, that he would have to consult his party, and that a place in the government must be reserved for Mikolajczyk. Mikolajczyk felt that he could not ignore such a firm answer by Witos, and that he could not take part in the consultations in Moscow without some contact with Witos or other representatives of the Peasant Party in Poland. This account of his thoughts is based on reports of Mikolajczyk's talks with the Foreign Office, passed on to the British Embassy in Moscow, and thence to Harriman.

his mind. And Harriman, along with Clark Kerr, secured from Molotov a second bid for Witos, along with a promise of special medical care and comfort during his trip and sojourn. Then, after Witos had again said he could not come, he solicited an invitation to Kiernik, the Vice-President of the Peasant Party.

Mikolajczyk's qualms had been overcome. Churchill, despite his own morose view of the prospect, persuaded him to go, thinking that if he stayed away either the outcome of the consultation would be even worse than otherwise, or no accord would be reached—whereupon the associates in Communism would govern Poland by themselves. The Prime Minister appealed to Mikolajczyk on the basis of his duty as a patriotic Pole to use this last chance to play a part in the determination of who would govern Poland; and assured him that he could count on the support and influence of the British and Americans. According to Mikolajczyk, the Prime Minister concluded by saying, "If you back out now, I will wash my hands of the whole Polish case."[5]

On June 15, just before the talks with the Poles began, Molotov had told Harriman and Clark Kerr that he thought the Commission of Three must make its own point of view clear to the Poles. Clark Kerr had demurred, saying that he thought all three of them should be very careful; that Molotov would not have forgotten an event that occurred in Munich a few years ago, when a settlement was imposed on a people against its will; that the Commission must not do anything like that. Molotov had pounced. Why was the British Ambassador reminding him about Munich? "Neither the Americans nor the Russians were there and Chamberlain is dead." Clark Kerr had calmly explained that his government was opposed to having the Commission do anything that could be regarded as a dictated settlement. He was sure they could rely on the Poles themselves to build a new government on the basis of the old one; and he believed it best that they should bear

[5] Mikolajczyk, *The Pattern of Soviet Domination*, pages 134-35. In this book Mikolajczyk purports to give actual verbatim extracts of his talks with Churchill. Among other statements he attributes to the Prime Minister is a remark that the American and British governments were then in a better position to deal with Stalin than before, because Stalin wanted to get into the war against Japan; and he quotes Churchill as saying: "That's why he—and not us—asked for the meeting of the Big Three, which will be held in Berlin in July. We are in a good position there. We don't care if he comes into the war against the Japanese or not. We don't need him now."

The talks were in English. No one present was recording the actual words spoken. Presumably Mikolajczyk's later published accounts of these talks are based on memos written by him, or perhaps by someone accompanying him, soon after the talks, rather than merely on later recall.

the onus of doing so. Harriman leaned the same way as Clark Kerr, but not so far. He thought his British colleague was being hindered by his instructions from London, and compelled to raise issues against his own best judgment. Molotov posed as a tolerant negotiator. Since all three members of the Commission, he said, agreed to abide by the principle of the Yalta accord (whereby the Warsaw government was to be the "basis" or "nucleus" of the new), he would not insist on bringing that accord to the fore at the first meeting of the Poles. There is no risk in surmising that he knew there was no need for him to do so.

With the arrival of the Poles a continuous series of meshed-in talks had begun. The three groups conversed with one another, and the Commission had long sessions with each group separately and then all together. The individual members of the Commission talked with each and all. Without devoting scores of pages, it would not be possible to trace out the twisted filaments of these related and prolonged discussions. I shall not do more than summarize the main views and wishes of the protagonists.

Bierut, a Communist and President of the Warsaw government, and Osubka-Morawski, a Socialist and Prime Minister of the Warsaw government, both avowed that their government, and theirs alone, had the allegiance of the Polish people. But they assured Harriman and Clark Kerr that in order to receive American and British moral and economic aid they were ready to admit individuals from outside into the governing circle.

The other groups maintained that this was untrue; that the Warsaw government was mistrusted by all classes—peasants, workers, and intellectuals. They were confident that the four Polish democratic parties other than the Communist party (the Peasant, Socialist, Christian Labor, and National Democratic parties) had far greater support; and that the new government would not have a popular basis unless it gave these parties places proportionate to their strength. But they recognized it was essential that Polish policy be oriented toward the Soviet Union. Hence they were willing to compromise to attain at least some semblance of Polish independence. Almost all of them hoped that Mikolajczyk would be made Prime Minister. Some of them said they would be satisfied if the groups not now within the government were given a forty percent representation; others thought they ought to be given more, and even seemed to believe there was a chance they might obtain it.

The members of the Commission of Three had made it clear that all of their governments understood that the existing Warsaw regime was to have the main part in the new government. Otherwise as far as can be learned from the open record, they acted as mediators, or perhaps tranquilizers. There is no way of knowing, however, to what extent Molotov may have secretly checked any impulse of the Warsaw Poles to accord the others a real share of authority.

On the night of the 21st the several groups assembled informed the Commission that they had reached an agreement. Bierut read a statement setting forth its main points, and on that night and the next the Commission discussed these with the Poles.[6] While some were quite clear and complete, others were not. The most definite element was the selection of the individuals to be introduced into the government, and the distribution of offices. The members of the Warsaw government who were in the three most influential posts were to retain them: Bierut was to remain as President of the National Council, Osubka-Morawski as Prime Minister, and Gomulka as First Deputy Prime Minister. But out of the total of twenty Cabinet posts, six were to be given to independent Poles. These included Mikolajczyk, who was to become a Second Deputy Prime Minister as well as Minister of Agriculture, and Kiernik of the Peasant Party, who was to become Minister of Public Administration. Two of the other influential outsiders, Witos and Grabski, were to become members of the Presidium of the Polish National Council.[7] This was to be made more representative by the inclusion of other prominent Poles.

To this allocation of offices to named persons, there may have been added a vague promise, a slip of a promise, that in the ultimate outcome men who had once been or still were associated with the Peasant Party and the Socialist Party would fare as well as those connected with the Workers Party (Communist).[8]

[6] As far as I have been able to find out, this statement has not been published and I have not seen a copy of it. In the course of the discussion Bierut remarked that it had been hastily prepared, and though it had been accepted in principle, he thought it ought to be carefully revised. At the end of the meeting all agreed that, after review, it should be published as a communiqué of the Commission.

[7] The Polish National Council was the supreme legislative organ in Poland, and was to function during the period before the election of a regularly constituted parliament. It had been conceived that it would select the President, who in turn was supposed to choose the other members of the government. A small, carefully chosen Presidium exercised the power of the Council in the intervals between its meetings, and had dominating influence over it.

[8] On this point the report that Harriman sent to Washington (June 21) reads as follows: "There are some additional understandings on which agreement has been reached in principle only, such as that the National Council shall be reorganized to extend fair repre-

There were also allusions to various other principles that were to be observed in the further stages of reorganization, and to the policies that the resultant government should be obligated to carry out. The historian must screen these for himself, for they are buried under the gravel of unsystematic and at moments incoherent talk—poorly recorded. Summing them up negatively, it may be said that no group explicitly denied: that the new government was to proceed as swiftly as practicable to hold elections on the basis of universal suffrage; that all democratic parties would be allowed to participate in these elections without hindrance; that the elections were to be fair and with a secret ballot; that all groups were to have freedom of assembly before the elections; or that there was to be an amnesty for most, if not all, persons accused of political offenses within Poland.

On one matter that was introduced into the discussions on these two nights (June 21 and 22) all the Poles were of the same mind. Members of all three groups spoke in sponsorship of the most extensive territorial claims.

Mikolajczyk had taken the lead. He said he understood that by joining in this accord and entering in the government, members gained the right to give expression in the name of the Polish nation to the

---

sentation of the different parties represented in the government and that the men for the under-ministerial posts shall be selected in the same proportion as the distribution of the ministerial posts.

"The fundamental basis of the reorganized government is that the Workers Party, the Peasant Party and the Socialist Party shall each have six portfolios, and two are to be held by other democratic parties."

But study of the records of the discussions on the nights of the 21st and 22nd, and of the subsequent talks with the various groups of Poles, leaves me uncertain whether the Warsaw government group actually committed itself to any such future rearrangement of offices.

Mikolajczyk, pages 140-43, gives the text of what he terms an "internal agreement" by which the Provisional Government "might" be guided until the elections. While not explicitly saying so, he conveys the impression that the three Polish groups, including that representing the government at Warsaw, approved it. But there is no reference to any such detailed written accord in the American minutes of discussion with the Commission.

The text published by Mikolajczyk stipulates that the Peasant Party was to have a one-third share in all branches of the government, but makes no similar provision for the Socialist Party. This and other features suggest that the "internal agreement" may have been all or part of a proposal made by Mikolajczyk and some of his associates, rather than a confirmed accord among all the Poles.

At the end of his comments on the general accord announced on the night of the 21st, Mikolajczyk, according to the minutes, asked Bierut to confirm their understanding on the principle of proportional representation of the parties in the widening of the National Council. Bierut's answer was inconclusive, if not evasive; he merely repeated that it had been decided to expand the National Council by including representatives of political elements who wished for a new democratic Poland.

demand that the western boundaries envisioned at the Yalta Conference be recognized by the great powers. He asked Bierut to confirm this. Bierut did so with gusto. From his reference to the recognition in principle at Yalta of the need for extending Poland toward the west, Mikolajczyk progressed to the conclusion that the only just settlement would be one awarding Poland all the land extending to the Oder and Western Neisse rivers.

Clark Kerr, after reading the Yalta formula aloud, had pointed out that the final decision on the boundary question would have to await the peace conference. The Prime Minister of the new government, after recognition, would have every chance to press its claims. Molotov said that the Soviet government stood on the Yalta decision; it considered that Poland's wish to have all the lands extending to the line of the Oder and the Western Neisse was fully justified and well founded. Harriman remarked merely that he had nothing to add to the words of the Yalta decision. On the next day, when Gomulka, the Chairman of the Political Committee of the Warsaw government, asked him what the American government thought of Polish western boundary claims, particularly the inclusion of Stettin in Poland, Harriman said merely that they would have to be talked over by the three powers and settled at the peace conference.

Both he and Clark Kerr warned their governments to anticipate that at Potsdam they would be confronted by the same claims.

Having heard the report, and the exuberant avowals of all participants that they intended to cooperate for lasting unity, the members of the Commission had made their responses. Molotov seemed to Harriman to be elated over the outcome. Clark Kerr said at once that the British government would accept the agreement the Poles had reached, and when they formed the new government would swiftly accord it recognition. But then, and in later interviews with the Poles, he stressed that these promises were dependent ones—dependent, that is, on the assumption that the new government would be "properly formed" in accordance with the Yalta accord, and that it would hold elections of an impartial kind in which all democratic parties would have the same chance to strive for votes and office. Harriman tried hard to get definite confirmation that the Warsaw government group was obligated to carry out not only the one feature of the accord that was plainly recorded (that providing for the introduction of named persons into the government) but also the other principles that had been fused vaguely into the description of the accord. But all he could extract from Bierut was, rather than a lucid pledge, a rambling puff of assurance: that, after this agreement, all would strive to achieve lasting unity and to hold free elections and continue the broadening of legislative organs that had already begun. Molotov tried to check Harriman's quiz of Bierut and his group, on the score that it was not fitting to inquire into the affairs of the Polish government. Thus upheld, Bierut became pert, ending Harriman's probing by saying he was sure the accord was firm and the Poles could settle these questions without allied interference.

At the end of the session with the Poles Harriman had said to them that if President Roosevelt were alive he would be very happy indeed over the agreement they had reached. But in the report he sent to Washington after this meeting (on the 22nd) he indicated that he knew that the accord was murky and frail. He told of Molotov's objections to his attempt to clarify the verbal understandings. This he took to be a clue that the Soviet government might resist our future efforts to assure free elections. The Poles who had come from Poland but were not in the government had emphasized to him, he added, that only if the American and British governments maintained a close watch could they hope for reasonable personal and political freedom.

After the three members of the Commission had approved the lean and awkwardly phrased communiqué about the results of the consultations, it was released, at midnight on the 22nd. All it did was to detail the contemplated changes in the composition of the Polish government. Nothing was said about any other features of the compact. Had the Poles or the three members of the Commission tried to reduce them to writing it is probable that the accord would have gone up in smoke.

Because Roosevelt had been lured by Stalin to agree to the Yalta formula—by the assurance that the Provisional Government would hold elections within a few months—and because the later default on this assurance was so crucial, more ought to be told of the efforts of Harriman and Clark Kerr to get positive promises before the Poles left Moscow.

On June 26, at a press conference at the Polish Embassy in Moscow, Gomulka, First Deputy Prime Minister, was asked whether the expected elections in Poland would be run on the basis of a united democratic bloc (Communist style) or on an individual-party basis. He answered that this question would be settled by the parties themselves in the course of cooperation, and that each of the parties would be free to unite with others if any so wished. He was asked when these elections would be held. He said that was to be decided, taking into account primarily the return of Poles from abroad, of whom there were several million.[9] Mikolajczyk professed himself to be satisfied with these answers. But he made known his intention to do what he could to have the elections held soon, for he was not eager to have all the Poles who had taken Soviet nationality come back into Poland and vote Communist.

On the evening of that day, Clark Kerr, in a final talk with Bierut, returned to the subject. Since the British government attached great importance to the pledge about elections, would he not see to it that in one way or another all doubt was dissipated? Bierut squirmed. He said that although the Provisional Government fully intended to hold elections, it should not appear that this was due to foreign pressure. He said he would probably reaffirm publicly that he himself, and the regime he headed, accepted the Yalta decision in its entirety—that is, including the election pledge. That was all he could be brought to say. Nor had Harriman managed to break through this barrage of virtue-tinted professions. "He could not be pinned down," Harriman informed Washington. In informing the State Department of his frustration, Harriman advised it to hold up recognition until it actually knew what the new government was to be.

All of the Polish leaders, even those who were in the existing Warsaw government, had been outspoken, it might almost be said profuse, in their profession of a longing for friendly relations with the West, above all with the United States. They competed in their presentation of the hope that Poland would receive from the United States relief and aid in its economic tasks.

Harriman had inferred that all the Poles were eager to have a loan from the United States. He advised the State Department to consider starting talks at once about a small credit that would enable Poland to buy some of the equipment it needed most for reconstruction. In this way, he thought, we might enhance our influence on the political scene

[9] It could be honestly argued that a short delay was justified if the elections were to express the preferences of all the Poles. At least two million Poles who had lived in Poland before 1939 were still abroad—in Germany, England, Italy, and the Soviet Union. Those in the Soviet Union, having come from the eastern sections that were being incorporated into the Soviet Union, had been treated as Soviet citizens, but they were being given the right to reacquire Polish nationality. A migration of Poles into German Pomerania was taking place. The western frontiers of Poland had not yet been defined.

in Poland, particularly in regard to carrying out truly free elections. He urged some other striking gesture, as for example sending to Poland several hundred American trucks that were in Germany, or bringing quick relief help through UNRRA and the Red Cross. Harriman was afraid that if the American government seemed to be taking its time about coming to the help of the country, this could lessen its influence. Bierut, he noted again, had affirmed his wish for close and friendly relations with the United States, and he added: "While I cannot predict to what extent the Russians will attempt to put a brake on Polish desires for open contact with the west, it is my feeling that Bierut is sincere in his statement."

The State Department had resolved to make friendliness plain by showing a ready will to help the new Poland. It authorized the recently appointed American Ambassador, Arthur Lane, to tell the Polish authorities that the American government would see to it that the contemplated UNRRA program of relief to Poland, a very substantial one, was carried out; that while it could not grant a loan at once, because of a legislative ban, it would look for ways by which Poland could pay for its needs by exports, especially of coal; that it would supply Poland with one thousand surplus army trucks; that it would be glad to negotiate a new trade treaty with Poland; and that it would welcome in the United States a mission of Polish technicians and economists to tell us of Polish wants and study our methods of production. These were to be our proofs of trust.[10]

The chief members of the Provisional Government for National Unity had flown back from Moscow to Warsaw on Russian transport planes on June 27. On the next day the membership of the government was announced. Fourteen of the twenty-one top posts were allotted to men associated with the existing Warsaw government. Two new cabinet posts were created. The authority of one of these, the Ministry of Forestry, assigned to a Communist, overlapped with that of the Ministry of Agriculture and Land Reform, to which Mikolajczyk had been appointed.

This was short measure. Even so, Harriman had thought that the new members of the government might have some influence, and that they had been wise to accept the best they could get. He was bothered by the fact that the new government was retaining a separate Ministry of Internal Security, for this was evolving into a secret police on the

[10] Potsdam Papers, Document 523.

Russian model. All in all, however, he reckoned that there was a fair chance, if the American and British governments continued to take an active interest in Polish affairs and were generous in their aid, that things might not work out too badly.

The new government had taken office on the night of June 28. Osubka-Morawski, the Prime Minister, sent messages at once to Truman and Churchill, announcing its formation. He repeated the broad formula with which Bierut had parried Harriman's and Clark Kerr's queries about the prospects for free elections: that the new government recognized in their entirety the Yalta decisions on the Polish question.

A troublesome error had been noted in the text of the announcement sent out by the Polish Prime Minister. During the consultations with the Commission, Bierut had done his best to get Harriman and Clark Kerr to agree to the omission of the word "Provisional" from the title of the new government. They had refused, on the score that this was the designation used in the Yalta accord and they could not depart from it, pending the holding of elections. Bierut had appeared to accept this verdict. But in the message to Truman the word "Provisional" was omitted. In calling the attention of the State Department to the "slip," Harriman reported that the Moscow press was similarly forgetful in referring to the new government. He at once got in touch with the Polish Ambassador in Moscow and told him that the American government still insisted that the word be retained. At midnight on the 29th a member of the Polish Embassy, speaking for the Ambassador, said that a serious mistake had been made and that the message should include the word "Provisional."

President Truman had decided that no useful purpose would be served by delaying recognition. So on July 2 he proposed to Churchill that they act at once and together. Churchill objected to such haste. He explained why the British government needed more than a few hours' notice. It had to work out honorable arrangements with the abandoned Polish government in London, for its members and its large staff, which still ran an army of 160,000 men and was entitled to a little time to advise all its employees. The British government also needed time to decide what was to be done about the Polish military forces that had fought with the allies. Thus Churchill asked Truman for a brief postponement.

On July 5 they had simultaneously announced recognition of the new Polish Provisional Government of National Unity. In this and in various connected messages and statements they introduced references to the prescribed pledge to hold free elections. These, on purpose, im-puted high value to a guarded promise, a pledge to which the Warsaw authorities were refusing to affix a date.

The new government had been well received by most Poles. Even the liberal-conservative circles about the University of Cracow spoke of it in a friendly fashion, though the response from groups such as this was due less to enthusiasm than to recognition of the need for social, political, and territorial change, and to fatigue left by the war, Nazi occupation, and tension with Russia.

By the time the Potsdam conference met, it could be expected that the true intentions of the new government that had emerged from the Mos-cow consultations would have been more clearly revealed. Churchill's impression of the result—which he had accepted—was that it was a failure. As summoned up in his later memory, it was: "We were as far as ever from any real and fair attempt to obtain the will of the Polish nation by free elections. There was still a hope—and it was the only hope—that the meeting of 'The Three,' now impending, would en-able a genuine and honorable settlement to be achieved."[11]

But even in the brief fortnight between the granting of recognition and the gathering at Potsdam there had been signals that this hope was going to prove empty.

[11] *Triumph and Tragedy*, pages 583-84.

28. Poland: Debate on General Questions

STALIN at Potsdam was as bent as Churchill or Truman on discussing the affairs of Poland, for he was not sure that the Prime Minister would deprive the forlorn groups of Polish officials in London of all influence and perquisites. Therefore, at the session of July 18, he proposed that the three of them resolve to sever all relations with the abandoned Government-in-Exile; to enable the new government to take over all Polish property abroad; and to see to it that the Polish armed forces outside the country, and Polish naval and merchant vessels, come under the orders of the new government. Not only the men but their equipment, supplied by the British and the Americans, were wanted.[1]

To Stalin this course was but a routine march to a set political purpose. But to Churchill it would be a sad and cruel ending of a close and moving association. At the conference table his memory flared into a vivid review of what the Polish and British nations had gone through together; of how well the Poles who had come west and their dead comrades had served. He recalled how the British had given a home to the Poles when Hitler drove them out: the effort made and expense incurred in supporting the Polish refugees; the training of the Polish aviators, who had fought with reckless valor over the air of Britain when it was alone; the formation of the Polish army corps which had gone through the campaigns in Italy and Germany. The survivors, who numbered about 200,000 men "front and rear,"[2] the British government was resolved to treat in a way the world would approve. At which point Stalin, untouched by guilty memories, uttered a hearty "Of course."

Churchill said he had told the House of Commons that if there were Polish soldiers who had fought on the British side and did not want to go back to Poland, they would be taken into the British Empire, but British policy was to persuade as many of these men as possible to return. Hence he had been angry when he learned that General Anders, a good soldier, had told his Polish troops that if they went home they would probably be sent to Siberia. Anders would not be allowed to continue

---

[1] Potsdam Papers, Document 1120.
[2] Eden, in a note he sent to Byrnes at Potsdam on July 17, submitting the text of a joint Three-Power statement about future political developments in Poland to be issued at the end of the conference, estimated that there were some 250,000 Poles on British soil and in the armed forces under British command. Potsdam Papers, Document 1118.

to make such hurtful statements.[3] The British government would continue to encourage both Polish soldiers and civilians to return to their liberated homeland. But they needed and deserved a little time. Of course, the better affairs went in Poland, the sooner they would go home. If the new Polish government would assure them of their reception "in full freedom and under appropriate economic conditions, that would be of great help. He would like them to feel assured in returning to their home which had been freed by the victory of the Red Army. The Foreign Ministers might discuss this matter."[4] As for Polish property, the Government-in-Exile controlled little and the new government was welcome to that. There were the frozen gold reserves—but these would in normal course be turned over to the Central Polish Bank.

Stalin adopted an easy tone. The British, he commented, had sheltered the former rulers of Poland and yet these men had caused the British much trouble. All the Soviet government wanted to do was to put an end to this situation, for the reactionary remnants of the old government were still conducting their activities, through agents and the press. Churchill said he agreed. But in Britain individuals—and that included members of Parliament—were not stopped from talking because they lost office or their funds were cut off. After Mikolajczyk had resigned, neither he himself nor Eden had seen the members of the old government. Still, what was to be done if they wandered through the streets and talked with journalists? About the Polish army they had to be careful lest there be mutiny and possible bloodshed. "The British had the same objectives as the Soviets. They asked for help and a little time and also that Poland be made an attractive place for the Poles to return to."

Truman said he could see no real difference between Churchill and Stalin. But he also was interested in the Polish question. What was being done about the agreement reached at Yalta for the holding of free and secret elections as soon as possible? Stalin did not tell him.

In that state this whole muster of questions about Poland was consigned to the attention of the Foreign Ministers. They toiled over them for the next three days. The result—to cut the story short—did in some

[3] Actually, it may be inserted, a few days earlier General Anders, Commander of the Second Polish Corps, Italy, and Field Marshal Alexander had agreed that the Polish soldiers under Anders' command—some 110,000 of them—would be given a free choice as individuals to decide whether or not to return to Poland, and had promised to do everything possible to expedite the repatriation to Poland of those who chose to return. Potsdam Papers, Document 1123.
[4] *Ibid.*, Minutes, Second Plenary Session, July 18.

measure reward on paper the efforts made by Eden and Byrnes. But later events were to prove that the fractures of purpose had merely been taped over by diplomacy, not healed.

Eden and Byrnes advocated that the new Provisional Government be asked to affirm definitely that those Poles who returned home would enjoy the same personal and property rights as other citizens. Molotov maintained that this might be offensive to the Poles; that it was enough to say that the three powers "expected" that the returning Poles would have such equal rights. In the final statement, since Stalin had insisted that the sensibilities of the new Polish rulers must be so respected, the point was written this way.

Eden and Byrnes proposed that a clear recording be made of the understanding that the Provisional Government was pledged to hold free and unfettered elections on the basis of universal suffrage and secret ballot, in which all democratic and anti-Nazi parties would have the right to take part and put forward candidates. Molotov objected on the score that this language was not in accord with that of the Yalta agreement.[5] Moreover, he pointed out, when the new Polish government was formed it had given this pledge. Concluding correctly that small turns of language would not make any actual difference, the Americans and British agreed that the final draft might say instead that "The Three Powers note that the Polish Provisional Government in accordance with the decisions of the Crimea Conference, has agreed to the holding . . ." Eden and Byrnes had wished to add a sentence expressing the hope of the three powers that "the elections will be conducted in such a way as to make it clear to all the world that all sections of Polish opinion have been able to express their views freely, and thus to play their full part in the restoration of the country's political life." This was turned down by Molotov as unneeded and unpleasant for the Polish government, since it showed mistrust.

The most stubborn struggle was over the wish of the Americans and British to have it stated that the representatives of the allied press would have unrestricted freedom to report on developments in Poland before and during the elections. Vishinsky and Molotov said that since

[5] The pertinent sentence of the English-language Yalta agreement read: "The Polish Provisional Government of National Unity shall be pledged to the holding of free and unfettered elections as soon as possible on the basis of universal suffrage and secret ballot." As has already been told, the new Provisional Government, on receiving recognition, had promised to carry out all the provisions of the Yalta accord.

so little time had gone by since the end of the war, the Poles would find it difficult to accord "unlimited" freedom to the press, but that as conditions changed, greater freedom could be given. They argued, however, that this was a Polish question, which could not be decided without the Poles. As expressed by Stalin when the issue came before the Heads of Government at the Plenary Session on July 21: "The Poles are very touchy and they will be hurt. They will suspect us of accusing them of being unwilling to accord a free press." Therefore, would Churchill and Eden not be a little more amenable and omit this requirement, especially since foreign correspondents were in Poland now and were enjoying full freedom? No, answered Churchill; in fact, he hoped to strengthen the affirmation on this point, not weaken it.

In the end, however, it was probably not Churchill's firmness but Truman's plea that budged Stalin. "There are six million Poles in the United States. A free election in Poland reported to the United States by a free press would make it much easier to deal with these Polish people." And besides, it seemed to him that "the Polish Provisional Government knew that the Three Powers would expect the press freely to report the elections and would expect this matter to be raised." With a small change in language—in deference to Polish pride—the statement was preserved.

Both Churchill and Truman seem to have thought that the accord about these matters provided as much chance for a free and independent Poland—friendly to the West as well as to Russia—as could be had by words. Mikolajczyk, in Potsdam at the time, seemed to his Western friends sometimes hopeful, sometimes downcast over the prospect. He thought it essential to maintain sympathetic working relations with his Communist associates. But he was fearful over what was going to happen —once the new government felt safely in control.

Up to the eve of his departure from Potsdam, Churchill tried to make Bierut and his companions realize how deep and genuine was the British interest in having this program carried out in good faith: that Poland should be a land where personal and political liberties were respected, where there would be freedom of opinion, of press, and of religion. And when Attlee and Bevin took the place of Churchill and Eden, they likewise did all they could to keep the Poles and their Soviet mentors reminded that they were pledged to these liberating precepts and measures.

Overstepping the ordinary boundaries of this narrative, it may be told that on the basis of this accord the British authorities, as quickly as they could properly do so, broke the few remaining threads of official connection with the Polish Government-in-Exile. They arranged for the transfer of Polish assets under British control to the new regime. They urged all Poles, civilian and military, with whom they were in touch to return to Poland. The Warsaw government beckoned these back with welcomes and assurances, but only a small number returned. Though homesick and hard put to it to find a new place to settle and work to do, most of them chose this harder path. Of those who had served in the armed forces under British command, many gladly accepted the offer of British citizenship.[6]

[6] The saddest of all at the dissolution of the Polish Government-in-Exile, to which they had been faithful during the war, and at the acceptance of the new regime sponsored by Moscow, were General Anders and the forces that had fought under him in the hardest campaigns. He writes (page 282): "There came quite suddenly in the afternoon of August 10 unofficial reports of the end of the war with Japan. For a second time we Poles were unable to share in the glorious moments of victory. London, always so sober and steady, was going crazy with rejoicing. Huge and excited crowds flocked down the Strand, past the Savoy Hotel, where I was staying. I could understand their merriment but was unable to take part in it. I felt as if I were peeping at a ballroom from behind the curtain of an entrance door through which I might not pass. How often in an officers' mess at the front had we dreamed of the final moments of the war and of our joyful return home. How different was this day."

29. Poland: The Struggle over Frontiers

As soon as the three Heads of State, in a gust of amiability, approved the "Statement on the Polish Question," on July 21, they fell to about Poland's western frontiers. The Poles of all political colors were at one in wanting the line of the Oder and Western Neisse rivers. They were already there, and the Russians were determined that they should stay there. But before telling of the argument over the western frontier, we may pause to note the quick fixation of the northern limits.

As far back as December 1943, at Teheran, Stalin had said he would accept the Curzon Line as the Soviet-Polish frontier only if the Russians also received the northern part of East Prussia, running along the left (the southern) bank of the Niemen River, including Tilsit and the Baltic port city of Königsberg. The Soviet government, he had said, deserved this ice-free port and this piece of German territory. Moreover, this acquisition would contribute to security against future assaults for it would "put Russia on the neck of Germany." Neither Churchill nor Roosevelt had at the time denied this claim. From then on Stalin had taken it for granted that the Soviet Union was to keep this area, into which a large Soviet army afterward thrust.

On July 23 at Potsdam the Soviet delegation presented a proposal calling for a decision of three governments that "pending the final settlement of the territorial questions at the Peace Conference, the part of the western border of the U.S.S.R. adjoining the Baltic Sea should follow the line from the point on the western shore of Danzig Bay indicated on the map annexed hereto, eastward-north of Braunsberg-Goldap to the junction of frontiers of the Lithuanian S.S.R., the Polish Republic and former East Prussia."[1] The rest of "former East Prussia" was being assigned by common consent to Poland.

At the Plenary Session that day Stalin repeated his reasons for wanting this area: the need for an ice-free port on the Baltic at the expense of Germany,[2] and the wish to give satisfaction to the millions of Russians whom the Germans had caused to suffer.

Both Truman and Churchill at once agreed in principle to the transfer of territory. But Truman said he wanted time to study the details

---

[1] Potsdam Papers, Document 1020.
[2] The Soviet Union already had two ice-free ports on the Baltic. These were Windau (or Ventspils) and Libau (or Liepaja), in what had been Latvia before that country was absorbed as a unit of the U.S.S.R. But these were farther to the north and probably more easily blockaded.

of the Russian proposal. And Churchill pointed out that the language had several other implications. It would lead to an admission that East Prussia no longer existed and that the area was not under the authority of the Control Council for Germany. It would also commit the British and American governments to recognize the absorption of Lithuania in the Soviet Union. These, he thought, were matters that really should not be settled before the peace conference. Well then, said Stalin, all the Soviet government would ask at this time was that the British and American governments give and record their approval, and promise to support the transfer at the peace conference. To this Churchill and Truman assented.

In the search for a mutually acceptable phrasing of this understanding, for entry into the official record, a snag was met. How was the exact line to be determined between the part of former East Prussia that was to go to Russia and the part that was to go to Poland? The Soviet government thought it ought to be established by the experts of the Soviet Union and Poland alone, without outside surveillance.[3] But Attlee and Bevin insisted that this was a matter for all the United Nations to determine, not merely the two border countries. Byrnes once again acted as conciliator. He proffered an interpretation of the pertinent clause which would allow the two countries to try first to settle the question between themselves. Only if they disagreed would the experts of the United Nations be called in. So it was settled at the last session of the conference, after agreement had been reached on Poland's western boundary.[4]

Little or no effort was wasted to save the face of principle in this northern profile—but much was spent in trying to preserve it in the west.[5]

[3] According to Mikolajczyk, page 159, Bierut and Osubka-Marawski, who were to become President and Prime Minister of the Provisional Government, had made a secret agreement with Stalin as early as July 25, 1944, defining the frontier line; and Stalin subsequently browbeat them into keeping this agreement.

[4] The paragraphs dealing with East Prussia and the northern frontiers of Poland will be found in the Protocol, Supplementary Note 7.

[5] Another frontier adjustment that had taken place before Potsdam, about which the western allies were not consulted at all, was the agreement signed on June 29 by Fierlinger, the Czechoslovak Prime Minister, consenting to retention within the Soviet Union of the Sub-Carpathian Ukraine. This had formerly been a section of Czechoslovakia, and had been annexed by Hungary in 1939. It had never been part of Russia. Yet in the agreement the transfer of territory was called "a return" to the Soviet Union. As remarked in the *Economist* of July 7, 1945, "It is more correct to say the incorporation of the Sub-Carpathian Ukraine is merely the last episode in the 'collection' of all Ukrainian lands by Generalissimo Stalin." At Potsdam neither Churchill nor Truman asked Stalin about this transaction.

POLAND: THE STRUGGLE OVER FRONTIERS

The American and British governments were well aware that the
Soviet government would support the full claims of the Poles. Were
these not conceived as direct compensation for the loss of territory to
the Soviet Union? In May the Soviet authorities had assigned to Polish
control that segment of the Soviet zone extending to the Oder and the
Western Neisse, and Molotov had met with excusing evasions the strong
protests made by the British and American governments against this
action.[6]

Then on July 7, two days after the new Polish Provisional Government was recognized, General Zhukov, at the second meeting of the
Kommandatura for Berlin, had left no doubt that the resources east
of the line formed by the Oder and the Western Neisse would not be
available for Berlin or the western sections of Germany. He had based
his assertions on the ground that Germany did not exist, and that everyone knew that the Yalta conference had fixed the Polish frontier along
that line.[7] This, of course, was not so.

The Foreign Office, a few days before the start of the Potsdam
conference, had submitted to American officials ideas for two alternative
positive courses.[8] It was convinced that time would only aid the Poles,
with Russian support, to establish themselves permanently in all the
territory east of the Oder-Neisse line. Thus if the British and American
governments contented themselves with putting their views on record
while postponing settlement of the frontier, future troubles would be
increased and the Soviet government would have been allowed to flout
the authority of the Control Council over Germany.

The British government, continued the memo, was seriously opposed
to the line advocated by the Poles. It could scarcely be expected that
British public opinion would lastingly support a settlement that ampu-
tated about one-fifth of Germany, in which about ten million Germans
had formerly lived. Such action would prove to be a formidable ob-

[6] The vigorously worded memo that Kennan, as asked by Grew, had given to Vishinsky
on May 8 stated that in the opinion of the American government the changes disregarded
the principles of the agreements on zones of occupation and control of Germany. "The
Government of the United States," it concluded, "wishes to make it clear that the free city
of Danzig and occupied German territory now subject to Polish administration . . .
remain in fact enemy territory under Soviet military occupation, and must be held as such
pending the conclusion of such agreements and understandings as may be reached after full
and complete consultation and deliberation between the Allied powers concerned." Potsdam
Papers, Document 510, fn. 4.
[7] Ibid., Document 429.
[8] In almost identical memos given by the British Embassy in Washington to the State
Department on July 13 and by the Under Secretary of State for Foreign Affairs to Assistant Secretary of State Dunn on July 14 in Potsdam.

stacle to the maintenance of European peace. Certainly it would withdraw this large area from the authority of the Control Council, exclude
it as a source of both reparations and supplies needed for western Europe, and give undue advantage to Poland and Russia.

Taking into account the reasons for not simply leaving the question
in suspense, and the objections to the frontier sought by the Poles, how
might the British and American governments offset the Soviet-supported
demand?

The Foreign Office memo proposed that one way, the most promising way, would be jointly to state at Potsdam what the British and
Americans regarded as a reasonable boundary, and hold fast to and for
it. Poland should be allowed to acquire the Free City of Danzig, East
Prussia south and west of Königsberg, the Oppeln district of Upper
Silesia, the eastern part of Pomerania—and no more.[9] This was roughly
the frontier line favored by the State Department.[10] If the French
government also assented, they would agree to transfer of the territories
east of such a frontier to permanent Polish administration, subject to
ratification at the peace conference.

The memo continued that the other course to which the two governments might resort—if the Soviet government refused to join them in
getting the Poles to accept this delineation of Poland's western limits
—would be to state, first, that they would not give their formal consent
to the transfer to Polish administration of any parts of Germany except
those that all four controlling powers were prepared to allow Poland to
acquire permanently; and second, that if the Soviet government turned

[9] Before the war the city of Danzig had been a Free City under a High Commissioner
appointed by the League of Nations; almost all its inhabitants were German. The Oppeln
district of Upper Silesia included the area awarded to Germany in 1921 after a plebiscite;
it was a main source of coal, zinc, and iron and steel production. There Germans were
in the majority. The eastern part of Pomerania (east of the Kreuz-Dramburg line) was
one of the poorer farm sections of Germany, containing many Junker estates. Much of the
work on these was done by migrant Polish labor. To Poland this area would bring a
greatly extended sea frontage on the Baltic.

[10] As described in the Briefing Book paper dated June 29, 1945, prepared for the
Potsdam conference: "On Polish claims against Germany this Government agrees that
East Prussia (except for the Königsberg district), the former Free City of Danzig, German
Upper Silesia and a portion of eastern Pomerania should be ceded to Poland."

The State Department believed, however, that the British government was pledged to
support the transfer of greater areas. "The American Government would prefer that other
German territories east of the Oder should remain German. However, the British have
agreed to the cession to Poland of all territory east of the Oder and this Government would
probably not wish to stand out alone if the Russians insist on this point." The State Department had in mind Churchill's talk with Stalin in Moscow in October 1944, as reported
by Harriman. See U.S., Dept. of State, *The Conferences at Malta and Yalta*, page 203.
The British Foreign Office apparently did not regard this promise as rigid or official.

over other areas without their consent, thus reducing the capacity of Germany as a whole to pay reparations, the British and American governments would be compelled to insist on a proportionate reduction in the Russian share of reparations. Or they might go even further, and state that if a satisfactory agreement was not reached about this frontier, the western allies would not permit the transfer of any products from their zones in Germany to the Soviet Union, by way of reparations.

The American group of advisers at Potsdam had been impressed by the reasoning in this British memo, but at the start of the conference they were not willing to adopt either of these two positive courses. They were still loath to agree to the firm fixation of any frontier line before the peace conference met. Principle was at stake; the Polish vote in the United States was at hazard; and the Senate was on guard. Nor did the Americans then see what good could come of threatening the Soviet government with reprisals. So the British memo was read, noted, and filed. The American tactic was first to explore the possibility of compromise, merely raising the question without revealing our attitude toward the Soviet wish to secure for Poland the line of the Oder and the Western Neisse.[11]

Before the Heads of Government got round to the issue, they received identical letters from Bierut and from Osubka-Morawski, the President and Prime Minister of the Polish Provisional Government. These said that it was the unanimous and inflexible will of the whole nation that Poland's western frontier be one "that follows, beginning in the South, the former frontier between Czechoslovakia and Germany, then the Lausitzer [Western] Neisse river, then runs along the left bank of the Oder, and leaving Stettin for Poland, reaches to the sea west of the town of Swinemünde."[12] This boundary would be just, said the letters, and would assure successful development of the Polish nation, security to Europe, and lasting peace to the world.

Truman sailed boldly into the subject in the Plenary session on July 21. He had just finished reading the authoritative report from General Groves on the impressive result of the test of S-1 in the New Mexico desert. The ensuing discussion was of such historical moment that its main trail ought to be followed with care.

Germany (within its 1937 frontiers), the President said by way of

[11] Memo of Dubrow talk with Middleton of the British Embassy, July 13, Washington, Potsdam Papers, Document 518. Memo from Dunn to Byrnes, July 15, Babelsburg, *Ibid.*, Document 520.
[12] *Ibid.*, Document 1154.

introduction, was to have been occupied by the three of them, and their troops were now disposed within the allotted zones. But it now appeared that the Soviet government was, on its own, awarding Poland a separate zone. He was friendly toward the Polish Provisional Government, and full accord could probably be reached on what the Soviet government wanted. But, he concluded, it ought to be achieved by consultation.

Stalin's response would do credit to any advocate. Had not the Declaration at Yalta stated that Poland should be ceded territory to the north and west of its former frontiers? Had it not stipulated that the reorganized Polish government would at a suitable time consult with the three main allies about a final settlement of the western frontiers? Had not the Polish Provisional Government made known its views? Why then should this conference not state its opinion, final decision of course being left to the peace conference? Moreover, he continued, it was not quite accurate to say that the Soviet government had given the Poles a zone of occupation without consultation. True, the American and British governments had protested the admission of Polish administrators in certain areas before the boundaries were settled. But the Soviet government could not heed them, for the Germans in these areas had fled westward while the Poles had remained. The Red Army had needed a local administration to maintain friendly order behind its lines, but did not want to run it. Should it have set up a German administration, which might stab it in the back? Anyway what harm had been done, since Poland was to receive territorial cessions in the west and only Poles remained?

Now the full effect became plain of the failure to foresee what would happen if Poland's frontiers were not fixed before the war ended. No ordinary way was left to prevent the Russians and Poles from pushing too far westward. But perhaps the Soviet government would exercise restraint if it was made to realize that it would have to pay for its support of the Poles.

This Truman hinted, pointing out that if the Soviet government released part of its zone to the Poles, the German capacity to pay reparations would be reduced. Of that aspect of the decision Stalin professed scorn. The Soviet Union was not afraid of this, and if necessary would renounce reparations. Then with a straight face he went on to remark that everything the President had said was "interpretative." Although Poles were in charge of the administration of part of the Soviet zone, the western frontier question was open; the Soviet Union was not obligated. "You are not?" asked Truman. "No," answered Stalin. Still, Truman flatly said again that the Soviet government ought to have kept control of the whole of its zone—as the other powers were retaining theirs. Stalin retorted that "on paper" the areas under discussion were German territory, but practically, there were no Germans left; they had all fled.

At this juncture Churchill took up the argument. He disputed Stalin's statement that there were no Germans left in the disputed area, saying that he was informed that two and a half million Germans remained. And, he added, the more of them that fled into western Germany, the more would have to be fed there, kept warm, and provided with work. That might be so, Stalin answered in effect, but the Germans were mainly to blame for these difficulties; most of the Germans had fled the area before the Soviet army arrived. No single German remained in the territory to be given Poland. Between the Oder and the Vistula the Germans had quitted their fields, which were now being cultivated by the Poles. "It is unlikely that the Poles would agree to the return of the Germans." Only the Poles could grow the food and mine the coal.

Churchill was not to be quieted. Polish territorial claims were immoderate. What was asked would not even be good for Poland. The vast transfer of population that would ensue would be harmful to Europe and a great shock to Great Britain; and unless food from eastern Germany were available for the immense population of the Ruhr, the British government might be confronted with a condition similar to that in German concentration camps. Stalin indicated that he thought Churchill's worry about that was needless; could not the Germans buy food from the Poles? This query touched off the question that lurked in Truman's mind: how were the Germans to pay for what they needed if the exactions of the Russians and Poles prevented repair of their broken productive capacity. If they could not pay would the United States have to meet the bill, as it had after the First World War?

Against these stony ridges, the discussion, which was renewed at their next session, came to an impasse. Stalin, it may be surmised, believed that Churchill and Truman, while avowing other reasons, were really trying to protect and spare the Germans. For otherwise why should the two uphold the cause of the Germans against the Poles, whom they had so brutally treated, unless the Americans and the British wished Germany to become strong enough again to menace the Soviet Union? Churchill and Truman thought they had been tricked. Churchill was convinced that Stalin was bent on ensuring permanent Soviet control over Poland, as a menacing step forward against the West.

Truman was no less indignant. But he seemed to be primarily concerned over the fact that a "fifth occupation zone" in Germany was being created, which would make the American task in its zone harder. He still did not want to come to grips over the question of the permanent frontier. Thus he was inclined to let the issue rest, perhaps until after the conference. Churchill was convinced that temporizing was unwise; that the longer the decision was deferred, the more unchallengeable the local situation would be, as the Poles took steps to make themselves complete masters of the territory. Hence he rejected Stalin's suggestion that when the Council of Foreign Ministers met in September, as planned, they should consult with representatives of the Polish government and recommend a settlement. He feared the delay, he said, and thought besides that this would only pass on, not dissolve, the difficulty. Though Truman wavered, Churchill would not give in.

Then, asked Stalin, why not ask the Poles to come to Potsdam right away? Churchill said that in view of the urgency of the question he would prefer that, but he was mindful of Truman's recent objection to having representatives of the Yugoslav government summoned to Potsdam, and he foresaw that the Poles would ask far more than he could grant. Perhaps they could agree, without the Poles, on an arrangement for the transitional period—between the present and the peace conference. Let the Poles have territory east of a designated line, but west of it act only as agents of the Soviet government.

What Truman made of this proposal cannot be learned either from the minutes of the discussion or from his own later account.[13] Both contain statements that are more repetitious and emphatic than clear. He did not like the way in which Poland had acquired a zone without discussion among the three powers concerned; and he thought the main problem was that of their occupation of Germany. "That was his position yesterday, and that would be his position tomorrow."

As for Stalin, he correctly surmised that the dividing line Churchill had in mind was wholly along the Oder River—not along the Oder and the Western Neisse—and one that would leave Stettin and Breslau within Germany.[14] After walking around the table to show Truman, on the map, the line that he favored, Stalin said the question that required decision was the permanent frontier, not a temporary line. "They could settle the matter, and they could put it off, but they could not avoid it." Churchill's sally had failed.

[13] *Year of Decisions*, pages 372-73.

[14] The area between the two lines (that is, between the Western Neisse River and the upper reaches of the Oder) included parts of the Prussian provinces of Silesia and Brandenburg. It was a good farm region, with about 2.7 million people, almost all German. Potsdam Papers, Document 513, Attachment 6.

As a last chance it was agreed to call the Poles to Potsdam and see what arrangement could be made with them. Truman, who had up to then regarded this as unnecessary, now gave in—though he could hardly have thought that they would ask less than Stalin was affirming they should and must have.

The invitations were sped off. The Polish government was asked to send two or three representatives to Potsdam, by July 24 if possible. The Soviet authorities saw to it that they got there on time. The group that arrived included eight important members of the Polish Provisional Government—among them Bierut, Osubka-Morawski, and two deputy Prime Ministers: Mikolajczyk, most important liaison to the West, and Gomulka. They made a fluent, flamboyant show of national unity and patriotism.

The Poles used every hour of the days and nights to argue their cause. It is safe to assume that they saw Molotov, and perhaps Stalin, before anyone else. In the late morning of the 24th they met with the Foreign Ministers. To that group they pleaded their case in full—the President, Bierut, taking the lead.

He began by justifying his compliance with the Soviet acquisition of what had been the eastern part of Poland. The new Soviet-Polish frontier, he asserted, was in accord with ethnic facts, since the people that lived east of the Curzon Line were mainly Ukrainians, White Russians, and Lithuanians. Under Byrnes' questioning he did recall that about four million Poles had lived there, but, he said, most of them had probably already moved west.[15]

In view of Poland's great suffering during the war and its part in winning the war, it surely deserved compensation in the west, boundaries that would enable it to be secure and to prosper. Even if this wish were granted, Poland would be much smaller than before the war, and its population also smaller though homogeneous. The claimed land areas extending to the Western Neisse River were needed to resettle the four million Poles from east of the Curzon Line and some other three million who would return from other foreign lands. They were essential to provide a decent living for the Polish farmers and workers, who in the past had lived miserably in poor and overcrowded rural regions, or

---

[15] As recorded in a memo by Mikolajczyk of the talk at this meeting. Potsdam Papers, Document 1385. Mikolajczyk's own remarks on the occasion seem to indicate that most of these Poles had not yet been repatriated. The U.S. official summary of the statements made by members of the Polish delegation read: "The population east of the Curzon Line . . . had also included 4 million Poles which they expected would be repatriated to Poland." Potsdam Papers, Annex to the Minutes of Foreign Ministers Meeting, July 24.

been forced to serve in Germany as seasonal workers or to migrate abroad. The coal and minerals would be needed to make up for the losses to the Soviet Union of rich farm land and the oil fields of Galicia. The area ought and must not be partitioned, for unless Poland controlled the whole basin of the Oder River and its tributaries, the Germans might cut off the river flow. Stettin must be included because it was the natural sea outlet for Silesia, and the only adequate and sufficient port for Polish imports and exports; having it, Poland could become a great transit area for the Soviet Union and Czechoslovakia. Moreover, the frontier sought would be the shortest and easiest to defend, especially since Germany would have lost the terrain in the east in which it had prepared its earlier assaults and which had provided resources for its great armament industry.[16]

To this assembly of arguments various other members of the group contributed—not least among them Mikolajczyk. Gone were the thoughts that had caused him to protest so bitterly to Churchill and Roosevelt before and after Yalta: that if Poland were shifted to the west, Communism would travel with it; and that Poland would have to obey Moscow, for the new western frontiers, containing so much of what had been Germany, would be a lasting cause of German enmity. He spoke as though he had come to agree with Stalin and Bierut—that the change would improve the prospect for peace since it would take away from Germany the means of aggression.[17]

---

[16] The cession of this area to Poland—in addition to East Prussia, Upper Silesia, and other territory east of the Oder—would reduce the Polish-German frontier to around 250 miles, facilitate Polish-Czech communications, and provide Poland with primary railroad lines from the Baltic southward through Breslau. Bierut's contentions at Potsdam corresponded with the reasoning in the written statement that the Polish Provisional Government had presented to the British and American governments soon after they recognized it. This read in part: "The Odra-Nisa frontier, the doing away with the nest of the Junker tradition in East Prussia, will mean the liquidation of a convenient *place d'armes* making possible German aggression against Poland. Putting an end to East Prussia and making the [German-Polish] frontier line . . . considerably shorter (about 350 kilometers) will greatly facilitate defense. . . . It will mean the removal of the German wedge that existed between Poland and Czechoslovakia in 1939. Thus it may serve not only in regard to Poland, but also to the Soviet Union, and the whole Slavonic world, as the best rampart against the ever-possible German aggression." Potsdam Papers, Document 517.

[17] Insight into Mikolajczyk's purpose may be had from one of three memos he gave Harriman with a special request that his name be not associated with them. This cited other and different reasons why Bierut's request ought to be approved at once: to encourage the Poles east of the Curzon Line to come west before they perished; to stimulate the return of Poles from abroad, the sooner to have elections; to speed the day when the Soviet armies would leave; to enable Poland to normalize its economy and protect its independence. The author was no doubt aware that these reasons would appeal to the West, and they did. *Ibid.*, Document 1137.

After the Poles made their pleas Molotov spoke up in their behalf. The relation of the Soviet Union to the Polish frontier settlements, he said over and over, was different from that of others. The Soviet Union was obligated to favor Polish claims. But it was his duty to say also that this was a matter of justice, and that justice required that Germany be turned out of the whole of this area in the interest of the people of Europe and of the whole world. While Germany was thus weakened in her aggressive power, the Polish state could grow strong and democratic. Thus what the Polish government wanted it should have.

In the afternoon the Poles called on Churchill, who received them in the company of Eden, Clark Kerr, and Alexander. But before they could press their suit, Churchill lashed out with passion. Their proposals, he asserted, would deprive Germany of one-quarter of its arable land, cause a forced migration of eight or nine million people, and imperil the situation in the British zone of Germany. "We would oppose such a division, and were convinced that it was just as dangerous for the Poles to press too far to the west as they had once pressed too far to the east."[18] Bierut protested, and lamented Churchill's lack of insight. The Polish claims were modest and took account of the need for peace in Europe. He disputed Churchill's estimate of the number of people that would be caused to migrate. Only one and a half million Germans, he declared, remained in the areas that the Polish government was now seeking, including East Prussia; and most of these people, especially those in Silesia, were really Poles, although attempts had been made to Germanize them. Churchill shook his head and repeated his solemn warning that they were wrong in asking for so much.

Then the Poles went on to talk with Truman, in the company of Byrnes and Harriman. But this talk did not go so far or so deep, and after some twenty minutes it was ended, as the President had to leave for the Plenary Session. The President emphasized, as he had with Stalin, his dislike for the "arbitrary" way in which the Poles had acquired control of a part of the Soviet zone of occupation in Germany. Bierut did not dispute what he called the "legal point of view," but made it clear that he thought this had to give way to actualities. Thus the whole subject was left for another day, another argument.

On the 25th the Heads of Government met in the forenoon, as Churchill was due to leave for London. Although they decided to eschew the subject of Polish frontiers, since the Poles were still on their

[18] *Triumph and Tragedy*, page 662.

rounds, it crept into their talk in connection with the transfer of population.

Once again Churchill voiced his worries. The Poles were thrusting millions of Germans out of what was part of the Russian zone into the British and American zones. He did not think this ought to be done without heeding the effect on the food supplies for the whole of Germany and the chance of obtaining reparations from Germany. And once again Stalin spoke as though what was taking place were out of his control; he remarked merely that it ought to be appreciated that the Poles were taking revenge on the Germans for injuries suffered over the centuries. Whereupon Truman said, "We don't want to pay for Polish revenge."[19] He repeated that up to then there were only four zones of occupation in Germany, that none had been allotted to the Poles, and if they were to have one they were responsible to the Soviet Union for it. He wanted to be as helpful as he could but his position was that the frontier should be fixed at the peace conference.[20] It is hard to tell whether his repetition of these positive remarks was intended merely as a rebuke, as a way of confirming his opposition to Polish claims, or as a record useful at home. In any case they left the subject as much in the air as before.

Since this was Churchill's last chance before he left for London, he flung himself back into the discussion—without avail. The question of how far the Poles were to advance to the west, he said, lay at the very root of the success of the conference. If it dispersed in discord over this issue, the Poles in effect having been admitted as a fifth occupational power and with no plan for sharing food supplies equally among the German people, the meeting would have been a failure. Then all of them would have to hold on to everything in their respective zones in Germany, since he could not agree to an arrangement that would mean starvation in the British zone and the most fireless winter of the war. His animation drew from Stalin a cold set of answers: the Germans ought to pay, by exports, for the food they received; they could do so and also make reparation; and if the British needed to produce more coal in England they might use German prisoners of war in the mines.

Actually, both contentions were unreal—Churchill's, because even if the Poles were willing to share what was produced in the area they wished to acquire, they would have little coal or food for the rest of

[19] Potsdam Papers, Cohen Notes.
[20] Potsdam Papers, Minutes, Plenary Session, July 25.

Germany for the next year or two; Stalin's, because during the next year or two the Germans could not possibly supply themselves with essentials and pay substantial reparations.[21]

The nature of these concluding arguments indicates, I think, that the Americans and British had almost lost hope that the Poles and their Soviet advocates would retract their demands for territory. They were thinking of how to reduce the effect on their positions in Germany, and were resolving that the Soviet Union should be made to pay, as well as they.

But Churchill, in his subsequent account of this divisive issue, averred that he had intended, if reelected, to come to grips again with the Soviet government over it: ". . . neither I nor Mr. Eden would ever have agreed to the Western Neisse being the frontier line. . . . Here was no point of principle only, but rather an enormous matter of fact affecting about three additional millions of displaced people. . . . I had in view, namely, to have a 'showdown' at the end of the Conference, and, if necessary, to have a public break rather than allow anything beyond the Oder and the Eastern Neisse to be ceded to Poland."[22]

It is to be wondered whether Churchill, if he had returned to Potsdam, would really have gone through with his intention; and, if he had shown himself determined to take the risks of such a course, whether the Poles and their Soviet supporters would have compromised. Even if the British government, led by Churchill, had been willing to insist, would the American? A showdown might have led to the disruption of the United Nations even before its members met for the first time.

While the conference was waiting for Attlee to take Churchill's seat, and the Poles were having a last round of auditions for their case, Stalin

[21] The Poles would have just about enough grain, small surpluses of potatoes and sugar, but much less meat and fat than needed. Most of their surplus of coal they had already contracted to send to Russia and the Scandinavian countries, and for the rest, they wanted goods in return. So even if the Russians had been willing to agree to shipments of food and coal from the area under Polish administration to the west of Germany, the Poles would have refused to do so, except in return for goods. The Soviet government, however, was securing some reward for its support—for example, by obtaining coal from this area at a very low price.

These are just a few of the details of the Polish production situation, actual and prospective, reviewed in a long talk between an American group headed by Assistant Secretary of State Clayton and a Polish group headed by Minc, the Polish Minister for Industry, on July 28. Potsdam Papers, Document 1389.

[22] *Triumph and Tragedy*, page 672. Eden felt no less vigorously about this imposed boundary, and ended up his statement in the House of Commons when the accord on Poland was being debated (on August 20): "I would only say to our Polish friends that as, last time, they made a mistake in going too far East, so this time, I fear, they are making a mistake in insisting on going too far West."

gave the Poles a reception—on the night of the 27th. The Marshal repeated his vows of support for Polish claims. Bierut toasted Stalin.
Osubka-Morawski toasted Molotov. Mikolajczyk expressed his gratitude to Stalin and Molotov for their aid, and according to his memoir
of the occasion, Stalin turned to him just before the reception ended,
and said: "I know that you still have doubts and do not believe that we
sincerely want the Polish people strong, free, independent and truly
sovereign. You will see, after we have worked longer together; you will
become convinced of our intentions."[23]

A concurrent and hardly less vigorous argument had been going on
over German reparations; and as the two proceeded they became more
explicitly connected. Thus on this same day (the 27th), in a talk that
ended gruffly, Byrnes told Molotov that Soviet approval of the alienation to Poland of German territory—a large and productive part—
was one reason why he and the British were switching over to a different
kind of reparations plan. Instead of all three sharing in what could be
had from all of Germany, it would have to be each from its own zone,
with possible barter between them.

After Attlee returned, Truman briefly and gloomily reviewed with
him the two disputed questions. Then as the only way perceived of
bringing the conference to what could be regarded as a successful end,
he boldly offered to bargain off Western concessions on the one for
Soviet concessions on the other. But that will be better understood and
judged after we have followed the flow of talk and decision about
German matters, and listened in on the envenoming dispute about what
was to be taken from Germany as reparations.

[23] Potsdam Papers, Document 1388.

30. Germany: The Crucial Questions

THE central reason why the three Heads of Government had found it necessary to confer was that while they were bound to control Germany in combination, they had not yet agreed on the common policies to be pursued.

Early and late the negotiators, in the effort to formulate these, became snagged on the question: for the particular purpose in mind, what areas were meant by the name "Germany"? A preliminary supposition, a starting mark for discussion, was essential. Let it be, the three agreed, the Germany of 1937—that is, Germany before it absorbed Austria and Czechoslovakia. As has already been told, they almost immediately reduced that area by approving the division of East Prussia between Poland and the Soviet Union and the cessions of segments of Germany in the east and north to Poland.

Had France been as strong at the end of the war as the Soviet Union, it too might have been able to make effective its wish to detach from Germany and affiliate to France areas along their frontiers. But it had neither the diplomatic influence needed to persuade, nor the military means of defiantly taking what was wanted. Thus the requests that de Gaulle had made of the American and British governments were left in suspense. Neither sponsored them at Potsdam.

But the Russians thought they could be turned to advantage. Ivan Maisky, former Soviet Ambassador in England and member of the Reparation Commission, proposed at a meeting of the Economic Sub-committee on July 20 that as a security measure the Ruhr industrial district, containing some four million people, be internationalized under the control of the four powers—which would regulate its production "more or less permanently." He said his ideas about detail were still fluid, but a plan might be prepared for the Foreign Ministers and Heads of Government. The others did not respond.

Possibly because of the crunching argument over the German-Polish frontier in the east, the Soviet group did not revert to this proposal until agreement on that other issue neared. Then on July 30 Molotov gave Byrnes and Bevin a more precise written proposal: that they agree to the creation of an Allied Commission of the Four Powers to administer the Ruhr industrial district as a part of Germany, under the direction of the Control Council. And at the next meeting of the Heads of Government on the following day, Stalin urged the endorsement of

this drastic measure. Under the existing accord on zones, it may be recalled, the Ruhr district was under the jurisdiction of the Commander
of the British zone, subject to the joint direction of the Control
Council.[1] And under the new plan for reparations that was being discussed at this period of the conference, he would have final say as to
what could be taken out of the Ruhr as reparations. So it may be that
the Russians had this particular interest in mind, rather than a social
or political one.

In any case, because of Bevin's refusal to discuss the question in the
absence of the French, it was consigned to the future attention of the
Council of Foreign Ministers.

At the same time the idea of partitioning what remained of Germany
into a number of separate states was dropped once and for all. It is
pertinent to trace its fall from favor.

After Yalta, Churchill and his colleagues had drawn away from any
project for a division of Germany, even into two parts. They had concluded that the Soviet Union wanted to have a Europe that was pulverized into small states, the easier to dominate. In words the Prime
Minister used six weeks after Yalta: "I hardly like to consider dismembering Germany until my doubts about Russian intentions have cleared
away."[2] Roosevelt had remained uncertain, torn between anxieties: a
Germany left unified might again imperil the peace; a Germany separated into parts might devote itself to causing trouble. But the State
and War Departments and the Joint Chiefs were by then all advising
against partition. Their plans were being conceived in the thought that
there would be only one unified German state.

During these same spring months after Yalta, the impression had
spread among American officials in Washington and London who
watched for signs of Soviet intent that the Soviet Union too was turning away from this purpose, on which it had once been so determined.
Surmises about the reasons were as numerous as the memo writers. Perhaps the Soviet shift was due to fear that the British and Americans
might buy German surrender in the west by a secret promise not to
partition. Perhaps it was an effort to quiet the desperate fears of the
Germans of what would happen to them if they were at the mercy of
the Russians, which were thought to be causing them to relax their

[1] Potsdam Papers, Document 1027.
[2] Triumph and Tragedy, page 443.

resistance in the west while continuing to fight on furiously in the east. Perhaps—who was to know—the Soviet government was reckoning that if Germany were kept whole, and the awful destruction went on, it might be easy to bring the whole country under Communist domination later on. Whatever the reasons, the tone of the Soviet press and propaganda seemed to change during the last part of March and early April. Threats of extreme revenge were no longer heard. The Soviet leaders disavowed any attempt to destroy the German people, and began to open the way for a less punitive approach to the German masses after the war.

Thus it had come about that the committee that had been set up at Yalta to study the procedures for dismemberment (Eden as chairman with William Strang as deputy, and the American and Soviet Ambassadors in London, Winant and Gusev) talked over its assignment only long enough to agree that it had been canceled. On March 26, when the committee at last turned to the question, all three members had been diffident. The British member, William Strang, had prepared a paper for the occasion, a statement describing what he thought the committee's assignment to be. Whether by intent or not, this statement was expressive of a policy. It slanted toward the conclusion that the coalition should regard partition as a measure of last resort—to be considered only if the various control measures in mind for Germany were not deemed adequate to prevent German aggression. On that basis the only work that the committee need take in hand was the study of possible separate states and the measures that would have to be taken to assure that partition would be permanently effective.

Gusev, on accepting this statement as a basis for discussion in the committee, had said that the Soviet government also understood that under the Yalta decision dismemberment was not an obligation but a measure to bring pressure on Germany in order to render it harmless if other methods failed.[3] Strang corroborated this interpretation. Whether or not correctly, Winant took Gusev's observation to mean that the Soviet government was no longer bent on dismemberment, and so advised Washington. In commenting on Winant's report of this meet-

[3] The available sources of information about this discussion in the Committee on Dismemberment are not clear or satisfactory. As far as I know, no minutes were kept. I have not been able to locate Winant's report to Washington. This account is derived from a State Department memo submitted by Grew to the Cabinet Committee of Three (Stettinius or Grew, Stimson, and Forrestal) on March 29, and from Lord Strang's reminiscent account in *Home and Abroad*, page 7.

ing, Roosevelt said, "I think our attitude should be one of study and postponement of final decision."[4]

The impression that the Soviet government had renounced the idea had been reaffirmed when Stalin said in his victory speech, on May 9, "The Soviet Union celebrates victory, although it does not intend either to dismember or to destroy Germany." When Hopkins was in Moscow he had asked Stalin whether this meant a change in Soviet policy since Yalta. Stalin's answer showed that his version of what had happened at the meeting of the Committee on Dismemberment was different from the one Winant had conveyed to Washington. First he indicated he had been influenced by the fact that subsequent events had implied that his proposal in regard to dismembering had in effect been rejected at Yalta. He understood that in the meeting of the committee, Eden and Strang, on behalf of the British government, had interpreted the Yalta decision not as a positive plan for dismemberment, but as a threat to hold over Germany in the event of bad behavior; and that Winant had interposed no objection, although Gusev had done so. Hence he had concluded that both Great Britain and the United States had decided not to go through with this operation. Hopkins said this was not his understanding of the Yalta decision, and "he knew that President Truman was inclined towards dismemberment and in any event was for the detachment of the Saar, Ruhr and west bank of the Rhine under international control."[5] Hopkins agreed with Stalin that the British government was against dismemberment, but said he believed it would favor the separation of these areas in the west. The President, he thought, would want to thrash out these subjects when they met. Stalin said he would be glad to do so.

Who is to know whether Hopkins was correct in his explanation of Truman's thought at this time; or whether he was unaware of the changed trend of judgment in Washington; or whether he was trying to keep alive the project of dismemberment, on which he and Roosevelt had agreed, in face of the wish of others to let it expire?

In any case, by the time the conference met at Potsdam both American and British official opinion had become set against any forcible partition of Germany. Truman did not at Potsdam try to revive the idea. In the prolonged flow of talk about the treatment of Germany, only one passing reference was made to it. That was when Stalin, on presenting

[4] John L. Snell, *War Time Origins of the East-West Dilemma over Germany*, page 183.
[5] Potsdam Papers, Document 26, Bohlen memo, Stalin-Hopkins talk, May 28, 1945.

the Soviet proposal to place the Ruhr under four-power control, remarked that the views of all seemed to have turned against dismemberment. He was not contradicted. Soon after the end of the conference the committee that had been set up at Yalta to look into the matter was disbanded by common consent.

Looking forward to the Potsdam conference, the American and British governments had labored hard over the formulation of policies for Germany and its people. How was the authority of the Control Council to be defined? What principles should guide its members in enforcing the surrender terms, exterminating Nazi ideas and elements, reforming German political ideas and institutions, regulating economic affairs, and —not least—exacting reparations? What sort of better future could be fused out of the agony and the rubble? How were the Germans to live? How could they make retribution? How could they be taught to be peaceable—and forced to be, if they would not learn?

Such were the queries that wearied the workers in Washington and London who strove to perfect statements of policy—for a country that was still feared though its cities were in ruins, and for a people who behaved with abhorrent cruelty when under the spell of hatred or envy or insolent superiority.

There was another question that was hardly less troubling. Would any statement of policy that was being toiled over suit the Soviet government? In the interim between the surrender and the conference, the Soviet press versions of the western allies' actions and policies in their zones of Germany were tinged by critical suspicion, while in American official circles there was a deepening impression that the Soviet government was acting in its zone in the same way as in the satellites subject to its will. There were reports of dispossession, depredation, and terror, along with measures to help the people get back to peacetime work and trade, and of a shrewd courtship and encouragement of "antifascist" parties.

The American and British zone commanders were tempering their orders with discretion. The officers in charge of civil administration were giving way to an inclination to work with the more conservative and obedient elements. In contrast, the Soviet authorities were developing contacts with the more subversive elements in their zone, whose leaders had been taught in Moscow and trained to turn Germany toward Russia and Communism.

The western allies thought that the Soviet government was using for its own devious purposes former Nazi officials and military officers who had served under Hitler. The Soviet government thought that the western allies were being too indulgent to former Nazis, too disposed to permit Germans who had served in the government under Hitler to remain in local government positions, and to allow the groups that had controlled German industry under Hitler to retain their wealth and power.

Was it going to be possible at Potsdam to quench these suspicions, dissipate the criticisms, bridge the differences? Were the three governments who were to share (along with France) in the control of Germany going to be able to reach genuine accord on policies to be followed alike in their several areas of authority and for all of Germany? If they did so, their alliance might stay together. If not, it was sure to fall apart.

31. Germany: Political Principles

WHEN, at the First Plenary Session, Truman proposed that the Control Council for Germany begin to function at once, he submitted a statement of doctrines and measures for its guidance.[1] Here the description of the Control Council's authority was slightly different from that in the three-power agreement on Machinery of Control (November 1944). It read:

"The authority of the Control Council to initiate plans and reach agreed decisions on the chief military, political, economic and other questions affecting Germany as a whole shall be paramount in Germany, and those plans and decisions shall be carried out in each zone of occupation by the national Commander-in-Chief concerned. In matters exclusively affecting his own zone, each national Commander-in-Chief shall exercise supreme authority in accordance with directives received from his own government."[2]

Molotov asked the reasons for the new and rearranged language. He noted that in this version the supremacy of the Council was brought more to the fore than in the earlier accord. Was it intended, he asked, to increase centralized authority as compared with zonal? Byrnes denied there was any such purpose. Molotov asked why not then just use the same language as before? The statement ultimately adopted by the conference reverted in effect to the earlier one.

In essentials the political program presented by Truman was little different from that in the most recent Directive (1067/8 of May 14) that had been sent to Eisenhower to guide him first as Supreme Commander of Allied forces fighting their way through Germany, then as Zone Commander and prospective member of the Control Council.[3] Overworked and bewildered groups of military and civil-affairs officers were trying to put these measures into effect in the American and British zones.

For those whose memory of the policies sponsored by the American

---

[1] Because of differences told elsewhere, the Control Council did not hold its first regular meeting until July 30—when the Potsdam conference was in session and discussion was still going on about the political and economic principles that were to guide its decisions and activities.

[2] Potsdam Papers, Document 852.

[3] Montgomery had been advised by the British government to conform, as far as practicable, to the same general policies in the British zone. But he and his staff seem to have felt more called upon than the Americans to give the Germans an encouraging lead or push toward the restoration of peacetime conditions of life and work.

government may have been dimmed by time, a brief summary of the main features of Truman's proposal will serve as a reminder.[4] They will serve not only as a reminder of the conception that then prevailed, but also of the extent to which they were repudiated, as former friends in war became foes in peace.

1) The Germans were required to submit unconditionally to the orders of the Control Council and Zone Commanders.

2) Germany was to be completely disarmed and kept disarmed; all military forces were to be disbanded and forever forbidden.

3) National Socialism was to be extinguished as a government, a party, or an ideal; and all Nazis were to be removed from public and semi-public office, and from responsible positions in important private undertakings.

4) All Nazi laws and decrees that contained discrimination on grounds of race, creed, or political opinion were to be nullified.

5) Individuals accused of war crimes and atrocities were to be prose-cuted before a jointly formed tribunal, and those found guilty were to be punished.

6) The formation of a central German government was to be in-definitely postponed. But the Control Council might use central Ger-man administrative machinery for economic activities of national scope.

7) The German political structure was to be decentralized, and local responsibility developed.

8) All political parties except those of a Nazi character were to be allowed to function freely.

9) Education in Germany was to be controlled and directed in ways to further democratic ideas and forms of government and society, and eventual peaceful cooperation with other countries.

10) Steps were to be taken to assure freedom of speech, of the press, of religion, and of trade-union organization—subject to allied control for reasons of security.

To follow point by point, step by step, the evolution of this Ameri-can proposal into the text adopted by the Potsdam conference would lead us into a book-long thicket. Actually this first statement was *as a whole* approved by all three conference groups as a fair fusion of their ideas. All reaffirmed their wish to have in all Germany the same policies and practices, and to have these so inscribed in the statement of political principles that "so far as practicable, there shall be uniformity of treat-ment of the German population throughout Germany." This declaration

---

[4] The full text of Truman's proposal is in Potsdam Papers, Document 852.

corresponded with the genuine intentions of each and all of its several sponsors in one aspect but not in another. They were roughly of one mind as regards the suppressive elements in the program for control of Germany. But they were apart in their conceptions of the new society to be formed in Germany under their supervision.

Turning to particulars, we should take note of the points on which the American proposals were challenged and changes of more than minor significance were made.

The Soviet spokesmen were bothered by the stipulation that local self-government should be restored in all parts of Germany through elective councils, and the British seemed hardly less so. Even though Byrnes pointed out that the Control Council would have discretion as to when any elections should be conducted, Molotov feared they might be held "prematurely." He wanted to omit specific reference to elections. The provision in the final version was made to read "Local self-government shall be restored throughout Germany *on democratic principles and in particular* through elective councils *as rapidly as is consistent with military security and the purpose of military occupation*" (new language italicized). It was agreed that representative and elective principles should be introduced into the higher political units as rapidly as was justified by experience with them in local self-government.

These provisions were flexible. They could be molded by each of the occupying powers to suit the pace of its wish to turn over responsibility to the Germans in its own zone and its preference of ways and means.

The Soviet critics found a loose seam in the text of the provision banning Nazis from public and semi-public office and positions of responsibility in important private undertakings. It was made tight. And an affirmative sentence was added: "Such persons shall be replaced by persons who, by their political and moral qualities, are deemed capable of assisting in developing genuine democratic institutions in Germany."

The scope of the ban on all forms and kinds of military or paramilitary units and institutions was extended to include any that might keep alive the military tradition in Germany—including clubs and associations of war veterans.

The Russians wanted the decreed cancelation of Nazi laws to be extended to include *all* laws enacted while the Nazis were in power—not only those that made for discrimination on the basis of race, creed, or political opinion. They deferred to proof that this would do more harm than good. But in turn one of their supplementary suggestions was adopted: "The judicial system will be reorganized in accordance with the principles of democracy, of justice under law, and of equal rights for all citizens without distinction of race, nationality or religion."

One other amendment was a screen for actuality rather than a guide to it. The American proposal had stipulated that all weapons and specialized facilities for their production be "seized or destroyed." What about such technical facilities as wind tunnels? asked the Prime Minister at the session on July 18. Could they not be taken over and used in common? Stalin remarked that "they were not barbarians and they would not destroy research institutions." Churchill said he meant they could share them and use them together. Stalin said "this could be done." At the next meeting of the Foreign Ministers the clause was changed to read "held at the disposal of the allies or destroyed." No passing remark gave a clue to the competitive effort already under way to secure the services of German scientists and engineers with knowledge of military or economic value. Nor did anyone allude to the urgent inspection of German centers of research, invention, and experiment that was going on in all zones, or to the hurried removal of parts, special machines, blueprints, and formulas. In all these activities the Russians were being as diligent as bank robbers, and the Americans and British not lazy.

The whole vast program for shaping the political and social future of Germany was approved by the Heads of State with what in retrospect seems amazing ease.[5] Reread now, its provisions seem almost as taut and definite as any text of the sort could be. It was to become clear, however, even before the Potsdam summer was over, that in many ways they were not governing.

The configuration of political and social life and institutions that were emerging in West and East were even then becoming less, not more, alike. In the Western zones the military authorities were slow and cautious about allowing local political units to exercise authority. And in selecting or approving persons for official posts, favor was shown to former liberals, conservatives, socialists, whose avowed outlook and ideals were akin to those of the United States and Britain. In the

---

[5] The full text is contained in the Protocol of the Proceedings of the Conference, which is given in Supplementary Note 7. The statement of policies was not made public until March 1947. But all its main points and features were made known long before by the Control Council or the Zone Commanders.

Soviet zone the Russians were carrying out with speed and vigor a positive program in aid of a group of "anti-Fascist democratic parties," similar to those they were nurturing in countries of eastern and southeastern Europe. All were effectively under Communist influence and control. The German Communist Party had been officially reconstituted in the Soviet zone—and was taking the lead in an effort to form a united front with liberal and leftist parties.

In short, hardly had the Heads of Government signed their names to the statement of political principles for all of Germany when many were bent differently in the Western and Eastern zones. If they had been observed impartially they would have hindered what the Western occupants came to regard as essential tasks or duties of relief and reconstruction in their zones, and have prevented the Russian occupants from going forward with their program for change and domination in their zone.

32. Germany: Economic Principles

WHILE the conference was progressing toward an accord on political principles it was stumbling over the task of writing down a set of rules to guide the direction of German economic activity.

In the ordinary way the shape and substance of the economic life of a nation slowly form out of its own resources, needs, and the nature of its people. At Potsdam the members of the coalition tried to forge them out of their desires. But the task was most perplexing. Offsetting needs and aims had to be balanced and reconciled. A coherent pattern had to be woven out of a great complex of connected questions; what was to be done about each of these bore upon what ought to be done, or could be done, about all the others. Thus the task would have been hard even if all four occupants had been in roughly the same economic condition, had been devoted to the same vision of society, and had been without fear or rivalry. But none of this was so.

The Soviet Union needed and wanted more from Germany than did the United States or Great Britain. Its rulers were more set than those of the West on using this chance to smash Germany once and for all. The suffering that the Germans might thus have to endure would be small penalty for what they had caused. The Russians were not worried lest the Germans revolt if treated harshly. They were sure they could take care of that eventuality.

The ideas and attitude of the British government were in flux. It was becoming more and more worried over the prospect that the Soviet Union (and its associates) might obtain such superior strength that not even western Europe could be kept out of its grasp. So the British were leaning toward the conclusion that Germans must not be left in such distress that they might turn to Communism, and that Germany should be allowed to regain enough productive strength to correct the impending excess of Soviet power in Europe.

The French people hated the Germans for what they had done in France. They were afraid of those determined capabilities that the Germans had shown after their defeat in the First World War. But the French government, led by de Gaulle, was aggrieved at the western allies and mistrustful of the Soviet Union. So its interest in German economic affairs was self-centered. Its policy was directed toward enlarging the basis of French economic strength by taking away from

Germany the great resources of the Ruhr and Saar and farm areas of the Rhineland.

The American government was trying to blend in its policy four components that would not stay in stable mixture: detestation of a Germany that had debased itself under Hitler; a belief that it must be prevented from ever again assaulting others; anxiety that a Germany left in misery would be harmful and dangerous; and a resolve not to be compelled to provide the Germans with means of support.

It is little to be wondered then that the conferees often seemed lost, as, line by line, clause by clause, they went over the statement of principles for the direction of German economic affairs which the President drew out of his well-worn brief case.

Although the import of this proposal is still well-remembered, an enumeration of its main essentials may be helpful to historical accounting. 1) All of Germany was to be treated as a single economic unit. 2) In organizing the German economy, effort was to be directed primarily toward the use of the land and industries that would provide goods for peaceful pursuits. 3) There was to be a diffusion of economic power. 4) Uniform policies were to guide the exercise of control in all zones. 5) Similarly, as far as possible, ration scales were to be the same everywhere. 6) Only such controls were to be imposed on the German economy as were deemed necessary for a few elementary purposes; the prime one was to assure the production of goods and services (a) needed by the occupying forces and displaced persons, or (b) essential to prevent starvation, disease, or great unrest. 7) These controls were to be managed by the Germans themselves.

What a tribute this essay in re-creation was to the hope that Western and Communist systems of life could tolerantly adjust to each other!

In the discussions of this American prescription by the Economic Sub-committee of the conference, by the Foreign Ministers and the Heads of Government, many changes in substance and form were considered. But only a few were significant.

The American proposal read simply: "During the period of occupation Germany shall be treated as a single economic unit." Molotov wanted to qualify or condition this principle by inserting the clause "according to detailed instructions to be issued by the Control Council." The intent was to assure that all acts in execution of this policy would be subject to Soviet approval. But Molotov did not insist on the change.

A poorly recorded discussion in the Economic Subcommittee meeting of July 19 centered on the clause in the American proposal authorizing the controls necessary "to assure the production and maintenance of goods and services to meet the needs of the occupying forces and displaced persons in Germany, and *essential to prevent starvation, disease or civil unrest.*" This was perceived to leave so open a field for judgment that a zone commander could at his discretion maintain any factories he might desire. So for the clause I have italicized there was substituted another. This, it may be remarked in passing, turned out to be just as hard to define precisely: ". . . *essential to maintain in Germany average living standards not exceeding the average of the standards of living of European countries* (the United Kingdom and the Soviet Union excluded)." This was approved all along the line, and was included in the final statement. It was a more lenient level than the one set down in Eisenhower's Directive.[1]

The American text provided that in the absence of special reasons to the contrary, each of the zones of occupation, including the Greater Berlin area, was to draw its supplies as far as practicable from the areas of Germany from which they had come before December 1937, whether or not any part of such territory was administered by or ceded to another state. The need for affirming this had been sharpened by the Russian refusal to provide food and fuel to the people in the western sectors of Berlin, although the whole city had formerly obtained its supplies from the areas under Russian and Polish control.[2] But Molotov would not agree to the American formulation. He argued that changing conditions made it impossible to foresee how much food, coal, and other products could be had in the several parts of Germany; and he urged that therefore it would be best to let the Control Council deal with the matter in the light of later knowledge. Besides, he stressed,

[1] For details see Supplementary Note 4.

[2] At the meeting between the western commanders and Zhukov in Berlin on July 7, Zhukov had insisted that the western occupants accept proportionate responsibility for bringing in food and coal for the people of Berlin. He argued that sufficient supplies would not be available from the Russian zone, and none could be had from the areas taken over by the Poles. Clay had agreed, as an interim arrangement, to send in some coal from the Ruhr and some food. The American government had feared this would impair our basic position in regard to turning over part of the Soviet zone to the Poles, and also deprive other countries that needed coal from the Ruhr and Saar of greatly needed supplies.

Any historian who is not weary of irony can bemuse himself with the thought of how the Berlin situation would have developed if the Russians had agreed at this time to provide all sectors of Berlin with food, coal, and other essentials, and if therefore this relation of dependence of the western sectors on the western allies and West Germany had not developed. Presumably had the western sectors of Berlin procured most of their essentials from the east they would have had to export most of their products to the east.

as did Stalin, no matter what was written into this statement the Poles could not be *compelled* to produce for shipment to Germany. To these resistant reasons the Americans and British yielded. The provision was omitted.

The language of the American proposal imposing restraints on heavy industries was deemed by the Russians to be inconclusive. Thus it was revised to read: "In order to eliminate Germany's war potential, the production of arms, ammunition and implements of war as well as all types of aircraft and seagoing ships shall be prohibited and prevented. Production of metals, chemicals, machinery and other items that are directly necessary to a war economy shall be rigidly controlled and restricted to Germany's approved post-war peacetime needs. . . . Productive capacity not needed for permitted production shall be removed in accordance with the reparations plan . . . or if not removed, shall be destroyed."

Then there was the cluster of disputed points bearing, one way or another, on the question of how primary and dominant the quest for reparations was to be. Was this to rule over or be subject to other purposes and wants; and if subject, to what extent and in what ways? How little or much regard should be shown for the condition of the Germans, the revival of German industry, the preservation of a system of private ownership and activity?

The American officials and experts had not been able to formulate a precise set of rules for the adjustment of these related considerations. Too many of the pertinent facts were not predictable. But they had leaned on previous experience—leaned too hard in fact. Prospectively reparations were to be collected in two main forms. One was by removal from Germany of industrial and other equipment not needed for approved peacetime production. The other was by exports from stocks and future production. The Americans were determined that the United States should not again be called on to provide the means to enable the Germans to pay reparations to others. Thus they wanted to have it plainly stated that German export capacity was to be used to pay for approved essential imports before it was expended in reparations. Only the excess not needed to meet this bill should be deliverable as reparations.[3]

[3] As expressed in the first proposal submitted by the American delegation, "The United States Government . . . must insist that such necessary imports as are approved by our governments shall constitute a first charge against exports of current production and stocks of goods." Potsdam Papers, Document 894.

The Russian attitude slanted in the reverse direction: the Germans should first be made to meet such obligations as were imposed on them; and imports into Germany should be restricted to whatever the Germans could pay for after they had met this prior condition. Otherwise, the Soviet officials argued, the German and foreign capitalists would want to profit from foreign trade and skimp reparations for those who had suffered. The Germans, as a way of escaping reparations, would exaggerate their need for imports to live. After all, Maisky said to the other members of the Economic Subcommittee on July 20, the Germans would not have to import much in order to live as well as the people of Central Europe on whom they had trampled; and a national economic plan could be worked out on this basis. But the Americans and the British denied this supposition and rejected the proposed ways of validating it.

As it became clear that they would not give in, Molotov (on July 23) proposed a graduated formula: "After payment of Reparations enough resources must be left to enable the German people to subsist without external assistance. In working out the economic balance for Germany the necessary means must be provided for payment for imports approved by the Control Council. In case the means are insufficient to pay simultaneously on reparations account and for approved imports, all kinds of deliveries (internal consumption, exports, reparations) shall have to be proportionately reduced."

Was that not fair, Molotov asked? Byrnes and Eden said they did not think so. Nothing that was needed to compensate for approved imports into the western zones, they maintained in effect, should be turned over as reparations. Nor would they grant the Soviet government the chance, through the Control Council, unduly to reduce internal consumption in order to restrict imports into the western zones. They hinged their refusal on the idea that if imports were too small, then the Germans would produce less, say of coal, and the Western powers would have to make up the deficit.

Ultimately the circuit of argument over this point was broken by forgoing one of the forms of reparations that had been in mind—deliveries from stocks and future production. I will not here describe the involved version of the formula which was enmeshed in the final accord.

In my judgment the guide for policy adopted at Potsdam was not, as has so often been alleged, unjustly harsh to the Germans or forgetful of other countries' need for German production. But it was not well aligned with reality. The aims designated exceeded the means approved. The many provisions together constituted a prospectus—it might almost be said a plan—that could have been carried out only if German activities were greatly and rigidly controlled. Yet it was stipulated that the controls were to be slight. Perhaps this disparity was unavoidable: while the West and the Soviet Union could agree on spaciously described aims, they would not have been able to agree on adequate measures for achieving them. And the many beams of purpose were not coordinated. One of the central problems—one that was sure to arise—was left in a maze or haze: in what relative measure was each of the main requirements—imports, the standard of living, the removal of industrial equipment as reparations—to be cut down, if the need arose?

Even if the ideas of the four sponsors had been in consonance, they would have found it hard to turn this verbal exterior of an accord into reality. But actually, even during the years when the effort was made, the French government refused to heed the rules, and the differences between the Western and the Soviet participants in control became virulent. In Great Britain and the United States favor veered away from policies that had been approved under the spell of the war experience. The authorities—military and civilian—working in the western zones found the policies too drastic and grew inclined to sympathize with the Germans rather than to punish them. Business and banking people, not indifferent to the benefits for themselves of increased trade, did not find extreme the condemnatory judgment of a special article in the *Economist* of September 8, 1945, which began with the statement that "It is not difficult to demonstrate the utter lunacy of the Allies' policy toward Germany." The author reasoned that the Russians and Americans could favor such policies because to the closed economy of Russia and to the superproductive economy of the United States, the decline of Europe could not mean what it meant to unhappy Europeans; and he exhorted: "Britain has almost absolute control in the Ruhr. It can not only give a lead but make it effective. It should be the task of all the new Government to reverse the old errors, end the deadlock, and get to work."

This view—that the revival of the German economy was essential to the welfare of the whole of Western Europe—quickened the reversal of the Potsdam program. But the changes in policy would not have come about so quickly or been so thorough if this belief had not been companioned by a conclusion that a strong Germany was needed to resist the pressure of Soviet Communism upon the West. When nations change alliances, old principles, like old vows, are bartered for new ones.

But in recording these reflections I have wandered far forward from the discussion at Potsdam of that one subject in the economic field over which there was most dissension. What reparations was Germany to make, and in what ways?

33. Germany: Reparations

It had been thought that the Allied Commission on Reparations, born at Yalta in February, would start work at once to produce a detailed plan. But several months had passed before it met. During this time the armies of the coalition fought their way to a junction on the Elbe. Even while they were doing so, American and British officials were becoming troubled over the conditions in western Europe and impressed by the need to revive production of essentials quickly. This awareness had begun to dim the reasons for reducing German industrial capacity, and to infringe on estimates of obtainable reparations.

Edwin Pauley, organizer and owner of oil properties in the Far West, and a skilled and aggressive negotiator, had been chosen to be United States member on the Commission. The instructions given him reflect the diverse and in some ways conflicting ideas that mingled in American official thought.[1] In compressed meaning these were:

1) As large as possible a part of the total of reparations should be secured out of the existing national wealth of Germany, as small a part as possible out of recurrent future production.

2) The removal of factories and machinery in German heavy industries would be the main and most satisfactory source.

3) Reparations from future production, in so far as it was found necessary to agree to them, should be of such sorts and amounts as not to require the maintenance of German war potential or continued dependence of other countries on Germany. This meant that they should be primarily raw materials and natural resources.

4) The American government advanced no fixed idea about what the total should be. But various elements in the instructions amounted in effect to a caution against the designation of an excessive volume or sum.

5) The division of the total among the various claimants was left open for discussion.

This program did not assign reparations a reliable priority over other uses for German production. Deliveries were to be contingent on the course of future judgment of the German situation. The authors must have realized that this would not please the Russians, or seem to them just.

---

[1] The text of these instructions is Appendix 5 to the Pauley-Lubin Report of September 20, 1945, to the President. The Report is in Potsdam Papers, Document 980, but this Appendix is printed in Footnote 3 to Document 363.

In any event, as soon as the Reparation Commission met at Moscow (in mid-June) Pauley had become aware of it. He learned that the Russians were still set in the belief that the total obligation should be set at twenty billion dollars—half to go to the Soviet Union. He did not openly resist the use of this figure "as the basis of discussion," to use the phrase approved by Stalin and Roosevelt at Yalta. But he let his colleagues on the Commission know that the American government thought it best not to try to fix any total until more was known about the German ability to make reparations. Time was needed to determine what that would be.

During the interval before the Potsdam conference the members of the Commission had agreed on certain principles that were roughly in accord with those outlined in the instructions to Pauley. But they had differed drastically on several elements, among them the crucial one of whether to fix a minimum sum which Germany would be obligated to pay as reparations, unconditionally.[2]

Pauley had wished to stipulate that only such excess of exportable German products as were not needed to pay for essential imports into Germany should be allocated as reparations. Otherwise the American government feared that the United States would again, as after World War I, be under duress to provide the means for sustaining Germany so that it could pay reparations.[3] The Soviet advocate on the Commission had tried to dispose of the problem by saying in effect that the United States should let the Germans get along as best they could. Who could foretell with certainty whether there would be any excess?

Then Pauley had tried to get the Commission to agree that the Control Council should be authorized to prevent the transfer of any item as reparations when it deemed that its loss would reduce the available economic means in Germany below the minimum necessary for the other purposes of the occupation; if the members of the Council were unable to agree, each zone commander should be judge in regard to removals from his zone. This in essence would have meant that each of the occupant governments could restrict the flow of reparations from

[2] The range of agreement and disagreement is set out in the telegrams that Pauley sent to Washington between June 19 and July 14. Potsdam Papers, Documents 356, 366, 367, 370, and 375. The text of the principles that the members of the Reparation Commission agreed to recommend for guidance of the Control Council in preparation and administration of the reparations plan was submitted as an Annex to the Proposal made by the American delegation at Potsdam on July 17. *Ibid.*, Document 894.

[3] It is notable that Truman, in his later account of his ideas on setting out for Potsdam, singles out one "pitfall" that he was determined to avoid: "We did not intend to pay, under any circumstances, the reparations bill for Europe." *Year of Decisions*, page 323.

its zone—the British from the Ruhr, in particular. Any such leeway seemed to the Russians to endanger the value of the whole accord.

Regretfully the President and the Secretary of State had accepted the necessity to concern themselves with these issues at Potsdam. The Soviet government had been put on notice.

The discussion turned into one of the most sustained contests at the conference. It enlivened the American and British sense that the Soviet Union was indifferent to the fate of western Europe. And it nurtured the Soviet belief that the western allies would rather spare the Germans than enable the Russian people to get just redress and aid. American resistance to Soviet wishes became more firm as the days went by, when it was seen how set the Russians were in support of detachment of part of their zone for the Poles. British resistance was stimulated by worry over how the dense population in Britain's zone, augmented by the inflow of refugees from the east, was to be kept alive, healthy enough to work, and obedient.

Who would want now to follow the many coils of the argument? The purpose of recall and reflection will be served by a brief summary of those points on which, during the first week of the conference, the animated discussions centered. In regard to two of these, American and British official judgment had been gradually changing and hardening since Roosevelt and Churchill had talked over the subject with Stalin at Yalta.

The governments of the western allies became set in their refusal to agree to the designation of any fixed total sum—in terms of dollar value—of the reparations to be exacted. They had concluded that it was not prudent or sensible to try to do so, for they would thereby lose freedom to shape reparations policy by future facts. If any figure acceptable to the Russians was set, various disagreeable probabilities were foreseen. The United States might well be compelled to support the Germans; or to witness prolonged misery and discontent in Germany; or to agree to the exercise of state controls of German economic life which would ease the way toward Communism.

The Russians retreated from twenty billion—the sum originally asked —to the lesser sum of eighteen or sixteen billion. They contended that without some such indication of the dimensions of the German obligation, the Soviet Union would have no assurance of substantial reparations. Deliveries from the western zones, especially capital equipment from the Ruhr, would be subject to the judgment or whim of the western allies and the Germans. In more blunt language than the Russian negotiators allowed themselves, a reparations plan without a firm guiding mark would be no plan at all, and possibly a disappointing cheat.

To all the many repetitions of this contention Byrnes and Eden (and Bevin) answered over and over that it would cause future trouble if a fixed total were set, since so many elements of the German future could not be forecast. Byrnes remarked that it was a mystery to him where the volume of reparations sought by the Russians was to come from, since so much German property had been destroyed. In immediate prospect, the United States would have to give products to the Germans, not receive products from them. Similarly Eden stressed that the problem faced by the British in the Ruhr was how to prevent starvation, since the Soviet government would not send in food and other supplies. Here was the origin of the idea of arranging a formal exchange between zone authorities of capital equipment from the Ruhr in return for food and coal and other products from the east.

It had been conceived that the Germans were to pay part—though only the lesser part—of their reparations by delivering goods that they would produce during the next ten years. But further study of the situation had led the American and British officials to realize that in order to meet this obligation and pay their way in trade the Germans would have to be allowed to retain a large structure of production—large enough, it was estimated, to enable Germany again, if control were relaxed, to produce weapons, or at least be a valued ally or associate in some aggressive purpose. Moreover, the amount of surplus capital equipment that might be taken as reparations would be less. For these reasons the Americans and the British came to think it best that reparations in the form of recurrent deliveries from future production should be forgone. To this the Russians do not seem to have strongly objected; they were more intent on getting equipment and machines with which to manufacture products for themselves than on obtaining products from the Germans. Perhaps they figured also that the Germans would resort to the same type of measures they had followed after World War I, in order to evade any obligation to make recurrent deliveries, and that the benefit would not be worth the trouble.

The Americans sought to restrict by definition what was to be taken out of Germany as "restitution" and "war booty," as distinct from reparations.[4] The Russians wanted approval for a wide range of recaptures or seizures in these forms, since their country had been, in their words, plundered by the Germans "almost to the last nail and thread."[5] As the end of the conference neared, the views and wishes on this were as contrasting as they had been at the start. But when the basis of the reparations plan was converted, so that each occupant was to derive reparations primarily from its own zone, the need for uniform definition of these two kinds of acquisitions was no longer judged essential, and the conference desisted from the effort.

This change in the proposed system of securing reparations was crucial. The Americans and the British had entered the conference disposed to agree that it was best and feasible to allocate an "overall percentage" of an unspecified total to each of the three powers—to be applied to Germany *as a whole*. But as the argument went on they renounced that idea. They thought the basis had been impaired by the detachment of part of the Russian zone. And they judged it would work to the disadvantage of the western allies, since the Russians were taking so many industrial plants from all parts of Greater Berlin and East Germany that little would be left for delivery as reparations to the West or to support the German economy.[6] For these and other reasons they concluded that the conception of sharing out reparations from Germany *as a whole* had best be abandoned.

Byrnes first openly broached the new basis in an informal talk with Molotov on the morning of the 23rd. He said he was wondering whether it might not be wise to alter the plan so as to authorize each of the occupants to secure reparations from its own zone—with a supplementary accord for an exchange of products between zones, such as trading equipment from western zones for food and coal from the Soviet zone. The Russians resisted the change: they offered to compensate for what they had already taken from their zone by reducing

---

[4] For a more extensive summary of American and Soviet views and proposals on this question see Supplementary Note 5.

[5] A vivid and detailed contemporary description of the plight of the Soviet Union and the needs of its people is presented in the book by the American newspaper correspondent Harrison Salisbury, *Russia on the Way*, published in 1946.

[6] The Russians were in turn accusing the Americans of having removed optical and laboratory equipment and experimental apparatus from those sections of the Soviet zone they had occupied. Zhukov had described these removals in a report to Stalin, and had sent a copy to Pauley, who on July 29 passed on a summary of it to Truman at Potsdam. Pauley thought Zhukov's report was a smoke screen for what the Soviet government was doing before the approval of a reparations plan.

their claims from ten to nine billion; suggested that the property obtained by the Poles in the area turned over to them be treated as the Polish share of reparations; insisted that it was essential to them to get a fixed allotment of reparations from the Ruhr; cited their information that only a small part of Ruhr industrial capacity—ten to fifteen percent—had been destroyed, and the rest remained; maintained their opinion that if the will was there, it would be quite possible for Germany to meet Russian reparation demands, and submitted analyses to prove it. The experts of neither side convinced the politically aware on the opposed side.

The American group at Potsdam may not have realized the full import of this change in policy which it sponsored. The Russians, when they agreed to let the Poles detach part of their zone, had made the first rent in the prospect that the three allies would stay together in the control of all of Germany as a joint concern. The American decision to change over to a separate zonal basis of reparations was the second one. Neither can be said to have created differences of interest. But both were admissions that such differences existed, and made them deeper.

During the following days of conference the issue was left open. Attention turned to other matters. The last attempt to bridge the differences waited on the coming of the new English Prime Minister and Foreign Secretary.

34. The Springing Arch of the Conference

THE conference had been going on for almost a fortnight. The argument about the western frontier of Poland was rotating in a fixed orbit. That over reparations was snagged. As the Americans and the British pondered what was likely to happen if the conference dispersed without accord on these two focal issues, the possibilities seemed somber. Would the Russians then be even more willful and grasping? How could they be deterred, without going to war, from doing what they wanted in areas under their control? How might an acknowledged break affect plans for Soviet entry into the war against Japan and Soviet actions in the Far East? Would it not impair the formation of the United Nations, and mar the prospect that the peace might be made enduring and just by that association? The conclusion formed was that the more prudent course would be to pay tribute to the power of the Soviet Union to have pretty much its own way in Poland—if thereby greater protection could be had against Soviet intrusion toward the west.

Resigned to the fact that Stalin would not refuse the Poles any of the area of Germany they were claiming as their own, determined to frustrate Russian designs in or against the western zones of Germany, and swayed by the wish to align Italy with the democracies, Byrnes devised what in later idiom has come to be called a "package deal." He resorted to an offer to assent to the western frontier the Poles were seeking if the Soviet government would give in to his terms in regard to German reparations and the refurbishment of Italy. If agreement were reached on such a reciprocal basis, the conference would have been of use in disposing of the problems of Europe, its prime purpose. Terminal could be—would be—considered a "success." After all, who with any knowledge of history could expect the United States and its friends to have all their own way, to secure settlements that were wholly what they wanted? The usual results of diplomacy were work-a-day compromises.

Truman, by then baffled and eager to get away from these trying sessions of talk, fell in with the idea. Attlee and Bevin had deeper pangs and felt greater concern over having Poland—under Russia—come so far west. But the British did not have the strength to prevent it, or the willingness to use such strength as they had. So they could not continue to stand out. Moreover, their country was going to have a hard time to get through the coming winter and manage its zone in

Germany; it would need all the relief and aid it could get in these tasks through a betterment of the prospect for western Europe.

Thus a proposal was written out which wrapped together "solutions" for all three of these conference issues. This meant, in a sense, converting decisions about each of them into a single decision whether the conference was to leave the war allies in political touch or separated.

The 29th was a Sunday, with free time in the morning after church. Truman asked Stalin to come and see him so that they might try to clear up the matters that were delaying the end of their work. But Molotov drove over instead. He explained that Stalin had a cold and that the doctors would not let him out of the house. The President then asked Byrnes to inform Molotov of the matters he had in mind to talk over with Stalin. The Secretary of State named Polish western boundaries and German reparations as the main ones. If, he went on, they could reach an accord on reparations along the lines of his proposals to Molotov, the American government would go further to meet Soviet wishes in regard to Poland's western frontiers. He gave Molotov a paper defining the degree of our willingness. Its crucial paragraph read:

"The Three Heads of Government agree that, pending the final determination of Poland's western frontier, the former German territories east of a line running from the Baltic sea through Swinemünde, to west of Stettin to the Oder and thence along the Oder River to the confluence of the eastern Neisse River and along the eastern Neisse to the Czecho-Slovak frontier, including that portion of East Prussia not placed under the administration of the USSR in accordance with the understanding reached at this conference and including the area of the former free city of Danzig, shall be under the administration of the Polish state and for such purposes should not be considered as part of the Soviet zone of occupation in Germany."[1]

The new American concession was in the last clause. It was a hard and grave one to make, for by then it must have been foreseen that despite all the formulas in the preamble, it meant the permanent detachment of this part of Germany. Molotov did not say outright that the Soviet government did not think the offer good enough. He chose instead to poise his resistance on the fact that the Poles were insistent on retaining also the administration of the country between the eastern and western Neisse rivers. Byrnes admitted this was so. He pointed

[1] Potsdam Papers, Document 1151.

out that his proposal did not necessarily mean that Poland would be denied this further area; it might be had later by award of the peace conference. The President asked Molotov to submit his proposal to Marshal Stalin. Molotov said he would.

It may be reported, before telling of the other elements of this talk with Molotov on the morning of the 29th, that Stalin's cold did not prevent him from receiving Bierut that same evening. If an entry made by Mikolajczyk in his notes is reliable, Stalin had the impulse to repay the Americans a little for their eager wish for an accord. He seems to have made a passing effort to persuade Bierut to be content with a little less. The entry records Stalin as telling him that the Americans had "presented their boundary proposal based on the eastern Neisse and the line of the Oder, including Stettin"; and as asking him whether, in view of the fact that the Americans had given in somewhat, the Poles would not do likewise and agree, for example, to "the line of the Queis [Kwisa] instead of the Lausitzer [the western] Neisse." The diary entry goes on to state that "After consultations with experts it was decided that we [the Poles] should possibly agree not to the Lower Neisse, but only with regard to the watershed lying between the Queis and the Lausitzer Neisse. That would deprive us of some water installations but not affect the industry of Silesia."[2]

About the revised American plan for reparations, which Byrnes had asked him to consider, Molotov in this talk ceased to object in principle. But he inquired how much capital equipment his country could count on getting from the Ruhr (in addition to what was had from its own zone). Byrnes said one-quarter of what was available as reparations. Molotov then drily remarked that one-quarter of an unknown quantity meant very little. To make the obligation firm, they ought to agree on a definite money sum or physical quantity—say two billion dollars or six billion tons. And would the Russians get this equipment without compensation, or would they have to give in exchange products from the eastern areas? These questions were left over at the end of Molotov's talk with Truman and Byrnes. But thereafter the tussle over reparations ceased to revolve around concepts and turned into a bargain about "how much."

[2] The only available record of this talk with Stalin is a diary entry by the Polish Deputy Prime Minister Mikolajczyk, headed Babelsberg, July 29, 1945. The first line reads: "In the evening Mr. Bierut was invited to see Marshal Stalin, who informed him . . ." This presumably means that Mikolajczyk was not present. But he may well have been a participant in the consultations among the Poles and in the decision to accept a compromise line. The diary entry is printed in the Potsdam Papers, Document 1391.

Either the recorded report of the talk between the Poles and Stalin on the evening of the 29th is incorrect or misleading, or the Americans were not informed of it. In any case, overnight they decided, having talked again with Attlee and Bevin, to make their ultimate concession. They improved their offer about the Polish frontier and clarified their offer about German reparations. And they introduced a third element into the bargain: Soviet assent to a new version of the provision to ease the way toward the conclusion of a peace treaty with Italy and its admission into the United Nations.

In another talk with Molotov on the afternoon of the 30th, just before the Foreign Ministers met in formal session, and with only interpreters present, Byrnes exposed his repacked proposal.

The American government, he said, would accede to the Soviet wish that Polish administration extend to the western instead of to the eastern Neisse River. The revised paper he gave Molotov on this point read: "pending the final determination of Poland's western frontier the former German territories east of a line running through Swinemünde, and thence along the Oder River *to the confluence of the western Neisse and along the western Neisse to the Czechoslovak frontier* shall be under the administration of the Polish State and for such purposes should not be considered as part of the Soviet zone of occupation in Germany"[3] (my italics). Molotov said he was very pleased.

In regard to the entry of Italy into the United Nations, Byrnes explained that he had sought a compromise between his British and Soviet friends. After looking at its text, Molotov remarked that while he could not say so finally, he thought it would be acceptable.

Then Byrnes went on to what he called the "most difficult" of all the questions—reparations. On that he had new terms in mind also. In these, however, he made clear, the British had not yet concurred. As already envisaged, the chief source of reparations for the Soviet Union was to be its own zone. But the Soviet would also be accorded the right to receive, without any payment, fifteen percent of such industrial equipment in the Ruhr as was found to be not necessary for the German peace economy, and another twenty-five percent for an equivalent value in food, coal, and other products. Out of these receipts it was to satisfy Polish claims.

Who would decide what equipment in the Ruhr should be made available for reparations? The British, Byrnes thought, would have to have the last say, for the Ruhr was in their zone and they would

[3] *Ibid.*, Document 1152.

know what must be left there. Molotov, however, was of the opinion that the allies ought to make the determination jointly, through either the Control Council or the Reparation Commission. Byrnes indicated his willingness to consider this method, though final authority would have to be left with the zonal commander.

Molotov urged that the share to be allocated to the Soviet Union without payment be increased to twenty-five percent. Byrnes said he did not think the British would assent. Why then, Molotov asked, confine the offer to the Ruhr; why not agree to turn over to the Soviet Union a share of the surplus (in the understood sense) industrial equipment from all western zones—say, ten percent free and fifteen percent on exchange? Byrnes demurred on the ground that the United States, from its own zone, would have to take care of the claims of others—France, Holland, Belgium, Yugoslavia.

At the end of their talk Molotov remarked that he thought progress had been made. Before they went on to the waiting formal session of Foreign Ministers, he handed Byrnes a paper recalling the Soviet wish to have a separate four-power administration for the Ruhr—which has been described.

Up to the very last hour of the last session of the conference all three conference groups chiseled away at the façade and edges of the proposed bargain, reshaping a detail here or there, omitting or rewriting a clause or sentence.

At the session of the Foreign Ministers right after his talk with Molotov (on the 30th) Byrnes submitted his proposal formally. He asked that the three elements be accepted or rejected as a group, and stressed that the American government, in a spirit of compromise, was acting against its judgment about Polish western frontiers. Nevertheless, if conjoined accord could be reached on all three matters, he would be content. If not, the three Heads of Government would have to decide whether to keep on trying. Refusal of the American offer would have meant, although Byrnes did not say it, that Russia would get no reparations from the western zones. But he did point out that lack of an accord in these fields would hinder—if not prevent—settlement of many other questions, including the economic treatment of Germany.

In the ensuing discussion Bevin showed a firm preference for an arrangement whereby the equipment to be given to the Soviet Union, as an uncompensated addition to what it would get from its own zone, should come from all western zones, not merely the British one. Byrnes gave in, halving the proportions in the original offer to the Soviet Union.

Bevin also did not favor the reparations arrangements providing for an exchange between zonal authorities of products from the western zone for products from the east. He was afraid that such a plan would lead to disputes. Moreover, as a Socialist he thought it would be contrary to the concept of free economic movement through all of Germany and its control as a unified whole. His view was that the supply of goods in Germany ought to be treated separately. But in this regard he deferred to American judgment.

In all these offers Molotov found the same incisive fault. They were only percents of an unknown figure. Again he asked why not fix a total money value or tonnage total? Again Byrnes explained why this could not be done. When the Soviet Foreign Minister realized that Byrnes would be unyielding he directed his efforts toward getting other improvements. First he tried for a bigger percent; this Byrnes refused to consider. Next he tried once again to make sure that the Soviet government would have a chance to determine, through either the Reparation Commission or the Control Council, which equipment could be taken out of all zones. Byrnes was willing to agree to this, provided, as he once again proposed, that each zone commander had the right to refuse to allow the removal of anything from his zone that he thought was needed for the other purposes of the occupation.

Byrnes tried to assuage Molotov's criticisms of the reparations plan by referring again to "the proposal with regard to the Polish western frontier which involved a greater concession on our part than this one from the Soviets. The paper referring to the United Nations [admission of Italy and relations with the other satellites] involved a concession on the part of our British friends." He knew it was "a concession for the Soviets to agree to percentages," but if we made concessions, "the Soviets should also."[4] Molotov retorted, as paraphrased in the Minutes, that "It was a concession to Poland, not to them." "Had he not," Byrnes asked, "heard his friend, Mr. Molotov, make a more eloquent plea for this frontier than the Poles?" But Molotov would not yield; with convinced stubbornness he maintained that it was essential to fix a definite total obligation that Germany should be required to meet.

Byrnes concluded that the only step left was to see whether the three Heads of Government might be able to knit up the differences. Before them was the apparition of the condition of Europe; and in their ears

[4] Potsdam Papers, Minutes, Meeting of Foreign Ministers, July 30.

were reports of the wish of their peoples for a tranquilizing settlement that would enable them to get back to work, grow food, repair their houses and factories and roads, reopen schools, and have warmth in their homes. Against such needs, was it not better to accept less than seemed right, and trust the passing years to cover over imperfections?

On the next afternoon, the 31st, when Byrnes reported to the Heads of Government in Plenary Session, Stalin and Molotov objected to linking up the three questions. Each, they contended, should be decided on its own merits. But Byrnes, with Truman's support, maintained that the American government would acquiesce in the proposed Polish western frontier only if accord were reached on the other two matters as well. Stalin said that "Mr. Byrnes can use such tactics as these if he wishes, but the Russian delegation will vote on each question separately."[5]

As regards reparations, Stalin said he would renounce the Soviet wish for a guaranteed money or quantity total. He also accepted the principle that each country should exact reparations from its own zone —provided that in addition the Soviet Union would get industrial equipment from the western zones, part free, part in exchange for other products. But how soon would the amount of equipment be determined? Would three months not be enough? When Bevin said it would not be, Stalin agreed that six months should be allowed. What of the percentages? Was the Soviet Union not entitled to larger ones? And should it not get in addition shares in German industrial and transport companies in the western zones, and about one-third of German gold and assets abroad?

Truman and Byrnes were disposed to accord the Soviet Union a larger percentage of the excess industrial equipment in the western zones (fifteen and ten instead of twelve and a half and seven and a half) if the Russians would forgo their claims for shares in German companies, gold, and foreign assets. But Bevin was loath to do so. He maintained that the offer, as it stood, was liberal. But to Stalin it was "the opposite of liberal." The United States, he observed, was willing to meet the Soviet wishes. Why was Britain unwilling? After again trying to persuade Stalin of the reasons and again failing, Bevin at last said, "All right then." Stalin expressed his thanks.[6]

[5] Potsdam Papers, Cohen Notes.
[6] Potsdam Papers, Minutes, Plenary Session, July 31. Little historical importance attaches to the final discussion in subcommittees of the conference about various secondary · and still unsettled points in the reparations accord. Stalin renounced his claim to shares in

So ended for the time being the bout over German reparations, if not the conflict of purposes behind it. The accord was in reality frail,[7] for it rested on the intent to deprive Germany of a substantial part of its industrial capacity, and to maintain rigid restraint on its industrial development. And even if this purpose had been sustained, the program could have brought satisfaction only if all four participants in the control of Germany had used the same gauge in their treatment of the Germans and in their measurement of what the Germans needed for a peace economy (the allowed level of industry); and if the principles had been carried out with wholesome and mutual good faith.

But on this occasion no one chose to sermonize. The negotiators turned with relief to the details of the other two matters. About the Polish frontier settlement, Bevin was inquisitorial. He said that his instructions were to stand for the eastern Neisse, and he would like to ascertain what was involved in the new proposal. How was the transfer of this part of the Soviet zone to be regarded? Would the area remain "technically" under allied military control? If not, it would in effect be a transfer of territory before the peace conference, for which the approval of the French was also required.

The cross volley of comments that followed remains of interest.[8] Stalin retorted that this concerned the Russian zone and the French had nothing to do with it. Bevin asked whether the British could give away pieces of their zone without approval from other governments. "No," Stalin said in effect; this could be done in the case of Poland,

---

German enterprises located in the western zones of Germany, and to German foreign assets in all countries, in return for the exclusive right to take shares in the German enterprises in the eastern zone and German assets in Bulgaria, Finland, Hungary, Romania, and eastern Austria. He gave up any claim to German gold captured by allied troops.

At the last session, after Attlee said he was anxious that France become a member of the Reparation Committee, Stalin assented to that also.

But in one of his related aims—to secure for the Soviet Union a third of the captured or surrendered German fleet and naval vessels that were in the hands of the British and Americans—Stalin secured full satisfaction. An account of the vigorous negotiation about this matter before and at Potsdam is given in Supplementary Note 3.

[7] None was readier to profess the contrary belief—that this reparations accord was clear, conclusive, and workable—than Pauley and his staff. They did not want the job of turning this Potsdam accord into a program. All of them resigned and returned to the United States. Pauley, in an interpretative memo he wrote at the request of the U.S. zone commander before his departure from Potsdam, explained this action on the ground that the policies laid down in the Potsdam agreement to guide reparation removals were "clearly defined and complete though of a very general character." This memo is referred to in Potsdam Document 990, but is not printed. Its main substance is summarized in Ratchford and Ross, *Berlin Reparations Assignment;* see *ibid.,* pages 46-47, for Pauley's August 4 letter to Clay and the authors' comments.

[8] Potsdam Papers, Minutes, Plenary Session, July 31.

for there they were dealing with a state that had no western frontier, but this was the only such situation in the world.

Byrnes spoke up reassuringly. "They all understood," he said, as reported in the Minutes, that "the cession of territory was left to the peace conference. They confronted the situation where Poland, with Soviet consent, was administering a good part of this territory; by this action the three powers agreed to the administration in the interim by Poland in order that there would be no further dispute between them in regard to the administration of the area by the Polish Provisional Government."

Bevin ended his resistance to a decision that the British government thought unwise. He said he would not press the matter. But he asked again what would now happen in this "zone." Would the Poles take over and the Soviet troops withdraw? Stalin said they would if this territory did not constitute a line of communication with their army in Germany. "There were two roads there, one to Berlin to the north and the other to the south. These two roads were the ways by which the troops of Marshal Zhukov were supplied, in the same way that Holland and Belgium were used by the British." Would the Soviet troops, Bevin then asked, be limited to these lines of communication? Yes, said Stalin; in fact, four-fifths of the Soviet troops in Poland had been brought home, and thought was being given to further recall.

Truman took the measure of the moment, saying that then "all agreed on the Polish question." The others nodded.

Then without ado the third American proposal, having to do with the admission of Italy into the United Nations, was approved.[9]

The most trying issues were thus settled. The climax of the conference was past. A parting in wrath had been averted. The negotiators —none more impatient than the Americans—could soon start for home.

On the next day (August 1) Truman, on behalf of the three participants in the conference, informed the Poles, who had stayed in Potsdam, of the agreements about their country. The responsibility of the Polish government for the administration of the territories within the described boundaries was confirmed, he said, in accordance with its

[9] Stalin was prevailed on to forgo his demand that Italy be required to pay reparations. The Soviet delegation had contended that it ought to be made to pay, since it had caused so much havoc to all the allies. The Russian view was that it could pay six hundred million dollars over a six-year period. But the Americans and British denied that possibility, pointing out that they had already felt it necessary to send a half-billion dollars' worth of goods to Italy to prevent disease and unrest, and that any reparations would come out of their own purses. The Russians, rather than prolong the conference, gave in.

desires. Moreover, the Russians had agreed to withdraw their armies from these areas, except those along the lines of transit across Poland. Then the President went on to refer to the other features of the conference resolutions on Polish affairs: the transfer of Polish property abroad to the Provisional Government; the agreement to help Polish soldiers and civilians abroad to return to Poland; the confirmation of the condition that the Polish Provisional Government was to hold free elections as soon as possible. All, he ended, were unanimous decisions.

Bierut thanked him formally. Mikolajczyk thanked him personally. The Polish Communists were most justified in their satisfaction. From this time on the Americans and the British could not effectively deter them. Much as they might need and want economic aid from the west, they could get along without it if the Soviet Union stood by them.[10]

Since I cannot always resist noting the ironies of history, let me add one other reflection about the Polish frontier—brought to mind by certain current events. Suppose the Americans and British had had their way, instead of the Poles and Russians, and the line between Germany and Poland had been set further to the east. In that event, the eastern part of Germany—the area that was the Soviet zone—would presumably now be larger and more populous, and have greater coal, industrial, and land resources. Thus it would be more able to challenge the effort of West Germany—formed out of the American, British, and French zones—to represent all Germany. Poland would have been weaker, perhaps less afraid of future German attempts to regain its territory, but perhaps more dependent than it is on the Soviet Union. The way the situation has worked out up to now is one of those numberless instances in history which show how often results are different from anticipations. This is no excuse for not trying to be foresighted. But it is a reason for recognizing how hard it is to be.

Throughout the discussion of frontiers in Central Europe the thoughts of the British and the Americans were darkened by worry over what was to be done about the millions of Germans who had been living in the

[10] In the Protocol the provision about frontiers was slightly reworded and read: "The three heads of government agree that, pending the final determination of Poland's western frontier, the former German territories east of a line running from the Baltic Sea immediately west of Swinemünde, and thence along the Oder River to the confluence of the western Neisse River and along the Western Neisse to the Czechoslovak frontier, including that portion of East Prussia not placed under the administration of the Union of Soviet Socialist Republics . . . and including the former Free City of Danzig, shall be under the administration of the Polish state and for such purposes should not be considered as part of the Soviet zone of occupation of Germany."

parts of Germany taken over by the Russians and the Poles, and in Czechoslovakia and Hungary.

In the section of East Prussia that was being absorbed into the Soviet Union, some hundreds of thousands of Germans had made their homes. But by the summer of 1945 almost all of them either had been taken captive or had fled before the Red Army. In the other former sections of eastern Germany—including those nominally in the Soviet zone but actually in control of the Poles—there had formerly been some eight million Germans. How many of these had remained there, and out of captivity, was in dispute. The Poles and Russians professed that almost all had gone, leaving the towns, the farms, the factories, and the mines abandoned. But the best official estimates of Washington and London were that between two and three million still remained, though each day many thousands more were fleeing or being cast out.[11] In that part of Czechoslovakia known as the Sudetenland some two and a half million Germans had lived. Some were prisoners of the Russians and Czechs and others had fled. But it was thought that over a million—perhaps many more—still lingered.

The Soviet government regarded the historic experience as finished. The Germans who had surged east had been sent running back to the west. It felt no obligation to care about their condition or fate. Neither did the Poles, so many of whom had lived through the years of agony under the Germans.[12] They wanted all that still were in the area assigned to them to leave quickly to make room for their own people. The Poles were moving west out of areas east of the Curzon Line and from crowded and poor regions elsewhere in Poland. They were eager to take possession and begin to produce wanted food and coal and start on the work of rebuilding. The attitude of the Czech authorities, inflamed by similar memories and inspired by similar purposes, was the same.

The American and British governments recognized how strong, and in a way just, was the wish and will of these nations to thrust the Germans back into what was left of Germany. They were distressed, however, at the suffering that abrupt expulsion was causing old and young, poor and rich, healthy and sick. They thought it the duty of any humane people to subdue their impulse to punish and to show com-

[11] A vivid and well-detailed account of the expulsion of the Germans from Silesia is to be found in Rozek, *Allied Wartime Diplomacy*, pages 70–74.

[12] The Polish military losses had been heavy; about 2.5 million Poles had been transported to Germany as forced laborers; and about 3 million Polish Jews had been exterminated in ghettos and concentration camps. *Zachodnia Agencyou Prasow*, summarizing a report made in 1947 by the Office of War Reparations of the Polish Government.

passion for those who were losing their homes. They foresaw that the more miserable the experience of the migrants, the more likely would it be that they would remain hostile to the states in the east which had cast them out, and look long for a chance for revenge. And they were worried over how they could, within their ravaged zones of occupation in Germany, take care of this influx of millions. How were they to be fed and given medical care; where were they to be housed; how was work to be found for them; how could they be prevented from being a threat to civil order?

For these reasons the American and British governments tried to turn this flight of Germans into a gradual and orderly movement adjusted to the means and measures for taking care of the migrants and resettling them. Once they had the hopeful idea that the Russians and Poles might be willing to have the Allied Control Council work out some plan to that end—acceptable to the governments of the countries of departure. But they found out that Stalin was grimly indifferent to what was happening. When Churchill said that it was necessary to give thought to where the Germans would go, Stalin's first comment was that the Czechs had already evacuated those in the Sudetenland into the Russian zone of Germany, throwing them out on two hours' notice. Obviously he thought there was nothing to be done about that. Churchill answered that that might be so, but something might be done about the Germans that the Poles were thrusting out of areas within the zone originally assigned to Russia. Stalin said they were allowing about a million and a half Germans to remain until the harvest was over, and they would then force this remainder to leave also—for they were taking revenge on the Germans for injuries the Germans had caused them over the centuries. Churchill, with Truman supporting him, maintained that the Poles did not have the right to expel Germans from what was part of the Soviet zone into the American and British zones, where there was too little food and fuel.

In deference to their protests, Stalin did agree to ask the three Foreign Ministers to try to develop a program for the regulation of this forced return of Germans. A proposal was made to entrust the Control Council with the duty of striving to insure that it was carried out with care and foresight. Molotov did not turn down the idea of such joint supervision. But he advanced the opinion that all that the Council would be able to do was to prevent the Germans from crossing into Germany; it could not give orders to the governments of Poland, Hungary, or Czechoslovakia. Sir Alexander Cadogan, who was acting as spokesman for Britain until Bevin arrived in Potsdam, thought that these governments might be prevailed on to cooperate.

The Heads of Government took up the subject again on the 31st, after they had at last reached accord on Poland's western frontier. Before them was a proposal originating with the Foreign Ministers which, among other provisions, called on the Polish, Czechoslovakian, and Hungarian governments to suspend further expulsions pending an examination by the Control Council as to how they could be well managed. Both Molotov and Stalin found reasons for critical indifference. Molotov said that the recommendation was apt to be misconstrued. Stalin said he was doubtful whether it could be carried out, since all three governments were asserting that the Germans wanted to leave and that they did not wish to stop them from doing so. Let us find out whether that is so, Byrnes argued, by adopting this proposal. If the Germans were leaving of their own free will, the attempt would have no effect, but it would do no harm. If, as he believed, these governments were making it either impossible or unsafe for them to remain, it might lead to an orderly solution. In the end Stalin shrugged and said he would agree to the effort to find out if any such arrangement would be of use. For this Truman expressed appreciation. Perhaps, he remarked, the document would not change the situation very much, but it would help.[13]

But before the Control Council was well enough organized to carry out this assignment, the main inflow of miserable refugees was well under way. The roads were crammed day and night with destitute human beings looking for a place in which to rest or stay, and the military governments in the western zones were being forced to take temporary care of several million Germans from the east.

[13] The statement on this subject is in paragraph 20 of the Protocol, printed in Supplementary Note 7.

35. A Backward Glance at the Accords about Germany

BEFORE going on to what was done about the other situations dealt with at Potsdam, we may pause long enough for a few short reflections on the several accords having to do with Germany. The impulse to look back is quickened by the transformation that has since taken place in the relation of Germany to the war allies. Even though any conclusions that now come to mind must be curved if not controlled by the later experience, they may be granted a page or two.

The Potsdam accords were not, in intention or in effect, unjust or cruel to the Germans. The central conceptions—to allow the Germans to experience the same kind of deprivation and misery they had brought on others; to cast out and debar from influence those who had served the Nazi cause ardently; to reduce German industrial power to make war; to forbid the Germans all military forms and organizations; to redirect their political life in the hope of shaping it into a peaceful democracy—all these were good.

But the nature of the effort needed to effectuate them was not appreciated: the sturdy intent, the patience and superior skill and character that would be required of all four executors. They were defying the past and trying to change the pattern and values of German national life. To do that they would have to dominate their own fears and rivalries, be true to their common vows, and live in unassailable trust and mutual regard. Otherwise, no matter how complete, coherent, and clear the statements signed, how full the power of the four to command Germany, failure and fury would follow. And in various ways the accords were neither complete, coherent, nor clear.

Reviewing what has happened since, the mind is impelled to seek other possible courses that might have served the world better. Boldly, some may be suggested. If they stand up at all, it is only as a group.

1) Even though it might have caused the collapse of the conference and the Poles might have refused to retreat, assent should have been refused to the extension of Polish administration beyond the eastern Neisse.

2) The contemplated period of joint occupation and control of Germany should have been much shorter—only long enough to carry out definite measures such as disarmament, the destruction of the Nazi system, and arrest of war criminals.

3) It should have been stipulated that as soon as these tasks were done all foreign forces would leave Germany, and the zonal system of control would be ended.

4) Instead of prolonged occupation, the four powers should have (a) worked out adequate permanent arrangements for inspection in Germany to assure the effectiveness of the ban on arms; (b) entered, along with other European member states of the United Nations, into a mutual protection pact against possible future German aggression; and (c) compelled Germany to agree to remain permanently neutral.

5) The plan of reparations should have been differently conceived. It might have included the acquisition of some German industrial plants, those not needed for peaceful production even in thriving times. But the main source of reparations should have been future German productivity, over not too long a period of years, increased as that revived. The total could have been stated as a part or percent of that production —to be made available in kind.

The only value now of such a retrospective sketch of the other routes that could have been followed is to sustain the view that the subsequent division of Germany and the dangerous struggle over its affairs might have been averted. But this is a belief that must appeal more to faith than to history. The agonizing tendencies that surge out of the record of the past challenge it. Seldom have nations, after so deep a war, worked out arrangements that did not bring on later conflicts. Seldom have war coalitions between great powers lasted. For survival itself, however, the nations must now transcend the usual run of history. They cannot undo what has been done. But each can and must henceforth, by word and act, make up for the failure at Potsdam to turn victory over Germany into unfearing peace among themselves.

36. Austria

When the Heads of Government gathered at Potsdam, the Soviet authorities were still barring the way into Vienna and hindering the advance of the American and British contingents into their zones. On July 16, General Petrov, Chief of Staff for Koniev, the Soviet Commander in Chief in Austria, had bluntly told the American, British, and French Deputy Commanders (Gruenther, Winterton, and Cherrière) that they would have to wait until their governments had ratified the accords still under discussion in the EAC. But he had agreed that specialist officers of the four countries might meet in Vienna to discuss the use of roads, railways, and airfields, incident to the prospective joint occupation of the city. The visitors had found the Soviet officials obliging and reasonable. Their work enabled the Deputy Commanders to clear away the remaining differences about the use of airfields in Vienna, the dimensions and locations of the sectors, and related matters. On learning from the Chiefs of Staff of the progress made, Truman on July 19 authorized Winant to give notice that the American government approved the accord on zones, and on the next day the President signed the formal document.

But Churchill, either because news was not conveyed to him so quickly or because he wished to make it plain that he thought the Soviet government had behaved in an unfriendly way, complained about the Austrian situation at his meeting with Truman and Stalin on the 20th. Two full months before, he recalled, the British government had "humbly" asked that British officers be allowed to go to Vienna to look into accommodations there. After many talks and petitions, consent had been given. But the British troops were being kept out of Vienna, and prevented from taking over that part of Styria that was assigned to them. The Soviet forces had liberated Austria three or four months ago. How much longer were its allies to be compelled to wait before they were received as equals? Their right to ask an end to the delay was all the greater since they had retreated into their own occupation zones in Germany.

Stalin answered quietly. Could the newcomers fairly expect to take up their positions in Austria and Vienna until the agreements determining them had been completed? Now that this had been done, the troop movements could begin that very day or the next. He wished also to comment on a report made by Field Marshal Alexander, to which Churchill had referred, reproaching the Russian government for the situation. Alexander was himself to blame for some of the troubles in arranging for the advance of British troops into their zone. He had spoken and acted as though Soviet troops were under his control. That had caused ill-feeling. Churchill defended Alexander. He reminded Stalin that the American military commanders directing the movement into the American zone in Austria were also far from satisfied. Truman agreed. But this brisk examination of the reasons for the long enforced halt ended amiably.

Within a few days the movement into zones was well under way. The first arriving American and British officials found great congestion in their zones—especially in Linz and Salzburg, where many thousands of Germans and Hungarians were staying until they could be evacuated. So the American and British commanders paused before sending their national garrisons into Vienna. They waited until they knew whether their governments were going to have to support the people in their sectors. Formerly the whole city had obtained its supply of food from eastern Austria. Would the Soviet authorities take all the surplus food in their zone for the Red Army, or for export to Russia, and leave none for the western sectors of Vienna and of Austria?

Alexander was summoned to Potsdam. As he entered the conference room (at the Seventh Plenary Session on July 23) Stalin rose from his chair and walked round the table to shake his hand. Alexander and Churchill explained that they did not have the food to provide for the five hundred thousand people in the British sector of Vienna. Truman said that the United States did not have enough transport to send food for those in the American sector—some three hundred and seventy-five thousand. They desired, therefore, that Russia would see to it that the people of the city were fed from the east, as before. Stalin showed doubt whether the food situation in Vienna was really worrisome. He would talk it over with Marshal Koniev.

The next day he informed Churchill and Truman that the Red Army was ready to issue rations to all zones in Vienna until such time as the British and Americans could make other arrangements. They had to be satisfied with that retractable promise. The first Western troop units marched into Vienna a few days after the conference at Potsdam dispersed.

The Control Council did not begin to function until over a month later. The Russians were slow in sending instructions to Marshal Koniev, who was to be the Soviet member. He was reported to be ill. Then

General Mark Clark, who was to be the American member, was delayed on a good-will mission to Brazil. The arrangements for feeding Vienna were still not completed, nor were they when the Control Council met formally in Vienna for the first time, on September 11. At the end of that meeting the members of the Council issued a statement to the Austrian people, declaring that they were assuming supreme authority in Austria on matters affecting the country as a whole.

The directives that the American and British governments had issued to their prospective representatives on the Control Council were in accord with the intentions long since announced by all three members of the coalition. Austria was to be treated as a liberated country, free and independent within its former frontiers. Nazis were to be expelled and all German domination was to be ended. All military organizations were to be dissolved. The production of weapons was prohibited and all facilities specially designed or adapted to produce them were to be transferred, converted, or destroyed. Military control was to be exercised for these ends. It was also to seek to develop a sound Austrian economy devoted to peaceful pursuits and not dependent on Germany. Local self-government and the formation of a freely elected government were to be fostered. As soon as these were established the Austrians were to be given a chance to run the country under allied guidance and supervision. In economic matters Austria was to be regarded as a unit—with freedom of domestic trade and a centralized system of currency, finance, and transport.[1]

It was hoped that the instructions to the Soviet member of the Council were shaped on the same principles.

The question was put to the test in the Potsdam tussle over whether or not Austria was to be made to pay reparations. The Americans and the British had gone to Potsdam resolved to resist the Soviet demand for a mortgage on the Austrian economy, and if compelled to agree to it in principle, to restrict it in practice. They were aroused by the way in which the Russians were carrying out of Austria all kinds of equipment and reserve stocks, on the score that it had all belonged to the Germans (which much of it had). This meant, they foresaw, that they would have to give economic and financial aid to the Austrians, even if the pillage ended. The conclusion, as set down in the paper in the American Briefing Book, was that a program of reparations "limited to the transfer of existing capital equipment clearly in excess of the healthy peacetime requirements of the

[1] The full text of the detailed Directive issued on June 27, 1945, to General Mark Clark is in the State Department *Bulletin* of October 28, 1945.

Austrian economy, such as machinery in the armament plants erected since 1938 . . . need not necessarily conflict with the policy of this government."[2]

The Russians at first proposed that the Austrians be compelled to deliver over a six-year period industrial products to the value of two hundred and fifty million dollars, and maintained that they could do so. Byrnes, upheld by Cadogan, refused to agree to the imposition of any fixed obligation, or to any transfer except of machinery in war industries of no use for producing anything but weapons. Molotov went into a tirade: the Austrians ought not to go unpunished, since they had caused great damage and suffering to the Russian people.

This was at the Ninth Meeting of the Foreign Ministers, on July 27, while the clash over German reparations and Polish frontiers was most tense. But in the end, after these other issues were settled, Stalin gave in. Having consented to the rejection of the Soviet proposal, he said he was willing to have it recorded in the Protocol that "It was agreed that reparations should not be exacted from Austria." He asked, however, that this decision not be made known. As Molotov explained, publication might tie the hands of the occupying authorities unnecessarily; it was better to let the Austrians hope for this leniency than to know it had been granted.[3] Presumably what he had in mind was that if the Austrians did not know that he had agreed to renounce reparations, they would be less troublesome over Russian exactions under another name, or no name at all.

As part of the settlement, however, Truman and Attlee deeded to the Soviet Union all German assets in the Soviet zone of Austria, possibly because they thought the Russians would take them over with or without permission. The Soviet government subsequently claimed that almost all the large plants in eastern Austria were German-built or owned by Nazis, and therefore legitimate forfeit.

The policies confirmed at Potsdam reflected the difference between the victors' attitudes toward the Germans and toward the Austrians. This was evident in every phase of their conduct and experience in control.[4]

---

[2] Potsdam Papers, Document 273.
[3] Potsdam Papers, Cohen Notes.
[4] This has been well described and analyzed in a perceptive later review of the operations of the Allied Council in Balfour, pages 313-20, which ends with the comment: "Finally . . . there was a difference of character between the Austrian and German peoples. . . . It was symbolized in their preference for the light comedies of Mozart as against the massive heroics of Wagner. There can have been few members of the Allied Commission who remained wholly unaffected by its subtle and disarming influence."

At Potsdam the affront caused by Soviet recognition of the Renner administration as the Provisional Government of Austria was rubbed out. More thorough examination of its nature and conduct had ended in a good report. The members of the government had spoken and acted moderately, and its Prime Minister had entered into friendly and useful association with Austrian political groups that had no affiliation with the Communists. The revision of judgment is recorded in the ponderous paper in the American Briefing Book that was taken to Potsdam: "in terms of the men themselves and in terms of representation of political forces, the Renner government is as good a coalition as could be devised at the present time." And so it was deemed sensible "to proceed with recognition as soon as our desiderata with respect to zones of occupation and control machinery are met." When this was done, it was suggested, the Allies should stipulate that the Renner government hold "supervised" elections for a constituent assembly.[5] The British official attitude had been going around the same bend, though more slowly.

On July 23, after the amiable ending of the bout of argument over the reasons why Western forces were still kept out of their zones and Vienna, Stalin urged the Americans and British to allow the Renner government to extend its authority to their zones. He implied that this might aid in the collection of food. Truman and Churchill answered cautiously. But after Stalin, on the next day, said that the Russians would issue rations to all zones in Vienna, they both promised to consider this step as soon as their garrisons were in the city. In prinicple, they said, they thought it could be taken. This was recorded in the Protocol in the following way: "The Conference examined a proposal by the Soviet government on the extension of the authority of the Austrian Provisional Government to all of Austria. The Three Governments agreed that they were prepared to examine this question after the entry of British and American forces into the city of Vienna."

As postscript it may be observed that the Renner government managed to keep on good terms with all members of the Allied Council, and to prove useful both in carrying out their policies and in guiding the Austrian people toward a decent peacetime existence. In October, after changes sought by the western allies were made, the Council declared that the authority of the Renner government was extended to the whole of Austria. To acquire greater authority and secure recognition from the West, that government arranged for elections before the end of the

[5] Potsdam Papers, Document 268.

year. The way in which they were conducted brought respect for its freedom and reliability. The Communists' vote was very small (5.42 percent). Perhaps that is why the Soviet government did not resort to measures and maneuvers to displace the Renner regime in favor of one closer to Moscow.

All four allies recognized the elected Provisional Government early in 1946. A miserable and prolonged quarrel, akin to those over the recognition of the governments formed in Poland and the smaller satellites, was avoided. Austria was the one country in Central Europe over which the western allies and the Soviet Union did not glare at each other. Perhaps it ought to be made host to the diplomacy of the world.

37. Yugoslavia and Greece

EVEN though troubles with and over Yugoslavia had continued to ruffle relations between the allies, they were given only passing attention at Potsdam. Churchill and Truman tried to induce Stalin to join them in pleas or pressure directed toward Tito. They were still seeking to get the Yugoslav leader to comply with their view of accords into which he had entered: his agreement with Alexander for the division of control over the Italian province of Venezia Giulia (including Trieste and the Istrian Peninsula); and his compact with Subâsič (the last Prime Minister of the Royal Yugoslav Government-in-Exile) about the balance of political elements in his government and measures for converting it into a representative democracy on Western lines. But to follow what was done at Potsdam about these two running causes of dissatisfaction, let us pause and look back.

It may be recalled that in late May an accord between the western allies and Tito, on the division of Venezia Giulia into separate zones of control, was coming into sight. But it had remained out of reach.

On May 31, while Hopkins was still in Moscow, Truman had reported on the situation to Stalin. Tito, he said, was trying to impose troublesome conditions on his acceptance of the proposed arrangement. The Supreme Commander in the Mediterranean (Alexander) must have adequate authority in the area under AMG to carry out his task and protect the interests of all concerned. He must have final say about the way in which civil administration was carried out therein, and about the number of Yugoslav troops that might remain. Churchill sent word to Stalin that he concurred in these opinions.

In the wake of these messages to Stalin, the American and British Ambassadors had handed Tito a note explaining the attitude of their governments and submitting the text of the accord into which they were ready to enter. After a week of talk between General Morgan, speaking for Alexander, and Yugoslav military representatives, an agreement emerged. Having been approved by the Combined Chiefs, it had been signed on June 9 by the Ambassadors and the Yugoslav Foreign Minister. Since almost all those sections of Venezia Giulia in which the Italians were most numerous were kept out of Tito's grasp, it was foreseen that the Italians would not make too much of an outcry.

The province was divided into two zones of temporary occupation along what came to be known as the Morgan Line. The area west of the line—Zone A, which included Trieste, the railways and roads from there to Austria via Gorizia, Caporetto, and Tarvisio, as well as Pola (on the Istrian Peninsula)—was to be under the command and control of the Supreme Allied Commander. Yugoslav forces in that area were to be limited to two thousand troops, and be subject to the allied command; the rest were to be withdrawn. It was stipulated that while the area was under Allied Military Government, "Use will be made of any Yugoslav civil administration which is already set up and which in the view of the Supreme Allied Commander is working satisfactorily. The Allied Military Government will, however, be empowered to use whatever civil authorities they deem best in any particular place and to change administrative personnel at their discretion." The area east of the line, Zone B, was left in Yugoslav control.

Ritualistic form had been observed in the last article: "This agreement in no way prejudices or affects the ultimate disposal of Venezia Giulia west of the line. Similarly the military occupation and administration by Yugoslavia of the parts of Venezia Giulia east of the line in no way prejudices or affects the ultimate disposal of that area."[1]

This accord, it had turned out, was neither complete nor conclusive. Within a fortnight new quarrels had started. The British and American governments were offended by Yugoslav removals of property and conscription of Italians in Zone B. They asserted that this contravened the understanding. The Yugoslavs denied the charge, on the score that the Belgrade agreement did not ban the seizure as "war booty" of industrial plants owned or operated by "Fascists." On the other side of the line, Allied Military Government concluded that it could not fuse in its operations the local governments and courts that Yugoslavs had set up in the area with the older and very different Italian system of administration. Nor was it found feasible to adopt a dual system, allowing the Yugoslav committee system to operate in communes with a Slovene majority, and the Italian system of prefectural administration in communes with an Italian majority. Thus AMG proceeded to supplant the Yugoslav-sponsored organizations. Tito regarded this as a violation that justified him in transgressing other provisions.[2] The American and British governments warned him (on June 15) that they took a serious view of what they regarded as Yugoslav derelictions.

General Morgan, Chief of Staff in SAC, with assurance enough to

[1] U.S., Department of State, Executive Agreement, Series 501.
[2] An analytical account of these difficulties is to be found in Harris, pages 342-46, where details not related here are clearly and impartially recounted.

treat Alexander's orders as guidance, not commands, had planed away some of the abrasive edges of the first accord—in a supplementary one signed at Monfalcone on June 20. But others remained. The sharpest of these was the question whether the local Yugoslav administrations in the AMG zone were to be ousted and replaced by Italian forms and persons.

Then on the 21st, Stalin, under the impression that the negotiations were still at an impasse, had espoused Tito's views, in messages to Truman and Churchill. He attributed the trouble to the refusal of the Allied Command to entertain even the minimum wishes of the Yugoslavs, to whom, Stalin went on, credit was due for liberating the area from German invaders, an area moreover where the Yugoslav population predominated. He said he was loath to aggravate the situation, but felt impelled now to stress the opinion that the haughty tone used by Alexander in dealing with the Yugoslavs was inadmissible; his indiscretion, in a public address, in comparing Tito with Hitler and Mussolini was unfair and insulting to Yugoslavia.[3] The message had concluded, however, with a calm statement of hope that the rightful interests of the Yugoslavs would be respected, especially since on the main points they had met the allies halfway.

Churchill's answer (dated June 24) had ignored the complaints. He hoped that as the situation had now been "happily adjusted" at Belgrade (Monfalcone) they might, if necessary, discuss the position when they met at Berlin. He added that although he had not seen the terms of Alexander's statement before it was issued, he could assure Stalin that Alexander was entirely well disposed toward both Russia and Marshal Tito, and that he was sure that Marshal Tolbukhin would confirm this opinion.[4]

[3] Alexander had said "Marshal Tito's apparent intention to establish his claims by force of arms . . . [is] all too reminiscent of Hitler, Mussolini and Japan. It is to prevent such actions that we have been fighting this war." *New York Times*, May 20, 1945.

[4] This short message is in Stalin Correspondence, vol. 1, page 370. This collection does not contain the longer and more vigorous rejoinder to Stalin, dated June 23, which Churchill (in *Triumph and Tragedy*, pages 560-61) states that he sent in answer to Stalin's message of June 21; and Churchill does not refer to the shorter message of which I have given the substance.

In this longer answer Churchill bluntly accused Tito of using violent pressure to take territory to which he was not entitled. And he forthrightly refused to make any excuses for Alexander's public criticism of Tito's tactics. He concluded with a fling at the menacing Russian expansion: "It seems to me that a Russianized frontier running from Lübeck through Eisenach to Trieste and down to Albania is a matter which requires a very great deal of argument conducted between good friends."

It may be surmised that the longer message was written before Churchill received word of the supplementary military accord that had been signed by General Morgan on June 20 at Monfalcone. Morgan may have deferred dispatch of the news and substance

Truman, who was in Olympia, Washington, had been informed of the concluded accord—which may have caused him too to moderate his answer to Stalin. This asserted that due regard had been shown to the legitimate interests of both the Yugoslavs and the Italian populations. He repeated the point that the Allied Commander in his zone must have adequate authority to carry out the tasks entrusted to him and safeguard the interests of all concerned. In that connection Truman pointed out that no effort had been made to interfere with the responsibility of the Yugoslav commander in the region entrusted to him east of the Morgan Line. Referring to the "fundamental principle" of the agreement of June 9—that no action could be permitted that would prejudice the ultimate disposal of the area—the President said he had the impression that the Yugoslav government might not have made clear to the local commanders the full meaning of the accord. But, having upheld the opinion that Tito was being fairly treated, Truman like Churchill remarked that they would have the chance at Potsdam to talk over "any further aspect of the agreement" which Stalin felt ought to be considered.[5]

Stalin, in terse acknowledgments, had said that he did think there were points that needed clarification, and that he was ready to examine them at their prospective meeting.

Before setting off for Potsdam, Churchill and Truman had heard again from Alexander and the Italian government. Alexander reported that Yugoslavs were still trying to provoke trouble and to discredit the allied authorities in their zone by strikes, such as the one going on at the time in Trieste. The Italian government was bothered more by the way in which the Yugoslavs, in that section of Venezia Giulia under their control, were taking away the property of the Italians, mistreating them, and drafting them into the Yugoslav army.

Tito and Subâsic joined in messages to Truman and Churchill, while they were in Potsdam, which once again accused AMG of reinstating Fascist laws and administrators. They appealed for the use of the "democratic institutions" that the Yugoslavs had set up in Yugoslavia. And

---

of the accord until after he had a chance to explain and justify it in a meeting at SAC on June 22; there he related how hard it had been to negotiate with the Yugoslavs, and how necessary it had been to give and take in order to get General Jovanovic to sign the document. Message from Ambassador Kirk to Secretary of State, June 22: Potsdam Papers, Document 556.

Whether this longer message was actually sent, and then followed up by the shorter one, which evidently reached Stalin, I leave for others to find out.

[5] Potsdam Papers, Document 570.

they urged that elections for local governments be held very soon in all the part of Venezia Giulia under Allied Military Government.[6] But the three Heads of Government evidently judged that although these converging complaints were trying, the danger of real trouble was past. In any case they decided to leave them to ordinary diplomatic discussions.

But they did spend time arguing over the form and future of the Yugoslav government. Was it to be a dictatorship in which only Tito's adherents would have power, or was it to be turned into a representative democracy in which a diversity of political parties might contest for office and freely advocate their policies?

Again we must glance backward. Tito had continued to ignore the advice that the Heads of Government, together at Yalta, had passed on to him.[7] The various peoples in Yugoslavia had not been given a free chance to choose their form of government or select their rulers. The National Liberation Front (Tito and parties that supported him and his ideas and actions) had kept dominant control of all executive powers. Membership in the legislature had not been made more inclusive. In all six of the "federal" states that had been set up, Tito's friends were installed in office without consulting popular opinion. The political police were repressing all opposition. Political committees were acting as courts and making law as they went along. Those who did not belong to the favored groups were given smaller food rations than those who did. Industry was being rapidly taken over by the government, and all external trade brought under its control.

Despite inducements offered by Tito for their cooperation, Subâsić and other political leaders had abstained. They had counted on outside support to enable them to resist and to continue to fight for an open, free political system. The American and British governments—provoked

---

[6] *Ibid.*, Document 1207.

[7] This, it may be recalled, was directed toward effectuating the agreements signed by Tito and Subâsić on November 1, 1944. One of the agreements had stipulated that "The new government will publish a declaration proclaiming the fundamental principles of democratic liberties and guaranteeing their application. Personal freedom, freedom from fear, freedom of worship, liberty of conscience, freedom of speech, liberty of the press, freedom of assembly and association will be specially emphasized and guaranteed; and in the same way the right of property and private initiative." A second agreement had provided that elections for a constituent assembly were to be held within three months after the liberation of the whole country—in accordance with a law on elections which would guarantee a secret ballot and the right of all political parties that had not collaborated with the enemy to present lists of candidates. The text of the Tito-Subâsić accords is given in U.S., Department of State, *The Conferences at Malta and Yalta*, pages 251-54.

as they were by Tito's bold attempt to get and keep control over the whole of Venezia Giulia—had resolved they would not be friendly with his regime or give it economic aid unless it corrected its course. Curiously, they seem to have hoped that they could induce Stalin, when he was in their presence at Potsdam, to join them in laying down the law to Tito —in telling him that they thought it essential that truly free and democratic elections be held in his country, as a prelude to the operation of a constitutional government.

At Potsdam, Truman looked to Churchill to pursue the matter. The Prime Minister's first try showed that he was not going to have an easy success. On the 18th, when he dined with Stalin, he reviewed the troubles his government was having with Tito. Harking back to the compact he had made with Stalin when he was in Moscow at the end of 1944, that they should have equal influence in Yugoslavia, Churchill lamented that Britain had none at all. Whereupon Stalin said it could not have less than the Soviet government, which often did not know what Tito was about to do. That may have been nearer the truth than it was thought to be at the time.[8]

On the next day the Prime Minister submitted a proposal that in substance would, first, put the three allies on record as being of the opinion that the principles set out in the Tito-Subâsič agreement had not been put into practice; and second, lead to the issuance of a joint statement recalling that they had recognized the Yugoslav government in the belief that the agreement would be effective, and saying they expected it to be carried out in the near future.

Stalin thought they could not discuss the question unless the Yugoslavs were present—or in any event could not achieve results without them. Why not, he asked, call representatives of the Yugoslav government to Potsdam? Churchill asked whether Stalin meant Tito or Subâsič. Stalin said they could call in anyone. In that way they could find out whether Churchill was correct in thinking there were extreme differences among the Yugoslavs; the Yugoslav government should not be put on trial without being heard. Churchill agreed this was not a bad idea. But Truman objected. He is recorded as saying that he was in Potsdam "as a representative of the United States to discuss world affairs. He did not wish to sit here as a court to settle matters that would eventually be settled by the UNO. If we do that, we shall become involved in trying

---

[8] Even though Tito, in a speech he made on June 17 which caused grimaces in the State Department and the Foreign Office, had said "Long live our great ally, the Soviet Union, with its leader, our genius, Stalin."

to settle every political difficulty and will have to listen to a succession of representatives, de Gaulle, Franco and others. He did not wish to waste time listening to complaints but wished to deal with the problems which the three Heads of Government had come here to settle. If they could not do that their time was wasted."[9] Whereupon Stalin, who a moment before had argued that they could not do anything about the situation unless the Yugoslavs were heard, now heartily agreed that it was not necessary to hear them. He remarked that he found Truman's observation "correct." Churchill was taken aback. Stalin suggested that they pass on to another topic.

Just before the conference adjourned, the Secretary of State received word from our Embassy in Belgrade that the three chief dissenting political leaders, one of whom was Subâsič, were proposing new laws regarding the enlargement of the legislative body, the constituent assembly, elections, and voting procedure. But they did not think they could bring about such important changes without Western support. The Chargé expressed the belief that this was the last chance for the great powers to display support for the principles for which these men were striving. But by then it was too late to summon the Yugoslavs to Potsdam. And there was no reason to believe that Stalin had changed his mind and would approve any statement encouraging reform of the government unless the Yugoslavs had been given the same chance to justify their action as the Poles. So no new initiative was taken.

The discussion of the Yugoslav internal situation was the more touchy because at the time excited broadcasts and editorials in the Yugoslav radio and press were accusing the Greek government of persecuting Slav minorities in Greek Macedonia and provoking frontier incidents. Some even went to the extreme of accusing the governing circles of Greece of intent to invade Yugoslav territory and to persuade Brit-

[9] Potsdam Papers, Minutes, Plenary Session, July 19. It is difficult to be sure what was in the President's mind. The text of the American minutes could be read to mean either that he did not want to enter on a discussion of the Yugoslav political situation at all, which would be singular because he was insisting on discussion of the similar situation in Poland; or that he thought the three of them could tell the Yugoslavs what to do without consulting them, which seems belied by Stalin's response.

His own subsequent account of his statement leaves the impression that he was just impatiently drawing a line. "I told them frankly," he recalls, "that I did not wish to waste time listening to grievances but wanted to deal with the problems which the three heads of government had come to settle. I said that if they did not get to the main issues I was going to pack up and go home. I meant just that. Stalin laughed heartily and said he did not blame the President for wanting to go home; he wanted to go home too." *Year of Decisions*, page 360.

ish troops in Greece to occupy Southern Albania. The Greek government was denying these allegations, and in turn was accusing Tito of sending armed bands into Greece and stirring up trouble wherever he could.

The Soviet delegation at Potsdam submitted two proposals that were meant to be a warning and reproof to Greece. The British delegation submitted proposals that were meant to be a warning and reproof to Yugoslavia.

It was apparent that none could win unanimous assent. So when at one of the late sessions of the conference Bevin suggested that they be dropped, Stalin quickly said "Yes, welcome," and Truman said "I am satisfied."

Russian support before Potsdam of the agitation in the Yugoslav press and radio about alleged intentions of the Greeks was in line with the flow of comment in the Soviet press and radio about the government in office in Greece. It was accused, in concert with the British, of suppressing by force all democratic elements and denying political freedom and justice to the Greek people. Such statements were customary counter-attacks to Western assaults on the existing regimes in the countries of central and southeastern Europe that were Soviet wards.

They had an element of truth in them; the Greek authorities were dealing harshly with their revolutionary opponents and trying to disperse their leadership. But measures were being shaped that would enable the Greek people to express their political opinions freely and without fear. Plans were being considered for elections for a constituent assembly and for a plebiscite to decide whether the country would retain or dismiss the monarchy.

The American government, wishing to stay out of the Greek political struggle, had hitherto left it to the British to bear the onus of intervention and support for the conservative coalition they had helped to power. But in June its reluctance had given way. How could it ignore charges not only by dissident groups in Greece and in Soviet circles, but by more impartial witnesses, that the elections in Greece would be controlled by the Greek government, while seeking assurance that they would be free and fair in Poland, Yugoslavia, and elsewhere in Europe? So when consulted by the British government in mid-June, it had recognized that it would have to make an active effort to assure creditable political conduct by the Greeks.

On July 4—just before leaving for Potsdam—Byrnes had signed a memo to the President which had evolved out of talk between the State Department and the British Foreign Office. This had recommended that the American and British governments jointly tell the Greek government that they were willing to participate in the supervision of the prospective Greek elections; and that they assumed the Greek government would want to ask the *three* Yalta powers (and conceivably France) to do so. Byrnes explained that his idea was to ask the War Department to provide five hundred qualified Americans for this assignment; and that he thought someone other than the Ambassador in Athens should head the group, in order not to risk prejudicing his status (presumably by involving him in arguments among the Greeks). Truman had at once approved the program.[10]

The British government had been so advised. But the statement of ideas which the State Department gave the British Embassy on July 5 contained an additional point: that it also be recommended to the Greek government that elections for a constituent assembly precede the plebiscite on the monarchy—which might well be postponed until six months after an elected government took office. To this the Foreign Office objected. The suggestion, it stressed, was both contrary to the order of action on which the Greek factions had agreed, and most controversial; therefore the question whether the elections or the plebiscite should be held first should be left for the Greeks to decide. The American government agreed to omit the criticized provision.[11]

The British and American Ambassadors had made their parallel presentations to the Greek Prime Minister, Admiral Voulgaris, on July 13. He agreed, making no objection to the prospect of Soviet membership in the on-looking group. The British Foreign Office had at once written out invitations to the Soviet and French governments to join

[10] It may be surmised that the sponsors of this program realized that even if the Greek government assented to such outside supervision of the elections, the Soviet government might excuse itself. This is indicated in a State Department Paper, "Elections in Greece," from which Byrnes' proposals were derived. One passage read: "In this connection, however, it must be remembered that Marshal Stalin in a recent message to Prime Minister Churchill has stated his belief that the participation of foreign observers in the Greek elections would be an insult to the Greek people and an interference in Greek internal affairs. The Marshal is of course reluctant to see established a precedent which might be used to urge similar supervision of elections in other countries in Eastern Europe in the so-called Soviet sphere." Potsdam Papers, Document 443.

[11] Acting Secretary of State Grew, in the instruction that he sent Ambassador Mac-Veagh on July 11 telling him to go ahead, after pointing out the omission, said: "However, if you think it advisable you may informally indicate to the Greek Government that the Department perceives no objection to modifying, reversing or combining procedures for plebiscites and elections if mutually agreed upon by the Greeks themselves." The available documents do not tell whether the Ambassador conveyed this message to the Greek government.

in the supervision of the Greek elections. These glided over the issue whether the plebiscite should come before or after the elections by stating that the observers were to supervise "the forthcoming plebiscite and elections in Greece." Copies of this text were given to the State Department and (on July 15) to the American group at Potsdam.

Truman chose to put the program for Greece before Stalin as part of a general proposal for the "Implementation of the Yalta Declaration on Liberated Europe," rather than by and of itself. The text introduced by him at the first session of July 17 suggested merely that "the three Governments consider how best to assist any interim governments in the holding of free and unfettered elections. Such assistance is immediately required in the case of Greece, and will in due course undoubtedly be required in Romania and Bulgaria, and possibly other countries."[12]

Churchill in his talk with Stalin on the next night was more explicit. After expressing the flat opinion that the conference should make it plain to all the smaller Balkan countries, including Greece, that none would be allowed to trespass or fight, he suggested to Stalin that since Greece was to have a plebiscite and free elections "the Great Powers should send observers to Athens."[13] Stalin said he thought this would show a want of confidence in the honesty of the Greek people.

The written comment that Molotov presented a few days later (on July 20) at the meeting of Foreign Ministers was combative. The pertinent section in regard to Greece read: "But there is one country—Greece—in which no due order still exists, where law is not respected, where terrorism rages directed against democratic elements which have borne the principal burden of the fight against German invaders for the liberation of Greece. . . . In accordance with the aforesaid the Soviet government considers [it] necessary . . . to recommend to the Regent of Greece [Damaskinos, Archbishop of Greece] to take immediate measures toward the establishment of a democratic government."[14] In the outspoken discussion that followed, Eden called the Soviet proposal on Greece "a complete travesty of fact." He stressed that the press of the whole world would go to Greece and report, and that the Greek government had pledged itself to hold elections open to all parties and had invited observers from outside to regulate them. Molotov, need-

[12] Potsdam Papers, Document 745.
[13] *Triumph and Tragedy*, page 635. Churchill does not tell whether he made it clear that the intention was to have the observers "supervise" the elections.
[14] Potsdam Papers, Document 1064.

less to tell, only repeated charges. Nor was he silenced by Byrnes' statement that the American government was impressed by the action of the Greek government in inviting all of them, the Soviet government as well as the American, British, and French, to supervise the elections. The argument came to a desultory end.

The tedious later discussions led to a meager conclusion: that since they could not agree, they should abstain from any joint expression of attitude toward Greece or the next political measures to be taken by the Greek government. This left the British and American governments free to act as they wanted. But the dissent of the Soviet government was another sign that the war allies would no longer be able to appear as one in their treatment of the countries of southeastern Europe. Nor, as will next be related, could they show a united front in their relations with Turkey. At Potsdam they veered away from each other when their thoughts went in that direction.

38. Turkey and the Black Sea Straits

STALIN had been able to confirm the right to have and to hold all gains derived from the accord he had made with Hitler in 1939. But one of the notable facts about Soviet diplomacy at the time of Potsdam was the attempt to garner as well those benefits that Hitler had refused to confer.

During Churchill's visit to Moscow in October 1944, Stalin had said he would like to see a modification in the Montreux Convention regulating transit through and navigation in the Straits of the Bosporus and Dardanelles (from the Black Sea to the Mediterranean).[1] He thought Russian warships ought to have the right of passage at all times. Churchill, as a proof that the British government was no longer bent on preventing Russian entry to any or all of the seas of the world, had said that in principle he was not against a revision of the Convention.

Stalin had reverted to the subject at Yalta. He again remarked that he thought it only fair that the Convention be revised, since Russia could no longer tolerate the fact that Turkey had "a hand on Russia's throat." How could it be done in such a way as not to harm Turkey's legitimate interests? He proposed that the three Foreign Ministers (British, Russian, and American) might well consider this matter at their first meeting. Churchill responded amiably. He agreed that Russia's use of the narrow exit from the Black Sea—on which its lands bordered—should not be subject to the volition of Turkey. He would be glad to have Eden talk this over with his colleagues. But he thought the Turks ought to be told that the subject was under discussion; and if and when the Convention was changed, Turkey should be given a joint guarantee of its independence and unity. Stalin seemed to be satisfied with this response. Roosevelt's only comment was tangential—that it would be wonderful if all national boundaries would eventually be unarmed and unfortified, like the U.S.-Canadian frontier.

After Yalta, Turkey had put aside the guise of neutrality and declared war on Germany and Japan—thus becoming an ally. Nevertheless the Soviet government had come to want more, nothing less in fact

---

[1] The Montreux Convention had been signed in July 1936 by Turkey, the Soviet Union, United Kingdom, France, Japan, and four Balkan countries. The United States was not a party to it. The provisions pertinent to the Soviet demand for revision are given in Supplementary Note 6.

than command of the Straits. This was revealed when in June the Turkish government sought to enter into discussion about a new treaty in place of one that the Soviet government had denounced in March. Molotov, who had just returned to Moscow from San Francisco, told the Turkish Ambassador that before entering into a new accord it was thought best to settle various "outstanding questions."

The Soviet price for a treaty, as first reported to their governments by the British and American Embassies in Ankara, was threefold. The first requirement was the return to Russia of areas yielded to Turkey in 1921. That cession, Molotov remarked, had been arranged when the Russians were weak and now they were strong. Until that injustice was corrected the Soviet government could not discuss an accord whereby, presumably, it would pledge itself to respect, and maybe to defend, Turkey's territorial integrity. Molotov, it was learned later, did not definitely describe the territorial change desired. But his words were taken by the Turkish government in Ankara to mean that the Soviet Union wanted the return of the vilayet of Kars, including Ardahan. Second, the Russians insisted on prior agreement between the two governments concerning the changes to be made in the Montreux Convention. Molotov stressed that under its existing provisions the fate of two hundred million Russians might be settled by Turkey. And the third requirement was assent to the maintenance of Soviet military bases on Turkish territory within range of the Bosporus. This, it may be interjected, was one of the conditions Molotov had laid down as far in the past as November 25, 1940, in the response he gave Schulenburg, the Nazi Ambassador in Moscow, to Hitler's proposal that the Soviet Union join the Axis and agree with Germany on their respective spheres of influence.[2] Now at this later time Molotov justified the Soviet proposal on the score that the war experience had shown that Turkey, by itself, was not strong enough to defend the Straits.[3] In this talk the Turkish Ambassador had received the impres-

[2] As stated in the Molotov answer to Schulenburg, this condition read: "Provided that within the next few months the security of the Soviet Union in the Straits is assured by the conclusion of a mutual security pact between the Soviet Union and Bulgaria, which geographically is situated inside the security zone of the Black Sea boundaries of the Soviet Union, and by the establishment of a base for land and naval forces of the U.S.S.R. within range of the Bosporus and the Dardanelles by means of a long-term lease." U.S., Department of State, *Nazi-Soviet Relations, 1939-1941*, page 258.

[3] In 1946, in connection with the question of automatic five-year renewal of the Montreux agreement regarding the Straits, the Soviet government published a selection of captured documents of the German Ministry of Foreign Affairs concerning German-Turkish relations during the war, and delivered a note supporting its complaint that the Turkish government had not kept Axis naval vessels out of the Straits during the war. *Soviet News* (English-language publication of the Soviet government), August 14, 1946.

sion that Molotov was vaguely hinting that if Turkey broke away from its alliance with Great Britain the Soviet government might be less exigent on all three points.[4]

The answer of the Turkish government (of June 22) had been unafraid. It said that it would not even consider the cession of territory or the establishment of Russian military bases in the Straits; and that many other governments were entitled to a share in any decision about the revision of the Montreux Convention.

The British Embassy in Washington had informed the State Department that, in accordance with the Anglo-Turkish Treaty of Mutual Assistance of 1939, the British government intended to uphold the Turks in their refusal, especially since these Soviet stipulations seemed far in excess of any intimated by Stalin at Yalta. Would the American government join it in notifying Moscow that they believed that other nations, not only Russia and Turkey, had a proper interest in all three items in the Soviet bill of desire? To such an affirmation the British government thought there might be appended a reminder that territorial settlements ought to be worked out only by orderly processes, and not by force, intimidation, or blackmail. Grew asked time to consider. In any case, he told the British Ambassador, he thought it advisable to defer action until the Conference at San Francisco ended (June 23, according to expectations). There would be time enough left before the assembly at Potsdam.

While the American government was waiting, Molotov had talked again with the Turkish Ambassador in Moscow. Then he proposed rather than pushed. Would not the Turkish government think the situation over and see "if we cannot work out something useful on these points?"[5] But, annoyingly, he made several comparisons with Poland. After the First World War that country too, he blandly remarked, had negotiated a treaty "unjust" to the Soviet Union; but it had recently repaired this injustice and laid a basis for lasting friendship between the two nations.

The anxieties of the Turkish government had not been allayed by its Ambassador's account of this second talk. As first received it reported Molotov as saying that the Soviet government would also want to present certain questions about Turkish relations with the Balkan states.

---

[4] Memorandum of Conversation, Minister in the British Embassy in Washington (Balfour) with Acting Secretary of State Grew, June 18, 1945, and message from U.S. Ambassador in Ankara (Wilson) to State Department, June 18, 1945. Potsdam Papers, Documents 683 and 684.

[5] Message, Wilson to State Department, June 22. *Ibid.*, Document 686.

A fortnight later, however, the Turkish Foreign Office, which had been giving out an excited version of this new presumed Soviet design, corrected it. The American Ambassador was told that Molotov had not, after all, made any such statement, the inference that he had done so having been drawn from a garbled cable.[6]

Meanwhile the Turkish government had asked the American government for its "views" regarding Soviet intentions. The State Department decided that the situation did not yet warrant direct interposition. The Soviet government, it reasoned, had not threatened to compel Turkey to yield to its wishes. If a plea for restraint should become necessary, the Russians might pay more heed if it were made at the coming conference, and in connection with a promise to review the Montreux system of control of the Straits. So the answer sent from Washington to Ankara was meant to be moderating. It remarked that the Turkish-Soviet exploratory talks seemed to be taking place in a friendly atmosphere, without menacing clouds. Why not continue them with due respect for each other's point of view?[7]

The Turkish government had not known what to make of this advice. What was meant by the suggestion that it should show respect for the Soviet point of view? It regarded the proposals made by the Soviet government as projections of a comprehensive design: to extend its control from the Caucasus through Turkey to Alexandretta and the Mediterranean, and through Iran and Iraq to the Persian Gulf, and in course of doing so, to close the Black Sea Straits to all countries not in its orbit. The Acting Foreign Minister, Sumer, expressed the hope that when the question was discussed at the coming conference, the American government would "take [a] position supporting respect for equal sovereignty and independence [of] all states."[8]

A similar answer had been made by Grew to the British proposal. But the Foreign Office judged the policy of waiting dangerous. Lest inaction be construed as indifference, it went ahead on its own to make its views known to the Soviet government. The American government maintained its reserve in the face of Turkish forecasts of ominous Soviet intentions. It noted attentively, but calmly, insinuating articles in the Soviet press, such as one printed on the anniversary of the "glorious

[6] Message, Wilson to State Department, July 7. *Ibid.*, Document 701.
[7] Message, Grew to Wilson, June 23, *Ibid.*, Document 689.
[8] Message, Wilson to State Department, June 26. *Ibid.*, Document 691. On July 7, in talking with Grew, the Turkish Ambassador had gone further, saying that the Turkish government felt very strongly that vigorous representations by the American government in advance of possible trouble would have a powerful effect on the Soviet government. *Ibid.*, Document 702.

victory" of the Russian over the Turkish navy in 1770, and reports in the Turkish press that President Inonu and the Turkish Chief of Staff were inspecting Turkish defenses in Thrace.

American policy at Potsdam, it was conceived by the officials who wrote the papers for the guidance of the delegation, ought to be positive but circumspect. It should be made clear that the American government would oppose any threats to the independence and integrity of Turkey. But it would be advisable to refrain from coming out, as had the British government, in flat support of the Turkish government, lest it assume an attitude that might be regarded in Moscow as provocative. As set down in one of the Briefing Book papers, the American diplomats were to strive to maintain a detached and watchful attitude toward both Soviet and British policies, as long as these were in keeping with the principles of the United Nations. Thus as friend of all we would be able to make an impression if a crisis should come.

At Potsdam, Churchill did not wait until the subject came up in the planned flow of conference business. He exposed his thought about the reported Soviet demands on Turkey when he and Stalin dined together on the 18th. He repeated what he had said to Stalin during their talks in Moscow: that he would welcome Russia as a great sea power, and that he wished to see Russian ships sailing across the oceans of the world. Russia—in the image that leaped to his tongue—was like a giant with its nostrils pinched by its narrow exits from the Baltic and the Black Sea. But there were the Turks! They were naturally worried over the conditions the Soviet government had attached to a new treaty, and by reports of large Soviet troop assemblies in Bulgaria near the Turkish frontier. Stalin denied that any threatening demands had been made. He said that if Turkey had not sought a treaty of alliance, which would involve the Soviet government in a guarantee of Turkish frontiers and security, the Russians would not have asked for the return of Kars and Ardahan. And since the Turks said they could consider neither this adjustment of territory nor the type of revision sought for the Montreux Convention, the Soviet government could not consider a treaty of alliance.

This talk had at least the effect of inducing the Soviet government, despite its preference to deal only and directly with the Turkish government, to state openly what changes it was seeking to bring about in the control of the Black Sea Straits. At the Plenary Session on July 22, Stalin asked approval of three connected affirmations: first, that the

Montreux Convention would be terminated as no longer corresponding to current conditions; second, that the determination of the governance of the Straits—the only sea passage from the Black Sea—should fall within the province of Turkey and the Soviet Union as the states chiefly concerned; and third, that the new arrangements should provide that Turkey and the Soviet Union would both have military bases in the Straits in order to defend them against any enemy of the Black Sea powers.[9]

This led to a short but lively bout between Churchill and the Russians, to which Truman listened in silence. Churchill said it was his firm opinion that the Montreux Convention could be changed only after discussion between all the parties to it (with the exception of Japan). All—and not only the Soviet Union and Turkey—should have a part in settling the future regime for the Straits. And, he added meaningfully, the matter could be satisfactorily discussed between the Soviet Union and Turkey only in a peaceful atmosphere.

He reviewed again the reasons why the Turkish government was much alarmed over the integrity of its country and its power to defend Istanbul. Added to the frightening proposals made by the Soviet government and the continuous attacks in the Soviet press and radio was the reported concentration of Bulgarian and Soviet troops in Bulgaria, near the Turkish frontier.

Molotov did not apologize for the Soviet bid for part of Turkey. In his view the area that the Soviet Union was asking had been in 1921 "torn from Soviet Armenia and Soviet Georgia." But, he added, if the Turks decided they did not want to continue discussion of an alliance and territorial adjustment, the Soviet government was ready to make an agreement on the Straits alone, between the Black Sea powers.

Churchill reiterated that while he was ready to welcome an arrangement for the free movement of Russian ships, naval or merchant, into and out of the Black Sea, he felt in no way obligated to accept the new Soviet proposals, and he was sure that the Turkish government would not.

Truman brought this contention to an end by saying he was not ready to express an opinion and therefore would like to defer the question. The Joint Chiefs of Staff were advising him to do so until the subject of the Straits could be considered along with other territorial issues at the future peace conference. If he could not do so, however,

[9] *Ibid.*, Document 1369.

they thought that the American government might agree to a revision of the Montreux Convention along the lines of internationalization and free use suggested by the State Department; that it ought to favor demilitarization of the Straits; and that certainly it ought to oppose any plan granting any nation, other than Turkey, bases or other rights for direct or indirect military control of the Straits.[10]

The President was allured by the chance to gain acceptance, in connection with a new agreement about the Straits, for a plan of great scope about various other international waterways, especially the Danube and Rhine rivers. The State Department and the Joint Chiefs of Staff were both urging him to put it forward.[11]

He made a sanguine try at the seventh session, on the 23rd, after listening to Churchill and Stalin again state their ideas about what Russia was asking of Turkey. This time Stalin really made an effort to convince his audience that Soviet intentions were peaceable and Soviet wishes reasonable. He denied that the Turks had any reason for believing that the Russians were trying to scare them into yielding. There were, he asserted, fewer Russian troops in Bulgaria than the British had in Greece. The Soviet request for the transfer of Kars and Ardahan was justified if Turkey wished the protection of a treaty. But whether or not an alliance was made between them, the existing regime of the Straits was distinctly unfair to the Soviet Union, for the Turkish government was authorized by the Montreux Convention to prevent the movement of Soviet shipping in and out of the Black Sea not only if Turkey was at war but if it thought there was a threat of war. That was ridiculous. They could imagine, he continued, "what commotion there would be in England if a similar regime existed in Gibraltar or in the Suez Canal or what a commotion there would be in the United States if such a regime existed with regard to the Panama Canal." Soviet shipping ought to be able to pass to and from the Black Sea freely; and since Turkey was too weak to assure this in all circumstances the Soviet Union would like to be able to defend the Straits by force if necessary, just as the American navy defended the Panama Canal and the British navy defended the Suez Canal. If the Turks would not agree that the

[10] *Ibid.*, Document 1363.

[11] The State Department, Eisenhower, and the Joint Chiefs of Staff, for a variety of military and economic reasons, had been impressing on Truman and Byrnes the importance they attached to having navigation on these two main river systems restored and freed throughout their length from sectional, national controls.

Soviet Union have naval bases in the Straits, then let them provide some other base where the Russian fleet could repair and refuel and, in cooperation with its allies, protect the Straits.

This restatement of Russian desires loosened Truman's tongue. He too favored a change in the regime of the Straits. But the one Stalin proposed would merely enable the Soviet Union to share in control of this route of passage; it would be better to make it a free waterway open to the whole world, guaranteed by the three great allies. Then he launched into the sea of history, which is public domain for all. He had come to the conclusion after long study that all the wars of the last two hundred years had started in the area from the Black Sea to the Baltic, and from the eastern frontier of France to the northern frontier of Russia. It should be the aim of their work here at Potsdam, and of the peace conference to which they looked forward, to end this tragic recurrence. One measure that might help to do so would be to assure not only the Soviet Union and Great Britain, but all nations, of unhindered passage for their ships and products to all the seas of the world.

The President then read what was the boldest paper submitted at Potsdam, and what could have been the most transforming:

"The United States Government proposes that there be free and unrestricted navigation of such inland waterways as border on two or more states and that the regulation of such navigation be provided by international authorities representative of all nations directly interested in navigation on the waterways concerned.

"As an initial step there should be set up as soon as possible interim navigation agencies for the Danube and the Rhine. . . . Membership in these agencies should include the United States, the United Kingdom, the USSR, France and the sovereign riparian states recognized by these governments."[12]

He was making this proposal, Truman explained, because he did not want to engage in another war twenty-five years hence over the Black Sea Straits or the Danube. Americans wanted a Europe that was sound economically and could support itself—a Europe in which Russia, England, France, and all other countries were happy and with which the United States could trade pleasantly and profitably.

Churchill did not dissect closely either the President's history or his proposal. But his remarks were, in trend, supporting. He recognized

[12] Potsdam Papers, Document 755. A revised proposal, including the Kiel Canal and the Black Sea Straits, is in Document 758.

that alike in peace and war Soviet merchant vessels and warships ought to be able to pass through the Black Sea Straits at will. He agreed with Truman that this should rest on a guarantee by "all of us." Would not Stalin consider this as an alternative to his quest for a base near Constantinople? He thought that the Kiel Canal, which controls the converging entries into the Baltic Sea, should be similarly treated; and he attached great importance to free navigation of the Danube and the Rhine.

Stalin's response was dry and curt. He would have to read Truman's proposal carefully before he could discuss it. Then he at once turned to get a decision out of hand about the transfer to the Soviet Union of Königsberg and that part of East Prussia north of it.

That same evening Stalin once again showed that he never let a chance go by to pursue a wish that had been denied him. Churchill was host at a farewell dinner. The toasts had gone round and were reaching a spacious level of goodwill when Stalin, beckoned by Churchill, emptied, in duo, a potion (a small-size claret glass) of brandy. As remembered by the doughty Prime Minister of Britain: "We both drained our glasses at a stroke and gazed approvingly at one another. After a pause Stalin said, 'If you find it impossible to give us a fortified position in the Marmora could we not have a base at Dedeagatch [on the Aegean coast of Greece, very close to the Turkish border]?' I contented myself with saying 'I will always support Russia in her claim to her freedom of the seas all the year round.' "[13] For the moment the Straits were drained of animosity.

To the very end of the conference Truman strove for adoption of his releasing program for the inland waterways of the world. At the next Plenary Session (on the 24th) he asked Stalin if he had done his thinking. Stalin, not easily diverted, remarked that the President's proposal dealt with the Danube and Rhine rather than the Black Sea Straits. What about the Soviet proposal concerning the Straits? Truman said he would like to have the two questions considered at the same time. This was taken by Stalin to be an evasive dodge rather than a genuine attempt to separate the future from the past.

His response was negative. Why not, since their views were so different, stop talking about the Straits from the Black Sea to the Mediterranean? But neither Churchill nor Truman was reassured by this sulky rejoinder. Churchill tried to impress Stalin with the value of the American willingness to join the company of nations that would control the

[13] *Triumph and Tragedy*, page 669.

Straits and guarantee freedom of navigation through them. Obviously that did not appeal. Molotov belittled it by asking why, if this was such a good rule, should it not also be applied to the Suez Canal?

Truman tried to lead Stalin away from his particular wish for a controlling position in or over the Straits. Once more he proposed that they arrange for freedom of ingress and egress for all nations on all international rivers and straits of Europe, for any and all purposes. And once more Stalin said, in a matter-of-fact tone, that since their views about the question of the Black Sea Straits were so different, let it be postponed so that they could turn to more urgent matters. When the time came around, the Soviet government would resume its talks with the Turks. The United States and Great Britain could talk with them too. He was not sure Turkey would agree to international control. Let each of them just continue to see what it could do about the matter.

That was Stalin's last and conclusive word. A laggard try to get Soviet subordinates to talk over an improved proposal failed. They were, as they said, without instructions. And they stayed out of sight and out of call on the telephone.

The British government, having told the Turks of the course of the discussion at Potsdam, advised them to keep calm. Their soundest course would be to continue to resist Russian attempts to force them into direct negotiations, and to maintain that the revision of the Montreux Convention could be made only after discussion by all interested countries. The Prime Minister of Turkey (Sarajoglu) was not won over to the American vision—which would mean that the Straits, unguarded by any military installations, would be open to the merchant ships and war vessels of all nations, under international superintendence. Certainly, he said, the Turkish government would not agree to abandon its defensive structures on the Straits unless the Soviet government firmly guaranteed that it would not try to acquire any Turkish territory. A report of this opinion quenched the slight remaining hope that the question could be settled during the Potsdam conference.

Truman's expansive project about international waterways expired. Stalin did not even want it to be mentioned in the statement about the conference to be issued to the world. Truman had to be content with an agreement that the Protocol would contain note of the fact that it had been brought to the attention of the conference, and with an understanding that he was free to reveal what he had proposed. In that regard Stalin remarked crisply "Of course, that is your privilege."[14]

[14] Potsdam Papers, Cohen Notes, Twelfth Plenary Session, August 1.

The record reveals that the Russians were interested only in changing the control of the Straits. They were already in a position to control navigation on the Danube from Austria to the Black Sea. In any plan for control of the Rhine they would have only the lesser say. And the talk showed that the British would not yield control of the Suez Canal, or the Americans of the Panama Canal. No wonder then that nothing came of this discussion. But perhaps the mere fact that the Russians were brought openly to disclose and defend the terms on which they would sell insurance to Turkey made them more circumspect. They were made aware that use of force to impose their will on Turkey, in regard to either the border provinces or the Straits, would encounter strong resistance not only by Great Britain but also by the United States.

39. Iran, the Levant, the Italian Colonies, Tangier

OF THE other uneasy territorial situations calling for attention, that in Iran was best known. It will be recalled that Iran had served as an essential military base and transit route into the Soviet Union throughout the war, and as a way station to the Far East. It had been occupied by Soviet troops in the north and by British troops in the south. American army service forces were operating the rail and road transport system from the Persian Gulf to the Soviet frontier.

In the Anglo–Soviet–Iranian treaty signed in 1942 it had been stipulated that all foreign forces would be taken out of Iran within six months after the end of the war. But its authors had not made it clear whether they meant the war in Europe or the war in the Far East. At their conference at Teheran, November 1943, Roosevelt, Stalin, and Churchill had issued a public declaration confirming this promise and their benevolent intentions toward Iran. The Iranians had been much pleased, for it met four of their wishes: acknowledgment of their part in the war; a promise of economic aid at the end of the war; nourishment for their self-respect; and a joint pledge to maintain Iran's independence, sovereignty, and territorial integrity.

But an internal conflict had shaped up as the end of the war came in sight. Discontented elements (led by the revolutionary Tudeh party) assailed the Persian landowning groups who dominated the central government and the village administrations. Each side used violence and terrorism against the other. In the northern provinces, where the Russian troops were stationed, authority in the chief towns was taken over by the revolutionary partisans.[1]

Two weeks after the German surrender, the Iranian government had decided to ask the British and Soviet governments when they were going to withdraw their troops. In the opinion of the Shah, they were obligated by the terms of the 1942 treaty to have them out, at the very latest, by six months after the end of the war between the allied powers and Germany and her associates. This interpretation of the treaty was disputable.

The Shah had not at this time shown any desire to see the American

---

[1] An excellent account of the situation in 1945, and of the intricacies of internal politics and the activities of the Tudeh party, is to be found in Kirk, *The Middle East and the War*, pages 56 ff.

troops leave also. But all branches of the American government wanted to get American forces (all service, not combat troops) out of Iran as soon as practicable. It was being gradually done. The War Department wished to retain there certain small contingents, about 4,500 in all, at least until Japan was defeated. Some were needed to take care of American installations in Iran until they could be properly liquidated. Others were wanted for work at the Air Transport Command base at Abadan, which was a staging point for combat aircraft going on to China and for other American air traffic in support of the American forces in the Burma–India–China theaters.

The British officials had been in another sort of dilemma. They thought it prudent to keep British military units in southwestern Iran to protect the oil fields and the refinery at Abadan. But they knew that unless all British (and American) troops were taken out of Iran, the Soviet forces would not leave. And they feared that if Soviet troops stayed much longer in the north, that area might be brought under permanent Communist control, or that the Soviet power to intervene would be used to force the induction into office in Iran of a government obedient to Moscow.

The Soviet government had not yet made its attitude clearly known. It might seek to cancel or evade the obligation to call back its troops. Or conceivably it might try to gain popularity in Iran by calling for immediate and complete withdrawal of all foreign forces.

In the days before the Potsdam conference convened the Shah had openly discussed his fear of Russian intentions with the American Ambassador. He said that he was afraid to install a vigorous Prime Minister because the Soviet government would accuse him of Fascism; but that unless he did so, administration in Iran would become even less effective, the economy could not be straightened out, and political disorder would spread—with Soviet-supported left-wing groups gaining in influence.[2] The American as well as the British Ambassadors were of the opinion that the Soviet government was intent on having a Cabinet favorable to it in office before withdrawing the Red Army and before Iranian elections were held.[3]

[2] Potsdam Papers, Documents 1327 and 1329.
[3] In an American Briefing Book paper a program had been outlined for which British and Soviet assent might be secured at Potsdam. This looked toward an agreement between the three war allies who had troops in Iran to refrain from any and all intervention in Iranian internal affairs; to work together to enable the Iranian government to assume full responsibility and functions for the governing of the country, and evolve into a legitimate and strong government representative of the people and responsive to their needs; to withdraw quickly all armed forces in Iran whose presence was not needed to

At Potsdam the British took the initiative, because of their closer and longer connection with Iran. Eden (on the 21st) proposed that British and Soviet forces be withdrawn at once from Teheran, the capital, and then in several gradual stages from all the rest of Iran.[4] When the Heads of Government got around to discussing this, Stalin demurred. He was willing to agree to the prompt evacuation of Teheran. But his inclination was to let the troops remain elsewhere in Iran for a while longer—perhaps until six months after the end of the war against Japan. Let us take more time to consider our further course, he suggested. Churchill, not entirely averse, because of a wish to retain watch over oilfields and refineries, assented to postponement of the schedule of withdrawal. It was agreed that when the Foreign Ministers met in September, they would talk the matter over again. Truman said abruptly that he expected to have all American troops out in sixty days, since they were needed in the Far East. Whereat Stalin remarked that the United States was certainly entitled to guard its supplies, and then he added, "So as to rid the United States of any worries we promise you that no action will be taken by us against Iran."[5] Truman thanked him.

While not conclusive, the agreement to begin the evacuation from Teheran at once, coupled with Stalin's assurance, was regarded in Washington as a step forward. Besides, the American government was not obliged to hurry out the troops guarding supplies or the personnel operating the air transport service and its facilities. The Iranian government, in fact, was willing to have these remain and carry on their activities.

The announcement of the accord was welcomed in Teheran. But among the Iranian officials and their circle it did not wholly allay the fears of Soviet intentions or the resentment of British presence in the south. Iran remained a focus of anxiety.

The situation in the Levantine states had also continued to trouble. The dual quarrels in which the French government was engaged with the local governments and the British government were still dragging on.

---

carry on the war in the Far East—or, if the Soviet government would not consent to take its troops out while any British and American forces stayed, even in working services for the Pacific war, it was proposed that the Russians and British be asked to agree to a progressive and proportionate reduction of their forces and of the areas occupied by them.

[4] *Ibid.*, Document 1330.
[5] *Ibid.*, Minutes, Plenary Session, July 23.

The situation had remained on the verge of open conflict between native extremists and the French authorities. The British military had taken control of more and more areas, and the French were discredited. Late in June our minister in Lebanon and Syria (George Wadsworth) had informed the State Department that the Syrian and Lebanese troops under French officers were deserting rapidly. The Syrian and Lebanese governments were saying that native troops must be transferred to their command, and that all French troops must be taken out of their countries before a discussion of a political settlement began. Actually there were only about two thousand French troops in Syria at this time, mostly confined to barracks. As epitomized by the President of the Syrian Legislative Chamber in a talk at the Aleppo Mosque, "we have one present aim, to force France to quit our country."

The French government had tried to allay this ill feeling, which was sweeping out French influence and interests. It had announced the gradual transfer of command of the native troops from French officers to the local governments. It had let it be known that it would agree to withdraw the French troops from Syria and Lebanon at the same time as British troops might be taken out. It had given up plans to seek a naval base in either country. But these concessions had come too late to end the antagonism.

The French and British governments had teetered on the edge of talks. The French authorities would not go to London for the purpose. The British were reluctant to go to Paris, as they were at this time encouraging the French and Syrians to settle their quarrel directly. The French government was again trying to do so, having, it would seem, had second thoughts about the value of a five-power conference on the whole Middle East.[6]

American official judgment about the situation had coagulated against France. The State Department papers in the Briefing Book for Potsdam reveal an intent to make it clear to the British, and through them to the French, that we would oppose any settlement that infringed on the independence or sovereignty of Syria or Lebanon, or discriminated against the United States. An effort was to be made to induce the French and British to begin at once to withdraw their troops, concurrently and progressively.

But at Potsdam neither the President nor the Secretary of State went into the situation with the British on his own initiative. They were dragged into it by Stalin. He proposed that Churchill and Truman

[6] *Ibid.*, Documents 636, 644, and 645.

join him in an expression of favor for a conference with the French government about the situation in these countries, if it were willing. This led Churchill at the plenary session on the 23rd into a long harangue. He portrayed British intervention there as a disagreeable but necessary duty. He had told de Gaulle that British troops would be taken out of these countries as soon as he made an acceptable treaty with them. If they were withdrawn before then, fighting between the small French contingents and the natives would start again: French civilians might well be murdered and French troops routed, and turbulence and warfare would spread throughout the Middle East. Lines of communication through the Suez Canal, in use in the war against Japan, would be endangered. Great Britain had "no wish to remain there one day longer than necessary," and would be "delighted to withdraw" from what was "a thankless task assumed in the interest of the allies." It had borne the whole burden and so would not welcome a review of the sort proposed. But of course, if the United States wanted to take their place that would be "a different matter."

"No thanks," Truman responded. Then, taking heed of a passage in the Prime Minister's statement—that de Gaulle might reach a settlement which, while guaranteeing the independence of Syria and Lebanon, would "preserve for the French some recognition of their cultural and commercial interests"—Truman said he did not think France deserved a special position, in view of its behavior. All should have equal rights. Churchill explained that the British government, at a time of weakness, had promised France that it might have a preferred position—if Syria and Lebanon would accord it. After all, French activities and efforts went back to the Crusades. They even had a song that went "Nous partons pour la Syrie." But after Truman said he was sure the Syrians would not grant the French special rights, Churchill bowed out. Great Britain, he said, could not obligate others nor had it made strenuous efforts to enable the French to retain such rights. But "If they could get them the British would not object and would smile benignly on their achievements."

Stalin seemed to lose interest in the subject. After remarking that he thought the Syrians would be reluctant to show special regard for the French, he said that he withdrew the Soviet proposal. Both Churchill and Truman were pleased, for they feared Soviet entry into a fracas that they hoped was nearing an end.

The relief was the more real because the Soviet government was showing a lively interest in the disposition of the Italian colonies on the Mediterranean shore. Both Stalin and Molotov were displaying a wish for Soviet trusteeship over one of them—probably Libya. If this were granted, the Russians for the first time would have gained a strategic position south of Turkey and the Persian Gulf.

At the first plenary session Stalin referred to the earlier notice the Soviet government had given of its wish to discuss the question of allocation of trusteeships.[7] What he meant, he explained in answer to Churchill's questions, was a trusteeship for "some territories of the defeated States." He had in hand a circumambient written proposal: that the conference authorize the Council of Foreign Ministers to consider measures to bring into effect the trusteeship system provided in the United Nations Charter. In doing so they were to be "guided by the necessity of solution in the nearest future of the problem relating to the terms of trusteeship on the former colonial possessions of Italy in Africa and in the Mediterranean, having in view herewith the possibility of establishing the trusteeship system exercised by individual states or by the USSR, USA and Great Britain jointly."[8]

At the meeting of the Heads of Government on the 22nd Molotov said that he recognized it would not be possible to pursue this subject of trusteeships in detail during the conference. But some progress could be made. They could start by discussing what was going to be done about the Italian colonies. As reported in the Minutes, he had read in the foreign press "that Italy had lost its colonies once and for all. The question was who had received them and where had this matter been decided."[9]

[7] This was a reference to a series of documents: a letter Gromyko had sent to Stassen at San Francisco on June 9; Stettinius' answer to Novikov, in which he said that the American government was ready to support the Soviet wish to obtain a trusteeship; a letter from Gromyko to Stettinius on June 20, saying that the Soviet government would like to define the matter more clearly while the representatives of all at San Francisco were engaged in formulating the trusteeship provisions of the Charter; Stettinius' answer of June 30, saying it had been agreed that there was not to be any discussion at San Francisco of the disposition of particular areas, but he would be glad to hear Soviet views on his return to Washington. Within a few days, however, he was out of office. Gromyko at Potsdam gave Byrnes copies of this previous correspondence. Potsdam Papers, Document 734.

[8] *Ibid.*, Document 733, submitted at meeting of Foreign Ministers, July 20.

[9] What Molotov particularly had in mind, as he made clear at one of his meetings with Byrnes and Eden the next day, was, first, press reports of the affirmative answer Eden had given on October 4, 1944, to the question whether he would "assure the House [of Commons] that His Majesty's Government is opposed to the return of the colonies to Italy, and that their declaration that the Italian Empire in Africa is irrevocably lost will be strictly adhered to"; and second, Eden's statement in the House of Commons on January 17, 1945, that "The future of Italy's prewar possessions in Libya and Tripoli must await consideration by the United Nations at the conclusion of peace," together with his restatement of the British position in answer to questions: "It is that the Italian Government have no right to the return of any one of their colonies. What is done about the colonies is a matter, in some part, for discussion in the future."

Churchill was provoked to an indignant reply. He said that the British army had conquered these colonies and, except in Tunis, had conquered them alone; and at a time when the island homeland was under heavy attack. Moreover, despite Britain's heavy losses it had made no territorial claims—no Königsberg, no Baltic States, "nothing." This was the record of rectitude with which the British government approached the question of the Italian colonies. Eden had said in the House of Commons that he regarded Italy as having lost these colonies. He had meant that Italy had lost its claim to them as a matter of right. This did not, however, preclude the peace conference from restoring some to her.[10] He did not say that he favored such a disposition. The Council of Foreign Ministers and the peace conference were free to discuss it, when dealing with peace for Italy. At present the British held these colonies. Who wanted them? If there were claimants "they should put forward their claims."

The President hastened to say that the United States did not want them, or a trusteeship over any of them. Well then, Churchill asked, did Stalin wish to put forward a claim to one of these Italian colonies? Stalin did not answer the question directly. What he wanted to learn, he said, was whether this conference would consider Italy's colonies; if it was to lose them, they could decide to what states they would be transferred in trusteeship; if it was premature to deal with the matter, they could wait. Experience in the war, he explained, had shown that Soviet vessels that were damaged or seeking to escape attack did not have any refuge near the Dardanelles Straits; for that reason he thought the Russians wish for a base on the African shore was deserving. Churchill had thereupon somberly commented, as recorded in the Minutes, that "he had not considered the possibility of the Soviet Union desiring to acquire a large tract of the African shore. If that were the case it would have to be considered in relation to many other problems."

The Foreign Ministers resumed the discussion the next day. Then,

---

The identification of the statements Molotov had in mind is contained in a memo written by George V. Allen, Deputy Director of the Office of Near Eastern and African Affairs in the State Department. In this memo, however, the discussion at which Molotov recalled these statements to Eden is dated July 22. The official American minutes of the 22nd do not contain any reference to a discussion of Italian colonies. It was talked about by the Foreign Ministers on July 23rd.

[10] The Foreign Office had been preparing a preliminary treaty of peace with Italy. Field Marshal Alexander confided to our Ambassador in Rome, Alexander Kirk, that while in London he had looked it over, and thought it far too severe. His view was that Tripoli should be returned to Italy without conditions, and Eritrea and Italian Somaliland with conditions. Potsdam Papers, Document 471. Kirk's report was retransmitted to Byrnes at Potsdam.

after Byrnes emphasized that the question of the disposition of the Italian colonies could not be settled before the peace conference, it was agreed to make a start at the first meeting of the Council of Foreign Ministers in September, in connection with the peace treaty for Italy. This was affirmed in the Protocol.

The Soviet solicitation of a colony or base on the African shore of the Mediterranean (probably in Libya), under guise of a trusteeship, was taken by Byrnes to be a clear signal of a design to obtain a strategic position from which the Soviet Union could threaten the West. It could not be related to Soviet security, as the territorial claims in areas adjacent to former Soviet frontiers might be. The Secretary of State also got the impression that this Soviet foray into a region where the British had shown their valor, and so close to the Suez Canal and the Persian Gulf, shook up Churchill more than any other episode at the conference.

Nor was this the only place along the Mediterranean shore into which the Soviet government tried to pry its way. It was seeking admission into the group that would govern the city and zone of Tangier, which, located on the Straits of Gibraltar, were of great strategic importance.

Up to June 1940 these had been administered as an international zone by a council selected by the governments that were parties to the ruling statute of 1923 (Spain, France, Portugal, Great Britain, Holland, Belgium, Italy, and Sweden). At that time—when France was falling and it seemed as though German victory was near—the Spanish government had sent its troops into the area. It had averred that it was doing so to preserve the neutrality of the zone during the war. The other participants in the administration, most of them either occupied by the Germans or in dire danger, had acquiesced.

After the German defeat, the Spanish government had let it be known that it was willing to relinquish control. Although the United States had not hitherto shared in the administration of the zone, the British and French governments consulted it about arrangements for transfer of authority. The three agreed that as an interim or temporary measure the zone should be placed under a joint civilian administration in which Great Britain, France, Spain, and the United States should have equal part. But on two other points they got into a snarl.

The American and British governments had contemplated that later on an international conference would be convoked to work out a new statute to take the place of the obsolete one. But the French government wanted merely to return to the former regime, in which France had the greatest, almost dominant, influence.

Then the American government had been of the opinion that if the Soviet government expressed a wish to take part in these preliminary talks, this should be granted. The British and French governments were willing to inform the Soviet government of what was in mind, but they thought it unwise to include it in the talks. And the Spanish government served notice that it would ignore any consultations if Soviet officials were included in them. The American government let the others draft and send the communication. This described the nature of the talks in prospect, and promised to keep the Soviet government informed of the results.

On July 2, the day before the consultation of experts was to begin in Paris, the Soviet Ambassador in Washington (Gromyko) had informed the State Department that his government, because of its interest in Tangier, was surprised that it had not been invited to take part in these talks. He asked that they be deferred until the Soviet government had a chance to exchange opinions and to instruct the Soviet officials selected to be present. Similar requests were made of the British and French governments. Grew did his best to make the Soviet government accept the explanation that the reason the United States had been invited, and the Soviet Union had not been, was that the Soviet government had not previously shown any interest whatever in Tangier. He said that the American government would welcome Soviet presence, but was itself in a sense only a guest at the meeting. The French and British authorities would be told, he promised, that we favored the Soviet wish, but the decision was up to them. They had been so advised.

The French Foreign Office had commented in effect: "We told you so; the trouble could have been avoided if it had been decided merely to return to the situation as it was in 1939." This was still, they maintained, the best course to take. The British Foreign Office was also upset by the Russian request, but it was loath to incur blame for opposing it. Moreover, it did not want to have the United States left out of the temporary administration of the zone, as it would be under the French proposal.

At this juncture the Spanish government had strongly denounced the Soviet request, saying that while it would be glad to talk with the Western powers about the withdrawal of Spanish forces and the restoration of an international system, it would not discuss these matters with any other powers. The American Ambassador in Madrid (Norman Armour) advised the State Department not to disregard this declaration. If it did, he forecast that the Spanish government would refuse to take its forces out of Tangier, since it was convinced that the Russians would take advantage of being there to embarrass and weaken the Franco regime. But the State Department refused to be governed by Franco's fears or threats. It told the Ambassador that it thought the Soviet interest in the zone legitimate and deserving of recognition. Nevertheless it was aware that the course it might be compelled to pursue could hurt American relations with Spain and spoil the chance of using that country as a source of supply and a transport base.

These differences of purpose and opinion, and others that I will not trace out here, had been whirling around at the eve of the Potsdam conference. The opinion of the British government prevailed: that the talks about the future of Tangier should be postponed until Soviet ideas and intentions could be probed at Potsdam. Another reason given for waiting until then was that the Soviet rulers might be persuaded to grant the western allies, in return for admission into the talks about Tangier, a more genuine part in the direction of the affairs of the countries in eastern Europe.

At Potsdam, Stalin, whose initiative about Spain was being rebuffed, as has already been recounted, soon made it clear that the Soviet government thought itself entitled to a share second to none in determining what was to be done about Tangier. He wanted the conference to go on record as resolving that the Spanish occupation of the zone of Tangier should be ended; that the zone should again be put under international control; that representatives of the United States, Great Britain, the Soviet Union, and France should work out an appropriate new status for the zone; and that Spain should be invited to adhere to this new status after a democratic regime was established in that country.[11]

Eden took the lead in reining in these proposals, at the meeting of the Foreign Ministers on the 23rd. He too thought that the international administration for Tangier should be restored. He too thought talks should soon start to consider how best to bring this about; and he would be glad to have representatives of the Soviet government take part in them. But he contended that they ought not discuss at Potsdam what should be done, since France, which had so great an interest in the question, was not present; and that before any final decisions were

[11] Potsdam Papers, Document 1356.

taken, all governments that were parties to the Act of Algeciras (1906) —to which the governments of the United States and Imperial Russia had both been signatories—should be brought into conference. Byrnes agreed.

Molotov, for once, did not try to beat down this opposition. Probably he had won all that he had hoped to win—a chance for the Soviet Union to share in the determination and, as must have seemed likely to him then, the control of the zone. It was agreed that the four should meet soon to discuss "the question of Tangier." It was thought prudent by all concerned that this accord not be revealed in the joint public release to be issued at the end of the conference. But it was inscribed in the Protocol.

40. France

BEFORE leaving this tale of the conference at Potsdam we ought to revert to the fact that France was not there. De Gaulle's petition had been denied. He had called the refusal unfair to France, and reserved the right to treat as he saw fit any decisions that might be made. It has been seen how some issues were settled in accord with known French wishes; how others were settled without reference to them; and how still others, of which the most important was the future status of the Ruhr, the Rhineland, and Tangier, were postponed because it was judged that they either could not be or ought not be settled without consultation with the French government.

If de Gaulle had been at Potsdam the trudge toward the word-wrapped accords reached there would have been even more wearing than it was. There is little or no reason for thinking that they would have lasted longer. What the interplay of personal relations between de Gaulle and the other three would have been bests the imagination. All that can be said is that since the French government was not obligated by the Potsdam accords, it felt freer to combat their application in an effort to bend them to its purposes.

The first response of the French people to the communiqué that was issued about the doings of the conference was not unfavorable. They seemed pleased because their government had been invited to join in the Council of Foreign Ministers, taking this as evidence that France's rightful place of equality among the great nations was being recognized. But there were various criticisms and some speculations about "unpublished" decisions.

The French government was advised in advance (July 31, August 1 and 2) of the main decisions about European affairs. On August 7, Bidault, the French Foreign Minister, summoned the American, British, and Soviet Ambassadors and handed them identical notes commenting on these decisions. The French government, he said, accepted with pleasure the invitation to participate in the work of the Council of Foreign Ministers and the Reparation Commission (which was about to disband). It found no fault with the arrangements about Poland and Italy. But it had reservations about several elements of the program for Germany. Of these the most significant bore on the statement of political principles. As expressed in the official French notes (August 7):

"Some of the measures advocated seem to assume that a given po-

litical evolution of Germany will occur; while it is impossible to foresee at the present time whether such an evolution corresponds to the
interests of European peace and to the wishes of the populations involved.

"In this regard the French government has particularly in mind the
reconstruction of political parties for the whole of Germany, and the
creation of central administrative departments which would be directed
by secretaries of state whose jurisdiction would cover, it seems, the
whole of the German territory, which is not yet defined.

"For its part the French government believes that it would be
preferable before defining such conditions to take into account the ex-
periences which the four occupying powers will not fail to gather during the initial phase of control."[1]

About two weeks later Bidault reviewed the whole field more fully,
in a personal talk. Byrnes explained why the type of accord reached
on reparations was the only one possible, and why the provision regarding the division of receipts among the various claimants was as good as
could have been negotiated. Bidault's grumbling complaints could have
been foretold. The fate that had excluded France from arguing about
her share was cruel and harmful to good relations; and prospective receipts were far less than desired. France wanted restitution of what had
been taken by the Germans—and coal, and machinery, and German
labor services. The stipulation that Germany would have to pay for
its imports out of exports would be hard on France, since it would compel France to pay in dollars for the German coal it needed. Byrnes
abstained from retorting, except to point out that while the American
government was not asking for any reparations, the American people
were unwilling to provide the means to enable Germany to pay reparations to others.

Then Bidault dissected the security aspect of the accords. He noted
that German territory had been whittled down in the east but not in
the west. France would find it hard to bear with the prospect that
while German cities in the east, like Königsberg, Breslau, Frankfurt-on-
the-Oder, and Küstrin, would pass to Russian control, Saarbrücken in
the west was still to be regarded as part of Germany. He did not think
Germany would become a threatening military power for a long time.
But he feared that a unified Germany would fall under Soviet influence.
For these reasons, and for protection against a possible resurgence of
Germany such as took place after the last war, the French government

[1] Potsdam Papers, Document 1411.

"must insist that a section of territory be cut off in West Germany similar to that in East Germany."[2] The French government, like the Soviet government, wanted an international system established in the Ruhr Basin. About the left bank of the Rhine, no definite decision was sought at the moment. But the going arrangement, that of French occupation, should be continued, without interference. France could not agree to having that area revert to Prussia.

Byrnes tried to be reassuring. It was not contemplated, he explained several times over, to allow or create a central German government, but merely some essential central offices for administration. The United States would not repeat the mistake of again granting Germany loans for reconstruction. If we were fools enough to do so, he said, we should deserve the fate that would inevitably overtake us. The people of the United States were determined to do everything to prevent Germany from rearming. He did not see how amputation of German territory in the west could be more effective than the force of the whole world, organized in the United Nations.[3]

The talk foreshadowed the period of strife between the French and other members of the Control Council which hindered the attempt to develop a system of controls and initiatives for the whole of Germany, and the effectuation of common policies. Agitated and obstructive in its effort to have its way, the French government was going to be a very trying companion in the contest with the Soviet Union which was turning into a cold war.

[2] Potsdam Papers, Document 1414, Conversation, Byrnes-Bidault, August 23.
[3] *Ibid.*

41. Potsdam: Impressions and Epilogue

THE three Heads of Government did not draw together at Potsdam in the same warm, personal association in a common cause as at the two wartime meetings at Teheran and Yalta. Then the chief figures were under a bond of mutual military dependence to get along with one another. At Potsdam they were not. Previously they could submerge or postpone issues that might estrange them. At Potsdam they could not.

The impulse to strive together to transform the nature and relations of nations had waned. National diplomacy was relapsing into old habits of thought and reckoning, which so short a time ago had been judged outworn and inadequate. Conflicts of desire and opinion were emerging. In the West fear of broken Germany was overcast by fear of Soviet Communist domination of Europe. In the Soviet Union brief trust in the true good will of the West was giving way to the belief that the West was bent on depriving the Soviet Union of the benefits of its victory. As before, a friend who opposed Soviet aims was regarded as an enemy.

All these and other turns of time debarred easy and close contact between the three individuals and their advisers. They could have been in some measure transcended. But they could not have been wholly cleared away by wit, goodness, or firmness, or by skillful deceit. As the sessions went on, and each spoke his lines, the negotiators seemed to be learning *about* one another rather than *from* one another. And yet the outcome, the end of the play, was not decided only by the surge of national wills and ways. It was affected in some measure by the aptitudes and natures of the three men, by the way they thought and acted and treated each other.

Stalin, as twice before, had his wish about the locale of the conference. He would not venture outside the realm controlled by Soviet forces, so the other two, since they were more earnest in their wish to preserve wartime unity, went toward him.

Though the Soviet ruler had suffered a slight heart attack before leaving for Potsdam, and arrived a day late, no sign of reduced will or vigor of mind was discernible during the sessions, nor any sign of abnormal outlook. Seemingly never in a hurry, he maintained a steady hold on whatever subject was under discussion, appearing to know what he wanted and how to go after it. His presentations were usually phrased in terms of Western political and social ideals, never in those of Marxist ideology. His utterances were seldom illumined by visions of a new order of international society in the future. Humorless, and living within himself, he was a most able, though short-sighted, proponent of the traditional Russian instinct to expand and absorb.

At the conference table Stalin ordinarily spoke in low tones to Pavlov, the Russian interpreter, who was sitting at his side, while Truman and Churchill, since they wanted to be heard by all their American and British associates around the table, raised their voices.

Truman, perhaps covering over an inner lack of assurance, at times spoke abruptly or assertively. Having little knowledge of some of the issues he was suddenly called on to face, he tried to substitute a presumed deep insight into the lessons of history. He was irked by the need to go far afield to meet Churchill and Stalin, rather than elated by the prospect. For him it was an errand that had to be run, not a mission he was eager to pursue. To some of his staff he seemed unwilling to hear them out. Nor was his memory of what he had been told always exact. Perceiving that Stalin and Molotov were wont to argue a matter over and over again as a way of wearing down resistance, he disliked the ordeal; and believing that Churchill often talked overly long, either as a sort of purge or for the record, he tended to regard these discourses as an assault on his patience.

His was the image of a man of brisk decision, a person who, having once heard the pertinent facts, made up his mind swiftly and firmly— some observers thought impetuously. His sense that the three of them, the chief executives of their nations, could hurry through their business if they would, was given expression in his first talk with Churchill and Stalin about the matters before them. To quote from his own subsequent account: "I told Stalin and Churchill that we should discuss the next day some of those points on which we could come to a conclusion. Churchill replied that the secretaries should give us three or four points —enough to keep us busy. I said I did not want just to discuss. I wanted to decide. Churchill asked if I wanted something in the bag each day. He was as right as he could be. I was there to get something accomplished, and if we could not do that, I meant to go back home."[1]

Ten days later (on July 28) he was writing to his mother and sister Mary: "Well, here another week has gone, and I'm still in this God-forsaken country awaiting the return of a new British Prime Minister.

[1] *Year of Decisions*, page 349.

I had hoped we'd be finished by now, but there are some loose ends to clean up, and we must meet again to do it."[2]

Churchill was depressed at the pull of the Soviet Union on Europe, and at the refusal of the American government to adopt his ideas of political and military strategy. Although he thought it likely that he would win the elections, he was not sure. He probably detected that many people in his country, now that the combat was over, were giving way to exhaustion and turning toward purposes and promises sponsored by the Labour Party rather than by himself. Those who were present remember the boyish look on the face of the Prime Minister as, at the dinner he gave just before returning to London, he spoke somewhat as follows. "I must apologize for having to leave here and interrupt the sessions of the conference. But, as you know, I am going back to England to take part in what is a very important element in English democratic processes—the counting of the ballot. We will be back here Monday,"—at which point he paused and directed his gaze down at Attlee who was sitting by him—then resumed, "in such order as the British people may determine." Stalin looked at Attlee who was hunched down in his chair and remarked, "Mr. Attlee does not seem very eager."

Truman has told us that he had "an instant liking" for Churchill. But some of his advisers had imparted to him mistrust of the Prime Minister's motives and judgment, and had put him on guard against his winning ways. Davies' presence at Truman's side at the conference sessions is a clue to his readiness to regard Churchill's views as formed by concern over British interests rather than by devotion to progress and harmony, and to find them imperial if not imperious. He was, again according to some of his staff, afraid of being misled by the renowned veteran.

The President had accepted the opinion of those who tutored him in the record that Stalin had broken or was breaking agreements reached with Roosevelt. Still, at Potsdam, Truman was impressed by the man. He was pleased by traits that eased the work of the conference, by Stalin's directness, by the way in which he stuck to the main point, by his signs of wanting to do business quickly, and even by his on and off geniality. Though aware how willful the Soviet dictator was and how relentless a bargainer, he did not always see through the dissembling mind and words. Thus Truman retained the hope that acceptable accords could be reached if he made up his mind as to what the United States could or could not approve and firmly stood by it.

[2] *Ibid.*, page 394.

Stalin was courteous to the President. As seldom as possible did he enter into direct argument with him. As often as possible he took advantage of Truman's impatient wish to get business over and done with. Toward Churchill he was more mettlesome. Perhaps he was confident that in crucial matters the British government, in the end, would abide—would feel that it had to abide—by the American decision. He did not always refrain from scoffing at the Prime Minister's views or words. Churchill, the great and courageous leader, he had admired; Churchill, the head of a country and empire left weakened by the war, he felt free to challenge roughly.

Churchill entered into an amiable relationship with Truman and showed a marked disposition to agree with him as far as he could. He was pleased by Truman's vigor and declarativeness. But it is unlikely that he was impressed by the President's foresight or adeptness in dealing with Stalin. Toward Stalin, the Prime Minister's address and response were in continual flux. Now he was challenging, soon after conciliatory; now stubborn in maintaining his views, soon after yielding. Perhaps he was made unsure because of a sense that Truman was as likely to let him down as hold him up.

There was no burbling overflow of talk at luncheons and dinners, in the intervals between appointed meetings, as there had been at Teheran and Yalta.[3] Even on such social occasions the Heads of Government, and the groups around them, were not at ease or open with one another. Was this wholly due to the greater strain of business? May it have been in part because Roosevelt, with his air of geniality, was not there? Or because Stalin and Churchill were older and more tired? Or because the Martini (Roosevelt), the Vodka (Stalin), and the Whiskey (Churchill) were less in evidence as promoters of mutual friendship?

Music was called on to make the air around the table festive—maybe also as an antidote to boredom or as protection against the perils of intimate talk. During and after every dinner at which the Heads of State entertained one another, music rose above the toasts—not soft music, heard from a little way off, but loud music, piano, band, or choral. Truman set the example at the first evening occasion. For this he hunted up a young American pianist in uniform, Eugene List. The

---

[3] This seems to be borne out by the fact that there are no American minutes of the talk on any social occasions; and in the narratives of the course of the conference that I have so far read—with the exception of Churchill's record of his conversation with Stalin on the night of the 18th—there is no reference to consequential talk on these occasions.

President wanted him to play his favorite Chopin waltz. To get a score, all Europe had to be scoured. It was found in a collection flown in from Paris. Since the pianist did not have time to learn the piece by heart, the President turned the pages as he played. Stalin, not to be outdone, brought notable concert artists from Moscow for his formal dinner. Churchill, who was bored by music, chose a remarkably spirited Royal Air Force band when he was host.

Whether for any or all of the reasons on which I have touched, or only because it was judged the way to make progress, the Heads of Government turned over more of the ground work to the Foreign Ministers than they had at Teheran and Yalta. They tried to hold themselves as adjusters of differences rather than initiators. They usually waited for the Foreign Ministers to worry over a subject and report to them before entering into a systematic discussion of it. Truman was guided by Byrnes, who assiduously briefed him, more than Roosevelt had been by anyone around him. And Stalin used Molotov more actively and gave him more rein.

In so far as it lessened the chance that differences over policy would turn into personal clashes, which might accentuate the differences, this procedure was justified. Quite possibly it made for a more even flow of business, a more thorough examination of it, and a less haphazard outcome. And yet the historian is left with the rueful wish that instead of this regulated method there had been a great spurt of conciliatory spirit and revival of trust between three men, transfigured by concern for all the nations of the world.

The only groups that did not draw apart during the Potsdam period —in fact grew closer—were the American and Soviet military staffs and commanders. Among the Americans were General Eisenhower and General Marshall and his colleagues on the Joint Chiefs of Staff, in whose minds what counted most was the Soviet promise to join in the war against Japan, and so ease and shorten that struggle.

It is notable that while the American and Soviet military staffs at Potsdam discussed thoroughly their strategy in the war against Japan, the treatment of political situations in the region was slight and desultory. Truman was satisfied with Stalin's brief and unrecorded assurances that he did not seek to obtain for Russia more than what he had already been promised in the Yalta accord. Stalin did not try to secure from Truman definite assurances about the future regime and control of

Japan. The plan for the exercise of a joint trusteeship for Korea was not translated into an operative program.

All seemed willing to let these and other Far Eastern political questions wait a while longer. Perhaps this was in part because of the crush of other business. Probably it was in part connected with the thought that the war against Japan would go on for quite a while, and that there would be adequate later chance to talk over these issues. Or avoidance of discussion may have been calculated, for events in the Far East were about to come to an ultimate climax: the Americans may have reckoned that their position would be stronger after the full power of the atomic weapon had been revealed and our forces had landed in Japan; while the Russians may have reckoned that their position would be stronger after their armies had driven the Japanese out of Manchuria and Korea and perhaps overflowed into China.

As at Teheran and at Yalta the final main agreements were fused in haste. After a first trying week, analytical dissection of problems gradually turned into a quest for acceptable compromise. During the last two important days of the conference (July 31 and August 1) both Truman and Stalin reached the limits of their political creativeness. Attlee and Bevin, having just taken over the government of England, seemed fresher of body, and Bevin livelier in view and words. But they did not bring any significant new conceptions or proposals to the conference. More exhausted than any were the assistants and advisers, who worked day and night on the communiqué to be given out and on the official record (the Protocol).

Although the Heads of Government, on parting, paid tribute to their friendly association during the conference, no deep inner glow of friendship is to be found beneath their words. All three encouraged the world to believe that what they had done was sound and enduring. But their statements, I think, expressed a hope rather than a conviction.

Here is Truman's summary impression of the experience: "As I left for home I felt that we had achieved several important agreements. But more important were some of the conclusions I had reached in my own mind and a realization of what I had to do in shaping future foreign policy."[4] Two of these conclusions were of immediate consequence: a confirmation of the resolve not to share knowledge about the atomic weapon with the Soviet Union unless and until there was a satisfactory

[4] *Year of Decisions,* page 411.

accord about control and inspection; and a resolution not to yield the Soviet government a part in the control of Japan.

Churchill, as already remarked, was tired and dejected even before he left Potsdam. His electoral defeat left him with a sense that fortune was twisted. He had led his country through its most perilous pass, only at the end to be deprived of the chance to repair some of the mistakes he thought were in the making, and perhaps still to bring about a good peace. He reverted to earlier angry judgments of the ominous character of the Soviet regime.

Of the three, it may well be that Stalin was most nearly content at what had been done at Potsdam, for the Soviet position in regard to those European matters of most direct interest had come through unscathed. But the conference could hardly have been regarded by him or his colleagues as a triumph. Several of their strong desires had been thwarted. The United States and Great Britain were less responsive than they had been during the war, and less inclined to trust the Soviet word. The western allies were standing out against both Soviet expansionism and Communist social ideals.

Terminal was a bleak ending. The major accords made there soon began to break apart.

The determination of the Soviet government to bring into power in Poland and the small states of central and southeastern Europe "peoples' democracies" of the kind it favored, and to suppress all elements friendly to the West, was no longer to be denied. The Soviet government disregarded objections to its policy. Western admiration of the valorous Russian part in the war became dimmed by fear of Soviet ruthlessness and power, and by a realization that the followers of Moscow in the West would, if they could, destroy the existence of free government. The West was also alarmed by the way in which the Soviet Union, even though it was absorbing so large an area in the center of Europe, was seeking entry into points on its circumference; by its effort to get Norway to turn over Spitzbergen; its bid for one of the Italian colonies on the North African shore; its demand for control of the Black Sea Straits; its menacing ways in Iran. And in the Far East the Soviet union was set to extort from China special privileges that could be converted into control of Manchuria and Korea.

In Germany, the close wartime military association between the western allies and the Soviet Union continued for a while longer to lock them together. Both groups responded to a sense of necessity to continue to work together in some sort of joint program for the control of Germany. But the differences of memory and interest, and of visions of a good public and private life, proved to be too deep to make genuine cooperation possible once the common danger was past. Despite its deep revulsion against Nazi Germany, the West could not bring itself to be as ruthless toward the defeated Germans as were the Russians. Possibly because their countries had not been invaded by the brutal Nazi forces, the Americans and the British lost their fear of Germany more quickly than the Russians. They began to believe that the more promising protection against revival of efficient and ruthless ambition was to be had by bringing the Germans back into the political and economic community of the western democratic world. But the Soviet government was not willing to chance this—even when the western allies offered to join in a combined guarantee against possible future German aggression. The Soviet authorities—along with the Czechs and the Poles—had not forgotten Munich, and they lapsed into mistrust of the western will to keep Germany down. They preferred to test further the chance that the Germans, if left long in distress, might adopt Communism. Or if that did not happen, they thought their safety would be better protected by maintaining control over the area of Germany that they occupied.

The time of Potsdam should have been a time of exaltation. The enemy was prostrate. The suffering and separation were over. Great vows had been kept, and greater valor shown. The United Nations had the chance and the means to make over the world nearer to the visions of freedom, justice, peace, and fair well-being. But while populaces rejoiced, government officials knew that the prospect was overcast. As they looked over the scene of their triumph, their thoughts were brushed by the cold snow of mutual mistrust and dislike—between the western allies and the Soviet Union.

Maybe, despite the dreary and repetitive battle of yeas and nays that is going on as I write these closing pages, after much wearing turmoil the West and the Communist realm will reach a mutually tolerable adjustment of their quarrels. Ironically enough, the chance that they will do so derives mainly from the "mutuality of terror"—from their power to destroy each other.

But how long will it be effective against the push of national rivalries and resentments if these are not subdued? Not forever, certainly. Long enough, it must be hoped, for all to learn to improve their ways and for time to bring about peaceful change. Truly in these years men and women are hearing the summons: "I call heaven and earth to record this day against you, that I have set before you life and death, blessing and cursing; therefore choose life that both thee and thy seed may live."

To choose life, the great nations must one and all live and act more maturely and more trustfully than they did during the months that followed the end of the war against Germany. They must invalidate the historic lessons about national behavior that were illustrated during this period. The capability of men to respond to reason—and to master their passionate purposes and fancies—is undergoing its ultimate test.

Supplementary Notes

Main Sources Cited

Index

Supplementary Note 1

On the Use of a Short Instrument of Surrender for Germany

The European Advisory Commission had by the early spring of 1945 completed the text of an instrument of surrender to be signed by the German authorities. The American, British, and Soviet governments approved it in March. This was comprehensive, containing provisions to govern not only the submission and disposition of all German military forces and equipment but also the conduct and treatment of German civilian institutions and political and economic affairs.

It was based on the supposition that when the time of surrender came, there would be in existence a central German civilian authority, which would sign the document together with the German High Command; it would be signed also by the four allied Commanders-in-Chief on behalf of their own governments (as recounted by Lord Strang, the British member of the EAC, in his book *Home and Abroad,* page 222).

By the middle of April, however, when the Nazi government went to pieces, the possibility emerged that there might be neither a German political nor military authority that could carry out an effective surrender. It was supposed that in that event the victors might join in the issuance of a Proclamation stating the terms on which they would accept the surrender of German armed forces and assume control over Germany. The British member of the EAC produced a suitable draft of a Proclamation, written with this circumstance in mind. Notably, it did not use the explicit phrase "unconditional surrender." Moreover, it included statements on various points on which the four powers in the EAC had not quite reached accord. The Russians, quick as always to attribute hidden motives to others, became mistrustful. They gave signs of a belief that in proposing the variant text the American and British governments were intending to change their general policy toward Germany. On being advised to this effect, the State Department merely passed on to Winant, the American representative on the EAC, a message consisting of a single statement from the President: "I do not wish any document or proposal changing unconditional surrender terms."

Both the State and the War Departments became perplexed by the difficulties of composing a formal Proclamation such as was being discussed in the EAC, and bringing it into close accord with the comprehensive surrender instrument that the members had approved. So on the 19th of April, Winant was advised that they would prefer the issuance of a brief declaration, instead of a Proclamation converted from the surrender instrument. It would be adequate, he was told, if this declaration contained merely a few basic elements: 1) a statement of Germany's complete defeat and the imposition of the requirement of unconditional surrender; 2) the assumption of control authority by the four allied powers; 3) the establishment of the Control Commission and the delineation of zonal responsibilities; 4) an injunction to the Germans to comply with allied orders under warning of severe punishment if they did not; and 5) notice that further resistance to the United Nations forces would be considered unlawful and dealt with accordingly.

Having conveyed these views to Winant, however, the State Department concluded by telling him that it did not wish needlessly to hinder his effort to reach an accord with his colleagues on the EAC, and if in his judgment it was desirable to go forward with the idea of converting the long surrender instrument into a Proclamation, the American government would accept the verbal formulas for the change of which Winant had informed them.

The members of the EAC were still working on this task of conversion when agents of the German government and High Command sought terms of surrender. The way and order in which the several German proposals flowed into Eisenhower's and Montgomery's headquarters have been recounted in Section 2. It appeared that there was an acceptable German authority (the German High Command) that could be required to sign a document of surrender and be held responsible for its execution.

But the original long instrument of surrender prepared in the EAC was not used. In its place General Walter Bedell Smith, acting for General Eisenhower, presented to the Germans a much shorter statement of unconditional surrender. This was derived from a draft written long before by Assistant Secretary of War McCloy, which had been reposing in the files of SHAEF. It required only the signatures of an authorized representative of the German High Command (acting for the German government) and General Eisenhower, as Supreme Commander for the allies—and perhaps that of a representative of the Soviet High Command.

The State Department was taken aback by the unexplained substitution. Even now the reasons for it are conjectural. A copy of the original EAC surrender instrument, and of the State Department letter to the Joint Chiefs recording the approval of the three governments of the text as it then stood, had been forwarded as early as March 20 to the Commanding General of ETOUSA (European Theatre of Operations, U.S.A.) for information and guidance. But the EAC had then become engaged in amending the instrument to include France, as had been agreed at Yalta. At the time of the surrender talks with the Germans, various proposed small changes had not yet been approved by all four governments, and their representatives on the EAC were still awaiting formal authority to sign the amended instrument. Thus the Combined Chiefs of Staff had not been asked by the EAC or the governments to transmit that final text to Eisenhower.

In these circumstances Eisenhower decided to use the shorter military instrument SHAEF had in hand. The Joint Chiefs probably were informed of the decision in advance, for according to Strang, Churchill was, and he approved the decision. Whether or not the Soviet liaison officer at SHAEF or the Soviet High Command was consulted about this matter, the records available to me do not tell. In any case, it is probable that Winant was correct in his opinion that one other reason for the use of the shorter document was the belief in SHAEF that the acknowledgment of complete defeat could thereby be had with least discussion and delay.

Winant, on learning on May 5 that this was going to be done, got in touch with Churchill and General Smith. He persuaded them to include an article in the briefer document stipulating: "This act of military surrender is without prejudice to, and will be superseded by any general instrument of surrender imposed by or on behalf of the United Nations and applicable to Germany and the German armed forces as a whole."

This article warded off any possible German protest later on, when the allies imposed the terms defined in the longer document and the four Commanders-in-Chief issued a declaration assuming supreme authority in Germany.

Supplementary Note 2

American Policies in Regard to the Provision of Lend-Lease Aid for the Soviet Union and Great Britain after the Ending of the War Against Germany

The main features of our policy vis-à-vis the Soviet Union, as fixed during May-June 1945, were: 1) the ships at sea carrying Lend-Lease supplies should be allowed to proceed to their destination; 2) the vessels, both dry cargo and tanker, then being loaded would get their full cargo and also be allowed to leave for the Soviet Union; but 3) no further ships should be loaded with supplies in the Atlantic or Gulf ports, pending an examination of the current program in the light of organized resistance in Europe; 4) in the Pacific the loading programs for May and June would be completed as planned, since these supplies would so largely be of use to Russia in the war against Japan; 5) the scheduled shipment of supplies from the West Coast for the Arctic program would be carried forward, while that from the Atlantic Coast should be reexamined; 6) most important, deliveries under the programming of Annex III of the Fourth Lend-Lease Protocol, which included military supplies, raw materials, industrial equipment, and food, would be continued without interruption (these were for use by the Soviet Union in the war against Japan); 7) supplies needed to complete industrial plants in the Soviet Union which had already been made available in part under previous agreements would be delivered; 8) supplies on order in the United States, but not yet shipped and not part of any program toward which we had assumed an obligation, should be ended at once, and as far as practicable such goods and the related shipping tonnage would be diverted to supply programs for western Europe; 9) any further future supply program for the Soviet Union would be decided on the basis of adequate information regarding the essentiality of Soviet military requirements, in the light of all competing demands and the changing military situation; 10) there would be no more Lend-Lease shipments of oil from Abadan or Bahrein to the Soviet Union.

On May 28, two days after Stalin had complained to Hopkins about the abrupt American slash in Lend-Lease aid, Molotov and Mikoyan submitted to Harriman the Soviet program for Lend-Lease deliveries during the second half of 1945. The goods asked were in addition to the unfilled balances of the Fourth Protocol. The new requests mounted up to 570,000 tons. The

Soviet presentation stated that all these requests were directly related to the support of projects visualized under Annex III of the Fourth Protocol, particularly for the programs to the Arctic, for airways and fishing programs, and for certain equipment promised under the Fourth Protocol which had not been delivered by July 1, 1945. Taken altogether, and including these new requests, the total tonnage involved in this six-month period would have been 1,800,000 tons, of which 400,000 tons were oil.

The American Embassy in Moscow at once started a close examination of the program, and submitted its recommendations to Washington. There the Protocol Committee, acting under directives of the Chiefs of Staff, proceeded to authorize only a part of the newly requested materials, less than half. But almost all the undelivered goods under the Fourth Protocol were subsequently delivered, as were almost all Soviet requirements under Annex III, with the exception of some railroad cars and planes.

This is a very approximate and general summary of what was done for the Soviet Union in the way of providing it with Lend-Lease supplies during the period between May and September 1945. The purpose is merely to indicate that the complaint made by Stalin to Hopkins was at least partially effective, although the American authorities continued to exercise strict judgment in passing on the question of whether goods asked by the Soviet Union were really needed for the conduct of the war, as contemplated in the Lend-Lease legislation.

The question of the effect of the curtailment of Lend-Lease on Soviet-American relations must be considered in connection with the gradual disappearance of the idea of a large credit for the Soviet Union, and also in relation to the disputes over the scale of reparations to be taken from Germany.

The American Executive, after the defeat of Germany, thought it was required by law to terminate Lead-Lease aid to the British Commonwealth, except what would serve the combat effort against Japan (Potsdam Papers, Document 542, footnote 4).

Churchill reviewed British requirements in a message to Truman on May 28 (*ibid.*, Document 537, footnote 5). Truman responded in a memo for Churchill on July 17 (*ibid.*, Document 1189). In this he said that the American government intended to furnish Lend-Lease aid to the British Commonwealth for the prosecution of the war against Japan, but the amount in total or on individual items would not necessarily be as previously estimated; and he asked the Prime Minister to relax restrictions on dollar payments for certain items owing to the United States. Churchill pointed out in return that the munitions requirements of the Commonwealth for the first year after the German surrender had already been scaled down from 2.8 billion to 1.8 billion, and that Washington agencies seemed to be construing the law "in the narrowest possible sense" and so reducing munitions supply to the vanishing point (*ibid.*, Document 1190).

Consequent discussion of the issue took place in the meetings of the Joint and Combined Chiefs of Staff at Potsdam between July 20 and July 24, in connection with their report on Basic Objectives, Strategies, and Policies.

SUPPLEMENTARY NOTES

The British Chiefs of Staff argued that the limitation of Lend-Lease aid to what was needed for direct use against the Japanese did not adequately fulfill the basic strategic plans that were being jointly formulated. Their view was that the United States should continue at least to provide means of support not only for such forces in the liberated areas as could play an active and effective role in the war against Japan but also for such forces as were required "to maintain order in the interest of the war effort," especially in the liberated countries of Europe. The Joint Chiefs, however, refused to accept this responsibility.

The issues were presented to Truman and Churchill on July 24, when they met with the Combined Chiefs. The Prime Minister pointed out that because of the close meshing of British and American industrial effort during the war, based on various agreements and his talk with Roosevelt at Quebec, many British military units were supplied with American equipment. This could not be quickly replaced. Moreover, he feared that a rigid rule to maintain British warmaking capacity only in so far as it was connected with the prosecution of the war against Japan would be very hard on Britain. Truman said he was restrained by the fact that as Vice-President he had helped to work out the terms of the most recent renewal of the Lend-Lease Act, and at the time he had explained to Congress that the aid would be for war purposes only. He was trying to give the Act the broadest legitimate interpretation. He must ask Churchill to be patient, for he did not want to get into trouble with Congress.

The most difficult question was in essence whether the American government would continue to equip and supply the occupation forces of our allies in western Europe: British, French, Belgian, Dutch. Some of these, it could be foreseen, might be used later to repossess or garrison colonial possessions outside of Europe.

The provisions that were included in the "Basic Undertakings and Prosecution of the War," approved at the end of the discussions by the Combined Chiefs and by Churchill and Truman, read:

"Maintain the war-making capacity of the United States and the British Commonwealth insofar as it is connected with the prosecution of the war against Japan.

"Provide assistance to such forces of liberated areas as can fulfill an active and effective role in the present war in accordance with the overall conception [which included maintenance of military control of Germany and Austria]."

On July 28 President Truman sent to the Joint Chiefs a new interpretation of his Directive of July 5. This, in addition to the provision of military equipment for British Commonwealth and Empire forces for use in the war against Japan, in effect authorized a substantial amount of Lend-Lease equipment for allied occupation forces in Germany and in other foreign bases, for it accorded the Joint Chiefs discretion: 1) in supplying allied governments or forces when this would serve in direct support of redeployment of American troops, or of allied troops in connection with their redeployment for action in support of the war against Japan; 2) in supplying subsistence and equipment for such allied units as were serving American forces in any area. It also authorized the continuation, for several months longer, of Lend-Lease supplies for the replacement and maintenance of military units already equipped by the United States under the North Atlantic Rearmament Program, the Metropolitan Rearmament Program, and the Air Forces Program (*ibid.,* Document 1193).

Churchill also devoted himself to securing from the United States a more usual form of financial aid, so greatly needed to enable Great Britain to regain a self-sustaining peacetime situation. At lunch with Truman on July 18 he described Britain's "melancholy" position: more than half her former foreign investments used up for the common cause; a huge external debt incurred for purchase of supplies during the war; the rundown condition of many British export industries and the stricken state of some British living areas; the current large dependence on American food. Truman responded sympathetically—reflecting that if Britain had not managed to fight on alone for a time, the United States might now be fighting the Germans on the American coast. He said he would do his utmost, but the Prime Minister would appreciate the difficulties he might have with American opposition.

As a result of the ensuing correspondence and talk it was agreed between Truman and Churchill, and Attlee when he followed up the matter after Churchill's departure, that the British government should send a special mission to Washington—probably in December. It would be sent for the purpose of reviewing with the American authorities the British postwar financial position and economic arrangements and possible American aid.

The discussions regarding a possible loan were tardily started, however. In the meantime, on August 21, a fortnight after the surrender of Japan, the American government directed that all Lend-Lease aid to Britain be discontinued. This order directed that all outstanding contracts for Lend-Lease be cancelled, except when the foreign government was willing to agree to take them over and pay for them, or when it was in the interest of the U.S. to complete them. Because of the lament in Britain over this action—following on the intimate association in the ordeal of war—Truman felt it necessary to explain publicly that the step was not meant as a blow at the new British Labour government. The reason was, he explained, that Lend-Lease was conceived as a weapon of war, that the war was over, and that furthermore when the law had been extended for the last time he had promised, as Vice-President, that it would end when the war was over.

The very next day, August 24, Prime Minister Attlee stated in the House of Commons that the end of Lend-Lease placed Great Britain "in a very serious financial position." He was planning to send emissaries to Washington at once to discuss the situation. Churchill, commenting on Attlee's statement, called it "very grave, disquieting news." The *Economist* (August 25, 1945) titled its report of the action "Lend-Lease Guillotine."

The American government took sufficient heed of this worried British response to form a committee of high officials to study the new situation that would follow the termination of Lend-Lease and make recommendations to the President. The long and severe bargaining struggle with the British about the terms of the reconstruction loan was about to begin when the Japanese envoys went through the final act of surrender on board the *Missouri*.

The full depth and dimension of British needs and difficulties were only slowly revealed in the coming years. And they were sympathetically appreciated only when the menace of Russia and Communist activity and ambition had begun to be plain.

The foregoing is an incomplete and fragmentary account of the complicated Anglo-American discussions that took place between May and September, 1945. For an adequate knowledge the inquirer is referred to the many documents in the collection of the Potsdam Papers.

Supplementary Note 3

Negotiations about the German Navy and Merchant Marine

Not long after the surrender of Germany, Stalin, in messages to Churchill and Truman, noted that Germany had turned over almost all its navy and merchant vessels to the British and Americans, almost none to the Soviet armed forces. He asked them whether they were willing to share these prizes of war with the Soviet government. One-third of each, he thought, would be fair as a minimum.

Neither the American nor the British government thought that the Soviet Union needed the naval vessels for any legitimate purpose. They were reluctant to contribute to an enlarged Soviet fleet, against which they might have to compete later. While they were considering the matter, Stalin complained to Hopkins—in their second talk, on May 27. He said that if his request was rejected, it would be very unpleasant. Hopkins told him that he knew that the American government did not want to keep any of these German ships permanently, and he thought the matter could be arranged when the Marshal met with the President and the Prime Minister. Both Churchill and Truman let Stalin know they were willing to discuss it when they met.

The State Department left it to the Joint or Combined Chiefs of Staff to advise about the disposition of the German fleet, since this was deemed to be in the military sphere. It saw no ordinary reason, however, for not turning over one-third of the German merchant ships to the Soviet Union. Admiral Leahy was of the opinion that this ought not to be done until after the defeat of Japan, so that the vessels might be used in that struggle. The Joint Chiefs of Staff came to the same conclusion. They advised the President (on July 17, just as the Potsdam Conference was starting) that in their opinion all captured or surrendered German merchant vessels should be divided among the allied nations at a suitable time, except for such coastwise and inland watercraft as might be essential for the minimum German economy; for the time being all ought to be placed in the common pool of shipping operated by the western allies, and every effort ought to be made to persuade the Russians to enter the United Maritime Authority agreement, which controlled the use of the ships in the pool; and in view of our urgent need for more ships to carry troops to the Far East, all captured or surrendered enemy vessels suitable for that purpose should be made available at once for that service.

As regards the German naval fleet, the Joint Chiefs of Staff conveyed their views to the President in Potsdam on July 17, just before the subject was brought into discussion. They had concluded that it would be best if all German naval vessels, except a few useful LSTs and some naval auxiliary ships, were sunk or scrapped. But if the American government could not get the Soviet and British governments to agree to that course, then it ought to propose that all the heavier vessels and submarines be sunk, and that the smaller and more lightly armed vessels be shared among the *four* main allies, that is, including France. If it could not gain assent even to that, then all four powers might share equally in the division of each category of ships. In any event, the Joint Chiefs concluded, we ought to insist that all submarines be sunk.

When the Foreign Ministers began to consider the order of business for the Heads of Government at Potsdam, Molotov showed that he did not intend to allow this subject to be forgotten. He tried to get Byrnes and Eden to agree to bring it up at once, along with matters of far greater range. But Byrnes objected. And Eden remarked that since this was one of the most simple of the matters they had before them, he thought it could well wait; he could promise that the German fleet would not be sunk in the meanwhile.

At the First Plenary Session of the conference, on the afternoon of the 17th, Stalin followed up Molotov's initiative by proposing that this subject be added to the list of topics Truman presented for discussion. Just before this session ended, he reverted to the matter, asking "Why does Churchill refuse to give Russia her share of the German fleet?" Churchill's answer seemed to indicate that he was attracted to the idea of destroying it rather than dividing it. But Stalin said "Let's divide it. If Mr. Churchill wishes, he can sink his share."

The Soviet government, on July 19, submitted a proposal that one-third of the total German navy, wherever located, including ships under construction or in repair, be handed over to the Soviet Union, along with one-third of all German reserve naval arms, ammunition, and supplies; and that one-third of the German merchant marine be so transferred. It suggested that the turnover of ships be begun in August and completed by November.

At the Plenary Session that day, Stalin urged the others to approve at once this Soviet proposal. The ensuing discussion was warm and rambling. Churchill discoursed. He was not opposed to dividing up the German navy, but he thought that its submarines, of which, he pointed out, the Russians had forty-five in the Baltic, were in a different class from other ships, since they had only limited legal use; hence he would like to see most of them sunk.

The Prime Minister saw no objection to the proposed division of the merchant fleet. But other countries also, such as Norway, which had lost so large a part of its shipping in the war, deserved a share. And he agreed with the President that the ships ought to be available for use in the war against Japan and for other immediate uses, such as the transport of food and other essentials to Europe and the relief of liberated countries, such as Greece and Norway and "our Russian ally." The ships in the Russian share, he suggested, could be earmarked, if they had any ears when the Japanese war was over, and if any were damaged they could be "made good from our general resources."

Stalin assumed an injured air: of course it was not possible "to depict the Russians as having the intention to interfere in the war against Japan," and the matter could not be put in a way to imply that they were "to receive a gift from the allies"; they were "not after a gift." If Churchill and Truman approved the Soviet request in principle, he would be satisfied, and would not object to having the Russian third of the merchant ships used as the others in the war against Japan.

There was one more point, Stalin added. The Russians had not yet seen the German naval fleet, or even been given a list of the vessels. Could they not inspect them? Of course, Churchill said, but the British in return would like to be given the chance to see German installations in the Baltic; he believed that the Russians had obtained forty-five German U-boats in Danzig; they would like an exchange. Truman said the Russians could see anything they wanted in the American zone on a reciprocal basis.

So in effect the Russian title to one-third of both the German merchant marine and the naval fleet was recognized at this early session, but subject to the understanding that those vessels that would be useful and needed would be kept under allied control until the Pacific war was brought to an end. Whether and how other countries were to share in the distribution was left for further discussion. And the promised turnover of naval vessels was subject to one further qualification, entered by Churchill. Twice, he recalled with feeling, Britain had almost perished because of submarine activity; nations like Britain, with dense populations living in small areas surrounded by water, did not welcome the acquisition or construction by others of this type of ship. So he would want to discuss further how many of the captured submarines were to be sunk; of those that were not, he agreed that the division should be equal. Stalin responded by saying that he too was in favor of sinking many of the U-boats. It having thus been indicated that the views of the three were near together, the working out of the accord was left to the last days of the conference. This meant that if the three great allies were still friends at the end, the Russians would get what they wanted; if they quarreled, the Russians would have to get along without these German vessels.

But final agreement on the precise terms and conditions proved harder and longer than expected. Bevin's stubbornness in the end brought Molotov to agree that all but thirty submarines were to be sunk. Bevin also wrung from Molotov acceptance of a provision that the Control Council should determine first of all how much and what kinds of merchant tonnage (inland and coastal ships) would be needed for the level of the German economy to be maintained, and that these should be excluded from the division. But Bevin, who had argued that because the western allies would have to turn over a substantial amount of the merchant tonnage to their smaller maritime associates, the Soviet Union should be satisfied with a quarter of the total divisible tonnage, gave in on this point: he agreed that it would have a third, of which it should turn over part to Poland.

The Potsdam protocol stipulated that the transfer of naval vessels should be completed as soon as possible, and not later than February 15, 1946. But the transfer of the merchant vessels was to be deferred until after the end of the war against Japan. That came more quickly than expected.

Supplementary Note 4

The Stipulations Regarding a Basic Standard of Living for the Germans in Directive for Eisenhower of May 14, 1945

Two different ways of describing the basic standards of living for which allied controls might, if necessary, be employed were in the directive that was sent to Eisenhower on May 14 (JCS 1067/8). Paragraph 5 authorized the use of such controls as were *"essential to protect the safety and meet the needs of the occupying forces and assure the production and maintenance of goods and services necessary to prevent starvation and such unrest as would endanger these forces"* (my italics). Paragraph 21 stipulated: "You will estimate requirements of supplies necessary to prevent starvation or widespread disease or such civil unrest as would endanger the occupying forces. Such estimates will be based upon a program whereby the Germans are made responsible for providing for themselves, out of their own work and resources. . . . You will take no action that would tend to support basic living standards in Germany on a higher level than that existing *in any one of the neighboring United Nations and you will take appropriate measures to ensure that basic living standards of the German people are not higher than those existing in any one of the neighboring United Nations when such measure will contribute to raising the standards of any such nation"* (my italics).

Supplementary Note 5

On "War Booty" and "Restitution"

One of the most trying issues both in the Allied Reparation Commission and at Potsdam was the question of what seizures of German property and what recaptures of allied property taken by the Germans should be accounted as outside the reparations program.

What could be properly taken as *war booty,* without being entered into the reparations account? Only finished military equipment and supplies produced for and belonging to the German armed forces, as the Americans proposed? Or any and all goods that had served the German military effort, including factories, trucks, and office equipment, as the Russians proposed?

What could be claimed and acquired as *restitution,* that is, as a return of stolen property, and thus not be regarded as reparations? Truman, at the First Plenary Session on July 17, submitted a definition conforming to what Pauley had been advocating in the Reparation Commission: "restitution" should be confined to identifiable artistic, religious, and cultural objects; other kinds of identifiable stolen property should be treated as reparations, with each owner country having a prior claim. The Russians, however, proposed that restitution cover all kinds of identifiable property, and replacement of any that had been damaged, lost, or destroyed.

The British government, before and at Potsdam, was half-heartedly willing to go along with the American government in its efforts to confine both of these kinds of property removals, but the British officials were dubious about the good sense and effectiveness of limiting definitions. They thought that these would hamper the western occupants, while the Russians would anyway take anything they wanted and could get.

Many additional and more systematic details of the different views and proposals in this complex field are to be found in the Potsdam Papers, particularly in Documents 376, 377, 380, and 894.

Supplementary Note 6

Provisions in the Montreux Convention of 1936
Pertinent to Soviet Demands for Revision

Under Article 2 of the 1936 Montreux Convention, *merchant vessels* under any flag and with any kind of cargo were to enjoy freedom of transit and navigation in time of peace; and under Article 4 they were to have this right also in time of war, if Turkey was not a belligerent. In time of war, with Turkey belligerent, the merchant vessels belonging to countries not at war with Turkey were to retain this right "on condition that they do not in any way assist the enemy," according to Article 5, but Turkey was authorized to require them to enter the Straits by day and follow a prescribed route. And, under Article 6, "Should Turkey consider herself threatened with imminent danger of war it could apply the same rules as under Article 5."

In time of peace, or in time of war when Turkey was not a belligerent, Turkey was authorized by Articles 10 and 19 to impose various rules and limitations on the passage through the Straits of the *vessels of war* of the Black Sea Powers (for example, capital ships could pass only singly, escorted by not more than two destroyers) and stricter rules and limitations on the vessels of war of other countries. Under Articles 20 and 21 "the passage of war ships shall be left entirely to the discretion of the Turkish Government" at any time that Turkey was at war or considered itself threatened with imminent danger of war.

The text of the Montreux Convention is in British White Paper Cmd. 5249 (1936).

Supplementary Note 7

Protocol of Proceedings of the Berlin Conference, July 17–August 2, 1945. Department of State Press Release, March 24, 1947

The Berlin conference of the three heads of government of the Union of Soviet Socialist Republics, the United States of America, and United Kingdom, which took place from July 17 to August 2, 1945, came to the following conclusions:

I. ESTABLISHMENT OF A COUNCIL OF FOREIGN MINISTERS

A. The conference reached the following agreement for the establishment of a Council of Foreign Ministers to do the necessary preparatory work for the peace settlements:

1

There shall be established a Council composed of the Foreign Ministers of the United Kingdom, the Union of Soviet Socialist Republics, China, France and the United States.

2

(I) The Council shall normally meet in London, which shall be the permanent seat of the joint secretariat which the Council will form. Each of the Foreign Ministers will be accompanied by a high-ranking deputy, duly authorized to carry on the work of the Council in the absence of his Foreign Minister, and by a small staff of technical advisers.

(II) The first meeting of the Council shall be held in London not later than September 1, 1945. Meetings may be held by common agreement in other capitals as may be agreed from time to time.

3

(I) As its immediate important task the Council shall be authorized to draw up, with a view to their submission to the United Nations, treaties of peace with Italy, Rumania, Bulgaria, Hungary and Finland, and to propose settlements of territorial questions outstanding on the termination of the war in Europe. The Council shall be utilized for the preparation of a peace settlement for Germany to be accepted by the Government of Germany when a Government adequate for the purpose is established.

(II) For the discharge of each of these tasks the Council will be composed of the members representing those states which were signatory to the terms of surrender imposed upon the enemy state concerned. For the purpose of the peace settlement for Italy, France shall be regarded as a signatory to the terms of surrender for Italy. Other members will be invited to participate when matters directly concerning them are under discussion.

(III) Other matters may from time to time be referred to the Council by agreement between the member Governments.

4

(I) Whenever the Council is considering a question of direct interest to a state not represented thereon, such state should be invited to send representatives to participate in the discussion and study of that question.

(II) The Council may adapt its procedure to the particular problems under consideration. In some cases it may hold its own preliminary discussions prior to the participation of other interested states. In other cases, the Council may convoke a formal conference of the state chiefly interested in seeking a solution of the particular problem.

B. It was agreed that the three Governments should each address an identical invitation to the Governments of China and France to adopt this text and to join in establishing the Council. The text of the approved invitation was as follows:

COUNCIL OF FOREIGN MINISTERS DRAFT FOR IDENTICAL INVITATION TO BE SENT SEPARATELY BY EACH OF THE THREE GOVERNMENTS TO THE GOVERNMENTS OF CHINA AND FRANCE.

The Governments of the United Kingdom, the United States and the Union of Soviet Socialist Republics consider it necessary to begin without delay the essential preparatory work upon the peace settlements in Europe. To this end they are agreed that there should be established a Council of the Foreign Ministers of the five great powers to prepare treaties of peace with the European enemy states from submission to the United Nations. The Council would also be empowered to propose settlements of outstanding territorial questions in Europe and to consider such other matters as member Governments might agree to refer to it.

The text adopted by the Three Governments is as follows:
(Here insert final agreed text of the proposal.)

"In agreement with the Governments of the United States, His Majesty's Government in the United Kingdom and Union of Soviet Socialist Republics, the United States Government, the United Kingdom and the Soviet Government extend a cordial invitation to the Government of China (France) to adopt the text quoted above and to join in setting up the Council. His Majesty's Government, the United States Government, the Soviet Government attach much importance to the participation of the Chinese Government (French Government) in the proposed arrangements and they hope to receive an early and favorable reply to this invitation."

C. It was understood that the establishment of the Council of Foreign Ministers for the specific purposes named in the text would be without prejudice to the agreement of the Crimea Conference that there should be periodical consultation between the Foreign Secretaries of the United States, the Union of Soviet Socialist Republics and the United Kingdom.

D. The conference also considered the position of the European Advisory

Commission in the light of the agreement to establish the Council of Foreign Ministers. It was noted with satisfaction that the Commission had ably discharged its principal tasks by the recommendations that it had furnished for the terms of surrender for Germany, for the zones of occupation in Germany and Austria and for the inter-Allied control machinery in those countries. It was felt that further work of a detailed character for the coordination of Allied policy for the control of Germany and Austria would in future fall within the competence of the Control Council at Berlin and the Allied Commission at Vienna. Accordingly, it was agreed to recommend that the European Advisory Commission be dissolved.

II. THE PRINCIPLES TO GOVERN THE TREATMENT OF GERMANY IN THE INITIAL CONTROL

A. Political principles.

[1]

In accordance with the agreement on control machinery in Germany, supreme authority in Germany is exercised, on instructions from their respective Governments, by the commanders in chief of the armed forces of the United States of America, the United Kingdom, the Union of Soviet Socialist Republics and the French Republic, each in his own zone of occupation, and also jointly, in matters affecting Germany as a whole, in their capacity as members of the Control Council.

[2]

So far as is practicable, there shall be uniformity of treatment of the German population throughout Germany.

[3]

The purposes of the occupation of Germany by which the Control Council shall be guided are:

(I) The complete disarmament and demilitarization of Germany and the elimination or control of all German industry that could be used for military production. To these ends:

(*a*) All German land, naval and air forces, the SS, SA, SD and Gestapo, with all their organizations, staffs and institutions, including the general staff, the officers' corps, reserve corps, military schools, war veterans organizations and all other military and semi-military organizations, together with all clubs and associations which serve to keep alive the military tradition in Germany, shall be completely and finally abolished in such manner as permanently to prevent the revival or reorganization of German militarism and nazism;

(*b*) All arms, ammunition and implements of war and all specialized facilities for their production shall be held at the disposal of the Allies or destroyed. The maintenance and production of all aircraft and all arms, ammunition and implements of war shall be prevented.

(II) To convince the German people that they have suffered a total military defeat and that they cannot escape responsibility for what they have brought upon themselves, since their own ruthless warfare and the fanatical Nazi resistance have destroyed German economy and made chaos and suffering inevitable.

(III) To destroy the National Socialist party and its affiliated and supervised organizations, to dissolve all Nazi institutions, to insure that they are not revived in any form and to prevent all Nazi and militarist activity or propaganda.

(IV) To prepare for the eventual reconstruction of German political life on a democratic basis and for eventual peaceful cooperation in international life by Germany.

[4]

All Nazi laws which provide the basis of the Hitler regime or established discriminations on grounds of race, creed or political opinion shall be abolished. No such discriminations, whether legal, administrative or otherwise, shall be tolerated.

[5]

War criminals and those who have participated in planning or carrying out Nazi enterprises involving or resulting in atrocities or war crimes shall be arrested and brought to judgment. Nazi leaders, influential Nazi supporters and high officials of Nazi organizations and institutions and any other persons dangerous to the occupation or its objectives shall be arrested and interned.

[6]

All members of the Nazi party who have been more than nominal participants in its activities and all other persons hostile to Allied purposes shall be removed from public and semi-public office and from positions of responsibility in important private undertakings. Such persons shall be replaced by persons who, by their political and moral qualities, are deemed capable of assisting in developing genuine democratic institutions in Germany.

[7]

German education shall be so controlled as completely to eliminate Nazi and militarist doctrines and to make possible the successful development of democratic ideas.

[8]

The judicial system will be reorganized in accordance with the principles of democracy, of justice under law and of equal rights for all citizens without distinction of race, nationality or religion.

[9]

The administration in Germany should be directed toward the decentralization of the political structure and the development of local responsibility. To this end:

(I) Local self-government shall be restored throughout Germany on democratic principles and in particular through elective councils as rapidly as is consistent with military security and the purposes of military occupation;

(II) All democratic political parties with rights of assembly and of public discussion shall be allowed and encouraged throughout Germany;

(III) Representative and elective principles shall be introduced into regional, provincial and state (Land) administration as rapidly as may be justified by the successful application of these principles in local self-government;

(IV) For the time being, no central German Government shall be established. Notwithstanding this, however, certain essential central German administrative departments, headed by state secretaries, shall be established, particularly in the fields of finance, transport, communications, foreign trade and industry. Such departments will act under the direction of the Control Council.

[10]

Subject to the necessity for maintaining military security, freedom of speech, press and religion shall be permitted, and religious institutions shall be respected. Subject likewise to the maintenance of military security, the formation of free trade unions shall be permitted.

B. Economic principles.

[11]

In order to eliminate Germany's war potential, the production of arms, ammunition and implements of war as well as all types of aircraft and sea-going ships shall be prohibited and prevented. Production of metals, chemicals, machinery and other items that are directly necessary to a war economy shall be rigidly controlled and restricted to Germany's approved post-war peacetime needs to meet the objectives stated in Paragraph 15. Productive capacity not needed for permitted production shall be removed in accordance with the reparations plan recommended by the Allied Commission on reparations and approved by the Governments concerned, or if not removed, shall be destroyed.

[12]

At the earliest practicable date, the German economy shall be decentralized for the purpose of eliminating the present excessive concentration of economic power as exemplified in particular by cartels, syndicates, trusts and other monopolistic arrangements.

[13]

In organizing the German economy, primary emphasis shall be given to the development of agriculture and peaceful domestic industries.

[14]

During the period of occupation Germany shall be treated as a single economic unit. To this end, common policies shall be established in regard to:

(*a*) Mining and industrial production and its allocation;

(*b*) Agriculture, forestry and fishing;

(c) Wages, prices and rationing;
(d) Import and export programs for Germany as a whole;
(e) Currency and banking, central taxation and customs;
(f) Reparation and removal of industrial war potential;
(g) Transportation and communications.

In applying these policies, account shall be taken, where appropriate, of varying local conditions.

[15]

Allied controls shall be imposed upon the German economy, but only to the extent necessary:

(a) To carry out programs of industrial disarmament, demilitarization, of reparations and of approved exports and imports.

(b) To assure the production and maintenance of goods and services required to meet the needs of the occupying forces and displaced persons in Germany and essential to maintain in Germany average living standards not exceeding the average of the standards of living of European countries. (European countries means all European countries, excluding the United Kingdom and the Union of Soviet Socialist Republics.)

(c) To insure in the manner determined by the Central Council the equitable distribution of essential commodities between the several zones so as to produce a balanced economy throughout Germany and reduce the need for imports.

(d) To control German industry and all economic and financial international transactions, including exports and imports, with the aim of preventing Germany from developing a war potential and of achieving the other objectives named herein.

(e) To control all German public and private scientific bodies, research and experimental institutions, laboratories, etc., connected with economic activities.

[16]

In the imposition and maintenance of economic controls established by the Control Council, German administrative machinery shall be created and the German authorities shall be required to the fullest extent practicable to proclaim and assume administration of such controls. Thus it should be brought home to the German people that the responsibility for the administration of such controls and any breakdown in these controls will rest with themselves. Any German controls which may run counter to the objectives of occupation will be prohibited.

[17]

Measures shall be promptly taken:
(a) To effect essential repair of transport;
(b) To enlarge coal production;
(c) To maximize agricultural output; and
(d) To effect emergency repair of housing and essential utilities.

[18]

Appropriate steps shall be taken by the Control Council to exercise control and the power of disposition over German-owned external assets not already under the control of United Nations which have taken part in the war against Germany.

[19]

Payment of reparations should leave enough resources to enable the German people to subsist without external assistance. In working out the economic balance of Germany, the necessary means must be provided to pay for imports approved by the Control Council in Germany.

The proceeds of exports from current production and stocks shall be available in the first place for payment for such imports.

The above clause will not apply to the equipment and products referred to in Paragraphs 4 (*a*) and 4 (*b*) of the reparations agreement.

III. REPARATIONS FROM GERMANY

[1]

Reparation claims of the Union of Soviet Socialist Republics shall be met by removals from the zone of Germany occupied by the Union of Soviet Socialist Republics and from appropriate German external assets.

[2]

The Union of Soviet Socialist Republics undertakes to settle the reparation claims of Poland from its own share of reparations.

[3]

The reparation claims of the United States, the United Kingdom and other countries entitled to reparations shall be met from the Western zones and from appropriate German external assets.

[4]

In addition to the reparations to be taken by the Union of Soviet Socialist Republics from its own zone of occupation, the Union of Soviet Socialist Republics shall receive additionally from the Western zones:

(*a*) 15 percent of such usable and complete industrial capital equipment, in the first place from the metallurgical, chemical and machine manufacturing industries as is unnecessary for the German peace economy and should be removed from the Western zones of Germany, in exchange for an equivalent value of food, coal, potash, zinc, timber, clay products, petroleum products and such other commodities as may be agreed upon.

(*b*) 10 percent of such industrial capital equipment as is unnecessary for the German peace economy and should be removed from the Western zones, to be transferred to the Soviet Government on reparations account without payment or exchange of any kind in return. Removals of equipment as provided in (*a*) and (*b*) above shall be made simultaneously.

[5]

The amount of equipment to be removed from the Western zones on account of reparations must be determined within six months from now at the latest.

[6]

Removals of industrial capital equipment shall begin as soon as possible and shall be completed within two years from the determination specified in Paragraph 5. The delivery of products covered by 4 (*a*) above shall begin as soon as possible and shall be made by the Union of Soviet Socialist Republics in agreed installments within five years of the date hereof. The determination of the amount and character of the industrial capital equipment unnecessary for the German peace economy and therefore available for reparation shall be made by the Control Council under policies fixed by the Allied Commission on Reparations, with the participation of France, subject to the final approval of the zone commander in the zone from which the equipment is to be removed.

[7]

Prior to the fixing of the total amount of equipment subject to removal, advance deliveries shall be made in respect to such equipment as will be determined to be eligible for delivery in accordance with the procedure set forth in the last sentence of Paragraph 6.

[8]

The Soviet Government renounces all claims in respect of reparations to shares of German enterprises which are located in the Western Zones of Germany as well as to German foreign assets in all countries except those specified in Paragraph 9 below.

[9]

The Governments of the United Kingdom and United States of America renounce all claims in respect of reparations to shares of German enterprises which are located in the Eastern zone of occupation in Germany, as well as to German foreign assets in Bulgaria, Finland, Hungary, Rumania and eastern Austria.

[10]

The Soviet Government makes no claims to gold captured by the Allied troops in Germany.

IV. DISPOSAL OF THE GERMAN NAVY AND MERCHANT MARINE

A. *The following principles for the distribution of the German Navy were agreed:*

1. The total strength of the German surface navy, excluding ships sunk and those taken over from Allied nations, but including ships under construction or repair, shall be divided equally among the Union of Soviet Socialist Republics, United Kingdom and United States of America.

2. Ships under construction or repair mean those ships whose construction or repair may be completed within three to six months, according to the type of ship. Whether such ships under construction or repair shall be complete or repaired shall be determined by the technical commission appointed by the three powers and referred to below, subject to the principle that their completion or repair must be achieved within the time limits above provided, without any increase of skilled employment in the German shipyards and without permitting the reopening of any German shipbuilding or connected industries. Completion date means the date when a ship is able to go out on its first trip, or, under peacetime standards would refer to the customery date of delivery by shipyard to the government.

3. The larger part of the German submarine fleet shall be sunk. Not more than thirty submarines shall be preserved and divided equally between the Union of Soviet Socialist Republics, United Kingdom and United States of America for experimental and technical purposes.

4. All stocks of armament, ammunition and supplies of the German Navy appertaining to the vessels transferred pursuant to Paragraphs 1 and 3 hereof shall be handed over to the respective powers receiving such ships.

5. The three Governments agree to constitute a tripartite naval commission comprising two representatives for each Government, accompanied by the requisite staff, to submit agreed recommendations to the three Governments for the allocation of specific German warships and handle other detailed matters arising out of the agreement between the three Governments regarding the German fleet. The commission will hold its first meeting not later than 15 August, 1945, in Berlin, which shall be its headquarters. Each delegation on the commission will have the right on the basis of reciprocity to inspect German warships wherever they may be located.

6. The three Governments agreed that transfers, including those of ships under construction and repair, shall be completed as soon as possible, but not later than 15 February 1946. The commission will submit fortnightly reports, including proposals for the progressive allocation of the vessels when agreed by the commission.

B. *The following principles for the distribution of the German merchant marine were agreed:*

1. The German merchant marine, surrendered to the three powers and wherever located, shall be divided equally among the Union of Soviet Socialist

Republics, the United Kingdom and the United States of America. The actual transfers of the ships to the respective countries shall take place as soon as practicable after the end of the war against Japan. The United Kingdom and the United States will provide out of their shares of the surrendered German merchant ships appropriate amounts for other allied states whose merchant marines have suffered heavy losses in the common cause against Germany, except that the Soviet Union shall provide out of its share for Poland.

2. The allocation, manning and operation of these ships during the Japanese war period shall fall under the cognizance and authority of the combined shipping adjustment board and the United Maritime Authority.

3. While actual transfer of the ships shall be delayed until after the end of the war with Japan, a tripartite shipping commission shall inventory and value all available ships and recommend a specific distribution in accordance with Paragraph 1.

4. German inland and coastal ships determined to be necessary to the maintenance of the basic German peace economy by the Allied Control Council of Germany shall not be included in the shipping pool thus divided among the three powers.

5. The three Governments agree to constitute a tripartite merchant marine commission comprising two representatives for each Government, accompanied by the requisite staff, to submit agreed recommendations to the three Governments for the allocation of specific German merchant ships and to handle other detailed matters arising out of the agreement between the three Governments regarding the German merchant ships. The commission will hold its first meeting not later than September 1, 1945 in Berlin, which shall be its headquarters. Each delegation on the commission will have the right on the basis of reciprocity to inspect the German merchant ships wherever they may be located.

V. CITY OF KOENIGSBERG AND THE ADJACENT AREA

The conference examined a proposal by the Soviet Government to the effect that, pending the final determination of territorial questions at the peace settlement, the section of the western frontier of the Union of Soviet Socialist Republics which is adjacent to the Baltic Sea should pass from a point on the eastern shore of the Bay of Danzig to the east, north of Braunsberg-Goldap, to the meeting point of the frontiers of Lithuania, the Polish Republic and East Prussia.

The conference has agreed in principle to the proposal of the Soviet Government concerning the ultimate transfer to the Soviet Union of the City of Koenigsberg and the area adjacent to it as described above, subject to expert examination of the actual frontier.

The President of the United States and the British Prime Minister have declared that they will support the proposal of the conference at the forthcoming peace settlement.

VI. WAR CRIMINALS

The three Governments have taken note of the discussions which have been proceeding in recent weeks in London between British, United States, Soviet and French representatives with a view to reaching agreement on the methods of trial of these major war criminals whose crimes under the Moscow declaration of October, 1943, have no particular geographical localization. The three Governments reaffirm their intention to bring these criminals to swift and sure justice. They hope that the negotiations in London will result in speedy agreement being reached for this purpose, and they regard it as a matter of great importance that the trial of these major criminals should begin at the earliest possible date. The first list of defendants will be published before 1 September.

VII. AUSTRIA

The conference examined a proposal by the Soviet Government on the extension of the authority of the Austrian Provisional Government to all of Austria. The three Governments agreed that they were prepared to examine this question after the entry of the British and American forces into the City of Vienna.

It was agreed that reparations should not be exacted from Austria.

VIII. POLAND

A. *Declaration.*

We have taken note with pleasure of the agreement reached among representative Poles from Poland and abroad which has made possible the formation, in accordance with the decisions reached at the Crimea Conference, of a Polish Provisional Government of National Unity recognized by the three powers. The establishment by the British and United States Governments of diplomatic relations with the Polish Provisional Government of National Unity has resulted in the withdrawal of their recognition from the former Polish Government in London, which no longer exists.

The British and United States Governments have taken measures to protect the interest of the Polish Provisional Government of National Unity as the recognized Government of the Polish State in the property belonging to the Polish State located in their territories and under their control, whatever the form of this property may be. They have further taken measures to prevent alienation to third parties of such property. All proper facilities will be given to the Polish Provisional Government of National Unity for the exercise of the ordinary legal remedies for the recovery of any property belonging to the Polish State which may have been wrongfully alienated.

The three powers are anxious to assist the Polish Provisional Government of National Unity in facilitating the return to Poland as soon as practicable of all Poles abroad who wish to go, including members of the Polish armed forces and the merchant marine. They expect that those Poles who return home shall be accorded personal and property rights on the same basis as all Polish citizens.

The three powers note that the Polish Provisional Government of National Unity, in accordance with the decisions of the Crimea Conference, has agreed to the holding of free and unfettered elections as soon as possible on the basis of universal suffrage and secret ballot, in which all democratic and anti-Nazi parties shall have the right to take part and to put forward candidates, and that representatives of the Allied press shall enjoy full freedom to report to the world upon developments in Poland before and during the elections.

In conformity with the agreement on Poland reached at the Crimea Conference, the three heads of Government have sought the opinion of the Polish Provisional Government of National Unity in regard to the accession of territory in the north and west which Poland should receive. The President of the National Council of Poland and members of the Polish Provisional Government of National Unity have been received at the conference and have fully presented their views. The three heads of Government reaffirm their opinion that the final delimitation of the Western frontier of Poland should await the peace settlement.

The three heads of government agree that, pending the final determination of Poland's western frontier, the former German territories east of a line running from the Baltic Sea immediately west of Swinemuende, and thence along the Oder River to the confluence of the Western Neisse River and along the Western Neisse to the Czechoslovak frontier, including that portion of East Prussia not placed under the administration of the Union of Soviet Socialist Republics in accordance with the understanding reached at this conference and including the area of the former Free City of Danzig, shall be under the administration of the Polish state and for such purposes should not be considered as part of the Soviet zone of occupation in Germany.

IX. CONCLUSION OF PEACE TREATIES AND ADMISSION TO THE UNITED NATIONS ORGANIZATION

The three Governments consider it desirable that the present anomalous position of Italy, Bulgaria, Finland, Hungary and Rumania should be terminated by the conclusion of peace treaties. They trust that the other interested Allied Governments will share these views.

For their part, the three Governments have included the preparation for a peace treaty for Italy as the first among the immediate important tasks to be undertaken by the new Council of Foreign Ministers. Italy was the first of the Axis powers to break with Germany, to whose defeat she has made a material contribution, and has now joined with the Allies in the struggle against Japan. Italy has freed herself from the Fascist regime and is making good progress toward re-establishment of a democratic government and institutions. The conclusion of such a peace treaty with a recognized and democratic Italian Government will make it possible for the three Governments to fulfill their desire to support an application from Italy for membership of the United Nations.

The three Governments have also charged the Council of Foreign Ministers with the task of preparing peace treaties for Bulgaria, Finland, Hungary and Rumania. The conclusion of peace treaties with recognized democratic governments in these states will also enable the three Governments to support applications from them for membership of the United Nations. The three Governments agree to examine each separately in the near future, in the light of the conditions then prevailing, the establishment of diplomatic relations with Finland, Rumania, Bulgaria and Hungary to the extent possible prior to the conclusion of peace treaties with those countries.

The three Governments have no doubt that in view of the changed conditions resulting from the termination of the war in Europe, representatives of the Allied press will enjoy full freedom to report to the world upon developments in Rumania, Bulgaria, Hungary and Finland.

As regards the admission of other states into the United Nations Organization, Article 4 of the Charter of the United Nations declares that:

"1. Membership in the United Nations is open to all other peace-loving states who accept the obligations contained in the present Charter and, in the judgment of the organization, are able and willing to carry out these obligations.

"2. The admission of any such state to membership in the United Nations will be effected by a decision of the General Assembly upon the recommendation of the Security Council."

The three Governments, so far as they are concerned, will support applications for membership from those states which have remained neutral during the war and which fulfill the qualifications set out above.

The three Governments feel bound, however, to make it clear that they, for their part, would not favor any application for membership put forward by the present Spanish Government, which, having been founded with the support of the Axis powers, does not, in view of its origins, its nature, its record and its close association with the aggressor states, possess the qualifications necessary to justify such membership.

X. TERRITORIAL TRUSTEESHIP

The conference examined a proposal by the Soviet Government on the question of trusteeship territories as defined in the decision of the Crimea Conference and in the Charter of the United Nations Organization.

After an exchange of views on this question, it was decided that the disposition of any former Italian colonial territories was one to be decided in connection with the preparation of a peace treaty for Italy and that the question of Italian colonial territory would be considered by the September Council of Ministers of Foreign Affairs.

XI. REVISED ALLIED CONTROL COMMISSION PROCEDURE IN RUMANIA, BULGARIA AND HUNGARY

The three Governments took note that the Soviet representatives on the Allied Control Commissions in Rumania, Bulgaria and Hungary have communicated to their United Kingdom and United States colleagues proposals for improving the work of the Control Commissions, now that hostilities in Europe have ceased.

The three Governments agreed that the revision of the procedures of the Allied Control Commissions in these countries would now be undertaken, taking into account the interests and responsibilities of the three Governments which together presented the terms of armistice to the respective countries, and accepting as a basis, in respect of all three countries, the Soviet Government's proposals for Hungary as annexed hereto (Annex I).

XII. ORDERLY TRANSFER OF GERMAN POPULATIONS

The three Governments, having considered the question in all its aspects, recognize that the transfer to Germany of German populations, or elements thereof, remaining in Poland, Czechoslovakia and Hungary will have to be undertaken. They agree that any transfers that take place should be effected in an orderly and humane manner.

Since the influx of a large number of Germans into Germany would increase the burden already resting on the occupying authorities, they consider that the Control Council in Germany should in the first instance examine the problem, with special regard to the question of the equitable distribution of these Germans among the several zones of occupation. They are accordingly instructing their respective representatives on the Control Council to report to their Governments as soon as possible the extent to which such persons have already entered Germany from Poland, Czechoslovakia and Hungary and to submit an estimate of the time and rate at which further transfers could be carried out, having regard to the present situation in Germany.

The Czechoslovak Government, the Polish Provisional Government and the Control Council in Hungary are at the same time being informed of the above and are being requested meanwhile to suspend further expulsions pending an examination by the Governments concerned of the report from their representatives on the Control Council.

XIII. OIL EQUIPMENT IN RUMANIA

The conference agreed to set up two bilateral commissions of experts, one to be composed of United Kingdom and Soviet members, and one to be composed of United States and Soviet members, to investigate the facts and examine the documents, as a basis for the settlement of questions arising from the removal of oil equipment in Rumania. It was further agreed that these experts shall begin their work within ten days, on the spot.

XIV. IRAN

It was agreed that Allied troops should be withdrawn immediately from Teheran and that further stages of the withdrawal of troops from Iran should be considered at the meeting of the Council of Foreign Ministers to be held in London in September, 1945.

XV. THE INTERNATIONAL ZONE OF TANGIER

A proposal by the Soviet Government was examined and the following decisions were reached:

Having examined the question of the Zone of Tangier, the three Governments have agreed that this zone, which includes the City of Tangier and the area adjacent to it, in view of its special strategic importance, shall remain international.

The question of Tangier will be discussed in the near future at a meeting in Paris of representatives of the Governments of the Union of Soviet Socialist Republics, the United States of America, the United Kingdom and France.

XVI. THE BLACK SEA STRAITS

The three Governments recognize that the convention concluded at Montreux should be revised as failing to meet present-day conditions.

It was agreed that as the next step the matter should be the subject of direct conversations between each of the three Governments and the Turkish Government.

XVII. INTERNATIONAL INLAND WATERWAYS

The conference considered a proposal of the United States delegation on this subject and agreed to refer it for consideration to the forthcoming meeting of the Council of Foreign Ministers in London.

XVIII. EUROPEAN INLAND TRANSPORT CONFERENCE

The British and United States delegations to the conference informed the Soviet delegation of the desire of the British and United States Governments to reconvene the European Inland Transport Conference and stated that they would welcome assurance that the Soviet Government would participate in the work of the reconvened conference. The Soviet Government agreed that it would participate in this conference.

XIX. DIRECTIVES TO MILITARY COMMANDERS ON ALLIED CONTROL COUNCIL FOR GERMANY

The three Governments agreed that each would send a directive to its representative on the Control Council for Germany informing him of all decisions of the conference affecting matters within the scope of his duties.

SUPPLEMENTARY NOTES

XX. USE OF ALLIED PROPERTY FOR SATELLITE REPARATIONS OR "WAR TROPHIES"

The proposal (Annex II) presented by the United States delegation was accepted in principle by the conference, but the drafting of an agreement on the matter was left to be worked out through diplomatic channels.

XXI. MILITARY TALKS

During the conference there were meetings between the Chiefs of Staff of the three Governments on military matters of common interest.

ANNEX I

Text of a letter transmitted on July 12 to the representatives of the United States and United Kingdom Governments on the Allied Control Commission in Hungary.

"In view of the changed situation in connection with the termination of the war against Germany, the Soviet Government finds it necessary to establish the following order of work for the Allied Control Commission in Hungary.

"1. During the period up to the conclusion of peace with Hungary the president (or vice president) of the ACC will regularly call conferences with the British and American representatives for the purpose of discussing the most important questions relating to the work of the ACC. The conferences will be called once in ten days, or more frequently in case of need.

"Directives of the ACC on questions of principle will be issued to the Hungarian authorities by the president of the Allied Control Commission after agreement on these directives with the English and American representatives.

"2. The British and American representatives in the ACC will take part in general conferences of heads of divisions and delegates of the ACC, convoked by the president of the ACC, which meetings will be regular in nature. The British and American representatives will also participate personally or through their representatives in appropriate instances in mixed commissions created by the president of the ACC for questions connected with the execution by the ACC of its functions.

"3. Free movement by the American and British representatives in the country will be permitted provided that the ACC is previously informed of the time and route of the journeys.

"4. All questions connected with permission for the entrance and exit of members of the staff of the British and American representatives in Hungary will be decided on the spot by the president of the ACC within a time limit of not more than one week.

"5. The bringing in and sending out by plane of mail, cargoes and diplomatic couriers will be carried out by the British and American representatives on the ACC under arrangements and within time limits established by the ACC, or in special cases by previous coordination with the president of the ACC.

[353]

"I consider it necessary to add to the above that in all other points the existing statutes regarding the ACC in Hungary, which was confirmed on January 20, 1945, shall remain in force in the future."

ANNEX II

Use of Allied property for satellite reparations or "war trophies."

1. The burden of reparation and "war trophies" should not fall on Allied nationals.

2. Capital equipment. We object to the removal of such Allied property as reparations, "war trophies" or under any other guise. Loss would accrue to Allied nationals as a result of destruction of plants and the consequent loss of markets and trading connections. Seizure of Allied property makes impossible the fulfillment by the satellite of its obligation under the armistice to restore intact the rights and interests of the Allied nations and their nationals.

The United States looks to the other occupying powers for the return of any equipment already removed and the cessation of removals. Where such equipment will not or cannot be returned, the United States will demand of the satellite adequate, effective and prompt compensation to American nationals and that such compensation have priority equal to that of the reparations payment.

These principles apply to all property wholly or substantially owned by Allied nationals. In the event of removals of property in which the American as well as the entire Allied interest is less than substantial, the United States expects adequate, effective and prompt compensation.

3. Current production. While the United States does not oppose reparation out of current production of Allied investments, the satellite must provide immediate and adequate compensation to the Allied nationals including sufficient foreign exchange or products so that they can recover reasonable foreign currency expenditures and transfer a reasonable return on their investment. Such compensation must also have equal priority with reparations.

We deem it essential that the satellites not conclude treaties, agreements or arrangements which deny to Allied nationals access, on equal terms, to their trade, raw materials and industry; and appropriately modify any existing arrangements which may have that effect.

Main Sources Cited

Anders, Lt. General Wladyslaw, C.B., *An Army in Exile: The Story of the Second Polish Corps* (1949)

Balfour, Michael, *see* Royal Institute of International Affairs

Bryant, Sir Arthur, *Triumph in the West* (1959)

Bundy, Harvey H., "Remembered Words," in *Atlantic Monthly* (March 1957)

Butcher, Harry C., *My Three Years with Eisenhower*, The Personal Diary of Captain Harry C. Butcher, USNR, Naval Aide to General Eisenhower, 1942 to 1945 (1946)

Byrnes, James F., *All in One Lifetime* (1958)

Churchill, Winston S., *The Second World War*, vol. 6, *Triumph and Tragedy* (1953)

Clay, Lucius D., *Decision in Germany* (1950)

Craven and Cate, *see* U.S., Air Force

Davison, W. Phillips, *The Berlin Blockade: A Study in Cold War Politics* (1958)

de Gaulle, Charles, *Mémoires de Guerre.*, vol. III, *Le Salut* (1959)

Doenitz, Admiral Karl, *Memoirs: Ten Years and Twenty Days*, tr. by R. H. Stevens in collaboration with David Woodward (1959)

Dulles, John Foster, *War or Peace* (1950)

Feis, Herbert, *The China Tangle: The American Effort in China from Pearl Harbor to the Marshall Mission* (1953)

Feis, Herbert, *Churchill-Roosevelt-Stalin: The War They Waged and the Peace They Sought* (1957)

Forrestal, James, *The Forrestal Diaries*, ed. by Walter Millis with the collaboration of E. S. Duffield (1951)

Gardner, Richard N., *Sterling-Dollar Diplomacy* (1956)

Grew, Joseph C., *Turbulent Era, A Diplomatic Record of Forty Years, 1904–1945*, ed. by Walter Johnson, assisted by Nancy Harvison Hooker (1952)

Halifax, The Earl of, *Fulness of Days* (1957)

Hammond, Paul Y., *The Origins of American Occupation Policy for Germany*, written under the auspices of the Twentieth Century Fund (manuscript)

Harris, C. R. S., *see* U.K., Military Series

Herodotus, *Works*, English translation by Alfred Denis Godley (1921–24)

Holborn, Hajo, *American Military Government, Its Organization and Policies* (1947)

Kirk, George, *see* Royal Institute of International Affairs

Leahy, Fleet Admiral William D., *I Was There: The Personal Story of the Chief of Staff to Presidents Roosevelt and Truman, Based on his Notes and Diaries Made at the Time* (1950)

McNeill, W. H., *see* Royal Institute of International Affairs

Mikolajczyk, Stanislaw, *The Pattern of Soviet Domination* (1948)

Montgomery of Alamein, Field-Marshal The Viscount, K.G., *Memoirs* (1958)

Morison, Elting E., biography of Secretary of War Stimson (Manuscript)

Mosely, Philip, "The Occupation of Germany," in *Foreign Affairs* (July 1950)

Penrose, Ernest Francis, *Economic Planning for the Peace* (1953)

Potsdam Papers, *see* U.S., Department of State

Ratchford, B. U., and William D. Ross, *Berlin Reparations Assignment* (1947)

Royal Institute of International Affairs, *Survey of International Affairs 1939–1946*, ed. by Arnold Toynbee and Frank T. Ashton-Gwatkin: *The Middle East and the War*, by George Kirk (1952); *America, Britain and Russia, Their Cooperation and Conflict, 1941–1946*, by William Hardy McNeill (1953); *Four-Power Control in Germany and Austria, 1945–46*, by Michael Balfour (1956)

Rozek, Edward J., *Allied Wartime Diplomacy: A Pattern in Poland* (1958)

Russell, Ruth B., *A History of the United Nations Charter, The Role of the United States 1940–1945* (1958)

Salisbury, Harrison, *Russia on the Way* (1946)

Sherwood, Robert E., *Roosevelt and Hopkins, An Intimate History* (1948)

Smyth, Henry De Wolfe, *Atomic Energy for Military Purposes; the Official Report on the Development of the Atomic Bomb under the Auspices of the United States Government, 1940–1945* (1945)

Snell, John L., *Wartime Origins of the East-West Dilemma over Germany* (1959)

Stalin Correspondence, *see* U.S.S.R., Ministry of Foreign Affairs

Strang, William, Lord Strang, *Home and Abroad*, Canadian ed. (1956)

Triumph and Tragedy, see Churchill

Truman, Harry S., *Memoirs*, vol. 1, *Year of Decisions* (1955)

U.K., Military Series, History of the Second World War: Civil Affairs and Military Government, vol. 3, *Allied Military Administration of Italy, 1943–1945*, by Charles Reginald Schiller Harris (1957)

U.N., Information Organization, *Documents on United Nations Conference on International Organization* (1945–54)

U.S., Air Force, Historical Division of Research Studies, *The Army Air Forces in World War II*: vol. 5, *The Pacific: Matterhorn to Nagasaki, June 1944 to August 1945*, ed. by Wesley Frank Craven and James Lea Cate (1953)

U.S., Congress, Report of Joint Committee on Atomic Energy, *Soviet Atomic Espionage* (1951)

U.S., 79th Congress, First Session, *Hearings* before the Committee on Foreign Relations, United States Senate, on H.R. 2013 (Lend-Lease) March 28 to April 4, 1945

U.S., Department of State, European and British Commonwealth Series 51, Publication 6757, *The Soviet Note on Berlin: An Analysis* (released January 1959)

U.S., Department of State, Foreign Relations of the United States, Diplomatic Papers, Publication 6199, *The Conferences at Malta and Yalta, 1945* (1955)

U.S., Department of State, Potsdam Papers: collection of papers and documents concerning the Potsdam conference, assembled by the State Department for publication

U.S., Department of State, Publication 3023, *Nazi-Soviet Relations 1939–1941: Documents from the Archives of the German Foreign Office,* ed. by Raymond James Sontag and James Stuart Beddie (1948)

U.S.S.R., Ministry of Foreign Affairs, *Correspondence Between the Chairman of the Council of Ministers of the U.S.S.R. and the Presidents of the U.S.A. and the Prime Ministers of Great Britain during the Great Patriotic War of 1941–1945,* Foreign Languages Publishing House (Moscow, 1957); this work is referred to throughout the present book as Stalin Correspondence

Vandenberg, Arthur H., *The Private Papers of Senator Vandenberg,* ed. by Arthur H. Vandenberg, Jr., with the collaboration of Joe Alex Morris (1952)

Wilcox, Francis Orlando, "The United Nations: Peace and Security," in *American Political Science Review,* vol. 49, no. 5 (October 1945)

Year of Decisions, see Truman

INDEX

Alanbrooke, Field-Marshal Lord, 172

Alexander, Sir Harold, British Field-Marshal, surrender of German forces to, 9, 12, 144; and the Venezia Giulia situation, 40–45, 47, 48, 48n., 49–51, 129, 130, 132, 144, 185, 187, 280–283, 308n.; and Polish forces in his command, 217n., 231; summoned to Potsdam, 274–275

Allen, George V., American diplomat, 308n.

Allied Military Government in Italy (AMG), 40, 45–47, 48, 50, 51, 129, 130, 131, 281–283

Anders, Wladyslaw, Polish General, 204, 204n., 216, 217n., 220n.

Anderson, Sir John, Chancellor of the Exchequer, 29

Antonov, Alexei E., General, First Deputy Chief of Staff, Soviet Army, 14, 16, 18, 20, 146

Argentina, admission into the United Nations of, 89, 99; invitation to San Francisco Conference, 90

Armour, Norman, U.S. Ambassador to Spain, 311

Arnold, H. H., Commanding General of U.S. Army Air Forces, 50, 164n.

Atomic bomb, (S-1) (T.A.), Interim Committee on, 80, 88, 172, 173, 174n., 176; Hopkins' knowledge of, 97; Harriman's knowledge of, 97; 139; Churchill-Roosevelt Hyde Park agreement about, 172; first explosion at Alamogordo of, 165–171; question of telling USSR about, 173–178; future control of, 173; use against Japanese of, 174, 179, 180

Attlee, Clement, Deputy Prime Minister, later Prime Minister of Great Britain, 161, 219, 222, 233, 234; and Polish frontiers at Potsdam, 259–267, 318; 321, 332

Austria, Control Council for, 74–76, 183n.; occupation zones in, 65–67, 143, 144, 149, 150; French occupation zone in, 150; Provisional Government of, 68, 69, 278, 279; American and British policy toward, 276; reparations from, 276–277

Bainbridge, Professor Kenneth, 167

Berlin, sectors of, 138, 141, 144, 248;

agreements for joint administration of, 141; question of access to, 145–149; visit of American and British missions to, 144, 145; entry of American troops into, 144, 145; Kommandatura for, 233; supplies for, 248–249

Bernadotte, Count Folke, head of Swedish Red Cross, 8, 9

Bevin, Ernest, British Secretary of State for Foreign Affairs, 219, 222, 235, 236, 259, 262–267, 271, 287, 321, 335

Beynet, Paul, French General, 133

Bidault, Georges, French Foreign Minister, 130, 132, 135, 136n., 313–315

Bierut, Boleslaw, President Polish National Council, later President Polish Provisional Government, 204n., 207, 208, 208n., 209n., 210–214, 222n., 225, 229, 230, 230n., 231, 234, 261, 268

Blumentritt, General Gunther von, 10

Bohlen, Charles E., American diplomat, 84n., 104n., 105n., 112n., 118, 177, 238n.

Bonomi, Ivanoe, Italian Premier, 46

Bulgaria, 62–64, 109, 188; peace treaty for, 181–184, 194, 197; Control Commission in, 191, 191n., 192, 193; supervision of elections in, 198–199, 289

Bundy, Harvey H., Assistant to Secretary of War, 174n., 175

Bush, Dr. Vannevar, 170, 174n.

Byrnes, James F., Secretary of State, 78; selected as Secretary of State, 82; 155; preparation for Potsdam by, 160, 161; and news of atomic bomb test, 164, 164n., 171, 174; and informing Stalin about atomic bomb, 177–178; and proposal for peace treaties and conference, 183; and proposals about Italy, 190, 194–197, 197n.; and satellite states of Eastern Europe, 195–199; and Franco Spain, 202; and discussion of Polish political affairs at Potsdam, 216–221; and discussion of Polish frontiers at Potsdam, 221–235, 225n.; 241, 243; and German economic questions at Potsdam, 250; and German reparations at Potsdam, 256–258; "package deal" proposed at Potsdam by, 259–267; and Austrian reparations, 277; and supervision of Greek elections, 287–289, 288n.; 297n.; and Italian colonies, 307n., 308n., 309; explanation to Bidault about Potsdam decisions, 313–315

INDEX

Cadogan, Sir Alexander, 95, 270, 277

Caffery, Jefferson, U.S. Ambassador to France, 129–130, 136

Chadwick, Sir James, 174n.

Chapultepec Conference, 89, 90

Cherrière, French General, 274

Cherwell, Lord, 175

Chiang Kai-shek, Generalissimo, 79, 112–114, 116, 177

Chiefs of Staff, British, 19, 30, 41, 45, 56, 76, 81, 162, 172, 187, 331

Chiefs of Staff, Combined, 9, 13, 14, 19, 40–46, 48, 129, 144, 177, 328, 330, 331, 333

Chiefs of Staff, U.S., 7, 19, 20, 28, 41, 42, 45, 50, 56n., 65, 74, 77, 78, 131, 141, 142, 145, 155, 157, 162, 164n., 187, 188, 236, 297, 328, 331, 333, 334

China, relations with Soviet Union, 99, 111–114; place on Council of Foreign Ministers, 182, 183

Churchill, Winston Spencer, Prime Minister of Great Britain, and German forces in Holland, 6; and Himmler offer of surrender, 9; and announcement of German surrender, 16, 17; and advance into Czechoslovakia, 19, 20; and termination of Lend-Lease, 29, 30, 330–332; and Yalta agreement about Poland, 31–34; and Polish frontiers, 31–33; and formation of new Polish government, 34–35, 106; admission of Warsaw Provisional Government to San Francisco Conference, 37, 38; and Tito, 40; and Venezia Giulia, 40–51, 280–283; and directives about policy in Germany, 57, 58; and German reparations, 59; and satellite states in Eastern Europe, 63–64, 188–199; and allied mission to Vienna, 66, 67, 69; and Austrian Provisional Government, 68, 69; and ideas about dealing with Soviet Union, 73, 78, 79, 124–127, 159; and withdrawal into zones in Germany, 74–77, 81, 140–144; and date and place for Potsdam Conference, 82, 83, 139, 140; and Hopkins' mission to Stalin, 83, 84; and the San Francisco Conference, 86; and voting procedure in the U.N., 92; and separate Truman-Stalin meeting, 124–127; talks with Davies, 124–127; and de Gaulle, 128–138; and crisis in Syria and Lebanon, 132–135; and invitation to Potsdam for de Gaulle, 138; and access to Berlin, 146; and entry of western forces into Vienna, 149–150, 274; and proposals for Potsdam discussions, 155; mood be-

fore Potsdam, 159; Hyde Park agreement with Roosevelt about atomic bomb, 172; and test of atomic bomb, 171–180; and informing Stalin about atomic bomb, 175–178; proposal for peace treaties and conferences, 182–183; proposals about Italy at Potsdam, 188–190; and Franco Spain at Potsdam, 200–202; view of Stalin-Hopkins accord on Poland, 203; recognition of Polish Provisional Government of National Unity, 214–215; and discussion of Polish political affairs at Potsdam, 216–221; and discussion of Polish frontiers at Potsdam, 221–234; and dismemberment of Germany, 236–239; and Potsdam proposals of political program for Germany, 241–245; and German refugee problem at Potsdam, 270–271; and recognition of Austrian Provisional Government at Potsdam, 278–279; and reform of Yugoslav Government at Potsdam, 283–286; and revision of Montreux Convention at Potsdam, 291; and Soviet demands on Turkey at Potsdam, 295–297; and Truman's proposal about international waterways at Potsdam, 297–301; and Iran at Potsdam, 304–306; and Italian colonies, 306–309; behavior and manner of, at Potsdam, 316–319; departure from Potsdam of, 318; and impressions of, 322; and division of German navy and merchant marine at Potsdam, 333–336

Clark, Mark, U.S. General, 146, 276, 276n.

Clay, Lucius D., U.S. General, later Commander-in-Chief of American zone in Germany, 56, 56n., 140n., 146–149, 248n., 266n.

Clayton, William L., Assistant Secretary of State, 56n., 137, 233n.

Cohen, Benjamin, State Department official, 161, 197n., 232n., 265n.

Combined Chiefs of Staff, see Chiefs of Staff, Combined

Commission of Three on Polish matters, 34, 106, 107, 203–215

Conant, Dr. James B., 170

Control Commission for Bulgaria, see Bulgaria, Control Commission for

Control Commission for Italy, see Italy, Control Commission for

Control Commission for Romania, see Romania, Control Commission for

Control Council for Austria, see Austria, Control Council for

[360]